JC
233
.M299
D7
PT.1
V.2

053

P9-CDU-983

0 0 2 3 7 3 7 5 6

Date Due

MAY 5/82		
NOV 2 1982		
MAR 1 0 1983		
JUN 9 1983		
Aug. 3/83		
APR 2 9 1992		
DEC - 2 1993		
MAR 1 6 1994		

JC233.M299D7 PT.1 V.2   A053106601

SENECA
FINCH
COLLEGE LIBRARY

KARL MARX'S
THEORY OF
REVOLUTION

KARL MARX'S THEORY OF REVOLUTION

by Hal Draper

I: STATE AND BUREAUCRACY

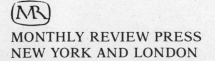

MONTHLY REVIEW PRESS
NEW YORK AND LONDON

Copyright © 1977 by Hal Draper
All rights reserved

Library of Congress Cataloging in Publication Data
Draper, Hal.
    Karl Marx's theory of revolution.
    Bibliography: p.
    Includes index.
    CONTENTS: I. State and bureaucracy
    1. Marx, Karl, 1818-1883—Political science—
Collected works. 2. Revolutions—Collected works.
I. Title.
JC233.M299D7   301.5'92   76-40467
ISBN 0-85345-387-X

First printing

Monthly Review Press
62 West 14th Street, New York, N.Y. 10011
21 Theobalds Road, London WC1X 8SL

Manufactured in the United States of America

CONTENTS

APPENDICES

15 | THE BONAPARTE MODEL

The tendency of the bourgeois state under pressure to revert back to more authoritarian and despotic forms of government does not arise only from a working-class threat from below. Another factor imparting the same tendency is one of the characteristics making for the political inaptitude of the capitalist class (as summarized in the preceding chapter): namely, the "exuberance of internal hostilities"—the fact that "no other ruling class is so profusely criss-crossed internally with competing and conflicting interest groups—the dog-eat-dog pattern."[1]

It may be helpful to think of these two factors as being, respectively, the vertical and horizontal components of social struggle in the system, without necessarily equating them in importance. The horizontal struggle takes place among sectors of the ruling classes themselves, not only between different blocs of the bourgeoisie but also pitting landowning interests (however bourgeoisified) against various bourgeois interests.

In practice, to be sure, such horizontal social struggles can rarely take place without involving the vertical class struggle of the exploited classes against the tops. Conflicts within the ruling circles tend to stimulate or unleash intervention from below, and conversely, the threat of subversion from below may divide the tops either on how to deal with the problem or in terms of whose interests are mainly endangered. In practice, therefore, these components of the historical social struggle tend to interpenetrate, with the driving force coming from below (vertically).

But whatever their source, if the internal conflicts become so unmanageable as to threaten the stability of the system, the resolution of the conflict by authoritarian means becomes the lesser evil for *every* stratum that shares in the benefactions of the status quo.*

If the bourgeoisie can no longer control the social jolts and tremors within the framework of democratic forms, its own preservation demands that, as a class, it yield up *direct* political power to other and firmer hands, the better to safeguard its socioeconomic rule. For Marx, the classic case that acted out this proposition was the situation in France leading from the February revolution of 1848 to the military dictatorship established by Louis Napoleon Bonaparte in a coup d'état on December 2, 1851. The analysis of this original "Bonapartism" was the subject of his work written directly after the events, *The Eighteenth Brumaire of Louis Bonaparte,* which was perhaps his most brilliant historical study.** Its prevasive theme is the relations between the state power and the various social classes and fractions thereof; and an outstanding characteristic is its painstaking dissection of the *complexity* of the historical situation, to which we will not be able to do justice here.

1. THE PROBLEM POSED

Today's reader has to recapture the contemporary historical background of *The Eighteenth Brumaire,* for it is not an abstract treatise but an analysis of the news of the day as it happened. In July 1830 the Restoration monarchy had been brought down by a timid bourgeois-republican effort at revolution which succeeded only in replacing the

---

* For a broader view of the historical pattern, this proposition should be linked with the explanation (in Chapter 11, section 7) of the three subsidiary tasks of the state. The third of these subsidiary tasks is precisely the resolution of internecine disputes that might otherwise disrupt the social fabric. This suggests that the other two subsidiary tasks may also play a role in the tendency of the state toward autonomization (and authoritarianism); and I believe they do—though to a lesser extent. From a fundamental standpoint, then, the present discussion could be derived directly from the statement about the tasks of the state.

** This was obviously Engels' opinion, judging by his many recommendations to students of Marxism. The present chapter will be devoted mainly to this work; it is the source of all quotations not otherwise ascribed. The title refers to the analogous coup d'état of November 9, 1799 (the 18th Brumaire in the calendar of the French Revolution) by which the first Napoleon established his military dictatorship. The analogy with the 18th Brumaire, and even the content of Marx's first paragraph, were given in Engels' letter to Marx the day after the coup.[2]

Bourbons with a constitutional monarchy headed by Louis Philippe, a bourgeoisified royalty. Never a very strong regime, the July monarchy of Louis Philippe hit the rocks with the industrial depression of 1847. The following year saw the outbreak of the first Europe-wide revolutionary upsurge; in France the Second Republic was proclaimed in February.

Louis Philippe's bourgeois monarchy, in which "a limited section of the bourgeoisie ruled in the name of the king," was now replaced by a bourgeois republic, in which "the whole of the bourgeoisie will now rule"—or so they thought.[3] The Constituent Assembly which was elected with the help of peasant and clerical support was thoroughly bourgeois, and set out to settle accounts with the main class danger from below, the Paris proletariat. The liberal Tocqueville reported: "I saw society split in two: those who possessed nothing united in a common greed [*sic*]; those who possessed something in a common fear. No bonds, no sympathies existed between these two great classes, everywhere was the idea of an inevitable and approaching struggle."[4] In the face of mass starvation among the workers, the bourgeois republicans provocatively cut down on the welfare program.

The workers' response was the "June insurrection, the most colossal event in the history of European civil wars"—up to then.

> The bourgeois republic triumphed. On its side stood the aristocracy of finance, the industrial bourgeoisie, the middle class, the petty-bourgeois, the army, the lumpenproletariat organized as the Mobile Guard, the intellectual lights, the clergy and the rural population. On the side of the Paris proletariat stood none but itself. More than 3000 insurgents were butchered after the victory, and 15,000 were transported without trial. With this defeat the proletariat passes into the *background* of the revolutionary stage.[5]

At this point, all other social strata and their political representatives were united against the vanguard proletariat of Paris. The savage (because terror-stricken) slaughter of the rebel movement eliminated the threat of proletariat revolution for more than two decades. But, as Marx stressed, the threat still remained in the background.

The foreground of the picture is going to concern the tug-of-war among the various strata of "those who possessed something"—the property-owning classes and their hangers-on. The problem which *The*

FROM FEBRUARY TO THE COUP D'ÉTAT

To aid the reader in following Marx's analysis of events in The Eighteenth Brumaire of Louis Bonaparte, *here is a chronological table of the main developments that took place between the February revolution and Bonaparte's coup d'état. In this work Marx divides the story into three main periods or phases as follows: (1) the "February period," headed by a provisional government; (2) the "period of the constitution of the republic," headed by the Constituent National Assembly; and (3) the "period of the constitutional republic," headed by the Legislative National Assembly, and brought to an end by the coup d'état.*

FIRST PERIOD

1848	Feb. 22	Uprising in Paris.
	Feb. 24	Louis Philippe abdicates; Second Republic proclaimed.
	Apr. 23	Elections to Constituent National Assembly; victory of bourgeois republicans.
	May 4	Constituent Assembly meets.

SECOND PERIOD

	May 15	Workers' demonstration invades Assembly; proclaims a revolutionary government; Blanqui, Barbès, others arrested.
	June 23-26	The June uprising: workers' rebellion in Paris suppressed by terror and Cavaignac dictatorship.
	Nov. 4	New constitution completed.
	Dec. 10	Louis Napoleon Bonaparte elected president of republic.
	Dec. 20	President Bonaparte installed, forms cabinet.
1849	Jan. 29	Constituent Assembly votes its own dissolution under pressure of troops in Paris.
	April	French begin attack on the Roman Republic.
	May 28	Legislative National Assembly meets.

THIRD PERIOD

	June 13	Suppression of demonstration (abortive revolt) by Ledru-Rollin's radicals.
	Oct. 31	President Bonaparte installs cabinet of his own men (D'Hautpoul cabinet).
1850	Mar. 10	Assembly by-elections: swing to left.
1851	July 15	Assembly rejects constitutional revision permitting second term for President Bonaparte.
	Dec. 2	Coup d'état: Bonaparte seizes power with help of army.

AFTERMATH

	Dec. 21	Plebiscite held by Bonaparte to sanction coup.
1852	Nov. 2	Empire ("Second Empire") proclaimed with Bonaparte as Napoleon III.

Eighteenth Brumaire addressed mainly was not the role of the state with respect to the proletariat, a role which had been amply demonstrated by the June Days: "It had revealed that here *bourgeois republic* signifies the unlimited despotism of one class over other classes."[6] (This class despotism is what Marx elsewhere called the "class dictatorship" of the bourgeoisie.)

The problem which Marx set himself to unravel was, rather, the subsequent role of the state with respect to the criss-crossing conflicts among the property-owning classes themselves, which had united to crush the June rising. The immediate subject is the role of the state with respect to the ruling classes themselves.

After June, the wide united front of the righteous upholders of "property, family, religion, order"[7] was going to narrow down, as one slice of it after another was cut off from political rule (like the famous salami). After the June scare, the simplest bourgeois-reform demand was going to be stigmatized as a subversive "attempt on society" and as "socialism," until the very heroes of law and order who had suppressed the proletarian insurgents were themselves cast aside like squeezed lemons. It is this process which we are now going to follow for the light it casts on the phenomenon of state autonomization.

2. BANKRUPTCY OF BOURGEOIS LIBERALISM

The next months marked the political rule, and then collapse, of the "pure" bourgeois republicans, one of whose leaders was General Cavaignac, the executioner of the June Days.

It was not a faction of the bourgeoisie held together by great common interests and marked off by specific conditions of production.* It was a clique of republican-minded bourgeois, writers, lawyers, officers and officials that owed its influence to the personal antipathies of the country against Louis Philippe, to memories of the old republic, to the republican faith of a number of enthusiasts, above all, however, to *French nationalism,* whose

---

* Note that here as elsewhere Marx repudiates the latter-day pseudo-Marxist notion that every party necessarily represents a separate class or social-group interest. This party reflected an *ideological* current within a class. (For the general issue, see the preceding chapter, p. 332 fn.)

hatred of the Vienna treaties and of the alliance with England it stirred up perpetually. . . . The industrial bourgeoisie was grateful to it for its slavish defence of the French protectionist system . . . the bourgeoisie as a whole, for its vicious denunciation of communism and socialism.[8]

This bourgeois party came to power not "through a liberal revolt of the bourgeoisie . . . but through a rising of the proletariat against capital, a rising laid low with grapeshot." Its ascendancy did not come about through an ascending line of progressive struggle, as it had once dreamed when it opposed the monarchy; its accession to power was not a "revolutionary event" but rather "the most counter-revolutionary."

It was this liberal bourgeois party which presided over the drafting of the constitution for the new republic. On the one hand, it wanted to extend the vote to the mass of the bourgeoisie itself; on the other hand, it was afraid of universal suffrage which went beyond bourgeois bounds. Still feeling the heat generated by the February revolution, it had to twist and turn:

> The narrow electoral qualification of the July monarchy [of Louis Philippe], which excluded even a large part of the bourgeoisie from political rule, was incompatible with the existence of the bourgeois republic. In lieu of this qualification, the February Revolution had at once proclaimed universal suffrage. The bourgeois republicans could not undo this event. They had to content themselves with adding the limiting proviso of a six months' residence in the constituency. The old organization of the administration, of the municipal system, of the judicial system, of the army, etc., continued to exist inviolate. . . .[9]

There were two consequences relating to state forms: (1) as Marx mentions later in the work, the old state apparatus was not smashed, it was merely taken over; and (2) the democratic liberties apparently guaranteed in the constitution were turned into frauds, and the executive power was separated from and counterposed to the legislative (representative), in the manner which we detailed in preceding chapters.[10] "Such was the Constitution of 1848" which collapsed before Bonaparte at a mere touch, Marx concludes.

While this constitution was being fabricated, the bourgeois-republican general Cavaignac was maintaining the "state of siege" (martial law) in Paris:

If the Constitution is subsequently put out of existence by bayonets, it must not be forgotten that it was likewise by bayonets, and these turned against the people, that it had to be protected in its mother's womb and by bayonets that it had to be brought into existence.

Thus these "respectable republicans," says Marx bitterly, "produced . . . a splendid invention, periodically employed in every ensuing crisis," eagerly adopted by other Continental powers: the "state of siege" device to keep the masses under military control at critical points.

But the military learned from this. If the armed forces of the state were "periodically laid on French society's head to . . . render it quiet," if they were periodically allowed to act as judge, censor, and policeman "as the highest wisdom of society and as its rector," then were not these same armed forces "bound to hit upon the idea of rather saving society once and for all by proclaiming their own regime as the highest and freeing civil society completely from the trouble of governing itself? . . . all the more as they might then also expect better cash payment for their higher services. . . ."[11]

Thus, by giving the armed forces their head to suppress the masses, "the respectable, the pure republicans" also prepared the ground for the coup d'état of Bonaparte's praetorians.

Having exhausted its role, this liberal bourgeois party was given its quietus when Bonaparte got himself elected president in December 1848: the squeezed-lemon syndrome. (Marx here refers readers to the analysis of this period which he had made in his earlier *Class Struggles in France.*)[12]

In sum: the liberals were defeated mainly by the massive peasant vote. But the result was also greeted by the army (which had garnered neither pay nor glory from the liberals in exchange for the dirty work it had done), by "the big bourgeoisie, which hailed Bonaparte as a bridge to monarchy," and also by the petty bourgeoisie and the proletariat, who saw in the vote a revenge on the hated party of Cavaignac for their own slaughter in June. (This is the famous pattern of "The enemy of my enemy is my friend" which has helped more than one despot to power.)

3. THE PATTERN OF PERMANENT COUNTERREVOLUTION

Now to the fore came "the mass of the bourgeoisie," especially the big bourgeoisie, the main body of the property-owning classes, as distinct from the ideological current which had been represented by the bourgeois liberals.

> This bourgeois mass was, however, *royalist.* One section of it, the large landowners, had ruled during the [Bourbon] Restoration and was accordingly *Legitimist.* The other, the aristocrats of finance and big industrialists, had ruled during the July Monarchy [of Louis Philippe] and was consequently *Orleanist.* The high dignitaries of the army, the university, the church, the bar, the academy and of the press were to be found on either side, though in various proportions. Here, in the bourgeois republic, which bore neither the name *Bourbon* nor the name *Orleans,* but the name *Capital,* they had found the form of state in which they could rule *conjointly.*[13]

This united front of the two kinds of royalists was the Party of Order, that is, the flag-wavers of the slogan of Law and Order, meaning systematic repression of even mild bourgeois-democratic reformers. The liberal republicans slunk out of effective existence "just as cowardly, mealy-mouthed, broken-spirited, and incapable of fighting" as they had been brutal in shooting down workers; they were through.[14] The Party of Order had helped Bonaparte to hound them and their Constituent Assembly out of existence, thereby helping to make parliamentarism a hollow shell, a shell which Bonaparte could easily crack later when he in turn had to get rid of his allies.*

With this turn in the situation, Marx pauses for an interim generaliza-

---

* Two decades later, Marx made the point more broadly:

In their uninterrupted crusade against the producing masses they [the bourgeois parliamentarians] were, however, bound not only to invest the executive with continually increased powers of repression, but at the same time to divest their own parliamentary stronghold—the National Assembly —one by one, of all its own means of defense against the Executive. The Executive, in the person of Louis Bonaparte, turned them out. The natural offspring of the Party-of-Order Republic was the Second Empire [of Bonaparte].[15]

tion. In the first French Revolution, the shift of political dominance from the Constitutionalists to the Girondins and then to the Jacobins followed an "ascending line": that is, as each political tendency brought the revolution as far as it itself could go, it was "thrust aside by the bolder ally that stands behind it." Now we have the reverse process; we are watching a revolution as it follows a descending line:

> The proletarian party appears as an appendage of the petty-bourgeois democratic party. It is betrayed and dropped by the latter on April 16, May 15, and in the June days. The democratic party, in its turn, leans on the shoulders of the bourgeois-republican party. The bourgeois-republicans no sooner believe themselves well established than they shake off the troublesome comrade and support themselves on the shoulders of the party of Order. The party of Order hunches its shoulders, lets the bourgeois-republicans tumble and throws itself on the shoulders of armed force. . . . Each party kicks back at the one behind, which presses upon it, and leans against the one in front, which pushes backwards. . . .[16]

In this situation, Marx explains, the period "comprises the most motley mixture of crying contradictions," contradictions which he proceeds to list in a brilliant vein of black humor.[17]

Among these contradictions was one which also provides the key for the next period. We have already mentioned it: the fact that the united royalists of the Party of Order could remain united only on the terrain of the republic which they both detested; for as soon as restoration of monarchy came on the agenda, they split on the royal house to be restored. Monarchism, which they shared, divided them; republicanism, which they hated, united them. This split among the royalists reflected more than simply the opposition of lily to tricolor:

> Under the Bourbons, *big landed property* had governed, with its priests and lackeys; under the Orleans, high finance, large-scale industry, large-scale trade, that is, *capital,* with its retinue of lawyers, professors, and smooth-tongued orators. The [Bourbon] Legitimate Monarchy was merely the political expression of the hereditary rule of the lords of the soil, as the [Orleanist] July Monarchy was only the political expression of the usurped rule of the bourgeois parvenus. What kept the two factions apart, therefore, was not any so-called principles; it was their material conditions of existence, two different kinds of property; it was the old

contrast between town and country, the rivalry between capital and landed property.[18]

Marx adds an important note on the relationship between these two rival forms of property, which qualifies the rivalry:

> Orleanists and Legitimists found themselves side by side in the republic, with equal claims. If each side wished to effect the *restoration* of its *own* royal house against the other, that merely signified that each of the *two great interests* into which the *bourgeoisie* is split—landed property and capital—sought to restore its own supremacy and the subordination of the other. We speak of two interests of the bourgeoisie, for large landed property, despite its feudal coquetry and pride of race, has been rendered thoroughly bourgeois by the development of modern society. Thus the Tories of England long imagined that they were enthusiastic about monarchy, the church, and the beauties of the old English Constitution, until the day of danger wrung from them the confession that they are enthusiastic only about *ground rent*.

Under the corporate business title of the Party of Order, this united front of royalists "exercised more unrestricted and sterner domination" over the rest of society than had ever been possible for it under either the Bourbons or Louis Philippe. Only "under the form of the parliamentary republic" could these two royalist divisions of the bourgeoisie pool their strength, and thus establish "the rule of their [whole] class instead of the regime of a privileged faction of it."[19]

But it was not only royalist sentiments which made these "republicans" hate and fear the republic:

> Instinct taught them that the republic, true enough, makes their political rule complete, but at the same time undermines its social foundation, since they must now confront the subjugated classes and contend against them without mediation, without the concealment afforded by the crown. . . . It was a feeling of weakness that caused them to recoil from the pure conditions of their own class rule and to yearn for the former more incomplete, more undeveloped and precisely on that account less dangerous forms of this rule [that is, monarchist forms].[20]

We pass over the section in which Marx summarizes how the Party of Order next proceeded to smash its remaining adversary in parliament,

the party to the left of it, previously called the petty-bourgeois democracy or Social-Democracy—the pinkish reformers led by Ledru-Rollin.*
Suffice to say that in this way the Party of Order also tore down the
Constitution and parliamentary prestige, facilitating Bonaparte's subsequent operation. With the reformist left put out of action, the Party of
Order remained alone as the dominant force in parliament, and thus
isolated, confronted the executive power which was named Bonaparte.

4. STATE GIGANTISM VERSUS DEMOCRACY

As an individual, Louis Bonaparte was a political adventurer. He was
neither the first nor the last such type to make his adventure successful
by gearing it to the historical need of the moment. Up to this point, the
dominant politicians had tended to scorn him as a nonentity, as
unnecessary; but these same politicians were now in process of making
themselves not only unnecessary but impossible. A vacuum was being
created by their inability to rule, that is, by the inability of the
bourgeoisie to rule as a class, which they reflected. The adventurer's
game was to move into this vacuum, thereby making himself useful, and
finally necessary, to a class which could not rule in any other form.

There was no doubt that the two-headed bourgeoisie ruled the
socioeconomic domain (civil society); but it was paralyzed in the
attempt to develop the state forms through which it could effectively
wield the reins of power in the political domain. When civil society is
paralyzed, there is only the state power to take hold of things and keep
them working. At the given moment, this meant Bonaparte.

Bonaparte's next step was to detach the cabinet (ministry) itself
from parliamentary control, and convert it into an agency of the
executive. The Party of Order lost every "lever of executive power."
Marx explains the significance of this step in a passage of great
importance:

> It is immediately obvious that in a country like France, where the
> executive power commands an army of officials numbering more
> than half a million individuals and therefore constantly maintains

* Besides this section in *The Eighteenth Brumaire*,[21] the same ground had been
covered in even greater detail in *The Class Struggles in France*.[22] This material will
be important for another subject, the nature of social-reformism.

an immense mass of interests and livelihoods, in the most absolute dependence . . .

We interrupt to note that, while Marx wrote this passage in 1852 and of
"a country like France," the picture he painted is increasingly true of
both the capitalist and "Communist" states in our own time; hence this
passage should be read with contemporary eyes. To continue:

> . . . where the state enmeshes, controls, regulates, superintends,
> and tutors civil society from its most comprehensive manifesta-
> tions of life down to its most insignificant stirrings, from its most
> general modes of being to the private existence of individuals;
> where through the most extraordinary centralization this parasitic
> body acquires a ubiquity, an omniscience, a capacity for accele-
> rated mobility and an elasticity which finds a counterpart only in
> the helpless dependence, in the loose shapelessness of the actual
> body politic—it is obvious that in such a country the National
> Assembly forfeits all real influence when it loses command of the
> ministerial posts, if it does not at the same time simplify the
> administration of the state, reduce the army of officials as far as
> possible and, finally, let civil society and public opinion create
> organs of their own, independent of the governmental power.[23]

Marx's remedy for this gigantism of the state was going to be even
more drastic later; the point now is his diagnosis of the condition. The
bourgeoisie (he goes on to explain) was incapable of opposing this
development; its contradiction was that it was simultaneously disarmed
and defended by one and the same process, cured and castrated by the
same operation:

> But it is precisely with the maintenance of that extensive state
> machine in its numerous ramifications that the *material interests*
> of the French bourgeoisie are interwoven in the closest fashion.
> Here it finds posts for its surplus population and makes up in the
> form of state salaries for what it cannot pocket in the form of
> profit, interest, rents, and honorariums. On the other hand, its
> *political interests* compelled it to increase daily the repressive
> measures and therefore the resources and the personnel of the
> state power, while at the same time it had to wage an uninter-
> rupted war against public opinion and mistrustfully mutilate,
> cripple, the independent organs of the social movement, where it
> did not succeed in amputating them entirely. Thus the French
> bourgeoisie was compelled by its class position to annihilate, on

the one hand, the vital conditions of all parliamentary power, and therefore likewise of its own, and to render irresistible, on the other hand, the executive power hostile to it.[24]

The bourgeoisie suffered from another contradiction. It could hope to stand up politically to Bonaparte's state apparatus not just by mobilizing moneybags but by mobilizing the people behind it. Yet "never did it display more ostentatiously the insignia of domination" in its capacity as an exploiting class. A symbol was its reestablishment of the wine tax, which hit the peasantry, already burdened by low grain prices. Out of social fear, the bourgeoisie leaned on the clergy for "the superintendence of the French mind," on the gendarme for the superintendence of action, and on bureaucratic prefects and spies to forestall subversion.[25]

And the slightest reform was denounced as *"Socialism!"* (This is 1850, not the 1950s.) "Even bourgeois liberalism is declared *socialistic. . . ."* There was class logic for this apparent silliness, as usual:

> The bourgeoisie had a true insight into the fact that all the weapons which it had forged against feudalism turned their points against itself, that all the means of education which it had produced rebelled against its own civilization, that all the gods which it had created had fallen away from it. It understood that all the so-called bourgeois liberties and organs of progress attacked and menaced its *class rule* at its social foundation and its political summit simultaneously, and had therefore become *"socialistic."* In this menace and this attack it rightly discerned the secret of socialism, whose import and tendency it judges more correctly than so-called socialism knows how to judge itself. . . .[26]

Along this road there followed "the logical conclusion that its [the bourgeoisie's] *own parliamentary regime,* that its *political rule* in general" must also be condemned as "socialistic." For its political rule under democratic forms opened the door to the use of these same weapons against its social rule, against capitalism. The parliamentary regime created "unrest" where the bourgeoisie needed tranquillity (apathy).

> The parliamentary regime lives by discussion; how shall it forbid discussion? Every interest, every social institution, is here transformed into general ideas, debated as ideas; how shall any interest, any institution, sustain itself above thought and impose itself as an article of faith? . . . [T]he debating club in parliament is

necessarily supplemented by debating clubs in the salons and the pothouses. . . . The parliamentary regime leaves everything to the decisions of majorities; how shall the great majorities outside parliament not want to decide? When you play the fiddle at the top of the state, what else is to be expected but that those down below dance? [27]

Here Marx is making his first detailed analysis of the basic incompatibility of capitalism with democracy; the analysis will be supplemented later when he works out the revolutionary alternative to parliamentarism.

5. THE KEY TO BONAPARTISM

Marx comes to the following conclusion:

Thus . . . the bourgeoisie confesses that its own interests dictate that it should be delivered from the danger of its *own rule;* that, in order to restore tranquillity in the country, its bourgeois parliament must, first of all, be given its quietus; that in order to preserve its social power intact, its political power must be broken . . .

Here we come to the key to Bonapartism: *In order to preserve the bourgeoisie's social power, its political power must be broken. . . .*

. . . that the individual bourgeois can continue to exploit the other classes and to enjoy undisturbed property, family, religion, and order only on condition that their class be condemned along with the other classes to like political nullity; that in order to save its purse, it must forfeit the crown, and the sword that is to safeguard it must at the same time be hung over its own head as a sword of Damocles. [28]

So Bonaparte was able to get away with breaking the political rule of the bourgeoisie as a class, expressed through its parliamentary domination. He wooed the workers with demagogic if empty reform schemes, with the help of Saint-Simonian "socialists," at the same time that he allied himself with high finance in the cabinet. He let the parliamentarians lull themselves with electoral "victories" while he gathered the police powers into his own hands. When the bourgeois parliamentarians showed their hand by outlawing universal suffrage, he came out for the suffrage, knowing that the levers to manipulate it were in his hands alone. And he organized his storm troops (called the Society of December 10) mainly out of the disintegrating "scum of all classes," the lumpenproletariat.

While he usurped the political power of the Assembly, he shouted that "France demands tranquillity." And the bourgeoisie did demand tranquillity. The Assembly was afraid to fight back: "By so doing it would give the nation its marching orders, and it fears nothing more than that the nation should move."[29] The danger of being defended from below is worse than that of being defeated from above: such is the principle of the Kerenskys in every epoch.

This socially determined cravenness of the bourgeoisie allowed Bonaparte to take over control of the army unchallenged; and thus "the Party of Order declares that the bourgeoisie has forfeited its vocation to rule."[30] The parliamentary majority opposed to Bonaparte fell apart, as desertions from its camp multiplied—"out of sheer egoism, which makes the ordinary bourgeois always inclined to sacrifice the general interest of his class for this or that private motive." The Assembly became a mere talking-shop, but the deputies went through the motions of winning meaningless parliamentary victories. This is "that peculiar malady . . . *parliamentary cretinism*"[31]—that is, the illusion that activity in parliament has a meaning independent of the social struggle outside.

Even now, with economic discontent growing among the lower classes, the Party of Order could have won back some mass support, thereby possibly throwing Bonaparte into its arms; but all Bonaparte's puppets had to do to stop this was "to conjure up the red specter."

> Instead of letting itself be intimidated by the executive power with the prospect of fresh disturbances, it ought rather to have allowed the class struggle a little elbowroom, so as to keep the executive power dependent on itself. But it did not feel equal to the task of playing with fire.[32]

By a maneuver threatening revision of the constitution, Bonaparte further set the two royalist factions of the Party of Order against each other, the split weakening both. Outside parliament, the mass of the bourgeoisie now yearned only for a "strong government," one which would ensure tranquil conditions for business and security against economic discontent. The leaders of high finance had gone over to

Bonaparte even before this. The London *Economist* declared: "The President is the guardian of order, and is now recognized as such on every Stock Exchange of Europe."

> By the aristocracy of finance must here be understood not merely the great loan promoters and speculators in public funds, in regard to whom it is immediately obvious that their interests coincide with the interests of state power. All modern finance, the whole of the banking business, is interwoven in the closest fashion with public credit. A part of their business capital is necessarily invested and put out at interest in quickly convertible public funds. Their deposits, the capital placed at their disposal and distributed by them among merchants and industrialists, are partly derived from the dividends of holders of government securities. If in every epoch the stability of the state power signified Moses and the prophets to the entire money market and to the priests of this money market, why not all the more so today, when every deluge threatens to sweep away the old states, and the old state debts with them?

Thus the growing interpenetration of finance capital and the state power was a weapon in Bonaparte's hands.

The industrial bourgeoisie also demanded tranquillity and strong government especially with the onset of business depression: "It proved that the struggle to maintain its *public* interests, its own *class interests*, its *political power,* only troubled and upset it, as it was a disturbance of private business."[33] Above all, the bourgeoisie demanded stability, and turned against its own parliamentary mouthpieces and ideologists, whose very squirmings were now upsetting to the status quo. By such servility to Bonaparte, "It declared unequivocally that it longed to get rid of its own political rule in order to get rid of the troubles and dangers of ruling."

At the same time, "This bourgeoisie, which every moment sacrificed its general class interests, that is, its political interests, to the narrowest and most sordid private interests," had the gall to denounce "the stupidity of the masses, the vile multitude" for the state of affairs[34]— the same masses it had helped shoot down every time they raised their head.

"Now picture to yourself the French bourgeois, how in the throes of this business panic his trade-crazy brain is tortured, set in a whirl and stunned by rumors of coups d'état and the restoration of universal suffrage" until he "madly snorts at his parliamentary republic: *'Rather an end with terror than terror without end!'* "[35] Under all these conditions, Bonaparte could finally pull off his coup d'état of December 2, 1851 without successful opposition.

6. THE AUTONOMIZED STATE AND THE CLASSES

Now the executive power had smashed the legislative power; now it seemed that "all classes, equally impotent and equally mute, fell on their knees before the rifle butt." In this way the executive power was reduced "to its purest expression," it was set up "as the sole target," against which the subsequent forces of revolution would concentrate.[36]

"This executive power with its enormous bureaucratic and military organization . . . this appalling parasitic body," summarizes Marx, had been created by the absolute monarchy and then proliferated into "a state authority whose work is divided and centralized as in a factory." It had been strengthened as a centralized repressive power by the parliamentary republic in struggle against revolution. "All revolutions perfected this machine instead of smashing it," notes Marx, in an early reference to the revolutionary task of dismantling the old state machine.* "The parties that contended in turn for domination regarded the possession of this huge state edifice as the principal spoils of the victor."[38]

Under the previous French regimes, the state bureaucracy, "however much it strove for power of its own," had been only the means through which the bourgeoisie prepared or carried out its class rule. "Only under the second Bonaparte does the state seem to have made itself completely independent." But this apparent independence of the state was conditional: ". . . And yet the state power is not suspended in mid-air. Bonaparte represents a class, and the most numerous class of French society at that, *the smallholding peasants.*"[39] *Represents* here meant that Bonaparte presented himself as the defender of the peasantry and thus based his power on them, a class "incapable of enforcing

* Four years after Marx, Tocqueville noted the same pattern—with approbation: ". . . since '89 the administrative system has always stood firm amid the debacle of political systems. . . . For though in each successive revolution the administration was, so to speak, decapitated, its body survived intact and active. The same duties were performed by the same civil servants. . . ."[37]

their class interest in their own name."* This, qualified Marx, was true
only of the conservative bulk of the peasantry, not of its radicalized
elements who were able to look beyond their small land-parcels.[41] But
it was the conservative bulk of the peasantry that provided both the
votes and the armed force for the establishment of the military dictatorship; as Engels later summarized it, "Louis Napoleon founded the
Empire . . . on the votes of the peasants and on the bayonets of their
sons, the soldiers of the army."[42]

Resting on this backward mass, the executive power manipulated a
simulacrum of universal suffrage as a plebiscitary device. Using the state
power, Bonaparte nourished "an enormous bureaucracy, well-galloned
and well-fed . . . an artificial caste, for which the maintenance of his
regime becomes a bread-and-butter question."[43] But while the broad
butt of this autonomized state rested on the peasant mass as its
support, Bonaparte knew well where economic power lay:

> As the executive authority which has made itself an independent
> power, Bonaparte feels it to be his mission to safeguard "bour-
> geois order." But the strength of this bourgeois order lies in the
> middle class. He looks on himself, therefore, as the representative
> of the middle class and issues decrees in this sense.

But there was a permanent contradiction in Bonapartism:

> Nevertheless, he [Bonaparte] is somebody solely due to the fact
> that he has broken the political power of the middle class and
> daily breaks it anew. Consequently, he looks on himself as the
> adversary of the political and literary power of the middle class.
> But by protecting its material power, he generates its political
> power anew.[44]

And in fact, as we know, the political power of the bourgeoisie *was*
going to regenerate itself eventually under the protection which Bonapartism gave to its socioeconomic power. "Industry and trade, hence
the business affairs of the middle class, are to prosper in hothouse
fashion under the strong government."[45] At this point, it was Marx's
prediction; when Engels looked back after four decades, it was possible
merely to report:

* Looking back in 1871, Marx put it this way: "The peasants were the passive
economical basis of the Second Empire"; or again, the Second Empire was "supported by the passive adherence of the peasantry. . . ."[40] (See Chapter 20, pp. 499
and 501, for additional comment on the phrase, "the state power is not suspended in mid-air.")

Louis Bonaparte took the political power from the capitalists under the pretext of protecting them, the bourgeois, from the workers, and on the other hand the workers from them; but in return his rule encouraged speculation and industrial activity—in a word, the upsurgence and enrichment of the whole bourgeoisie to an extent hitherto unknown.[46]

7. BONAPARTISM: THE CLASS EQUILIBRIUM

On December 2, 1851, when the adventurer Bonaparte established his dictatorship over France, no political observer or thinker understood that something new and different of world-historic importance had just occurred in the modern world, whatever analogues existed in the past. That applied to Marx and Engels like everyone else—for at least one week.

Engels' next-day letter to Marx was punctuated by words like *comedy, farce, silly, infantile, stupid,* and never left this superficial level; there was no hint of an insight into what had taken place.[47] As we have mentioned, this common contemporary reaction left its mark in the first sentence of Marx's great essay, a sentence which is as undeservedly famous as it is shallow. Leaving aside Hegel's inflated generalization that "all" great historical events occur twice, "the first time as tragedy, the second as farce,"[48] and granting the comedic elements in Bonaparte's rise to power, as in Hitler's, it was a concession to the shortsighted punditry of the time to view the advent of Bonapartism as a farce. This initial reaction was refuted by the rest of the work.*

Marx's first letter to Engels about the event avows frankly that he is "°quite bewildered° by these tragicomic events in Paris." He ventures the suggestion that

At any rate it seems to me that the situation has been improved rather than deteriorated by the coup d'état. It is easier to cope with Bonaparte than would have been possible with the National Assembly and its generals. And the dictatorship of the National Assembly was standing at the gate.[50]

* It appears that Marx wrote Chapter 1 in about three weeks after the coup d'état and sent it off for publication. Chapter 2 seems to have been written in January; Chapters 3–5 in February; the whole was not finished until March.[49] It is not until Chapters 3–4 that Marx's essential theory of Bonapartism is set down.

This was a week after the coup. The letter underlines how much Marx had to learn, very fast, about the nature of the state and revolution as illuminated by the phenomenon of Bonapartism.

What did he learn? Let us sum up the French experience on how the state machine achieved a formal autonomy from political control by the bourgeoisie or any other class of society, while the bourgeoisie surrendered all forms and channels of its political rule in exchange for the preservation of its socioeconomic dominance.

1. *The state moves toward autonomization insofar as an unresolved class struggle balances the power of contending classes against each other.*

The "secret" of Bonaparte's victory, wrote Marx in 1858, lay "in the mutual prostration of the antagonist parties," with the help of the onset of a period of prosperity following his coup. "It was the total apathy—the politically used-up, blasé state of mind—of these classes [the middle classes] which allowed Louis Napoleon to establish his power," wrote Engels the same year.[51] The precondition was mutual exhaustion of the contending classes in a struggle without issue.

The state power's balancing act could be effective because it could demagogically appeal to each class against the others in a situation that offered no good alternative to demagogy. Bonaparte, wrote Marx in 1856, "made his coup d'état on two diametrically opposite pretenses: on the one hand proclaiming it was his mission to save the bourgeoisie and 'material order' from the Red anarchy to be let loose in May 1852 [when elections were due]; and on the other hand, to save the working people from the middle-class despotism concentrated in the National Assembly."[52] But the class resentments whipped up could not be fought out:

> As against both the workers and the capitalists [wrote Engels in a pamphlet closely checked by Marx] Bonapartism distinguishes itself by preventing them from coming to blows. That is, it protects the bourgeoisie from forceful attacks by the workers, promotes a little peaceful skirmishing between the two classes, and, for the rest, deprives both of them of any trace of political power. No right to organize, no right to assemble, no freedom of the press; universal suffrage under such bureaucratic pressure that opposition votes are almost impossible; a police-economy which was unheard of up to now even in police-ridden France. Moreover, a section of the bourgeoisie as well as of the workers is

directly *bought:* the former through a colossal credit swindle, whereby the money of the small capitalists is lured into the pockets of the big capitalists; the latter through colossal state works, which, alongside the natural, independent proletariat, concentrate an artificial pro-Empire proletariat, dependent on the government, in the big cities. Finally, national pride is flattered by apparently heroic wars. . . . [This regime] exists only to keep the workers under a tight rein with respect to the bourgeoisie.[53]

In an article written about the same time that Marx was finishing *The Eighteenth Brumaire,* Engels explained for Chartist readers the "Real Causes Why the French Proletarians Remained Comparatively Inactive in December Last," that is, in face of Bonaparte's coup. First of all he explains that "whatever Louis Napoleon took from others, he took it not from the working-classes" but from the middle classes.

°°Not that Louis Napoleon would not, quite as gladly, have robbed the working-classes of anything that might appear desirable to him, but it is a fact that in December last [1851] the French working-classes could not be robbed of anything, because everything worth taking had already been taken from them during the three years and a half of middleclass parliamentary government that had followed the great defeats of June 1848. . . .

Thus the working-classes had, at the moment of the late coup d'état, very little, if anything to lose in the chapter of political privileges. But, on the other hand, the middle and capitalist class were at that time in possession of political omnipotence. . . . And for them it was indeed a hard case to be robbed of all this . . . and to be reduced at once to the state of political nullity to which they themselves had reduced the working people. . . .

The struggle, then, on the 2nd of December lay principally between the middle-classes and Louis Napoleon, the representative of the army.

But while the workers could hardly be moved to shed their blood in order to fight the enemy of their enemy, that did not mean they had no interest in the outcome, even if they had no "direct political privilege" to lose. What they had to lose were opportunities to struggle for power.

Thus, they could not let the occasion pass without showing the two opposing forces that there was a third power in the field, which, if momentarily removed from the theatre of official and parliamentary contentions, was yet ever ready to step in as soon

> as the scene was changed to its own sphere of action,—to the *street*.

The workers' problem was this: If they rose against Bonaparte, wouldn't they simply be helping to restore the rule of the bourgeois class enemy which had slaughtered their militants? "And if they at once declared for a revolutionary government, would they not, as was actually the case in the provinces, frighten the middle-class so much as to drive them to a union with Louis Napoleon and the army?" [54]

Thus the working class was in no position to strike out for itself, and declined to go into the streets on behalf of one or the other enemy. Under these conditions, the class struggle was not abolished but immobilized in equilibrium.

> The whole secret of Louis Napoleon's success is this, that by the traditions of his name he has been placed in a position to hold, for a moment, *the balance of the contending classes of French society*. For it is a fact that under the cloak of the state of siege by military despotism which now veils France, the struggle of the different classes of society is going on as fiercely as ever.

Though not by *forcible* means at the moment.

Engels emphasizes that Bonaparte's opportunity came only after *all* the social classes had demonstrated their incapacity to rule, and thus exhausted not only themselves but their credit. After the February Revolution had upset the power of the "large bankers and stock-jobbers," each class had a shot at power: first, the workingmen "during the days of the first revolutionary excitement"; then the republican petty bourgeoisie under Ledru-Rollin; then the bourgeois republicans under Cavaignac; lastly the bourgeois royalists of the National Assembly majority. "None of these classes had been able to hold fast the power they for a moment possessed. . . ." The royalists, uniting the landed interest and the "moneyed interest," feared lest power return to the hands "of the working-class, who themselves might be expected to have become fitter to turn it to account." Making use of all these divisions, Bonaparte used the peasant vote, the lumpen-demonstrators, and the army's force "to step in and assume a more or less absolute sway over those classes, none of which, after a four years' bloody struggle, had proved strong enough to seize upon a lasting supremacy." Hence the success of the coup.

Thus the reign of Louis Napoleon is not superseding the class-war. It merely suspends for a while the bloody outbreaks which mark from time to time the efforts of this or that class to gain or maintain political power. None of these classes were strong enough to venture at a new battle, with any chance of success. The very division of classes favored, for the time being, Napoleon's projects.[55]

In résumé, in the last section of the article:

We repeat: Louis Napoleon came to power because the open war carried on during the last four years between the different classes of French society have [*sic*] worn them out, had shattered their respective fighting armies, and because under such circumstances, for a time at least, the struggle of these classes can only be carried on in a peaceful and legal way. . . . Under these circumstances it is in a manner of speaking in the interest of all contending classes that a so-called *strong government* should exist which might repress and keep down all those minor, local, and scattered outbreaks of open hostility, which without leading to any result, trouble the development of the struggle in its new shape by retarding the recovery of strength for a new pitched battle. This circumstance may in some way explain the undeniable general acquiescence of the French in the present government.[56]

The repeated emphasis on the stalemate of the contending classes may well recall the beginning of the *Communist Manifesto,* which stated the historical generalization that the class struggle has always "ended, either in a revolutionary reconstitution of society at large, or in the common ruin of the contending classes."[57] Neither of these dénouements was yet the case, for the process had not ended; it was something in between, for the contending classes were not ruined but exhausted and deadlocked. The "recovery of strength for a new pitched battle" was still ahead.

8. BONAPARTISM: SOCIETY IN A PLASTER CAST

2. *The state moves toward autonomization insofar as there is no other alternative to prevent society from shaking itself apart in internecine conflict without issue.*

This summarizes much that we have already seen in Marx's and Engels' discussions. In *The Eighteenth Brumaire* and elsewhere, Marx stressed that the June defeat pushed the working-class threat to the background, but that does not mean it was pushed out of the picture. Behind the impotence of the upper classes to resolve the issue of power was their fear of moving in any direction that might open the way for a renewed proletarian assault.

°°When the volcanic upheavings of 1848 [wrote Marx and Engels] suddenly threw before the eyes of the astonished liberal middle classes of Europe the giant specter of an armed working class, struggling for political and social emancipation, the middle classes, to whom the safe possession of their capital was of immensely higher importance than direct political power, sacrificed this power, and all the liberties for which they had fought, to secure the suppression of the proletarian revolution. The middle class declared itself politically a minor, unfit to manage the affairs of the nation, and acquiesced in military and bureaucratic despotism.[58]

In the following summary view that Marx included in his essay on the Paris Commune, we direct attention to the last sentence:

The [Bonapartist] empire, with the coup d'état for its certificate of birth, universal suffrage for its sanction, and the sword for its sceptre, professed to rest upon the peasantry, the large mass of producers not directly involved in the struggle of capital and labour. It professed to save the working class by breaking down Parliamentarism, and, with it, the undisguised subserviency of Government to the propertied classes. It professed to save the propertied classes by upholding their economic supremacy over the working class; and, finally, it professed to unite all classes by reviving for all the chimera of national glory. In reality, it was the only form of government possible at a time when the bourgeoisie had already lost, and the working class had not yet acquired, the faculty of ruling the nation.[59]

The autonomized state, then, steps into a vacuum created by the frustration of class power on all sides.

3. *The autonomized state provides the conditions for the necessary modernization of society when no extant class is capable of carrying out this imperative under its own political power.*

In the present case, modernization meant industrialization above all, and industrialization meant bourgeoisification as long as the working class was still too immature to organize society under its own aegis. The Bonapartist state had to adopt the bourgeoisie's economic aims and interests as its very own: not simply as a concession to a business partner, but in its own interests as well. It needed a modern industrial and economic development to pursue its own aggrandizement too, in this era when imperial and military aspirations had become toothless without an economic capacity to give them bite.

The propertied classes could well afford to be content with the "strong government" which assured their interests along with its own, wrote Marx:

> °°When Louis Napoleon ... vaulted to a throne ... the sovereign princes and aristocracies of Europe, the great landowners, manufacturers, *rentiers,* and stockjobbers, almost to a man, exulted in his success as their own. "The crimes are his," was their general chuckle, "but the fruits are ours. Louis Napoleon reigns in the Tuileries; while we reign even more securely and despotically on our domains, in our factories, on the Bourse, and in our countinghouses. Down with all Socialism! *Vive l'Empereur!"*
> And next to the Military, the fortunate usurper plied all his arts to attach the rich and powerful, the thrifty and speculating, to his standard.[60]

The Bonapartist state served the socioeconomic interests of the classes that owned the instruments of production; and these propertied classes, in turn, willingly plied their profit-taking under the political domination of the Bonapartist state, as long as it did not get in their way. In these terms there was a special symbiosis between the socioeconomic ruling classes and the state they did not control directly.

But this arrangement bore the seed of its own dissolution. Accelerated modernization meant, on the one hand, that a maturing bourgeoisie would begin to feel its oats, and on the other, that the Bonapartist state would begin to outlive the value of the services it rendered to the socioeconomic order. In Chapter 18 we will return to the regime of Louis Bonaparte as its reaches the stage of dissolution; but first we must follow Marx and Engels as they broaden their historical conception of the nature of the Bonapartist state itself.

16 | BONAPARTISM: THE BISMARCKIAN EXTENSION

In *The Eighteenth Brumaire of Louis Bonaparte,* Marx worked out the class analysis of a particular historical development taking place in one country. In contrast, consider the following passage by Engels written over thirty years later, in which he succinctly sums up much that both he and Marx had written in the meantime.

Engels had just explained that the state is "as a rule, the state of the most powerful, economically dominant class, which, through the medium of the state, becomes also the politically dominant class." Only *as a rule*—not always? There are, then, exceptions to the rule that the class which dominates economically also dominates politically, that is, controls the state machinery?

> By way of exception, however, periods occur in which the warring classes balance each other so nearly that the state power, as ostensible mediator, acquires for the moment a certain degree of independence of both. Such was the absolute monarchy of the seventeenth and eighteenth centuries, which held the balance between the nobility and the class of burghers [*Bürgertum*] ; such was the Bonapartism of the First [under Napoleon I] and still more of the Second French Empire [Louis Bonaparte], which played off the proletariat against the bourgeoisie and the bourgeoisie against the proletariat. The latest performance of this kind . . . is the new German Empire of the Bismarckian nation: here capitalists and workers are balanced against each other and equally cheated for the benefit of the decadent Prussian cabbage-Junkers.[1]

A few pages later, we are reminded that "The cohesive force of civilized society is the state, which in all typical periods is exclusively

410

the state of the ruling class": plainly it is not so in atypical periods. But "in all cases [it] remains essentially a machine for keeping down the oppressed, exploited class."[2] What is in question, then, is not the class-repressive function of the state, which is fundamental to its role, but the variable relationship of the state to the ruling classes.

This applies not only to the regime of the Second Empire but that of Napoleon I, not only to France but Bismarckian Germany, and not only to the modern era but also the era of absolute monarchy. Later we will see still other types of regimes discussed in terms of this pattern.

We are dealing with an extension of the concept of Bonapartism made by Marx and Engels after the original analysis, an extension in which Bonapartism is not merely broadened in application but eventually becomes itself a special case of a still broader concept. These extended concepts of Bonapartism will be the subject of the next four chapters.

The application of the concept of the Bonapartist state to Bismarckian Germany was no great leap in itself. This step was adumbrated by Marx by the end of the 1850s, as the Prussian monarchy showed that it was carrying out certain aims and aspirations of the bourgeoisie while sternly excluding its representatives from political power. At this point the goal involved was the unification of Germany, albeit under Prussian hegemony and without Austria ("Little Germany"): the realization of a progressive aim in a reactionary form.

> The Reaction executes the program of the revolution. In this apparent contradiction lies the strength of Napoleonism [Bonapartism], which still today regards itself as the mandatary of the revolution of 1789. . . . To be sure, this program of revolution in the hands of Reaction turns into a satire of the revolutionary strivings involved, and thus into the deadliest weapon in the hands of the irreconcilable foe. The Reaction carries out the demands of the revolution in just the same way as Louis Bonaparte carries out those of the Italian nationalist party.[3]

Of course, Bonaparte carried out the demands of the Italian nationalists in the sense that he wanted to "liberate" Italy by replacing Austrian rule with his own. The implicit analogy was that Bismarck carried out the demands of the progressive bourgeoisie by unifying Germany—under the aegis of reactionary Prussian Junkerdom. Socially, the analogy was somewhat less than complete, for while the substitution of French oppression for Austrian would change little for Italians, the unification of Germany *even under reactionary auspices* would and did benefit the bourgeoisie by spurring the modernization of the society.

But the other analogy, between Bismarck's course and Bonapartism, was closer. Writing to Engels in 1862, Marx connected the enthusiasm of the German bourgeois progressives for the Bismarck cabinet with their enthusiasm for Louis Bonaparte: "Now they see what a 'Bonapartist' cabinet means in Prussia."[4] The Prussian Bonapartism of Bismarck was indeed welcomed by the bourgeoisie, which found its economic benefits more interesting than constitutional aspirations, even though Marx damned their dereliction: "That she [Germany] finds her *unity* at first in the *Prussian barracks* is a punishment she has amply merited."[5]

1. BISMARCK'S COUP

It was Engels who took up and developed the analogy between Bismarck's and Bonaparte's regimes, first in correspondence with Marx and then in a major work.*

For him, the turning point was Bismarck's announcement in April 1886 summoning a German parliament elected by universal suffrage. In preparation for war with Austria, it was the rabidly antidemocratic Junker monarchist who had become the champion of universal suffrage,

---

* On a couple of occasions Engels referred back to the fact that it was he who had specialized on this question, at least in print: in an 1883 letter he mentioned that the characteristics of the Bonapartist monarchy "were elaborated by Marx in *The Eighteenth Brumaire* and by me in *The Housing Question,* II, and elsewhere. . . ."[6] On the other hand, in an 1880 article he wrote that the General Council of the International had written "immediately after the war of 1870" that "You, Herr Bismarck, have overthrown the Bonapartist regime in France *only in order to reestablish it at home!*"[7] This would seem to refer to the council's Second Address on the War (September 1871), written by Marx; but there is no such statement there. Marx's report to the 1872 (Hague) congress contained a passage a little closer but not by much, in any case not related to Bonapartism. Assuming that Engels was acquainted with Marx's drafts for *The Civil War in France,* he may have been thinking of a passage in the Second Draft: "The Prussians who in coarse war exultation of triumph look at the agonies of French society and exploit them with the sordid calculation of a Shylock, and the flippant coarseness of the Krautjunker, are themselves already punished by the transplantation of the [Bonapartist] Empire to the German soil."[8]

not the bourgeois progressives. It was a sort of coup d'état in itself, the 18th Brumaire (or 2nd December) of Otto von Bismarck.

Before this, Engels, like Marx, had been tentative about seeing "Bonapartism" in the Prussian development. In an 1864 letter he had casually represented Bismarck as wanting to emulate the French emperor.[9] In an 1865 pamphlet on Prussian military and social policy, he had included a direct discussion of Bonapartism as a possible recourse of reaction, though the description of Bonapartism was pitched in French terms only. He had even explicitly raised the question, "what if the government were to . . . decree direct universal suffrage?"[10]

Four days after Bismarck's announcement, Engels ventured, in a letter to Marx, a first sketch of Bonapartism as an extended concept bearing on bourgeois development in general, not only locally.

> So Bismarck's universal-suffrage coup has been made, even if without his Lassalle [who, now dead, had urged him to this course]. It looks as if the German bourgeois will acquiesce in it after some kicking, for Bonapartism is indeed the real religion of the modern bourgeoisie. It is becoming clearer and clearer to me that the bourgeoisie doesn't have the stuff to rule directly itself, and that therefore, where there is no oligarchy as there is here in England to take over, for good pay, the managing of state and society in the interest of the bourgeoisie, a Bonapartist semi-dictatorship is the normal form; it carries out the big material interests of the bourgeoisie even against the bourgeoisie, but deprives the bourgeoisie of any share in the ruling power itself. On the other hand, this dictatorship is itself, in turn, compelled to reluctantly adopt these material interests of the bourgeoisie. So now here we have Monsieur Bismarck adopting the program of the Nationalverein [the pro-Russian bourgeois liberals].[11]

The political mechanism was, as in France, an equilibrium of classes, though not necessarily the same balance pattern of classes: Bismarck seeks "to play the Bonaparte as against the bourgeois with the Junkers behind him instead of peasants."[12] (In fact, Bismarck also counted on the Junkers' shepherding the peasant vote and on Prussophile leaders like the Lassalleans doing the same service in the working class.) Moreover, Engels saw that "Bonaparte's pupil, Bismarck" could not act simply as an agent of his own class, the Junkerdom. History had an ironic edge for Bismarck, who, so as to be able to carry on for a few months an apparently feudal and absolutist rule inside the country, on the outside pursues the policies of the bourgeoisie °with a vengeance,° prepares the way for the rule of the bourgeoisie, enters onto roads where progress can be made only with liberal and even revolutionary methods, and thereby day after day throws their own principles in the faces of his own cabbage-Junkers.

The feudal party, he chuckles, "is now choking over the crap they have to eat by command of their own leader."[13]

Eventually Bismarckism will have to converge with bourgeois aspirations more and more:

> Politically speaking, Bismarck will be obliged to base himself on the bourgeoisie, which he needs as against the princes. Perhaps not at this moment, since prestige and the army still suffice right now. But if only to make sure he has the necessary conditions for the central power with respect to parliament, he must give the bourgeoisie something, and the natural course of things will continually force him or his successors to fall back on the bourgeois again and again; so that even if Bismarck possibly avoids giving the bourgeoisie right now any more than he absolutely *has* to, still he is more and more pushed in the bourgeois direction.[14]

2. ENGELS' FIRST SKETCH

In 1872 Engels published a first sketch of the Bonapartist interpretation of Bismarckianism in his article on *The Housing Question*.

The context is important, for it comes right after his vigorous reassertion that "The state is nothing but the organized collective power of the possessing classes, the landowners and the capitalists, as against the exploited classes, the peasants and the workers." But, he asks, are the reactionaries right in claiming that in Germany, where the bourgeois do not rule as yet, "the state is still to a certain extent a power hovering independently over society, which for that very reason represents the collective interests of society and not those of a single class"? (One should note that there are two quite separate assertions involved here: one, that the state "hovers independently" over society;

and two, that it represents the collective interests of society.) Engels explains: "In reality, however, the state as it exists in Germany is likewise the necessary product of the social basis out of which it has developed." Whatever conclusions we may come to about this specific situation, the state will still be found explainable only in terms of the class structure of society, not primarily in terms of the "collective interests." In Prussia, Engels continues, the class structure looks as follows:

> There exists side by side with a landowning aristocracy, which is still powerful, a comparatively young and extremely cowardly bourgeoisie, which up to the present has not won either direct political domination, as in France, or more or less indirect domination as in England. Side by side with these two classes, however, there exists a rapidly increasing proletariat which is intellectually highly developed and which is becoming more and more organized every day.

This becomes the class basis of the Bonapartist equilibrium:

> Therefore, alongside of the basic condition of the old absolute monarchy, an equilibrium between the landed aristocracy and the bourgeoisie, we find here the basic condition of modern Bonapartism, an equilibrium between the bourgeoisie and the proletariat. But both in the old absolute monarchy and in the modern Bonapartist monarchy the real governmental authority lies in the hands of a special caste of army officers and state officials.[15]

Note that, whereas at first (1866) Engels had interpreted the Bismarckian class equilibrium as balancing primarily bourgeois against Junkers, he now sees this relationship as the obsolescent component still hanging on from the era of absolute monarchy. The distinctively modern component of Bonapartism is the bourgeoisie–proletariat equilibrium. This had not been so clearly visible in the French model because the proletariat had been pushed temporarily into the background. As Engels wrote later, Bismarck's "whole Bonapartist game consists in playing off, in turn, the workers against the bourgeois and the bourgeois against the workers, and thereby doing both in the eye."[16]

What is this bureaucratic "caste" (a loose term for a social stratum which does not play the role of a separate class)? In Prussia it is recruited partly out of its own ranks (father to son) and partly from the higher and lower aristocracy, "and least of all from the bourgeoisie." This caste enjoys a certain independence, but that does not mean the *state* is independent of class society: "The independence of this caste, which appears to occupy a position outside and, so to speak, above society, gives the state the semblance of independence in relation to society." But only the semblance. Under Prussian "pseudo-constitutionalism, a form which is at once both the present-day form of the dissolution of the old absolute monarchy and the form of existence of the Bonapartist monarchy," the old state forms are dissolving under the impact of industrial development.[17]

What is taking place is the social *fusion* of the governing bureaucracy and aristocracy with the bourgeoisie, through the growing bourgeoisification of the old ruling elements. The titled aristocrats enter "the whirlpool of speculation" in stocks, and the stock speculators enter the titled gentry. The bureaucrats, as well as the nobles, turn away from the traditional bureaucratic industry, embezzlement, in favor of corporation posts. As the elements of the old state decompose, "the non-bourgeois elements are becoming more bourgeois every day," and the transition quickens from the forms of the absolute monarchy to those of the Bonapartist monarchy. "In all economic questions the Prussian state is falling more and more into the hands of the bourgeoisie." The trend is held back only because the bourgeoisie itself is afraid of any of its own demands which also "provides the menacing proletariat with new weapons."

> And if the political power, that is, Bismarck, is attempting to organize its own bodyguard proletariat [Lassalleans and other pro-Prussian elements] to keep the political activity of the bourgeoisie in check, what else is that if not a necessary and quite familiar Bonapartist recipe which pledges the state to nothing more, as far as the workers are concerned, than a few benevolent phrases and at the utmost to a minimum of state assistance for building societies à la Louis Bonaparte?[18]

The reparations exacted from defeated France (the "French milliards") "have given a new, short reprieve to the independence of the Prussian state machine in regard to society"[19] by giving it an independent source of revenue, but being temporary, this cannot change the course of development.

In short: Engels does not take the wooden course of denying that, under Bonapartism, the state apparatus and the "caste" that operates it enjoy a certain autonomy with respect to the class society which they manage; but first, this autonomy is temporary—or better, conjunctural, that is, the outcome of a certain constellation of forces; and second, this fact does not in the least mean that the *state* is "a power hovering independently over society" or that it merely "represents the collective interests of society" rather than the actual resultant of class forces in a changing equilibrium.

True, this social reality could hardly be fully summed up in the aphorism that the state is "merely" a committee for managing the common affairs of the ruling class; but it illustrates that this aphorism is nothing more than an approximation, like Kepler's Laws of Motion in a far more exact science.

3. THE CLASS SHIFT

This first exposition of Bismarckian Bonapartism did not cover all the angles. In an article the following year, Engels emphasized the impotence and political emasculation of the bourgeoisie under the very regime that carried out its economic aspirations, while the Junkerdom that still seemed to be ruling politically was being undermined socially. For "Every government, including the most despotic, is compelled to govern with an eye on existing [social] relations, under pain of breaking its neck."

> Junkerdom, a necessity for old Prussia, was an encumbrance on the "Reich." Just as Bismarck had been obliged to put through freedom of trade, freedom of movement, and other bourgeois reforms—albeit in bureaucratically deformed manner—contrary to his previous views, so also the irony of history finally condemned him, the Junker *par excellence,* to lay the ax to Junkerdom. . . .[20]

But the bourgeoisie got what it needed, though what it got was bureaucratically deformed:

It took credit for the fact that Bismarck was compelled, by the historical position in which he had put Prussia and by the industrial progress of the last twenty years, to do that which the bourgeoisie itself had been too cowardly to carry through from 1848 to 1850. It did not even have the courage to force its Bismarck to carry out these little reforms in plain and simple bourgeois fashion, without making a police-state mess of it; it loudly exulted over the fact that Bismarck had to deal with its own demands of 1846 by—emasculating them. And, mind you, only its economic demands—things that a thousand Bismarcks could not have kept from being carried out even if they wanted to. As for *political* demands, turning over political power to the bourgeoisie, this sort of thing comes up in talk only as a concession to decency, at the most.

For fear of the class below, the bourgeoisie was happy to surrender political power to stronger hands, in exchange for cash payment:

> The Prussian bourgeoisie does not *want* political dominance; it is rotten before attaining maturity; without having ever enjoyed political rule, it has already reached the same stage of degeneration that the French bourgeoisie attained after eighty years of struggle and a longer period of rule. *Panem et circenses,* bread and theatricals—that is what the demoralized Roman plebs asked of their emperor; *panem et circenses,* swindlers' profits and animal-like luxury—this is what is asked of its emperor not by the Prussian people but by the Prussian bourgeoisie. The Roman plebs together with their emperor were swept away by the German barbarians; behind the Prussian bourgeoisie towers the threatening figure of the German workers.[21]

This autonomized state had been strengthened by its military victories of the 1860s followed by the smashing triumph over France; and its very increase in strength made it necessary for it to *shift its class base.* Engels wrote in another essay a year later: "In this way the very victories of the Prussian army shifted the entire basis of the Prussian state structure; the Junker domination became ever more intolerable even for the government." For now a big European power had to be a *modern* power: socioeconomic modernization was a necessity for a Reich, an empire. And economic modernization reinforced another class shift:

At the same time, however, the extremely rapid industrial development caused the struggle between bourgeois and worker to supersede the struggle between Junker and bourgeois, so that internally also the social foundations of the old state underwent a complete transformation.

This brought up the distinction we saw before: the obsolescent component was the class equilibrium held over from the era of absolute monarchy; the modern component was the specifically Bonapartist equilibrium of bourgeoisie against proletariat.

The basic precondition for the monarchy, which had been slowly rotting since 1840, was the struggle between nobility and bourgeoisie, in which the monarchy held the balance. From the moment when it was no longer a question of protecting the nobility against the onrush of the bourgeoisie, but of protecting all propertied classes against the onrush of the working class, the old absolute monarchy had to go over completely to the form of state expressly devised for this purpose: *the Bonapartist monarchy.*[22]

Bonapartism, Engels now stressed, is modern—it is "a modern form of state which presupposes the abolition of feudalism." That is why Junkerdom had to be sacrificed, even by the chief Junker, if he was to be a European power-wielder. "This, naturally, is being done in the mildest possible form and to the favorite tune of: *Immer langsam voran!*" (This echoed an old German song, translated by the U.S. Supreme Court as "with all deliberate speed.") The Junker was being transformed into something like an English squire, "and need not have offered so much resistance because the one is as stupid as the other." Thus Prussia was completing its bourgeois revolution in the form of Bonapartism.[23]

In exchange for the Bonapartist power's economic benefactions,

the bourgeoisie leaves all actual political power in the hands of the government, votes taxes, loans, and soldiers, and helps to frame all new reform laws in a way as to sustain the full force and effect of the old police power over undesirable elements. The bourgeoisie buys gradual social emancipation at the price of the immediate renunciation of political power. Naturally, the chief reason why such an agreement is acceptable to the bourgeoisie is not fear of the government but fear of the proletariat.[24]

4. ELEMENTS OF BONAPARTISM

In 1887 Engels began writing a summary account of the Bismarck era for use as an exposition of the relationship between political force and socioeconomic factors. (It was intended as the new fourth chapter, dealing with Germany, of a booklet whose main contents would be a reprint of the three chapters on the force theory in *Anti-Dühring*.) Although *The Role of Force in History* was therefore not focused on the problem of Bonapartism and, being unfinished, lacks whatever summation of the question Engels might have had in mind, let us review what it does contain for its partial recapitulations and special emphases.

1. *The historical role of Bonapartism is modernization of the society.*

In his "best period—up to 1870"[25] at any rate, Bismarck was willy-nilly engaged in this course. He realized that the Junkers were not a "viable class," that only the bourgeoisie had a future as a ruling class; and though concern for the bourgeoisie was not his motivation, yet "the existence of his new Reich promised to be so much the more secure, the more he gradually prepared it for the transition to a modern bourgeois state."[26] The Junkerdom was mostly past rescue in any case, its downfall imminent. By a policy of gradual and slow political concessions to the bourgeoisie which were anyway inevitable,

> the new Reich would at least be guided onto the road where it could fall in with the other West European states that were far ahead of it, finally shake off the last remnants of feudalism as well as the philistine tradition still strongly dominating the bureaucracy....[27]

It was wise of Bismarck "to steer toward bourgeois rule,"

> in short, to cut off Germany's immensely long old pigtail, and guide her consciously and definitely on the road of modern development, to adjust her political to her industrial state of affairs....[28]

Engels never suspected that such a role would one day be interpreted by self-styled revolutionists as a justification for giving political support to the Bonapartist modernizer. For him, it was objective evidence of how the old society, in one way or another, prepared the ground for eventual socialist victory. As he wrote in a letter, apropos of the rapid progress of industry in Germany: "in any case the old philistine Germany is finally beginning to become a modern country, and that is absolutely necessary to help us get ahead."[29]

2. *The bourgeoisie trades its political rights and power in exchange for the insurance of economic expansion.*

This aspect has already been sufficiently brought out. In *The Role of Force in History* Engels is particularly concerned with those economic concerns of the bourgeoisie which required the national unification of Germany; he explains in some detail why the split-up state of Germany "inevitably soon became an unbearable fetter on vigorously growing industry," and therefore why "the desire for a united 'Fatherland' had a very material background."[30] National unity was inextricably bound up with foreign policy, and here bourgeois aspirations matched Prussia's.

> Bismarck moved in. It was a matter of repeating Louis Napoleon's coup d'état, making the real relationship of forces utterly clear to the German bourgeoisie, forcibly dispelling their liberal self-delusions, but carrying out those national demands of theirs that coincided with Prussian wishes. . . .
>
> In the continuing conflict over the constitution, Bismarck had fought the parliamentary demands of the bourgeoisie to the uttermost. But he burned with eagerness to carry out its national demands: after all they coincided with the deepest-held heart's desires of Prussian policy.[31]

Marx had remarked that Bismarck "began by building up a despotism under the plea of unification,"[32] that is, the aim was his "despotism," the means to it, the espousal of national unity. For the bourgeoisie, the aim was unification; the price, Bismarckian "despotism," their surrender of political power to the old state.

3. *The Bonapartist state had to enforce the interests of the class even against the opposition of the class itself or its unenlightened sections.*

Bismarck, remarks Engels, "did the will of the bourgeoisie against its will," that is, carried out what the bourgeoisie really wanted even while the bourgeoisie fought him in the conflict over the constitution.[33] In part, this relationship depended on the previous point, the swapping of political rights for economic benefits. But in addition, there were different bourgeois elements involved, since the class consisted of disparate parts and individuals.

In particular Engels pointed—as Marx had done in *The Eighteenth Brumaire*—to the split between the practicing bourgeoisie and the ideological wing of the bourgeoisie. The ideological spokesmen in and out of parliament could not be as crudely indifferent as the real economic powers to the demands of political consistency and democratic rhetoric. They sometimes had to be left high and dry, still spouting. There was

> a contradiction quite similar to the one in France in 1851 between the bourgeoisie in the Chamber who wanted to keep the power of the President [Bonaparte] in check and the bourgeoisie outside who wanted tranquillity and strong government, tranquillity at any price—a contradiction which Louis Napoleon resolved by dispersing the squabblers in parliament and giving the mass of the bourgeoisie tranquillity. . . .[34]

Bismarck was equally ready to manhandle the constitution to suit his purposes; the introduction of universal suffrage forms by fiat from above was one means at hand.

> Hadn't Louis Napoleon shown there was absolutely no risk—if handled right? And wasn't it precisely this universal suffrage that offered a means of appealing to the great mass of people, and flirting a little with the newly arising social movement, if the bourgeoisie proved refractory? [35]

For the social movement of the proletariat was green and stumbling, and Bismarck had his "royal-Prussian socialists" (as Marx called them) just as Bonaparte had had his Saint-Simonians at heel.

The case was clearest with respect to the Junkers, who could not understand that the world was changing at all, nor that their own man Bismarck was doing well in letting them down easily; for their saurian mentalities understood only that they were being let *down*. To be sure, they could not get in Bismarck's way, for this class was a living fossil lacking effective energy. "The Junkers had proved this for sixty years during which the state continually did what was best for them against the opposition of these Don Quixotes" themselves.[36] Even when Bismarck put through a district ordinance that preserved as far as possible the Junkers' privileges in exploitation of the rural "helots," they could only rail at the introduction of any change at all:

> But what can one say about the stupidity of their excellencies the Junkers, who pulled a tantrum like spoiled children against this district ordinance which had been worked up solely in their own interests, in the interest of prolonging their feudal privileges, only under a somewhat modernized label? [37]

No more than F. Ebert or F. D. Roosevelt later did Bismarck get any thanks for saving a sickly class from its own shortsighted excesses. As Engels commented in 1890, "°°The aristocracy Bismarck never could rely on; they always considered him as a traitor to true Conservatism, and will be ready to throw him overboard. . . ." [38] Yet Bismarck was in fact trying to save as much of their class privileges as could be saved, just as the agrarian legislation of pre-1848 Prussia had tried "to save as much of feudalism as could be saved" (as Engels had remarked in another connection). [39]

4. *Bonapartism as a state form does not depend on the personal qualities of the dictator in charge.*

There was a considerable personal element in Marx's analysis of Louis Bonaparte's regime in *The Eighteenth Brumaire* and in his subsequent articles for the *New York Tribune.* On the one hand, Marx's close attention to the personality of the chief actor is a salutory antidote to the myth that Marxism simply negates the role of the individual in history; for it was necessary to explain how this development took place in a specific place at a specific time, and how the individual element became part of the fabric woven by dominant social forces. But there is an inherent difficulty when a scientist can examine only a unique specimen of a given phenomenon: where exactly is the line between the generic and the specific?

Bismarckism, as another case of the Bonapartist pattern, helped to clarify this question. On the personal plane, it was enough to see the difference between the lumpen-Napoleon and the super-Junker. "Bismarck," wrote Engels, "is Louis Napoleon translated from the French adventurist-pretender into the Prussian cabbage-Junker and German student fraternity man [*Korpsbursche*]." [40]

He tried to find common ground between the two: "Like Louis Napoleon, Bismarck is a man with a very practical head and great cunning, a born businessman and a crafty one, who in other circum-

424 Part II: The Theory of the State

stances would have rivaled the Vanderbilts and Jay Goulds on the New York stock exchange. . . ."[41]

> Had not Louis Napoleon become the idol of the bourgeoisie precisely because he dispersed their parliament but increased their profits? And didn't Bismarck have the same business talents that the bourgeoisie admired so much in the false Napoleon?[42]

But the indicated characteristics (even if taken to be true of Louis Napoleon) are not really specifically bourgeois; they are generally found among successful organizers and reorganizers of states in difficult situations, including Diocletian and Charlemagne, as well as in corporation manipulators. In the same passage, Engels points out pertinently that Bismarck, although so narrow-minded at bottom that he could not free himself of his specifically Prussian outlook, lacking originality of mind, yet was the artful user of others' ideas, and, unlike the bourgeois leaders, endowed with energy and will.

Each Bonapartism shared a similar sociopolitical content even though details naturally differed: "The bourgeoisie supplied him [Bismarck] the goal, and Louis Napoleon supplied the path to the goal; only the way he carried it out remained Bismarck's own work."[43] Also, the two regimes operated under different economic circumstances, which led to different short-range economic effects, and so on.[44] It need hardly be added that the two Bonapartes likewise became deadly rivals for supremacy in Europe.

It is not only the personality factor that has to be identified if the various adventitious elements of given Bonapartisms are to be separated from the *specifically Bonapartist* element. For, as in all real historical situations, Bismarck's regime was no more than Louis Napoleon's a chemically pure or laboratory-isolated distillation of Bonapartism—if such a thing can be imagined. Like all social phenomena, it is found in nature only in various admixtures. If the Germans (as Engels remarked in a letter) "are stuck in a mishmash of semifeudalism and Bonapartism,"[45] what belonged to the old and what to the new *ism?* What constituted the *differentia specifica* of Bonapartism?

5. *The crux of Bonapartism is the autonomization of the state power with respect to all the classes, including the ruling classes.*

We remind that this use of the term *autonomization* is ours, not Marx's or Engels'; but it represents the conception which Engels develops on Bismarckism's relation to the class structure.

"As things stood in 1871 in Germany," writes Engels, "a man like Bismarck was indeed thrown back on a policy of tacking and veering among the various classes." That in itself was no reproach: the question was, where was he heading? There were three possibilities. Toward eventual bourgeois rule? In that case, his policy would at least be "in harmony with historical development." Toward preserving the old Prussian state? In that case, it would be reactionary. Or was his policy headed in a third direction? "If it headed toward simply maintaining Bismarck's rule, then it was Bonapartist and bound to end like every Bonapartism."[46] Indeed, events showed that Bismarck's guiding star was the third aim, as he insisted on cutting the Reich constitution "to his own measure."

> It was one step further on the road to his personal one-man rule [*Alleinherrschaft*], by balancing the parties in the Reichstag and the particularist states in the Federal Council—one step further on the road to Bonapartism.[47]

Thus the specifically Bonapartist direction is clearly differentiated from a state policy directed either in the interest of the bourgeoisie or of the old Prussian ruling class. Subsequently, Engels made clear, Bismarck did veer in the direction of Junkerdom, reverting to his own class roots—and ensuring his downfall. To follow this line of thought more closely, we have to turn from the manuscript of *The Role of Force in History,* which breaks off soon after this point, and go on to his outline notes on how he planned to finish this chapter. Here his Point I is naturally sketchy but quite clear:

> I. Three classes: two rotten ones, of which one [Junkers] is in decay, the other [bourgeoisie] on the rise, and [the] workers, who only want bourgeois °fair play°. Thus, tacking and veering between the latter two [would be] right—but no! [This is not Bismarck's course; rather, this is his] Policy: Strengthening the state power in general and *especially* making it financially independent (railway statification, monopoly), police state, and principles of justice of provincial law.[48]

Under Point II, Engels notes the "restoration of the police state and antibourgeois legal system (1876), bad copy of the French." But then comes Bismarck's "complete swing-about toward Junkers," marked by the protective tariff, the "colonial swindle," and so on. Yet, following this "swing-about" is the following note under II.5: "Social policy à la

Bonaparte. (a) Anti-Socialist Law and crushing of workers' organizations and labor funds. (b) Social-reform crap."[49] The result, in a terse note: "Bismarck at the end—becomes reactionary, foolish. . . . The Junker comes to the fore, for lack of other ideas."[50] And then "after the war of 1870-71 . . . Bismarck's mission is fulfilled, so that he can now sink back again into the ordinary Junker."[51] There was still something of the "mishmash of semifeudalism and Bonapartism" in the admixture, but with Bismarck's fall the modern elements of bourgeois development asserted themselves more and more.

It is clear, then, that it is not the existence of a class equilibrium, the balancing of countervailing class pressures, which is itself the distinguishing feature of Bonapartism. This condition would confront any statesman under the circumstances, and would necessitate a maneuverist policy by any ruling-class leader. The crux of Bonapartism was the utilization of this condition to maximize the autonomous position of the state with respect to the classes—"strengthening the state power in general and especially making it financially independent"—an autonomization organized under a "personal one-man rule," the one man being an individual who is not functioning as the chairman of *any* class's "executive committee."

6. *Still, the objective historical result is a social transformation, a "revolution from above."**

The revolution from below had failed in 1848-1849. At that time the bourgeoisie had hoped to bring about a fusion of ruling classes with itself on top, and in its own way. Momentarily there had been a "triple alliance of Junkers, bureaucrats, and bourgeois now in power," as Engels had written in April 1849.[53] But this alliance refused to stabilize itself under the new hegemony. The alliance fell apart; but while the bourgeoisie remained excluded from political power, the tasks of the revolution *manqué* pressed heavily on society nonetheless. Something had to give, in the tension between the revolution that labored in the womb and the revolutionary class that could not give it birth. The same fusion of ruling classes had to be reestablished—only, under the hegemony of the old classes and with a different relation of forces. The

---

* The phrase "revolution from above" (according to Ladendorf) became current in Germany in the early nineteenth century, especially through F. von Schlegel, who in 1820 claimed its invention. He applied it to the first Bonapartism, that of Napoleon I, in whose hands "the revolution . . . had been transformed into a great despotism and revolution from above."[52]

revolution that had to come *came*, but in the most reactionary possible form. The Reaction executed the program of the revolution, and "this program of revolution in the hands of Reaction turns into a satire on the revolutionary strivings involved, and thus into the deadliest weapon in the hands of an irreconcilable foe," as Marx had foreseen well in advance.

> In short [wrote Engels of Bismarck], it was a thoroughgoing revolution, carried out with revolutionary methods. We are naturally the last to make this a matter of reproach. What we reproach him for, on the contrary, is that he was not revolutionary enough, that he was only a Prussian revolutionary from above. . . .[54]

It was "only half a revolution," stopping short with the interests of the bourgeoisie and the Junkers even if it did revolutionize the outmoded social conditions. Thus Bismarck "made his coup d'état, his revolution from above, in 1866, against the German Confederation and Austria, and no less against the Prussian *Konfliktskammer.*"[55]

The revolution from above by the autonomized state power was not accepted by Marx or Engels as a progressive substitute for revolution. During the 1850s and 1860s Marx's journalistic articles particularly carried on a drumfire of denunciation and indictment against the Bonapartist regimes that is not outdone by any of his other writings. The objective historical role of these regimes was a fact that had to be accepted; but also accepted was the fact that they were "the deadliest weapon in the hands of an irreconcilable foe." The first fact depended on a social analysis—a scientific determination of the lay of the land; the second, on a social taking-of-position—a choice of sides in a class war.

17 | BONAPARTISM AND THE "PROGRESSIVE DESPOT"

In the key passage (given at the beginning of the previous chapter) where Engels lists the types of states characterized by "a certain degree of independence" from the classes in equilibrium, we note that he includes the Bonapartism of the First Empire under Napoleon I as well as that of Louis Bonaparte. Whereas Bismarckism moved Marx and Engels to extend the Bonapartist pattern geographically, here we see them extending it back in time.

The word *Bonapartist* or *Bonapartism,* of course, was common under Napoleon, referring to his partisans; but in the passage under discussion Engels obviously used it in the new sense of a type of autonomized state power. This Bonapartism was less well developed under the uncle than under the nephew, but still visible. How did it manifest itself under the first Napoleon?

1. THE NAPOLEONIC STATE

One of Marx's earliest political attitudes was a deep hostility to Napoleon as a military despot and oppressor of peoples, but it was tempered by a willingness to grant his stature as a military and state-organizing genius and by recognition of his progressive social role in smashing the old regime outside France, especially in Germany. This combination was common enough among German liberals and leftists, especially in the Rhineland where Napoleon's armies had done their work most thoroughly. A letter by Marx's father to his nineteen-year-old son already denounced Napoleon as a suppressor of free thought, even though the father was no Francophobe but rather a pupil of the

428

Enlightenment.[1] The same year (to instance the positive side) Marx's juvenile "humorous novel" *Scorpion and Felix* illustrated the thesis that giants are succeeded by pygmies, geniuses by wooden philistines, with examples that included the contrast of Napoleon I with Louis Philippe.[2]

These cases reflect the political climate surrounding Marx's juvenile consciousness; but the same pattern essentially obtains in the first considerable reference to Napoleon in his political writings. In the 1843 exchange of letters published in the *Deutsch-Französische Jahrbücher,* the new-fledged socialist Marx depicts Napoleon as a despot who exemplifies the proposition that "Despotism's sole thought is contempt for man, dehumanized man," even if the despot is one "capable of great aims, like Napoleon prior to his dynastic frenzy."[3]

For decades afterward, Marx frequently echoed the giants-versus-pygmies comparison, especially in contrasting Louis Bonaparte with Napoleon, the "nephew" with the "uncle."[4] The progressive role of Napoleon's impact on Germany was not in question: *The German Ideology* duly acknowledged his services in "cleaning out Germany's Augean stables," for example.[5] During the 1848–1849 revolution, the Prussian regime's antidemocratic crimes could be compared only to the "Napoleonic despotism over the press"; still, it had to be acknowledged that, if the French sighed for Napoleon after the Bourbon Restoration, it was only "because the despotism of a genius is more bearable than the despotism of an idiot."[6]

Marx's germinal statement on the link between Napoleon and the concept of Bonapartism occurs, interestingly enough, long before he developed that concept in *The Eighteenth Brumaire,* and even before he had fully developed the class theory of the state. It is to be found in *The Holy Family.* The fact that it occurs so early means that we are dealing with the roots of the concept of Bonapartism, not its application.

The analysis in *The Holy Family* revolves around the relation between the French Revolution and the social classes. The revolution opened society to bourgeois rule; but Marx sees that the Jacobin left—here represented by the Terror—wanted to push beyond the bounds of mere bourgeois interests. Robespierre fails; the Thermidorean reaction leads to the Directory.

Under the government of the *Directory, bourgeois society*—which the Revolution itself had freed from feudal fetters and officially

recognized even though the *Terror* wanted to sacrifice it to an
ancient [form of] political life—burst out in mighty streams of
life.

It was against the flourishing of the liberal bourgeoisie under the
Directory that (Marx goes on to say) Napoleon directed his coup d'état
of the 18th Brumaire. Was, then, Napoleon simply antibourgeois? The
question is ambiguous. He did not wish to reverse the Revolution's
acceptance of bourgeois society (capitalism as a social system); still less
did he have any notion of turning social relations back to prebourgeois
channels. The bourgeoisie would dominate within civil society, sure
enough, but the Napoleonic state must dominate all of civil society
itself, including the bourgeoisie.

Let us see how Marx puts this crucial thought:

> *Napoleon* was the last struggle by the *revolutionary Terror* against
> *bourgeois society* . . . and its policy. To be sure, Napoleon already
> had the insight into the essence of the *modern state* that it rested
> on the basis of the unhampered development of bourgeois society,
> the free activity of private interest, and so on. He decided to
> recognize and protect this basis. He was no dreamy-eyed
> Terrorist.[7]

This was the probourgeois side.* Now the other:

> But at the same time Napoleon still regarded the *state* as an *end
> in itself,* and civil [*bürgerlich*] life only as the treasurer and as its
> *subordinate,* which must have no *will of its own.* . . . He satisfied
> the egoism of French nationalism to the point of complete
> surfeit, but he also demanded the sacrifice of bourgeois business,
> self-enjoyment, wealth, etc. whenever the political goal of con-
> quest required it. If he despotically suppressed the liberalism of
> bourgeois society—the political ideology of its day-to-day prac-

---

* The strongest statement of this side that Marx made subsequently occurs in
The Eighteenth Brumaire, but it does not differ essentially from what is already
said on this score in *The Holy Family.* Napoleon "created inside France the
conditions under which alone free competition could be developed, parceled
landed property exploited and the unchained industrial productive power of the
nation employed; and beyond the French borders he everywhere swept the feudal
institutions away, so far as was necessary to furnish bourgeois society in France
with a suitable up-to-date environment on the European Continent." But, he goes
on to say, this done, Napoleon had to disappear along with the other "ante-
diluvian colossi" to make way for the "true interpreters and mouthpieces" of the
bourgeoisie and "its real military leaders."[8] The Bonapartist side of Napoleon I is
not raised in this context.

tice—he showed no more consideration for its essential *material* interests, commerce and industry, whenever they came into conflict with his political interests. His contempt for industrial businessmen was the complement to his contempt for *ideologues*. Internally as well, what he fought in bourgeois society was opposition to the state, embodied by himself, as an absolute end in itself.[9]

To be sure, this Napoleonic concept of an autonomized state, which fostered bourgeois development so that the *state's* interests might thereby be aggrandized, had no future under the social circumstances. Marx had already written on a previous page of *The Holy Family* that bourgeois interests "were so powerful that they victoriously overcame the pen of a Marat, the guillotine of the Terrorists, and the sword of Napoleon, as well as the crucifix and the blue blood of the Bourbons."[10] However, it was Napoleon's striving in this direction that constituted the specific Bonapartism of the First Empire, no matter how surely doomed at the time.

A question-mark remains. We can certainly not assume automatically that a given analysis in *The Holy Family* represents a continuity of thought with the mature Marx, in the absence of a repetition of the same analysis later. Unfortunately, Marx never took the occasion later to take up the theme of the Bonapartism of the first Napoleon directly.* But Engels did, even if briefly; furthermore, in the case of both Marx and Engels it is worth noting the constancy of their general view of the man.

In 1860 a pamphlet by Engels linked Napoleon to the later Bonapartism in a minor aspect and in passing.** But much later the figure of

* The nearest approach is a remark in *The Eighteenth Brumaire* made collectively about "the absolute monarchy, during the first Revolution, under Napoleon." In all three cases, "bureaucracy was only the means of preparing the class rule of the bourgeoisie"—i.e., objectively, not by intention—whereas "Under the Restoration, under Louis Philippe, under the parliamentary republic, it [the state bureaucracy] was the instrument of the ruling class, however much it strove for power of its own."[11] We will return to this passage in Chapter 20.

** In *Savoy, Nice and the Rhine* Engels recalls the episode when the troops of General Anselme took Nice and, out of control, subjected the city to plunder and rape. "This was the original core of the later Army of Italy, with which General Bonaparte gained his first laurels," Engels continues, and then jumps to a comparison with the nephew: "Bonapartism, it seems, in its beginnings always has to base itself on the riffraff [*Lumpentum*]; without a Society of December 10th it would have gotten nowhere."[12] But in terms of historical analysis, a vicious soldiery is hardly the equivalent of Bonapartist storm-troops. Engels wants to link Napoleon with the later Bonapartism but does not really succeed here.

General Boulanger gave him another opportunity, as he commented on the new would-be Bonaparte's electoral victory in 1889. This, he wrote, reflects

°°a distinct revival of the Bonapartist element in the Parisian character. In 1798 [actually 1799: Napoleon's coup d'état], 1848 and 1889, this revival arose equally from discontent with the bourgeois republic, but it took this special direction—appeal to a saviour of society—entirely in consequence of a chauvinistic current.[13]

Bonapartism's antibourgeois side is stressed here, as also in a follow-up letter on the same subject, which links Napoleon I, Napoleon III, and Boulanger with the "recrudescence of Bonapartism, of an appeal to a savior who is to destroy the vile bourgeois who have quashed the revolution and the republic"—this reflecting "the negative side of the Parisian revolutionary character—chauvinistic Bonapartism. . . ."[14]

2. THE LITTLENESS OF NAPOLEON THE GREAT

Insofar as Marx's and Engels' general attitude toward Napoleon shifted in later life, it was only in the direction of a more virulent antipathy, less qualified by recognition of positive achievements.

While Marx's journalistic articles of the 1850s constantly scorned Louis Bonaparte in contrast with Napoleon as far as ability was concerned (a pattern set for all France when Victor Hugo labeled the epigone emperor "Napoleon the Little"), he was equally ready to condemn "the cruel despotism of Napoleon I." If he denounced Louis Bonaparte for filling the Paris salons with his police spies, he added: "quite as in the days of the [first] Emperor."[15]

What Marx attacked most often was any leaning toward a "Napoleon cult," such as is found even in the alleged libertarian Proudhon.[16] Marx lashed at "the traditional Napoleon superstition," the "Napoleon cult" or "Napoleon legend," in his major works on France; he linked Thiers as sycophantic historian of Napoleon to Thiers as butcher of the Paris Commune; the peasant cult of Napoleon was a "delusion" or fantasy, just as both Thiers and his imperial subject were notorious liars.[17]

"Both father and daughter [Jenny] hated Napoleon I," related Dr. Kugelmann's daughter, to explain why Jenny answered the question

"Characters of history I most dislike" with: "Bonaparte and his nephew." It was often to abuse the nephew that the "real Napoleon" could even be granted his genius, as when Marx repeated the jest that *"Napoléon le premier a eu génie, Napoléon le troisième a Eugénie."* Around the same time Marx asked Engels for a clipping from a recent history revealing the "wretched behavior of the hero" Napoleon so that daughter Jenny could win an argument.[18]

There are two longer denunciations of Napoleon in Marx.

He devoted a *New York Tribune* article to demonstrating that the current Bonaparte's suppression of liberty and press freedom only reenacted "the shabby part invented and played before by Napoleon the Great," and in fact objected to the title "Napoleon the Great" as furthering "Napoleon-worship." Marx added: "What is more useful to impress on the present generation is that Napoleon the Little [Louis Napoleon] represents in fact the littleness of Napoleon the Great."[19] This article was an elaboration of a remark that Marx had already made in a letter to Engels two months previously: Bonaparte "is only copying his alleged uncle. He . . . °personates [personifies] in a most admirable way° the °littleness° of the great Napoleon."[20]

Again: in a detailed indictment of French policy on Poland, Marx elaborated the thesis that Napoleon betrayed Polish independence; and even at home "that despot rather than have a truly *national* and *revolutionary war* in France after his defeat at Waterloo, preferred to succumb to the Coalition."[21] In his book *Herr Vogt,* Marx flayed Napoleon's betrayal of Venetian independence "to the despotic yoke of Austria."[22] Likewise, in referring to Napoleon's invasion of Spain, he criticized it as "the Napoleonic usurpation," yet also recognized the fact that where Napoleon's armies overran the country, there they "swept away from the soil all monastic and feudal institutions, and introduced the modern system of administration."[23] This two-sided appreciation is very much like Marx's appraisal of British imperialism's role in India, combining political hostility with recognition of imperialism's modernizing impact.

Later Marx introduced a new note even into his appraisal of Napoleon's relationship to European reaction. It appears in a change made between the first draft of *The Civil War in France* and the final version. In the first draft Marx writes of the overgrown French state apparatus, which "grew to its full development under the sway of the first Bonaparte," that under Napoleon "it served not only to subjugate the Revolution and annihilate all popular liberties, it was an instrument of the French revolution to strike abroad, to create for France on the Continent instead of feudal monarchies more or less states after the image of France." Here, as before, is the counterposition of despotism at home and a progressive impact abroad. But in the corresponding passage of the final version, Napoleon's "First Empire" is described merely as "itself the offspring of the coalition wars of old semifeudal Europe against modern France."[24] There is an appreciable shift here, from seeing the Napoleonic regime as "an instrument of the French revolution" even in one aspect, to seeing it as the "offspring" of European reaction itself in a definite sense.

Engels' course was quite similar. In his presocialist literary period of 1840–1841, he referred to Napoleon both with hostility as a despotic ruler and with respect as nonetheless responsible for progressive social gains—listing these gains as emancipation of the Jews, trial by jury, and a sound civil-law system. "Heine's Napoleon-worship is alien to the feelings of the [German] people," he insisted.[25] On the other hand, when Napoleon's body was moved to the Invalides, he published a poem combining relief at the passing of the Napoleonic era with respect for the man. It was good that "Europe's scourge, France's god" had died "like Alexander, without issue"; and now

> The Emperor sleeps, and hushed is the Te Deum;
> A stately pall hangs o'er the pious stone.
> The whole great chapel is his mausoleum!
> A dead god lies interred, and all alone.[26]

This two-sided view continued after his conversion to socialism, without essential change. Napoleon established "undisguised despotism," contrasted with Babeuf's goal of "real liberty"; at the same time, his progressive impact on Germany as "the destroyer of old feudal society" was appreciated, even though "the longer he reigned, the more he deserved his ultimate fate."[27]

In the later Engels, the references to Napoleon are more uniformly hostile.* The Code Napoléon was really the work of the Revolution and

---

* The main kind of exception continues to be Napoleon's progressive role in modernizing the German states; for example, "The creator of the German bourgeoisie was Napoleon."[28] In this respect Napoleon was criticized for failing to go far enough. "He is always revolutionary as opposed to the princes," noted Engels, but added: "Napoleon's mistake of 1806 was that he did not crush Prussia to the end."[29]

only "botched" by Napoleon himself; he was indeed something of a charlatan like Boulanger; the peasants' Napoleon figure was a "legend."[30] In a May Day greeting to Spanish socialists, Engels recalled the resistance to "the foreign invasion and tyranny of Napoleon"; then he started on a longer denunciation of Napoleon, "the so-called representative of the bourgeois revolution, in reality a despot inside his own country and a conqueror vis-à-vis the neighboring peoples," but left this out of the final version.[31] In his introduction to Marx's *Civil War in France,* he contrasted the Paris Commune with the bureaucratic state machine "which Napoleon had created in 1798." As we saw above, Marx had made the same connection in his first draft of the address on the Commune, when he wrote that the gigantism of the state machine "grew to its full development under the sway of the first Bonaparte" and that under him it served "to subjugate the Revolution and annihilate all popular liberties."[32]

Typically, the later Engels did not begrudge a passing bow to the progressive side of Napoleon's impact when the context was Russian czarism's expansionism, though he stressed Napoleon's betrayal of European national movements. In an 1890 article on Russian foreign policy, he reviewed the czar's relations with Napoleon. "The French Revolution had worn itself out, and had brought forth its own dictator—a Napoleon. . . . The rise of Napoleon now gave it [Russian diplomacy] the opportunity for new successes." Napoleon played along with Russia's game until they came to a parting of their imperialist ways over the czar's effort to dominate the German states. Austerlitz kept the Rhineland free of Russian domination, and of course Engels felt that Napoleonic domination was objectively preferable: "The French yoke, at least, was a modern one; at all events it forced the disgraceful German Princes to do away with the most crying infamies of their former political system." There is a good deal more on Napoleon's disregard of various national interests—Finland's and Turkey's as well as Poland's—as he played his imperialist chess game with Russia. Still, "the downfall of Napoleon meant the victory of the European monarchies over the French Revolution, whose last phase had been the Napoleonic Empire."[33]

3. THE LINE OF POLITICAL OPPOSITION

The significance of Marx's and Engels' hostility to the "progressive" despotism of the first Bonaparte has not usually been appreciated, especially if we keep in mind that this hostility mounted as their politics matured.

It is a good test case because, for one thing, the frequent allegation of a *personal* factor in Marx's political antipathies clearly has no basis in this instance. (In general Marx's pattern is that expressions of personal dislike flow from political enmity, not vice-versa.) For another thing, Napoleon I came along so early that he was not clearly counterposed to a proletarian movement, nor had socialism yet appeared as a viable alternative. This would seem to make him a good candidate for support as a historically progressive modernizer, despot though he be.

But such an approach was totally alien to Marx's and Engels' politics. They were quite capable of appreciating the historical progressiveness of a regime in an objective social sense without confusing this with the criteria for political support, any more than they would dream of becoming political supporters of or apologists for the "progressive capitalists" of the Industrial Revolution.* The touchstone of politics for them was the class struggle—the struggle of the lower classes against oppression and exploitation, in the present as in the time of Spartacus or Napoleon. A political position was a taking of sides in a class war.

Hence they felt not the slightest contradiction between recognizing the objective historical impact of a Bonapartism (Bismarck's, for example) and rallying the harshest political opposition against it. The objective progressiveness of a despot or exploiter meant merely that the enemy was compelled by history to help your cause despite himself: it could not for a moment induce you to change your mind about which side you were on. On the contrary, it was only the continued class struggle from below that could even squeeze the greatest historical advantage out of the "progressive" social forces which were propelling your enemy on his path.

---

* This question will come up again for discussion in connection with the politics of bourgeois revolution in Volume 2.

This was the attitude spelled out, firmly but ruefully, by Engels when it became clear that Bismarck was in position, by reason of Prussian military successes, to bring about the long-desired unification of Germany in his own way: the situation discussed at the beginning of the previous chapter. A progressive aim was being carried out, though not in *our* way; and so Engels allows that "we, like others, must recognize the *fait accompli,* [whether] °we may like it or not.°"

> The good side of this is that it simplifies the situation, facilitates a revolution by getting rid of the rows kicked up by the little state capitals, and in any case accelerates the development. After all, a German parliament is still something altogether different from a Prussian Diet. The whole mess of little states will be drawn into the movement, the worst influences toward local narrowness will come to an end, and the parties will finally become really national instead of merely local.
>
> The main drawback is the inevitable swamping of Germany by Prussianism, and this is a very big one. Then there is the temporary separation of German Austria, which will result in an immediate advance of Slavdom in Bohemia, Moravia, and Carinthia. Unfortunately, against *neither* of these is there *anything* to be done.
>
> So in my opinion we can do nothing but simply accept the fact, without approving it, and make use, as far as we can, of the greater facilities for the *national* organization and unification of the German proletariat that must now arise in any case.[34]

Marx replied agreeing: "I am entirely of your opinion that the filthy business must be taken as it is. Still it is nice to be far away during this honeymoon period"—while the German states cohabited under Prussia.[35]

The turn in the situation established a new starting point, but it was a new start for the struggle *against* the "progressive" Bonapartist. Bismarck was "facilitating a revolution" but the revolution could be furthered only by intransigent opposition to this facilitator. When the Lassalleans showed softness on Bismarck, Marx and Engels broke with them publicly.

4. THE CASE OF BOLIVAR

A case similar to Napoleon's, this time outside of Europe, was that of the leader of the South American liberation struggle, Simon Bolívar. Finding Bolívar's name on the list of articles to be done for the *New American Cyclopaedia,* Marx researched his subject and came up with an attitude of intense political hostility to the "Liberator" as a military dictator, authoritarian, and Bonaparte-type seeker of arbitrary power for himself.[36]

The issue is sharpened by the fact that Marx clearly assumed the progressiveness of the national liberation movement itself. His attack on Bolívar is always fully inside the framework of the view that the independence struggle was *weakened* by Bolívar's insistence on his personal dictatorship. The various revolutionary congresses exercised a popular mobilizing appeal to the masses insofar as Bolívar *failed* to control and abort them, whereas the leader's despotic methods kept the mass base of the revolution small.*

"Bolívar is a real Soulouque [one of the current sobriquets for Bonaparte]," Marx wrote to Engels, explaining the reason for the "partisan style" of his *Cyclopaedia* article, which its editor had questioned.[37] In the article itself, Marx had managed to link Bolívar with Napoleon I three times, however obliquely; mention of Louis Bonaparte would have been obviously intrusive.

If Bolívar was a "real Bonaparte," the leader of another contemporary national-liberation movement was another Bolívar, in Marx's view. This was Hungary's Louis Kossuth, of whom Marx's opinion was as scathing as of Italy's Mazzini. One of Marx's many denunciations of Kossuth's political role, written two years after his Bolívar article, began as follows: "The myth-creating force of popular fantasy has manifested itself in all times in the invention of 'great men.' The most striking example of this sort is indisputably *Simon Bolívar.*"[38] The dissection of Kossuth followed.

Marx saw these, and other, leaders as men who were *riding* a movement with progressive and liberationist aims, but who bestrode it with political aims of their own which were antithetical to the interests of the masses.

* A detailed discussion of these issues can be found in my article on the subject, *Karl Marx and Simon Bolívar* (see Bibliography).

18 | BONAPARTISM IN EXTREMIS

We can now return to the figure of the model Bonapartist, Louis Bonaparte himself, in order to view him from the same angle as Napoleon I and Bolívar: namely Bonaparte as Progressive Despot. Marx paid little attention to this aspect in his best-known works; when he wrote *The Eighteenth Brumaire* it had not yet emerged as strongly as it did later, and when he looked back in *The Civil War in France* it seemed a finished episode. In the meantime he had written it up cogently; and from today's perspective the subject has new interest.

1. BONAPARTE'S "SOCIALISM"

Even at the time of his "18th Brumaire," Bonaparte's *Idées Napoléoniennes* (the title of one of his books) played a role in giving him an antibourgeois posture, at the same time that his deeds assured the bourgeoisie of his antiproletarian and antirevolutionary bona fides. Other writings like *L'Extinction du Paupérisme* stressed his orientation toward state direction of the economy and social-welfare plans to appeal to a controlled working class. Government "is the beneficent mainspring of every social organism," he had written. Also: "Nowadays the day of class rule is over, the day of mass rule has begun. The masses must be organized so that they can formulate their will, and disciplined so that they can be instructed and enlightened as to their own interests." Bonaparte helped to clarify this rhetoric when he broke strikes, banned independent workers' organization, and worked to keep wages down. Through it all, he represented himself even as a sort of socialist, when appropriate; and in view of the amorphous history of that label, it would be a purely terminological enterprise to argue that he was "less socialistic" than certain figures discussed in histories of socialism. Indeed, some modern historians seriously present him as a sort of socialist in the same vague way that he put forward the pretense.*

There *was* a definite socialistic wing of the Bonapartist entourage. Its royal patron was the Emperor's cousin, Prince Napoleon ("Plon-Plon," or the Red Prince), who actually consorted with socialists of a sort. Marx liked to take thrusts at "the illustrious Plon-Plon, alias the *Prince Rouge*, the scion of the Bonapartist family, upon whom has fallen the lot of coquetting with revolution, in the same way that his bigger cousin dallies with 'religion, order, and property.' "[2] Bonaparte's economic brain trust was composed of disciples of Saint-Simon, who had been considered raving radicals in the 1830s and were now ravenous financiers and industrial expansionists: the Pereire brothers, Michel Chevalier, and others. It was through these Saint-Simonians that the biggest Bonaparte adventure in state-sponsored high finance was founded: the Crédit Mobilier, of which we will hear more.

There were other recruits from time to time. The "father of anarchism" himself, Proudhon, greeted Bonaparte's coup d'état with a book which fawned before his new power and invited him to be so kind as to institute the New Society.[3] Disillusioned eventually by the Emperor's failure to oblige, our "anarchist" returned to his former hostility, without however giving up hope in Plon-Plon. (Part of the difficulties of the Proudhonist-led French section of the First International was that its leadership was unwarrantably suspected of also being pro-Bonapartist.) Later, after Bonaparte's fall, two of Bakunin's chief lieutenants were going to come out as Bonapartist partisans—in the name of revolution, of course.[4] Bonaparte's secret payroll included known radicals like Karl Vogt—the same Herr Vogt who published a

---

* Specifically, J. M. Thompson's *Louis Napoleon and the Second Empire*, in which the facts and citations in the above passage can be found. Thompson accepts the Emperor's self-image not only as a socialist but as "a visionary humanitarian, a friend of the outlawed and the oppressed"—the evidence being that he said so himself. "The Empire, he [Bonaparte] thought, must be at once repressive and progressive." It must keep every class "contented and cooperative." This was "a Bourbon idea: Louis XIV would have understood it. . . . It was also a Napoleonic idea. . . ." The economy "needed discipline and direction." Strong government could overcome the antagonism of bourgeoisie and proletariat. Thompson especially leans on two English witnesses. The reformer Shaftesbury said that Louis Napoleon's course "makes my hair stand on end. Every working man that lives will on seeing these results shout *Vive le Despotisme! A bas les*

scurrilous book slandering Marx for dictatorial ambitions while at the same time he hailed the emperor as a "workers' dictator."[5] Among other more or less "left" Bonapartists were Sainte-Beuve (who called Bonaparte "an eminent socialist"), Auguste Comte, Frédéric Le Play, and Félix Pyat.[6]

If, as Bonaparte had written, "Today . . . one can govern only with the masses," it was necessary to look for Judas goats who could lead the masses in the proper spirit. Conservatives who did not understand the new game helped Bonaparte along by indignantly denouncing him as a socialist—old Guizot, for example, who greeted the news of the coup d'état by crying, "It is the complete and definitive triumph of socialism!"[7]

To Engels, Bonaparte appeared as a sort of True-Socialist (of the Hess-Grün tendency pilloried in the Manifesto) shading into bourgeois reform:

> As for [Louis] Napoleon [wrote Engels to Marx], didn't the man say to L. Blanc, when he went to France: *When I am President I will put your ideas into practice?* Anyway, one sees how financial necessity can drive even a True-Socialist like Louis Napoleon to typical financial-bourgeois measures, like conversion of bonds. The °shopkeeper° and small industry forgive twenty socialistic pranks for this one saving of 18 millions, and the *Daily News* admires the measure. Incidentally, it is impossible to say anything more stupid or disgusting on this business than the *Journal des Débats*. Altogether the old story: post office reform = socialism! conversion of bonds = socialism! free trade = socialism! I'm only afraid that Mynheer Napoleon, who despite everything went into his own socialistic things very timidly and in the mortgage question likewise does not go beyond the bounds of the bourgeois-Prussian loan institution, is finally under the pressure of circumstances transforming all his socialistic impulses into simple bourgeois reforms. . . .[8]

Marx likewise referred to Bonaparte's True-Socialism in this period right after the coup d'état.[9] A few years later, the original True-Socialist himself, Moses Hess, became a Bonapartist apologist.[10]

---

governements libres!" This seemed to refer particularly to the imperial public-works program and its state-made employment. Walter Bagehot saw Bonaparte as a "democratic despot," and his regime as "the best *finished* democracy which the world has ever seen," meaning an absolutism "with a popular instinct." Besides running the first popular democracy, Bonaparte was also a "Benthamite despot." So Thompson.[1]

2. THE CREDIT MOBILIER

It was the rise of the Crédit Mobilier and its subsequent scandals that turned Marx, in 1856, to his first close consideration of what he began to call "Bonapartist socialism" or "Imperial socialism," in an important series of articles.

The Crédit Mobilier was a banking institution set up as a sort of holding corporation to stimulate the development of industry and public works by concentrating the ownership of various enterprises in one common fund controlled by itself. It is "one of the most curious economical phenomena of our epoch," and may have "an immensely greater development in the future." It buys up the stocks of the various industrial concerns themselves; and this means "to make industry and public works in general dependent on the favor of the *Crédit Mobilier,* and therefore on the individual favor of Bonaparte, on whose breath the existence of the company is suspended."

°°Hence the *Crédit Mobilier* avows the intention of making itself the proprietor, and Napoleon the Little the supreme director, of the whole varied industry of France. This is what we call Imperial Socialism.

In practice the Crédit Mobilier goes beyond this, by proposing to make itself "not only the proprietor of such great industrial enterprises, but also the slave of the treasury, and the despot of commercial credit."[11]

The phenomenon had two sides: on the one hand, the Bonapartist higher-ups and speculators had a chance to enrich themselves by grabbing a piece of the flowing moneys before the whole thing blew up in a crash; on the other hand, there was the "socialistic" side. Bonaparte proposed to convert

all the property and all the industry of France into a personal obligation toward Louis Bonaparte. To steal France in order to buy France—that was the great problem the man had to solve, and in this transaction of taking from France what was to be given back to France, not the least important side to him was the percentage to be skimmed off by himself and the Society of December Tenth.*

* This is a variant of a similar passage near the end of *The Eighteenth Brumaire.* In 1855 Marx, in a letter to Engels, quoted the 1852 version, about Bonaparte's desire "to steal the whole of France in order to be able to make a

The method: through a credit operation.

> And there happened to be in France the school of St. Simon, which in its beginning and in its decay deluded itself with the dream that all the antagonism of classes must disappear before the creation of universal wealth by some new-fangled scheme of public credit. And St. Simonism in this form had not yet died out at the epoch of the coup d'état.[13]

Among the surviving representatives of this idea (Marx goes on) were the Pereire brothers, "who had sat at the feet of the Père Enfantin" in former days, and who had now become "the founders of the Crédit Mobilier, and the initiators of Bonapartist Socialism."*

> It is an old proverb, *"Habent sua fata libella."* Doctrines have also their *fate* as well as books. St. Simon to become the guardian angel of the Paris Bourse, the prophet of swindling, the Messiah of general bribery and corruption!

Another legal move by the government

> sanctions the expropriation of the mortgagors of the land, in favor of the government of Bonaparte, who by this machinery proposes to seize on the land, as by the Crédit Mobilier he is seizing on the industry, and by the Bank of France on the commerce of France; and all this to save property from the dangers of Socialism!

The next article, promises Marx, will explain

> the plain scheme of dragging all the industry of France into the whirlpool of the Paris Bourse, and to make it the tennis ball of the gentlemen of the Crédit Mobilier, and of their patron Bonaparte.[15]

That is, through the machinery of stock manipulation, "all the industry

---

present of her to France," and added that now he has "performed this task, within the bounds of pure reason. His loan manipulations are important experiments in this direction."[12]

* Four years later, Marx mentioned in a *Tribune* article that ex-Saint-Simonians had been involved in putting together the new commercial treaty between France and England.

> But, what is not known by the journals, is that *Père Enfantin*, the ex-high-priest of St. Simonism, was the principal actor on the French side. Is it not truly wonderful how those St. Simonians, from *Père Enfantin* down to Isaac Pereira and Michel Chevalier, have been turned into the main economic pillars of the second Empire.[14]

of France" is to be put under a single control, ultimately dominated by the Bonapartist state power.

3. THE STATE AND "INDUSTRIAL FEUDALISM"

The promised explication is given in the third and last article of this series. Marx explains that the speculative profits made by the manipulators of the setup (stockjobbers) will be "the base of the industrial development"; skimmed-off profits from the stock turnover are supposed to fatten the Crédit Mobilier holdings and increase the value of its stocks. "In this manner the Crédit Mobilier obtains command over a large portion of the loanable capital intended for investment in industrial enterprises." Obviously, this kind of operation offers plenty of opportunity for stockjobbing profits for the insiders too.

But Marx does not see the plan *simply* as a scheme for their personal pocket-lining. As he considers the potentialities inherent in the plan— quite apart from his prediction that the "unavoidable crash" of the whole structure was on the way—he theoretically projects its meaning into the future. This explanation starts by recalling that the Crédit Mobilier is required by its statutes to operate only on joint-stock companies:

°°Consequently there must arise a tendency to start as many such societies as possible, and, further, to bring all industrial undertakings under the form of these societies. Now, it cannot be denied that the application of joint-stock companies to industry marks a new epoch in the economical life of modern nations. On the one hand it has revealed the productive powers of association, not suspected before, and called into life industrial creations, on a scale unattainable by the efforts of individual capitalists; on the other hand, it must not be forgotten, that in joint-stock companies it is not the individuals that are associated, but the capitals. By this contrivance, proprietors have been converted into shareholders, *i.e.* speculators. The concentration of capital has been accelerated, and, as it[s] natural corollary, the downfall of the small middle class. A sort of industrial kings have been created, whose power stands in inverse ratio to their responsibility—they being responsible only to the amount of their shares, while disposing of the whole capital of the society—forming a more or less permanent body, while the mass of shareholders is undergoing a constant process of decomposition and renewal, and enabled, by the very disposal of the joint influence and wealth of the society, to bribe its single rebellious members. Beneath this oligarchic Board of Directors is placed a bureaucratic body of the practical managers and agents of the society, and beneath them, without any transition, an enormous and daily-swelling mass of mere wages laborers—whose dependence and helplessness increase with the dimensions of the capital that employs them, but who also become more dangerous in direct ratio to the decreasing number of its representatives. It is the immortal merit of Fourier to have predicted this form of modern industry, under the name of *Industrial Feudalism.*

To be sure, Marx goes on to say that the specific new invention by Bonaparte and his Pereires is not this setup itself but the idea "to render the industrial feudalism tributary to stockjobbing." But his article does not end there. He explains why a crash is inevitable; and he asserts his belief that "the real founders of the Crédit Mobilier have included it [a crash] in their calculations."

When that crash comes, after an immensity of French interests has been involved, the Government of Bonaparte will seem justified in interfering with the Crédit Mobilier, as the English Government did in 1797 with the Bank of England. . . . Louis Bonaparte, the imperial Socialist, will try to seize upon French industry by converting the debentures of the Crédit Mobilier into State obligations. Will he prove more solvent than the Crédit Mobilier? That is the question.[16]

We have, then, a vast prospect unrolled by a method of extrapolation from incipient tendencies, with several stages of future history seen close up (as always when a telescopic lens is used) even though they would not actually occur for most of a century.

There is, in the first place, the development of the capitalist corporation into the stage of evicting the mass of shareholders from effective control and concentrating the real corporate power in the hands of the "oligarchic Board of Directors," who in turn operate through "a bureaucratic body of the practical managers"—the development which Berle and Means, eight decades later, rediscovered *after* it had taken place. But that is only the beginning, for Marx is quick to give credit to a socialist predecessor, Fourier.*

Even more important, Marx does not see this taking place simply as an autonomous economic process, but in close association with the state power, in an eventual fusion, in personnel and role, of the state manipulators with the economic manipulators. The state power, at first standing behind its creature, will then have to step in openly to take over the economic power that will have been thus concentrated. Certainly Marx did give short shrift to the fantasy (reinvented by A. A. Berle in our day)[19] that the oligarchic corporations would develop a social conscience for the good of humanity. "Powerful engines in developing the productive powers of modern society," wrote Marx of the joint-stock companies, "they have not, like the medieval corporations, as yet created a corporate conscience in lieu of the individual responsibility which, by dint of their very organization, they have contrived to get rid of."[20]

4. TOWARD A BONAPARTIST STATE ECONOMY?

Marx did not return to this sweeping view. The definitive crash of "that curious mixture of Imperial Socialism, St. Simonistic stock-jobbing, and philosophic swindling which makes up what is called the Crédit Mobilier"[21] did not actually come about until a decade later, by which time Bonaparte's regime was in far too much serious trouble to dream of trying "to seize upon French industry." He did not "prove more solvent than the Crédit Mobilier" after all.

* For Fourier, "industrial feudalism" was to be the "pivot" period in the fourth (decay) phase of civilization; note that, being antagonistic to industrialism itself, he regarded both parts of the phrase as pejorative. The phrase, born in the 1820s, became a widely used socialist catchword for the next hundred years, not necessarily retaining its anti-industrial force. Fourierism's disciples took it up as an accusation, the Saint-Simonians as a program. Antibourgeois aristocratic dissidents used it for their own purposes, as did radicals as different as Proudhon and Blanqui. By 1902 an American socialist, W. J. Ghent, published a book on *Our Benevolent Feudalism* without mentioning Fourier at all.[17] The phrase *industrial feudalism* was usually applied to capitalism itself, especially in some monopolistic and hierarchized form, just as *industrial serfdom* was used for wage slavery. In this context it became merely a metaphor, though it had been more than that for Fourier. When Engels used the phrase in passing in an 1848 article, it definitely was merely a label for a monopolistic capitalism.[18]

But a monstrous crisis did break out in the autumn of the same year, 1856, and while the Crédit Mobilier did not collapse, it began to decline. Although a dozen years later Marx looked back with some pride to his analyses of "the real essence of the thing," [22] it is hard to say whether he continued to look on a Bonapartist takeover of the economy as one of the continuing possibilities. The answer seems to be: a possibility, yes; but less and less of a probability. The prospect that the Bonaparte regime would be swept away altogether seemed bright.

When the depression started, Marx (as often) saw a new 1848 coming, with a difference. For the European upper classes "are now discovering that they were themselves the instruments of a revolution in property greater than any contemplated by the revolutionists of 1848. A general bankruptcy is staring them in the face. . . ." Marx calls them "the official revolutionists." For in 1848 the movements preceding the outbreak "were of a merely political character. . . . Now, on the contrary, a social revolution is generally understood, even before the political revolution is proclaimed; and a social revolution brought about by no underground plots of the secret societies among the working classes, but by the public contrivances of the Crédits Mobiliers of the ruling classes." [23]

Engels opined that now "all socialistic °dodges°" had been exhausted by Bonaparte; but Marx wondered "what socialistic coups d'état Bonaparte is still capable of resorting to at the last moment." [24] He was still wondering a year later. One of the open questions continued to be the relationship of "swindling" (the personal-enrichment side of the operation) to the state-capitalist aspect.

> Swindling (which, to be sure, in turn also became a presupposition of *solid* commerce and industry) exists properly speaking only in the branches where the state is directly or indirectly the *actual °employer°*. However, it is certain that a capitalist of the size of the French government, even one that is bankrupt in itself (as Hegel would say), can make shift somewhat longer than a °private capitalist°. [25]

Bonaparte's plan "is evidently to make the Bank of France . . . the general entrepreneur of all his swindle-schemes," he guessed on another day. Engels expressed the opinion in a letter that "nobody believes in Bonapartist socialism any more." [26] But this was not the tone of a *New York Tribune* article in which Marx discussed Bonaparte's economic maneuvers to keep bread prices down for the masses while at the same time keeping agricultural prices up. Thus, wrote Marx, "he proclaims himself a sort of socialist providence to the proletarians of the towns, although in a rather awkward way, since the first palpable effect of his decree must be to make them pay more for their loaf than before. . . . At all events, we may be sure that the Imperial Socialist will prove more successful in raising the price of bread than he has been in attempts to reduce it." However, this did not mean to Marx that Bonaparte was thereby acting as executive-committee chairman for the bourgeoisie; rather, the emperor thereby served notice on the bourgeoisie that the state asserted control over their purses:

> The "savior of property" shows the middle class that not even the formal intervention of his own mock Legislatures, but a simple personal ukase on his part, is all that is wanted to make free with their purses, dispose of municipal property, trouble the course of trade, and subject their monetary dealings to his private cro[t]chets.

And "Lastly, the question is still to be considered from the purely Bonapartist point of view." The "purely Bonapartist point of view" is the point of view of the bureaucracy. The immense public works necessitated by the plan (granaries) will open up "a fresh field . . . for jobs and plunder," that is, more jobs for a lower officialdom and more plunder for the higher.[27]

5. THE AUTONOMOUS ECONOMIC POLICY

During this depression period Marx came to the opinion that the specific economic form represented by the Crédit Mobilier was a limited phenomenon. In a letter to Engels at the end of 1857, after referring to "the °general rottenness° of the bankrupt state" in France, he remarked that "At bottom, a Crédit Mobilier was possible and necessary only in a country so immobile" as France.[28] That is, it was the form necessitated by the previous stagnation of the economy ("immobile" is counterposed to *Mobilier*).*

---

* Three months later, Engels wrote that

I have quite come around to your view that the Crédit Mobilier in France was not an accidental swindle but a thoroughly necessary institution, and that Morny's gallows-worthy thievery in it was likewise inevitable, for without the prospect of such rapid enrichment a Crédit Mobilier would not have been realized in France.[29]

But Marx never changed his mind about what was implicit, or potential, in the possibilities open to "Bonapartist socialism" with its Saint-Simonian theoretical framework. About the same time as the above letter he was working out a train of thought in his *Grundrisse* notebook which ended up with almost as sweeping a statement about the Crédit Mobilier as the previous year's telescopic view of "industrial feudalism." The context was a discussion of the then-common panacea of a "labor bank"; Marx shows at some length that such a bank could not merely remain a simple exchange agency or replacement for the money system, but would have to go on to control buying and selling in general and indeed all production; that is, take over the entire economy: "Then, viewed with precision, the bank would not only be the universal buyer and seller, but also the universal producer." A basic comment then follows:

> In point of fact it [such a bank] would either be a despotic government over production and administrator over distribution, or else it would be in fact nothing but a °board° that kept books and accounts for a society based on labor in common. It presupposes that the means of production are held in common, etc., etc. The Saint-Simonians made their bank into the papacy of production.[31]

Thus, on the basis of the same presupposition, collectivism in production, two different courses branched out: in one the organizing authority set up as a controlling "despotism," a "papacy" over the productive system; in the other, the organizing authority simply served a free society as technical coordinator. The Saint-Simonian managers of the Bonapartist enterprise, Marx thought, were pointed in the first direction.

The fact that the potentiality did not work out historically, that the Saint-Simonian aims did not become Bonapartist realities, did not

---

The Duke of Morny, Bonaparte's half-brother and coup organizer, was something like the Goering of the regime. Engels' letter means that he had previously regarded the Crédit Mobilier *simply* as an ad hoc swindle, without roots in the economic development of France, as distinct from Marx's view of the institution as an organic feature of the economy. Marx had now qualified his view by limiting it to the French type of situation, and Engels was meeting him half-way from an *opposite* direction. Subsequently, Engels' back-references to Bonaparte's "socialism" tended to retain only the swindle aspect, as in *The Housing Question* and *Anti-Dühring*.[30] By that time, of course, it was clear that nothing had come of any other aspect, historically speaking; and there was a new context, the necessity of combating state-socialist illusions of another sort. We will discuss this material under the subject of state-socialism in Volume 3.

negate the theoretical meaning of "Bonapartist socialism" in Marx's view. Already in the article about industrial feudalism he had pointed out a specific national peculiarity of the Crédit Mobilier: it was the Bonaparte-Pereire way "to render the industrial feudalism tributary to stock-jobbing." Later, Marx discussed the limitations of the Saint-Simonian operation more fully in notes which became part of the third volume of *Capital.*

There, again expounding the economic meaning of Saint-Simonism on the basis of the Bonapartist scheme, Marx argues that the embryo of the Crédit Mobilier is already found in that doctrine. He remarks:

> This form, incidentally, could become dominant only in a country like France, where neither the credit system nor large-scale industry had reached the modern level of development. This was not at all possible in England and America.[32]

Saint-Simonism incubated the Crédit Mobilier because it looked to the bank and credit system for a takeover of the industrial structure; it was a victim of "the illusions concerning the miraculous power of the credit and banking system, in the socialist sense."

> The notion that the banks themselves should take over the management and distinguish themselves "through the number and usefulness of their managed establishments and of promoted works" (p. 101 [of a Saint-Simonian textbook]) contains the Crédit Mobilier in embryo. In the same way, Charles Pecqueur demands that the banks (which the followers of Saint-Simon call a *Système général des banques)* "should rule production." Pecqueur is essentially a follower of Saint-Simon, but much more radical. He wants "the credit institution . . . to control the entire movement of national production."[33]

Marx, to be sure, believes that it is illusory to think of taking over by this route: "there is no doubt that the credit system will serve as a powerful lever during the transition from the capitalist mode of production to the mode of production of associated labor; but only as one element in connection with other great organic revolutions of the mode of production itself."[34] But he discusses this illusion as a mistaken and eventually futile form of anticapitalism, not simply as a bourgeois dodge. This also provides the context for the Crédit Mobilier.

In short: Marx consistently interpreted the economic policy of the Bonapartist regime as autonomous from the bourgeoisie. This relative autonomy need not be interpreted as going any further than Napoleon I, who (as *The Holy Family* had explained) already knew that his state had to "recognize and protect" the "unhampered development of bourgeois society." Its driving force was not derived from hostility to the economic interests of the bourgeoisie, but rather from the aim of *subordinating* those interests to the autonomized state, which had its own aims of self-aggrandizement. Just as the bourgeois point of view was ruled by profits, so "the purely Bonapartist point of view" was ruled by the goal of "jobs and plunder" for the deserving Bonapartist cadres of the bureaucracy.

How far was it possible for these two interests to coexist peacefully? We consider this question next, in the light of Marx's coeval discussions of the political course of the Bonaparte regime.

6. WHAT CLASS SUPPORTS THE REGIME?

The year 1858 saw a high point in the revolutionary hopes of the anti-Bonapartist left—including Marx and Engels as well as the French radical emigrés and others.[35] While there were several reasons for the belief that the regime was on the skids, the main underlying drive was seen by Marx and Engels as the growing alienation between the Bonapartist state power and the developing bourgeoisie. In a *New York Tribune* article toward the end of that year, they summarized this pattern in essentially the same way as they did in later historical works.* After 1848–1849

> The middle class declared itself politically a minor, unfit to manage the affairs of the nation, and acquiesced in military and bureaucratic despotism. Then arose that spasmodic extension of manufactures, mines, railways, and steam navigation, that epoch of Crédits Mobiliers, joint stock bubbles, of swindling and jobbing, in which the European middle class sought to make up for their political defeats by industrial victories, for their collective

---

* For example, Engels in his pamphlet *The Prussian Military Question* and his introduction to *Class Struggles in France*.[36] Perhaps best known is Marx's summary in *The Civil War in France:* "Under [the regime's] sway, bourgeois society, freed from political cares, attained a development unexpected even by itself," etc.[37]

impotence by individual wealth. But with their wealth rose their social power, and in the same proportion their interests expanded; they again began to feel the political fetters imposed upon them. The present movement in Europe is the natural consequence and expression of this feeling, combined with that return of confidence in their own power over their workmen which ten years of quiet industrial activity have brought about.[38]

As the bourgeoisie's economic strength grew—thanks to the protection and stimulation given it under the aegis of the Bonapartist state—it sought a commensurate political power, such as Bonapartism denied it on principle. Five years before, too, Marx had thought to see this development reaching a breaking point, with the peasantry disillusioned, the proletariat still hostile, and the bourgeoisie pining "for a new change of power, to afford them at last 'a regular Government' and 'sound business.' "[39] Now, in 1858, it was perhaps the assassination attempt on Bonaparte's life by the Italian conspirator Felice Orsini in January that helped to crystallize revolutionary hopes; Marx thought the "coolness" of the public reaction was notable. The small bourgeoisie particularly feared "commercial ruin" and would welcome a change. "Boustrapa [Bonaparte] has perceived this and will now unleash the 'despot' as such. We shall see."[40]

What was "the 'despot' as such" that had not yet been unleashed? We shall see.

In a *Tribune* article, Marx marshaled the evidence pointing to the coming overthrow, in class terms. Bonaparte's victory had taken place on an upsurge of commercial prosperity;

> The commercial crisis, therefore, has necessarily sapped the material basis of the Empire, which never possessed any moral basis, save the temporary demoralization of all classes and all parties. The working classes reassumed their hostile attitude to the existing Government the very moment they were thrown out of employment. A great part of the commercial and industrial middle classes were placed by the crisis in . . . fear of the debtors' prison. . . . Another very large portion of the Paris middle classes, and a very influential one too—the *petits rentiers*, or men of small fixed incomes—have met with wholesale ruin. . . . That portion, at least, of the French higher classes which pretends to represent what is called French civilization never accepted the Empire, except as a necessary makeshift, never concealed their profound hostility to the "nephew of his uncle," and of late have seized

upon every pretext to show their anger at the attempt to transform a mere expedient, as they considered it, into a lasting institution.

This description certainly does not leave much of a civil ruling class to support the state.

Bonaparte (Marx continues) senses "the gathering storm." The "street enthusiasm" displayed for Bonaparte's escape from Orsini's bombs was organized by the police. The congratulatory addresses came exclusively from men who "one way or the other, belong to the Administration, that ubiquitous parasite feeding on the vitals of France." Bonaparte therefore demands new repressive laws, instead of pretending "to the more or less respectable forms of a regular Government." This shows "that the time of the sullen acquiescence of the nation in the rule of the Society of the perjured usurper has definitively passed away." The addresses of loyalty from the army "are simply the undisguised proclamation of pretorian rule in France."[41]

In his next article Marx continued the argument showing the disintegration of internal support to the regime, this time ending with the growing opposition among the peasantry.[42]

7. "THE RULE OF THE PRETORIANS"

In a special article Marx then squarely confronted the question of the class base and unique character of the Bonapartist state power in this, its period of dissolution. Its title took up a note that had already been sounded: "The Rule of the Pretorians."[43] The analogy, implied but not specifically discussed, was, then, the character of the state power in the epoch of the advanced dissolution of the Roman Empire—a long drawn-out epoch.

Marx's thesis in "The Rule of the Pretorians" is that by this time the state machine of Louis Bonaparte has gone all the way to a new relationship with society. The bonds connecting it with the social strata it has rested on (in its own peculiar way) have stretched and stretched, and now have snapped.

"France has become the home of Pretorians only," Marx emphasizes. Now "the rule of the naked sword is proclaimed in the most unmistakable terms, and Bonaparte wants France to clearly understand that the imperial rule does rest not on her will but on 600,000 bayonets."

If this means merely an ordinary military dictatorship, it is nothing new. Marx poses the key question in class terms with utter sharpness:

°°A great modern historian has told us that, disguise the fact as you like, France, since the days of the Great Revolution, has been always disposed of by the army. There have certainly ruled different classes under the Empire, the Restoration, Louis Philippe, and the Republic of 1848. Under the first the peasantry, the offspring of the revolution of 1789, predominated; under the second, the great landed property; under the third, the bourgeoisie; and the last, not in the intention of its founders but in fact, proved an abortive attempt at dividing dominion in equal shares among the men of the legitimate monarchy and the men of the monarchy of July. Still, all these regimes rested alike on the army. Has not even the Constitution of the Republic of 1848 been elaborated and proclaimed under a state of siege—that is, the rule of the bayonet? Was that Republic not personated by Gen. Cavaignac? Was it not saved by the army in June, 1848, and again saved in June, 1849, to be finally dropped by the same army in December, 1851?

It is clear, then, that all the preceding class regimes also rested openly on the army. (To be sure all class rule rests on armed force in the last analysis, but here Marx's point is that since 1789 all the French regimes rested on armed force in the first analysis.) Still, in all previous cases the armed force supported the socioeconomic power of different ruling classes. Marx continues: "What then forms the novelty in the regime now openly inaugurated by Louis Bonaparte? That he rules by the instrumentality of the army? So did all his predecessors since the days of Thermidor."

Now comes the answer: the novel phenomenon is that *this* state power supports no social class whatsoever, it maintains the rule of no group other than itself:

Yet, if in all bygone epochs the ruling class, the ascendancy of which corresponded to a specific development of French society, rested its *ultima ratio* against its adversaries upon the army, it was nevertheless a specific social interest that predominated. Under the second Empire the interest of the army itself is to predominate. The army is no longer to maintain the rule of one part of

the people over another part of the people. The army is to
maintain its own rule, personated by its own dynasty, over the
French people in general.

It is to represent the *State* in antagonism to the *society.*

This is state autonomization no longer as a mere tendency, not even
one that is realized in practice to a greater or lesser extent. This is state
autonomization driven, exceptionally, to its extreme conclusion. The
army is not the "instrumentality" of any of the social classes, of any
"specific social interest" of civil society; it represents the state itself in
antagonism to "society" *tout court,* to civil society in general.

This is the dangerous experiment under way:

It must not be imagined that Bonaparte is not aware of the
dangerous character of the experiment he tries. In proclaiming
himself the chief of the Praetorians, he declares every Praetorian
chief his competitor.

That is, he becomes vulnerable to military coups by his own generals.
Again, the obvious analogy is the pattern of the corresponding Roman
epoch, when one praetorian chief after another seized the imperial
throne.

This new system of government in France is not the result of any
seizure of power by the military in the usual sense; the head of state
himself has gone over to it, as his last resort:

We repeat that it is impossible to suppose Louis Bonaparte ignorant of the dangers with which his new-fangled system is
fraught. But he has no choice left. He understands his own situation and the impatience of French society to get rid of him and
his Imperial mummeries. He knows that the different parties have
recovered from their paralysis, and that the material basis of his
stock-jobbing regime has been blown up by the commercial earth-
quake [the crisis].

The reference to "the material basis of his [Bonaparte's] stock-
jobbing regime" may recall Marx's formulation of "jobs and plunder"
as the economic drive of the specifically Bonapartist cadres, the men
who "one way or the other, belong to the Administration, that ubiquitous parasite feeding on the vitals of France." This state bureaucracy, as
we have previously noted, had been intertwined by innumerable bonds
with the bourgeoisie in the orgy of self-enrichment which the Empire

had unleashed. Now the commercial and financial crisis had cut these opportunities. The nonmilitary sector of the state bureaucracy* was now itself treading air. Only the military cadres, the generals, could save the whole state machine that Bonaparte had put together.

> Consequently, he [Bonaparte] is not only preparing for war against French society, but loudly proclaims the fact. . . . The denunciation of *all parties* as his personal enemies enters, therefore, into the game of Bonaparte. It forms part of his system. He tells them, in so many words, that he indulges no delusion as to the general aversion his rule is the subject of, but that he is ready to encounter it with grape and musketry.

8. BY THE SWORD ALONE

This article, Marx's most direct statement on a case of complete state autonomy, raises important questions in hindsight. But first, to complete the picture, let us review Marx's subsequent analyses of the crisis of the Bonaparte regime, into 1859. All of his articles continue to be based on the premises laid out in "The Rule of the Pretorians"; we will not find any change in the conception, only variant formulations which may be useful especially for those unused to this area of Marx's thinking. Here are some highlights:

1. *Bonapartist state versus bourgeoisie and all other classes.* The eventual rising of the "revolutionary masses" will be helped by

> the decidedly anti-Bonapartist attitude of the bourgeoisie, the secret societies undermining the lower strata of the army, the petty jealousies, venal treacheries and Orleanist or Legitimist leanings dividing its superior layers. . . .[46]

---

* There is no theoretical reason to limit the term *state bureaucracy* to the civilian officialdom, though this is often done as a matter of terminological convenience. In this connection, one can look back to the passage quoted earlier in this chapter[44] in which Marx speaks of the Bonapartist regime as, from the beginning, a "military and bureaucratic despotism." This spells out the two main sectors of the state bureaucracy, to be sure; often enough Marx followed popular practice in labeling it merely a "military despotism." In fact, earlier in the same article "military despotism, the rule of the Caesars" is mentioned as the general form of government on the Continent. Elsewhere Marx referred to the Bonaparte regime as "the rule of the coup d'état in France" or "the coup d'état regime."[45]

Even now there is "coolness" toward the regime: "The masses show themselves °indifferent°. Direct and serious counter-remonstrations have come from: high finance, industry, and commerce; the clerical party; finally, the high military circles. . . ."[47] The European aristocracy and bourgeoisie are now disillusioned with Bonaparte:

> They knew him long since as a villain; but they deemed him a serviceable, pliant, obedient, grateful villain; and they now see and rue their mistake. He has been using *them* all the time that they supposed they were using him.[48]

In a *Tribune* article drafted by Engels, "The middle classes . . . are longing for a return of the time when they, or at least a fraction of them, governed the country. . . ."[49]

2. *The swindlers' regime.* The Bonapartist Empire

> had already dropped every pretense of being a regular Government, or the offspring of the *"suffrage universel."* It had proclaimed itself the regime of the upstart, the informer and the twelve-pounder [cannon]. It goes now a step further, and avows itself the regime of the swindler.

This introduces Marx's report on the new financial machinations of the Crédit Mobilier, amidst the financial and commercial rigors of the depression. In addition, there is an immense wastage of capital in "unproductive" public works, typified by the Haussmann urban-renewal program in Paris which features great boulevards suitable for using cannon and cavalry against barricades:

> Meanwhile, Bonaparte clings to his old way of sinking capital in unproductive works, but which, as Mr. Haussmann, the Prefect of the Seine, has the frankness to impart to the Paris people, are important in "a strategical point of view," and calculated to guard against "unforeseen events which may always arise to put society in danger." Thus Paris is condemned to erect new boulevards and streets, the cost of which is estimated at 180,000,000 francs, in order to protect it from its own ebullitions.[50]

3. *Bonaparte's "hankering for confiscations."* This phrase[51] refers to Bonaparte's plan to expropriate the landed property of the charity institutions in return for state bonds. The regime's finances are in a desperate state, and this time the Crédit Mobilier is in no position to help out. "There remains, then, nothing for Bonaparte but to return, in

financial matters, as he has been forced to do in political ones, to the original principles of the coup d'état." After plundering the Bank of France and the Orleans estates, now he moves toward "the confiscation of the property of the charitable establishments." But this operation "would cost Bonaparte one of his armies, his army of priests, who administer by far the greatest portion of the charitable establishments." An outcry has arisen "against this intended encroachment upon 'private property.' "[52]

4. *The "despotic military state."* Bonaparte is instituting a "system of domestic terrorism," a "reign of terror." As a result, "the French middle classes will soon be worked up to the point where they will consider a revolution necessary for the 'restoration of confidence.' "[53]

In this "despotic military state," Bonaparte bids fair to become the prisoner of his military instruments (as the late Roman emperors did):

> At the same rate that France grows impatient of the yoke of the army, the army waxes bolder in its purpose of yoking Bonaparte. After the 10th of December [1848], Bonaparte could flatter himself that he was the elect of the peasantry, that is, the mass of the French nation. Since the attempt of the 14th January [1858, by Orsini], he knows that he is at the mercy of the army. Having been compelled to avow that he rules through the army, it is quite natural that the latter should seek to rule through him.

This seems better nuanced than the subsequent flat assertion that "the army reigns in France."[54]

In the shift to a decisively military base and an inevitable outbreak of war, Marx sees the "beginning of the end" for the Bonapartist regime:

> . . . the commercial and agricultural distress, financial coup d'état, and the substitution of the rule *of* the army for rule *by* the army, are hastening the explosion. . . . [Meanwhile] war is believed to be imminent. Louis Napoleon has no other means of escaping speedy destruction. The beginning of the end is at hand.[55]

As late as March 1859, it was still Marx's opinion that " °°Louis Napoleon can never more be the demigod of the Bourse and the Bourgeois. He rules henceforth by the sword alone."[56]

9. LIMITS OF THE BONAPARTE MODEL

Let us now return to the interpretation of the Bonapartist state in dissolution given by Marx in "The Rule of the Pretorians," within the context of his running analyses of the Second Empire's crisis in 1858–1859.

The picture is of a state which has pushed its autonomization to the extreme point, where it is no longer the *resultant* of the actual class forces in society but rather stands in antagonism to all the social classes of civil society. To be sure, this state is the *result* of a historical process through which this class society has actually gone, but the result is that the political superstructure has torn loose from the social foundations which produced it. It has assumed an independent life of its own in the fullest sense.

It is evident that this picture is quite at variance with the narrow and cramped view of the "Marxist theory of the state" commonly presented by Marxist and anti-Marxist expositors, for whom Marx's and Engels' fairly extensive writings on the autonomized and bureaucratic state virtually do not exist.*

Two addenda are necessary.

1. The theoretical flight which Marx took in 1858 with "The Rule of the Pretorians" has to be put in the perspective of later developments.

Through 1858–1859 Marx evidently believed—and certainly hoped— that the Bonapartist regime, having broken its umbilical cord to civil society in a paroxysm of autonomy, had reached a point of no return. But we know, with twenty-twenty hindsight, that Bonaparte did "return," that is, make a turn back to accommodation with the social powers of bourgeois society; this was marked by a free-trade treaty with England in January 1860 and a revival of parliamentary life in November. In consequence, our history textbooks commonly date

---

* Marx's article "The Rule of the Pretorians" has never been reprinted, and its very text exists only in the not-very-accessible files of the *New York Tribune*. (In translation it is included in the Russian and German editions of Marx's and Engels' works.) Nor is it quoted, or even mentioned, in any work I know of that purports to discuss Marxist theory, with the single and outstanding exception of M. Rubel's *Karl Marx Devant le Bonapartisme*.[57] But then, it is rare to find even Marx's very accessible concept of Bonapartism presented, let alone explained, in this peculiar body of literature. Lest anyone be tempted to concoct a fable that

something called Bonaparte's "Liberal Empire" from that year. The despot had pulled back from the brink, realizing that he could not rule by the sword alone.

The extreme tensions induced by the autonomous course, which made Marx scent revolution, had had the same effect on the emperor. For the fully autonomized state power that was depicted in "The Rule of the Pretorians" meant a drastically unstable situation. If Bonaparte was "preparing for war against French society," it was the latter that was sure to win, for this bourgeois society was not only viable but on the rise: so Marx calculated, and so Bonaparte decided. As we have seen, Marx looked for revolutionary rumblings to begin quite soon, as "French society"—the classes that dominated the socioeconomic system—hardened in antagonism to the runaway state machine. The snapping of the bonds between this state and this society, therefore, marked a prerevolutionary situation (to use a modern term). The split between state and society had to be fought to a decision; the anomaly had to be resolved, the abnormal normalized.

It cannot be overemphasized that, in this case, the continued viability of bourgeois society was the underlying precondition for this conclusion. There was a state in dissolution, but there was no society in dissolution. On the contrary, we must recall that the roots of the conflict lay in the rapid growth of the bourgeoisie's economic strength: "with their wealth rose their special power . . . they again began to feel the political fetters imposed upon them." These material conditions prescribed the limits of state autonomization for the period. The limits of Bonapartism were defined by the historical position of the social classes it defied.

We need not inquire here whether the Bonapartist state really did reach the extreme point of autonomy which Marx saw in 1858; for even if we come to the conclusion that Marx's hopes were outrunning the facts, the question of state theory is nevertheless settled. What is established is Marx's lack of inhibition about envisaging the special case in which a state achieves full autonomization; what it settles is that

---

Marx forgot, dropped, or ignored his basic theory of the state at this time, or in articles for the *Tribune*, or in connection with Bonaparte: we may point in advance to one of the best brief statements that Marx ever set down on the relationship of the state as political superstructure to the class foundations of society. It appeared in an article for the *Tribune*, in the midst of the very articles we have been discussing, and on the subject of Bonaparte. Since this article is as little accessible as the other, the relevant section is given in Special Note C.

Marx's theory of the state includes provision for historical conjunctures in which a state, completely independent in the fullest sense, cuts loose from its foundations in civil society and turns on them.

In fact, there is no reason to believe that Marx even thought there was a special problem about it, or that it ever occurred to him that a rigid taboo against such notions would one day be considered "Marxism." For one thing, the formulations in the *Tribune* articles on the subject give not the slightest indication that the writer feels he is venturing into delicate territory. On the contrary, they are unusually brash—for Marx, who could become positively sibylline when he was on thin ice with respect to theory. For another thing: there is the evidence of the Marx-Engels correspondence, which was heavy during those years.* This evidence is like Sherlock Holmes's barking dog: the point is that, in the course of constant cross-discussions of developments in Bonaparte-land, the question at issue is *never* mentioned, either by Marx to get his friend's opinion or by Engels in comment.

2. Marx's 1858 analysis of Bonaparte's autonomous state throws a light, forward and backward, on two better-known writings in which the same question is raised but not answered sharply. These were written at the beginning and at the end of the Second Empire's life: in the one case before the autonomization process reached its apex; in the other, after the crisis thereby created was past.

In *The Eighteenth Brumaire*, Marx's formulation of the question is very tentative. He refers back to six previous periods and regimes in French history, from the absolute monarchy to the 1848 republic, each with its pattern of state–class relations, in order to make the point that the Bonapartist state is something new:

> Only under the second Bonaparte does the state seem to have made itself completely independent.** As against civil society, the state machine has consolidated its position so thoroughly that the chief of the Society of December 10 [Bonaparte] suffices for its head. . . .[58]

---

* A graph of the number of letters per year in the correspondence between Marx and Engels, from (say) 1852 to 1864, corresponds with interesting fidelity to the fever chart of Continental politics. The years 1857–1860 stand up on this chart like an alp, with steep walls on each side.

** Literally, "to have completely autonomized itself." The term *autonomized*, which we have been using, is unwonted in English, but it closely translates Marx's *verselbständigt*.

The key qualification is "seem": the state machine has not really made itself *completely* autonomous from civil society; the implication, not spelled out, is that it has, however, reached a high point of autonomy not previously seen. Marx then goes on to discuss what classes' interests are represented by Bonaparte, and how.

At this point, before the actual experience of the Second Empire, it is clear that Marx already has his eye on the problem.

In 1871 Marx, drafting *The Civil War in France*, started a passage on this problem with a statement similar to that in *The Eighteenth Brumaire;* then, once more emphasizing the relative novelty of the state form, he ended up with a strong statement that the Bonapartist state was the form needed for the social rule of the bourgeoisie. For this, indeed, was what it had turned into.

> °°The governmental power with its standing army, its all-directing bureaucracy, its stultifying clergy and its servile tribunal [judicial] hierarchy had grown so independent of society itself, that a grotesquely mediocre adventurer with a hungry band of desperadoes behind him sufficed to wield it. . . .

That much was a rewrite of *The Eighteenth Brumaire.*

> It appeared no longer as a means of class domination, subordinate to its parliamentary ministry or legislature. Humbling under its sway even the interests of the ruling classes, . . . sanctioned in its absolute sway by universal suffrage, the acknowledged necessity for keeping up "order," that is, the rule of the landowner and the capitalist over the producer . . . the state power had received its last and supreme expression in the Second Empire.

But this state, which humbled under its sway even the interests of the (civil) ruling classes, proved in fact the only political form through which the ruling classes of civil society (landowners and capitalists) could maintain their power over the producers (workers and peasants):

> Apparently the final victory of this governmental power over society, it was in fact the orgy of all the corrupt elements of that society. To the eye of the uninitiated it appeared only as the victory of the Executive over the Legislative, of the final defeat of the form of class rule pretending [that is, claiming] to be the autocracy of society [by] its form pretending to be a superior power to society. But in fact it was only the last degraded and the only possible form of that class ruling, as humiliating to those

classes themselves as to the working classes which they kept fettered by it.[59]

There is another passage, dotted with allusions to the autonomy of the state machine,* which also makes clear that this state protected the social interests of the ruling capitalists and landowners.

Only a vestigial reference to all this remained in the final version of *The Civil War in France* after the work of condensation. There is a quick reference to "The State power, apparently soaring high above society," and the heavy emphasis is on the conclusion that Bonapartism is

> the ultimate form of the State power which nascent middle-class society had commenced to elaborate as a means of its own emancipation from feudalism, and which full grown bourgeois society had finally transformed into a means for the enslavement of labour by capital. [62]

The Bonapartist experience left a model, the record of a striving, and evidence of a potentiality, but it came too early in the history of bourgeois society to develop into anything more. Its significance for the development of Marxist theory, however, was immense.

---

* Its interpretation is complicated by the fact that Marx's English in this draft is a little rough. It speaks of "this State usurpation" and "the centralized and organized governmental power usurping to be the master instead of the servant of society." Although this state destroyed the ruling classes' "parliamentary pretensions of self-government," it was "the last possible form of their class rule. While politically dispossessing them, it was the orgy under which all the economic and social infamies of the regime got full sway." It was the "last triumph of a *State* separate of and independent from society." But then, further along, Marx throws in the word *seeming*: this state machine was the "most powerful . . . expression" of the state, writes Marx, and (with good German syntax) he has "expression" modified by this phrase: "elaborated into seeming independence from society."[60] In the second draft, the formulation of this problem is a very brief summary of the foregoing:

> At first view, apparently, the usurpatory dictatorship of the governmental body over society itself, rising alike above and humbling all classes, it has in fact, on the European continent at least, become the only possible state form in which the appropriating class can continue to sway it over the producing class.[61]

19 | STATE AUTONOMY IN PRECAPITALIST SOCIETY

The formula version of Marx's theory of the state—"committee for managing the common affairs" of the ruling class—is the formula for relative normality, like most formulas that sum up experience. We have been testing the meaning of the theory by getting behind the formula, investigating the conditions under which the state tends to assert autonomy from the ruling classes to a greater or lesser extent.

To push this inquiry further, let us leave the boundaries of Bonapartism, as Engels did in the passage which inaugurated this discussion at the beginning of Chapter 16. He had broached the general category of *exceptional* periods "in which the warring classes balance each other so nearly that the state power, as ostensible mediator, acquires, for the moment, a certain degree of independence of both." As we saw, under this head he included three Bonapartists—Napoleon I, Louis Bonaparte, and Bismarck; but the first example he adduced was, as a matter of fact, not a Bonaparte at all: "Such was the absolute monarchy of the seventeenth and eighteenth centuries, which held the balance between the nobility and the class of burghers. . . ."

The absolute monarchy as a state form reigned over a long historical era—not "for the moment" but for a couple of centuries more or less, depending on the country. No Bonaparte figure was necessarily involved, the absolute monarchies being headed by individual monarchs of various shapes and sizes.* We have here an ongoing political *system* involving an autonomized state of a particular kind for a whole historical period, in a number of disparate countries.

---

* That Engels, like others, thought of Bonapartism as a form that tended to require a Bonaparte figure is attested by his remark that "There is no empire without an emperor, no Bonapartism without a Bonaparte. The system is cut to the man's measure; it stands and falls with him."[1] The context, in 1888, was the question how long Bismarck would last.

The absolute monarchy is not introduced by Engels as an example of Bonapartism. On the contrary, it is subsumed along with the three Bonapartisms under a broader head, to which no "ism" or other label is applied but which is described. They are all autonomized states resting on an equilibrium of contending class forces.

To generalize a point made in the last chapter, they are all cases reflecting a *system in dissolution,* and hence a crisis of a certain magnitude. In the case of Louis Bonaparte, we said, it was a particular political system that was on its last legs, but not the society itself; in different terms, the same would apply to the other Bonapartisms. But in the period of absolute monarchy, the political system was the outcome of a social system in dissolution—feudal society. The crisis was on an entirely different order of magnitude, and the persistence of the autonomized state for a whole historical era was of the same order.

1. THE STATE THAT SWALLOWED UP SOCIETY

As we know, Marx and Engels were quite aware of the possibility that the final crisis of a society might not be soluble even by revolution. They stated it in one of the most conspicuous places in all their writings, the opening statement in *The Communist Manifesto* of the proposition that all history (since primitive times) is "the history of class struggles."

> Freeman and slave, patrician and plebeian, lord and serf, guild-master and journeyman, in a word, oppressor and oppressed, stood in constant opposition to one another, carried on an uninterrupted, now hidden, now open fight, a fight that each time ended either in a revolutionary re-constitution of society at large, or in the common ruin of the contending classes.[2]

Engels repeated the alternatives much later in *Anti-Dühring,* not about the past, but with reference to the future: "its [the bourgeoisie's] own productive forces have grown beyond its control, and as if necessitated by a law of nature, are driving the whole of bourgeois society towards ruin, or revolution."[3] As the proletariat grows into a power, then "under penalty of its own destruction, [it] is forced to accomplish this revolution" which abolishes capitalism.[4]

In the Manifesto, Marx and Engels assumed everyone was aware of the great example in the past of "the common ruin of the contending classes." It was the disintegration without revolution of the society of the Roman Empire, an example which weighed heavily on all political thought and on its terminology. "Caesarism" later became a general catchword for personal and military dictatorship, but in terms of Marx's conception Caesar's dictatorship was undoubtedly one Roman analogue of Bonapartism. Caesar was the last step in the downfall of the patrician democracy (democracy for the ruling class as a whole, organized in the Roman Republic) after a long period of class struggles stemming from the bid of the rich plebeians for more political power and the ongoing battle between debtors and creditors. Caesar's state maneuvered between the class pressure of the patricians and the rich plebs, with an eye on its own interests.*

It is a pity that neither Marx nor Engels had occasion to take up the *political* forms in which the Roman state disintegrated, in the course of "the common ruin of the contending classes." Most of their writings were ad hoc, and this *hoc* never arose as a pressing theoretical problem. There are many animadversions to the Roman period in their works,[9] but nothing substantial on the politics of the period of social disintegration—the period when the imperial state more and more came forward as the only cement of the system, while no revolutionary class appeared with aspirations toward a new and progressive social transformation.

For present purposes, the pattern may briefly be summarized as follows: The state sought to maintain the status quo by patching here and there, substituting its own apparatus as necessary for the failing mechanisms of the old order. But this way of maintaining the status

---

* One may be misled by the fact that, in his 1869 preface to a new edition of *The Eighteenth Brumaire,* Marx expressed the hope of "eliminating the school-taught phrase now current, particularly in Germany, of so-called *Caesarism,*" because "this superficial historical analogy" forgets that the Roman class struggle took place inside the free minority, over the backs of the passive slave majority.[5] The specific analogy Marx was objecting to, in this passage, began flourishing in 1866, and has nothing to do with our subject; the term itself had become current about 1851 with one of the journalistic interpretations of Bonapartism.[6] Marx himself had made his own analogies with Caesarism more than once: in *New York Tribune* articles he had referred to the Bonaparte regime as "the Caesarism of Paris," and to "military despotism, the rule of the Caesars" in contemporaneous Europe; and when he discussed Bonaparte's decision for war in 1859 he brought out the phrase *"Aut Caesar aut nihil."*[7] For ourselves the main point is not that Caesar was a Bonaparte or Bonaparte a Caesar, but that both exemplified a more

quo became just another channel through which the unviable status quo changed into something else, for it could not remain the same. Since the status quo could not remain *quo,* the patchwork on the body started turning at long last into the body itself. By the time of Diocletian (around 300 A.D.) if not before, there could be no doubt about what had happened. The old ruling classes had disintegrated with their old social order; the state's role had changed, over centuries, from preserving an ongoing social system to replacing the organizer-classes of disintegrating civil society with its own cadres and mechanisms. *

One of the few places in which Marx touched on this process in passing dealt with another problem altogether: he wished to give an example of how the tillers of the land could be expropriated not by driving them off but by appropriating the product of their labor beyond the point of viability:

> In the last days of the Roman Empire the provincial decurions, which consisted not of peasants but of private landowners, deserted their homes, abandoning their land and even selling themselves into slavery, all in order to get rid of property which had become nothing more than an official pretext for harsh and merciless extortion.[10]

The merciless extorter in this case was the autonomized state, and the victims were part of the (former) ruling classes. The state that developed has been variously dubbed "state capitalism," "state socialism," "corporative state," and "fascism" by historians, anachronistically resorting to later historical phenomena to find a label for a special type of state arising out of "the common ruin of the contending classes." For when a whole civil society disintegrates, the only institution remaining to keep society together is the state: not to keep the old

---

inclusive phenomenon: state autonomization resting on a class equilibrium. The day after Bonaparte's coup d'état, Engels already had in mind the analogy between this event and "the rule of the pretorians." He wrote to Marx:

> It remains to be seen whether the pretorian regime of the days of the Roman Empire, which presupposed a widely extended state organized throughout on military lines, a depopulated Italy and the absence of a modern proletariat, is possible in a geographically concentrated, thickly populated country like France, with a large industrial proletariat.[8]

But they found that such broad social differences do not preclude broad analogies, when a common pattern is embodied in varying historical forms.

* The best short introduction to this question is by Walbank (see Bibliography), which also has a "Note on Books."

society together any more, but to keep *a* society, some kind of organized society, together on any terms.

The autonomized state becomes the residual legatee of society for a historical period. The political institutionalization of force, the state, infuses all the processes of society and subordinates everything to itself; the political and economic institutions fuse. The state is no longer simply a superstructure; it has swallowed up all of society.

This is what Engels saw happening in his own time, but, as usual, with the close-up telescopic view. In a summary passage of great power, moving in a few lines from the ancient slave societies to "present-day Europe," he notes the monstrous growth of state bureaucratization. The state power

> grows stronger, however, in proportion as class antagonisms within the state become more acute, and as adjacent states become larger and more populous. We have only to look at our present-day Europe, where class struggle and rivalry in conquest have tuned up the public power to such a pitch that it threatens to swallow the whole of society and even the state.[11]

An unexplained remark like this was possible because Engels assumed everyone knew that a state once had swallowed up "the whole of society."

2. THE FUSION OF POLITICS AND ECONOMICS

When we come to feudalism, there is a marked difference in the formulations of the early Marx (before *The German Ideology*) and the later Marx. An explanation is necessary before the nature of the difference can be appreciated.

The new feudal order crystallized in Western Europe out of the "statified" society in dissolution. In feudal society, land ownership and power went together; on the manor the feudal lord was also the embodiment of the state *automatically:* who held the land held the mastery of society. In this sense, one of the characteristics of feudalism as a social system was its specific way of fusing economic power and political power in the same hands.

Especially where feudalism is decentralized, where the power of the nobility has not yet been absorbed by a monarchy or princedom, the power of the ruling class can be (and has been) discussed in two apparently different ways, which are really one. The lord can be considered as the landowner (a socioeconomic category) and his land as his private property; at the same time the lord is the state power, which would seem to make the land the property of the state. There is no real contradiction; the difficulty, if any, exists solely in our habit of thinking of state power and economic power necessarily as two separate if related powers; that is, our habit of thinking in terms of the social relations of the bourgeois era and social systems in which property ownership does not directly entail political status.

Thus, in the third volume of *Capital* Marx casually lists "the slave-owner, the feudal lord, and the state (for instance, the Oriental despot)" as representing different social orders.[12] Obviously, at this point he is not thinking of the feudal lord as being *also* the state power, even if only on a duodecimo demesne. But the lord was indeed the state power on his manor.

In Western Europe, out of "the common ruin of the contending classes" of the ancient world, it was the relations of production, established locally between the tiller of the soil and the (military based) owner of the land, that gave rise to the specific state forms of the Middle Ages. The political power of the feudal lord was organically fused with his relationship as landowner to the actual producers. If the consequence was that the land was therefore state property, it was an entirely different form of state property than obtained under the Oriental despotism. Also different was the "state production" that Marx refers to as existing "in former epochs of Russian history on the basis of serfdom."[13] This is only another way of saying that, just as quite different social systems exist on the basis of private property as an economic form, so also there are different social systems based on state property as an economic form.

As we saw in Part I, the thinking of the young Marx on social issues was dominated by the Hegelian dichotomy between the particular and the universal, the particularity of private or personal interests versus the universality of public or state interests. The political sphere was the sphere of the universal; the economic sphere was that of the particular. And so the relationship of universal to particular translated into the relationship of political and economic.*

* For this, see Chapter 3 (especially the first few sections) and Chapter 1, section 1, and Chapter 2, pp. 70-73.

For this Young Hegelian, an overriding problem was how to fuse the universal interest and the particular into a genuine unity—how to make them identical, or reconcile their antagonism, through changed political forms and institutions. In this context, it was recognized that such a fusion *had* existed in the Middle Ages, in a specifically feudalistic way; the aim was not to return to those old forms, but to find a way of making the fusion on the basis of modern conditions.

This is why the young Marx had occasion so often to refer to the fusion of politics and economics as characteristic of medieval society (to use our terms, not his). As early as 1842, in his *Rheinische Zeitung* article on the wood-theft law, Marx referred to the "mixture of private law and public law such as we meet in all institutions of the Middle Ages." [14] But it is in his notebook critique of Hegelian politics (1843) that this is done to the greatest extent.

One important passage occurs in the section where medieval society was called the "democracy of unfreedom," discussed in Chapter 3. [15] If the broad and narrow meanings of *state* in Hegelese are recalled, [16] the following statement becomes clear. Under the Old Regime

The political sphere was the sole state sphere in the state, the sole sphere in which the content . . . was the true universal. . . . It stands to reason that the political constitution as such is developed only where the private spheres have attained an independent existence.

It is in modern bourgeoisified society that "the private spheres have attained an independent existence," that is, independent of the state power (political sphere).

The abstraction of the *state as such* belongs only to the modern period because the abstraction of private life belongs only to the modern period. The abstraction of the *political state* is a modern product.

. . . in the Middle Ages property, trade, society, men were *political;* . . . every private sphere had a political character or was a political sphere, or [in other words] politics was also the character of the private spheres. In the Middle Ages the political constitution was the constitution of private property, but only because the constitution of private property was the political constitution. In the Middle Ages the life of the people and the life of the state [*or read:* political life] were identical. [17]

Again, in his commentary on Hegel's Section 303, Marx, in the course of attacking Hegel's identification of the state bureaucracy as the universal class,[18] also attacks his (reactionary) way of doing away with the modern split between civil and political life. In Hegel, writes Marx, "The civil society's *class difference* becomes a political difference," and "The *separation of 'civil and political life' is to be abolished in this way and their 'identity' established.*" Marx points out that Hegel is trying to *re*establish the typically medieval state of affairs; Hegel himself admits that "identity" in *his* sense was at its peak in the Middle Ages.

> Here [in the Middle Ages] the *Stände* of civil society* [that is, the classes] in general and the *Stände in their political meaning* [the estates] were identical. The spirit of the Middle Ages can be expressed thusly: The *Stände* of civil society [classes] and the *Stände* in their political meaning [estates] were identical because civil society was political society, because the organic principle of civil society was the principle of the state.
>   ... The identity of the civil and political *Stände* was the *expression* of the *identity* of civil and political society. This identity has disappeared [in modern society].[20]

There is a good deal more of this: for example, of the medieval *Stände*, "Their whole being was political; their being was the being of the state."[21]

The same point recurs in Marx's essay "On the Jewish Question"; these passages have already been quoted in Chapter 5.[22] Likewise in the 1844 Manuscripts:

> In general, the sway of private property begins with landed property; that is its basis. But in feudal landed property the lord at least *appears* to be the king of the landed property. . . . The piece of real estate is individualized with its lord; it has his rank, it is baronial or ducal along with him, it has his privileges, his jurisdiction, his political position, and so on. . . . Hence the proverb *Nulle terre sans maître* [No land without a master], in which the growing together of the lordship and the landed property is expressed.[23]

* In this passage, the German *Stand* (pl. *Stände*) is used in two senses in order to distinguish them, as we explained in Chapter 1.[19] The *"Stände* in their political meaning" are the social estates of the medieval order, classes made corporate as a political institution; the *"Stände* of civil society" are the socioeconomic classes apart from their formal political status.

As for the tillers of the soil, "His [the lord's] status with respect to them is therefore directly political. . . ." Modern society now requires

> that landed property . . . be drawn completely into the movement of private property and become a commodity, that the rule of the owner appear as the pure rule of private property, of capital, abstracted from all political tincture. . . .[24]

> Thereby the medieval proverb *Nulle terre sans maître* is replaced by the modern proverb *L'argent n'a pas de maître* [Money has no master], which expressed the complete dominion of lifeless matter over people.[25]

Insofar as the state power is constituted *directly* by the feudal lord without intermediary, the state can hardly be called the executive committee or committee to manage the common affairs of the ruling class. That aphoristic formula requires an obvious readjustment in a society where economic power and political power are fused in the same hands. Insofar as each feudal lord in his own demesne could say *"L'état c'est moi,"* he had no need of any other formula. It was only as political power was centralized, in latter-day feudalism, in the hands of a more or less absolute monarchy that the (centralized) state had to function as the managing committee of the nobility as a class, precisely because land ownership no longer automatically conferred all sovereign political power on the landowner.

Next step: insofar as political power is separated from economic control, it first becomes possible for that political power to aspire to or move toward *autonomy* from the economic masters. This is precisely what happens under the absolute monarchy, when the history of state autonomization resumes. But before we can consider this, we must take up a loose end.

3. PRIVATE PROPERTY UNDER FEUDALISM

We have detailed the thinking of the young Marx on the fusion of politics and economics in feudalism; but what did the mature Marx have to say about this feature of the feudal social order *before the era of absolute monarchy?*

Very little one way or the other; and the above-stated view is reaffirmed very glancingly, never directly. The reasons for this appear to be two:

1. From *The German Ideology* on—that is, as soon as Marx develops the historical method which points him toward seeking the roots of modern society in the productive relations of previous history—his attention is overwhelmingly concentrated on the later period of feudalism. It is difficult to find even passing references to the earlier feudal period, just as it was difficult to find references to the long period of Roman society in dissolution. Marx's and Engels' interests—usually responsive to some contemporary political task, in the same sense that the writing of *Capital* was undertaken as a *political* need—focused on the transition from feudalism to capitalism, and to a lesser extent on the transition from primitive society to various succeeding forms including Oriental despotism. But they virtually ignored the historical problems of several centuries of European history, from the palmy days of the Roman world to the onset of absolute monarchy, including the transition from "the common ruin of the contending classes" to Western European feudalism.*

2. Where Marx and Engels do comment on the social relations of feudalism, their emphasis is always on the thesis that the underlying determinant of the system was the socioeconomic relation between the landowner and the actual producer (serf). The feudal lord is here considered as the owner of private property, as we have already discussed. At no time did Marx or Engels stop to take up the analysis of the nature of the state power under decentralized feudalism.

These emphases can be seen most clearly, perhaps, in *The German Ideology,* just because it lies on the border between the young Marx and the mature Marx. In this book, where the method of exploring the material factors in history is first being worked out, Marx's emphasis is that, under feudalism, "landownership played the chief role," and that in the feudal outlook it was landownership that determined "the whole structure of society."[26] He does not, however, go on to discuss directly what sort of state power was thus determined. Perhaps he thought the question sufficiently covered by his brief statement about the *origin* of feudalism:

* Here is an unexploited opportunity for the paranoidal school of marxology to explain that Marx was "paralyzed" by the thought of the Emperor Diocletian, since he never offered a theory of the late imperial state. Actually, the list of what Marx did *not* discuss is much longer, and therefore offers endless material for nonexplanations.

> The feudal system ... had its origin, as far as the [German] conquerors [of Rome] were concerned, in the martial organization of the army during the actual conquest, and this only evolved after the conquest into the feudal system proper through the action of the productive forces found in the conquered countries.[27]

And, elsewhere in the work: "The hierarchical structure of landownership, and the armed body of retainers associated with it, gave the nobility power over the serfs."[28] The feudal system, wrote Engels much later, was "in its very origin a military organization."[29]

The implications of these statements correct the one-sidedness of the emphasis on land ownership alone, but the implications are *not* brought out. Instead, Marx hurries on to latter-day feudalism, since it is this that leads to the historical roots of modern society.

Further on, there is a section devoted to "The Relation of State and Law to Property" which gives the feudal era short shrift: it gets little more than one phrase in a sentence which moves rapidly on to modern capital. Characteristically, we learn that it is not until the rise of modern capital that there comes into being "pure private property, which has cast off all semblance of a communal institution and has shut out the state from any influence on the development of property." It is, furthermore, only in the bourgeois-dominated state that, for the first time, "Through the emancipation of private property from the community, the state has become a separate entity, beside and outside civil society, . . ." and that "private property has become entirely independent of the community."[30] If this becomes true under the modern bourgeois state for the first time, then the case must have been otherwise under feudalism. But Marx is not interested in backtracking to cover that problem for its own sake.

A similar pattern is found in later writings, insofar as any attention is paid to the question at all. More than once it is implied in passing that under feudalism the relation between the political and the economic was different from today, but this difference is not in the center of the exposition. Thus in *Capital* there is the remark that "The leadership of industry is an attribute of capital, just as in feudal times the functions of general and judge were attributes of landed property."[31] These latter functions of feudal times were *state* functions. Elsewhere: when landed property is bourgeoisified, integrated into capitalist relations, it "receives its purely economic form by discarding all its former political and social trappings and admixtures"—"all those traditional accessories" of feudal landed property.[32] In a real sense, feudal landed property has to be *depoliticized* in order to be bourgeoisified. In other notes Marx makes the point that private property in land becomes exchange value only as "the product of capital and of the complete subordination of the state organism to capital."[33] But before capitalist relations become dominant, the state organism is not only not subordinated to capital, it is not subordinated to civil society in general; under feudal relations, the state power is inextricable from landed property.

The same goes for Engels. In his draft for the Manifesto, he wrote that, as distinct from "feudal and guild property," the rise of capitalism "created a new form of ownership—private ownership." This reflects a feeling that private ownership did not exist under feudal forms of property—obviously a vague formulation until explained. In *The Peasant War in Germany* he was not loath to write about the status of feudal vassals as "almost independent sovereigns" when the bonds of empire fell apart. There is a passage of similar force in his *Revolution and Counter-Revolution in Germany*.[34]

Such is the state of this question in Marx's and Engels' writings: very unsatisfactory. Fortunately, a quite different situation exists when we come to the more decisive period that followed, the era of absolute monarchy, with respect to the issue of state autonomization.

4. ABSOLUTE MONARCHY AND STATE AUTONOMY

The fragmentation of state power in the hands of the separate feudal lords, each sovereign in his demesne, had originally arisen as a means of organizing the disintegration of the ancient world; but this political fragmentation could not endure indefinitely in the face of the economic integration promoted by merchant capital, the growth of cities, and the use of money. These pressures necessitated a centralized state power. Without it, even the old feudal nobility could not survive: they exhausted their historical initiative in finding ways to kill themselves off—"devoured by the great feudal wars," or "annihilated in the peasant wars."[35] In England they were in a fair way of exterminating themselves in the so-called Wars of the Roses.[36]

This class as a whole had to be deprived of its sovereign political power in order to preserve its socioeconomic privileges—or more exactly, to preserve *as much as possible* of its ruling-class privileges. It had to be shorn of political power for its own good, as usual—which means: for the good of the social system in which it had a place. As before and after, state autonomization came in as a means of maintaining a system in dissolution, by rescuing its ruling class from their own incapacities.

The centralization of state power in the hands of one feudal lord, all others becoming dependent vassals, took the form of the absolute monarchy. This absolutism was the formal reflection of the need for state autonomization: the more absolute, the more autonomous; the more a duke here or a count there retained some of his former power, the less autonomous the centralized state. The feudal lord, as a member of a ruling class, remained a landowner, still exploiting enserfed labor and deriving his income therefrom. The land which was formerly both his private property and his state property now took on more and more the aspect of feudal private property only (later to merge into bourgeois private property)—and at the same time, ownership became more and more divorced from management of the demesne. "The landed noble turned into the court noble, the faster and surer to be ruined."*

In notes for a revision of his *Peasant War in Germany*, Engels remarked that the absolute monarchy

> *had* to be absolute just because of the centrifugal character of all elements. However, "absolute" [is] not to be understood in the vulgar sense: [it was] in constant struggle partly with the estates, partly with the insurgent feudal lords and cities. . . .

And he makes the interesting suggestion that the absolute monarchy should rather be called the *ständische,* or estate, monarchy; that is, it should be designated not by the new political form on top but by the way in which the underlying population was organized in sociopolitical estates. This monarchy, he adds, was "still feudal, feudal-in-decline and bourgeois-in-embryo." [39]

---

* So Engels.[37] In *The German Ideology* this idea was used to show how Max Stirner's "Ego" had derived its views on "My Self-Enjoyment" (one section of his book): "In modern times the philosophy of enjoyment arose with the decline of feudalism and with the transformation of the feudal landed nobility into the jovial, extravagant nobles of the court under the absolute monarchy."[38] (An even more telling example is that other "anarchist" classic, Rabelais' depiction of the Abbey of Thélème.)

This state was "still feudal" inasmuch as it began as the only possible way of saving the feudal lords from shaking their society apart with their blind-alley brawls. In notes for a history of Germany, Engels pointed to the confused tangle of feudal rights, among numerous reasons for a permanent state of internecine conflict.

> How could conflicts be avoided? Hence that century-long alternation of the vassals' attraction to the royal center, which alone could protect them against external foes and against each other, and of their repulsion from that center, into which that attraction inevitably and perpetually changed; hence that continuous struggle between royalty and vassals, whose tedious uproar drowned out everything else during that lengthy period when robbery was the only source of income worthy of free men. . . .

His conclusion:

> It is plain that in this general chaos royal power was the progressive element. It represented order in confusion, and the budding nation as opposed to dismemberment into rebellious vassal states. All the revolutionary elements taking shape under the feudalistic surface gravitated just as much towards royalty as the latter gravitated towards them.

Centralized monarchic power offered both protection and encouragement to the burgeoning bourgeoisie:

> The alliance of royalty and burgherdom dates back to the tenth century. Often interrupted by conflicts, because nothing pursued its course consistently in the Middle Ages, it was each time more firmly and vigorously renewed, until it helped royalty to its final victory [over the nobility], and royalty, by way of thanks, subjugated and plundered its ally.[40]

The basic conception that the absolute monarchy represented a form of relative state autonomy, balanced on the countervailing pressures of contending classes, already appeared in *The German Ideology*. There it comes up first as codicil to one of the earliest statements of Marx's characteristic theory of the state—that the state is "the form of organization which the bourgeois necessarily adopt both for internal and external purposes, for the mutual guarantee of their property and interests."

The independence of the state is only found nowadays in those countries where the estates have not yet completely developed into classes, where the estates, done away with in more advanced countries, still have a part to play, and where there exists a mixture; countries, that is to say, in which no one section of the population can achieve dominance over the others. This is the case particularly in Germany.[41]

Germany's retarded social development is linked with the fact that none of the social spheres (estates turning into classes) had been capable of asserting exclusive domination.

The necessary consequence was that during the epoch of absolute monarchy, which was seen here [Germany] in its most stunted and semipatriarchal form, the particular social sphere which, owing to the division of labor, was responsible for the administration of public interests acquired an abnormal independence, which was pushed even further in the modern bureaucracy. Thus the state constituted itself as an apparently independent power, and this position, which in other countries was only transitory—a transitional stage—it has maintained in German to the present day.

There were certain consequences in the ideological superstructure:

It is this position of the state which explains both the honest character of the government officialdom which is found nowhere else, and all the illusions about the state which are current in Germany, as well as the apparent independence of German theoreticians in relation to the burghers—the apparent contradiction between the form in which these theoreticians express the interests of the burghers and those interests themselves.[42]

The equilibrium thesis was put forward directly by Engels in 1847:

... the [Prussian] king, representing the central power of the state, and supported by the numerous class of government officers, civil and military, besides having the army at his disposal, was enabled to keep down the middle classes by the nobility, and the nobility by the middle classes, by flattering now the interests of the one, and then those of the other; and balancing, as much as possible, the influence of both. This stage of absolute monarchy has been gone through by almost all the civilized countries of Europe, and in those most advanced it has now given place to the government of the middle classes.[43]

And then this stage was mentioned in the *Communist Manifesto* as one of the steps in the development of the bourgeoisie, when it was "serving either the semifeudal* or the absolute monarchy as a counterpoise against the nobility, and, in fact, cornerstone of the great monarchies in general. . . ."[44]

Soon afterward, the equilibrium thesis was applied by Engels to countervailing social forces other than classes—namely, to the disparate national groups in the Austrian empire of the Hapsburgs, in combination with a class equilibrium. To begin with, the Hapsburgs "supported the city burghers against the nobility and the towns against the princes" as "the sole condition on which a great monarchy was at all possible."[45] But the developing bourgeoisie began to threaten the dominance of the nobility, and growing peasant opposition aroused old national struggles.

> In this state of affairs Metternich brought off his masterpiece. With the exception of the most powerful feudal barons he deprived the rest of the nobility of all influence over the conduct of the state. He deprived the bourgeoisie of its strength by winning over the most powerful finance-barons**—indeed he had to do this, under compulsion of the financial situation. Thus supported by the high feudal nobility and high finance as well as the bureaucracy and the army, he attained the ideal of absolute monarchy more completely than any of his rivals. The burghers and peasants of every nationality he kept in hand through the nobles of the same nationality and the peasants of all the other nationalities; the nobles of every nationality, through their fear of the burghers and peasants of their own nationality. The various class interests, narrowminded nationalist tendencies, and local prejudices, complicated as they were, were mutually held in check to the fullest, and allowed the old scoundrel Metternich the greatest freedom of movement.[47]

---

* *Semifeudal* is the loose translation, in the standard Moore-Engels English version, of the *ständische* monarchy, that is, the monarchy based on estates—the same term that Engels later suggested as a substitute for *absolute* monarchy.

** In a shorter version of this explanation in Engels' later *Revolution and Counter-Revolution in Germany, finance barons* and *high finance* become *large stockjobbing capitalists:*

> The government of Prince Metternich turned upon two hinges: firstly, to keep every one of the different nations, subjected to the Austrian rule, in check by all other nations, similarly conditioned; secondly, and this always has been the fundamental principle of absolute monarchies, to rely for support upon two classes, the feudal landlords and the large stockjobbing capitalists; and to balance, at the same time, the influence and power of either of these classes by that of the other, so as to leave full independence of action to the Government.[46]

5. ABSOLUTE MONARCHY: THE DOWN PHASE

There was a common pattern to the absolute monarchies, including the Austrian: at first, a push behind the rising bourgeoisie, in order to keep the nobility in line; then a bridling of the new class, to prevent it from taking the bit in its teeth. Thus the era of absolute monarchy had its ascending line, when as "a product of bourgeois development"[48] the royal power played a progressive role, and then it started downward on the path of decline, when it stood in the way of further progress.

In the first period, the bourgeoisie was not moved *above* the nobility but merely alongside, as recipients of the state's favors.

> Here [in Kautsky's article, wrote Engels] there is missing a lucid exposition of *how* the absolute monarchy came into existence as a naturally evolved compromise between nobility and bourgeoisie and how it therefore had to protect certain interests of both sides and distribute favors to them. In this process the nobility—politically put in retirement—got as its share the plundering of the peasantry and of the state treasury and indirect political influence through the court, the army, the church and the higher administrative authorities, while the bourgeoisie received protection through tariffs, monopolies and a *relatively* orderly administration of public affairs and justice.[49]

In the later period, the Crown was still trying to keep the bourgeois forces locked into this pattern in spite of their increasing economic power. But this was no longer possible on the basis of the old division of the plunder. The Crown therefore had to shift the direction of its thrust in order to try to maintain the old equilibrium; that is, in order to maintain the status quo, it had to alter the status quo. At this point the absolute monarchy turned against the current of economic development.

Now, "as a rule" such a turn means that the ongoing system is no longer historically viable and must eventually succumb.* For the absolute monarchy too, there was

---

* Engels in *Anti-Dühring*:

After the political force has made itself independent in relation to society, and has transformed itself from its servant into its master, it can work in two different directions. Either it works in the sense and in the direction of the natural economic development, in which case no conflict arises between them, the economic development being accelerated. Or it works

a period when the Crown played the burghers against the nobility, in order to keep one estate in check by means of the other; but from the moment when the bourgeoisie, still politically powerless, began to grow dangerous owing to its increasing economic power, the Crown resumed its alliance with the nobility, and by so doing called forth the bourgeois revolution. . . .[51]

The pattern of decline was discussed by Marx a little more fully in an 1847 article. The target of this article was the feudal-socialist tendency in Germany whose anticapitalism led it to support the absolutist regime against the bourgeoisie. Marx was therefore intent on emphasizing the reactionary role to which the absolute monarchy had descended. The bourgeoisie, he explained, originally helped the monarchy to victory against the great feudal lords, and later exploited the financial needs of the Crown to make it dependent on high finance.[52] Now the absolute monarchy was trying to check further progress:

> Having arisen out of the defeat of the feudal orders and itself taken the most active part in their destruction, it now tries to maintain at least the *semblance* of feudal distinctions. Formerly encouraging commerce and industry and simultaneously the rise of the bourgeois class as necessary conditions of both national power and its own resplendence, the absolute monarchy now stands in the way of commerce and industry, which have become more and more dangerous weapons in the hands of an already powerful bourgeoisie.[53]

True, a process of bourgeoisification takes place inexorably, but the absolute monarchy sets its face *against* this development; it tries to hold back the clock.

> But in Prussia, as previously in England and France, the absolute monarchy does not let itself be bourgeoisified amicably. It does not abdicate amicably. Besides their personal prejudices, the princes have their hands tied by a whole civil, military, and

---

against economic development, in which case, as a rule, with but few exceptions, force succumbs to it.[50] [The first part of this passage was discussed in Chapter 11, p. 248.]

If a rule allows exceptions, as most do, it is still necessary to explain the exceptions in terms of the framework established by the rule. In this case Engels is able to allow for exceptions because of the concept of state autonomy as a resultant of class forces.

clerical bureaucracy—components of the absolute monarchy which by no means want to change their status as rulers for one as servants with respect to the bourgeoisie. For another thing, the feudal orders hold back; for them it is a question of to-be-or-not-to-be, that is, property or expropriation. It is clear that the absolute monarchy, in spite of all the servile genuflections of the bourgeoisie, perceives its real interests to lie on the side of these feudal orders.[54]

Thus, when push comes to shove, the absolutist state "perceives its real interests to lie" on the same side as the decaying aristocracy. It is plainly not acting in this respect as the managing committee of the old aristocracy, now far gone in marasmus and political impotence. It is acting in its own real interests, including the interests of its components, the various sectors of the ruling state bureaucracy, which has the social power to tie the hands of the head of state.

6. FROM ABSOLUTISM TO BONAPARTISM

Given this analysis of the play of class forces producing the absolute monarchy in both its up and down phase, there is a plain relationship between this state form and the state form of Bonapartism. Both are autonomized states resting on an equilibrium of contending classes, but the classes in question are different. In the first case, "the basic condition of the old absolute monarchy" was "an equilibrium between the landed aristocracy and the bourgeoisie," while "the basic condition of modern Bonapartism" is "an equilibrium between the bourgeoisie and the proletariat."[55]

In the class struggle between proletariat and bourgeoisie [wrote Engels in a letter*] the Bonapartist monarchy . . . played a part

---

* Engels' letter was educationally addressed to E. Bernstein, then in the heyday of his revolutionary period as editor of *Der Sozialdemokrat.* A few months later Bernstein had occasion to show what he had learned, in an important lead article. In this article the pertinent passage is interesting because of its degree of generalization: "State absolutism," wrote Bernstein,

is the political expression of quite definite social conditions—it is found everywhere where a class that has been the ruling class up to then feels

similar to that of the old absolute monarchy in the struggle between feudalism and bourgeoisie.[57]

The "Bonapartist monarchy" here is the Prussian, under Bismarck. In Prussia the relationship between absolute monarchy and Bonapartism had a special feature, for the general social backwardness of German conditions caused one to *merge* into the other.

> The basic precondition for the [Prussian] monarchy, which had been slowly rotting since 1840, was the struggle between nobility and bourgeoisie, in which the monarchy held the balance. When the nobility no longer needed protection against the onrush of the bourgeoisie and it became necessary to protect all the propertied classes against the onrush of the working class, the old absolute monarchy had to go over completely to the form of state expressly devised for this purpose: *the Bonapartist monarchy.*[58]

Evidently the nobility no longer needed protection against the bourgeoisie after the ignominious collapse of bourgeois radicalism in 1848–1849. At the same time an impetus was given to the bourgeoisification of the bureaucracy itself as well as of the rural nobility.[59] Catching up with itself, Prussia ran the two state forms together, in the Bismarckian monarchy, the result being a "pseudoconstitutionalism" which "is at once the present-day form of the dissolution of the old absolute monarchy and the form of existence of the Bonapartist monarchy."[60]

If the absolutist monarchy could telescope into the Bismarckian (Bonapartist) state without any break in continuity, it was because of the continuity of the common feature: the autonomization of the state. What changed was the equilibrium pattern of the contending classes on which the state rested. The social formation that assured the continuity of the state *through the changeover in class basis* must have been, then, the one that Marx pointed to as a decisive component of the autonomized state: *the bureaucracy.* To this question we now turn, last but not least.

---

itself in decline while the new class that is developing is not yet strong enough to rule. Hence we find it everywhere at the close of the Middle Ages—in England, in France, in Germany.

Engels thought the article "very good," but his comment makes no specific reference to this passage.[56]

20 | STATE BUREAUCRACY AND CLASS

There has already been frequent occasion to refer to the role of the state officialdom or bureaucracy. Naturally: for the development of a *special* social stratum of state officials is already involved in the basic conception of Marx's theory of the origin of the state, as we saw in Chapter 11.

This is one of the distinctive features of Marx's political theory: the bureaucracy is not a mere accretion or an adventitious element in society, not simply an unfortunate tumor on the otherwise sound body of the state, but rather inherent in and inseparable from the very existence of a state. Therefore no political theory makes the officialdom, as an institution, more central to state theory as well as practice.

Within Marx's framework, the state cannot be defined without thereby defining the bureaucracy. Terms like *managing committee* or *special agencies* are collective nouns for the people who man them. The integral connection is most evident in Engels' summary:

> Society gives rise to certain common functions which it cannot dispense with. The persons appointed for this purpose form a new branch of the division of labor *within society*. This gives them particular interests, distinct too from the interests of those who empowered them; they make themselves independent of the latter and—the state is in being.[1]

Thus, the characteristic *detachedness* of the officialdom's relationship to the mass of the people, the gulf between this special body and the people it rules—this already exists in the Marxist conception of the state as "a power seemingly standing above society . . . and increasingly alienating itself from it."[2] In any case, who says *state* says *bureaucracy.**

In popular parlance and some academic systems, *bureaucracy* may be reduced to a conjunctural relationship: perhaps a set of bad habits (for example, arrogance, insensitivity, slothful organization) or bad governmental practices (overstaffing, red tape, swollen paper work) or bad intragovernmental relations (hierarchy). These are indubitably bureaucratic diseases or disease symptoms to be combated, but they do not define the diseased organism; they are consequences. This secondary meaning may be best represented by the term *bureaucratism*, to distinguish it from *bureaucracy as a social formation.*

In our present context, then, *bureaucracy* is used to denote a social stratum of officialdom which is an instrument of *rule from above* in society, institutionally detached from the mass it is organized to manage. Its internal hierarchy, with lines of command from the top down, is a reflection of its basic class function.**

* In 1849 Marx was led to make this point explicit in ABC fashion for the benefit of malicious German officials. It is worth reading since it is an odd marxological tenet nowadays that Marx was capable of discussing a state (the Oriental state) without it occurring to him that it had a bureaucracy. In a *Neue Rheinische Zeitung* article, Marx denounced the Düsseldorf authorities for planning to try Lassalle twice for the same speech: once for advocating "arming against the sovereign power" and again for advocating "forcible resistance against government officials." Marx treated this as a contemptible dodge, not worthy of serious debate:

> If in a speech I "call for arming against the sovereign power," doesn't it go without saying that I am calling for "forcible resistance against government officials"? The *existence* of the sovereign power is, indeed, precisely its *officials*, army, administration, judges. Apart from this its body, it is a shadow, a figment of the imagination, a [mere] name. The overthrow of the government is impossible without forcible opposition to its officials. If in a speech I call for *revolution*, then it is superfluous to add *"Forcibly oppose the officials."*[3]

It must be remembered that in the course of its millions of words, Marx's *NRZ*, like everyone else, customarily referred to the absolutist state power as the "Crown" or similar standard term of collectivity (monarchy, absolutism, and so on). It was only in a later century that this language could be considered vague. "The state is the officials [*Beamten*]" went an old German saying.[4] It is historians who popularize Louis XIV's alleged counterclaim that *"L'état, c'est moi,"* but the common man knew the state as a network of outstretched hands, hard faces, and armed men. Indeed, Louis is supposed to have made this famous assertion in interrupting a magistrate who dared to use the expression "the king and the state."[5] In his notes on the historian Maine, Marx remarked at one point: "This unfortunate *Maine has not the faintest idea* that . . . the state is by no means the *prince*; he only *seems* to be."[6]

** By analogy, bureaucracies, in the sense of institutionalized officialdoms not

1. THE VIEW FROM 1843

When Marx discussed bureaucracy so extensively in his notebook critique of Hegel in 1843, the term was still quite rare in serious political writing. It had *not* been used by Hegel himself for his class of officials; it was Marx who introduced it into the analysis.

What did it mean in 1843? Firstly, from its beginnings in French and German the term was strongly pejorative—as it still usually is today, especially outside academic circles influenced by Max Weber. It was possible for Marx to put it to use because his viewpoint was pointed against bureaucracy.

Secondly, the term had already bifurcated into its two areas of meaning: a ruling social formation of some kind, or merely a set of practices or attitudes. The former had characterized the term's first recorded appearance in a German book (by C. J. Kraus, 1808), where the *Büreaukratie* denoted a stratum which "blatantly rules" Prussia in place of the aristocracy. It had earlier been used in the German periodical press in connection with the French revolutionary developments after 1789.[8] The Brockhaus encyclopedia of 1819 had recognized it; and in the 1820s it became better known through use by the prominent publicist J. J. Görres, whose writings, familiar to the young Marx and Engels,[9] are said to have naturalized the term in German.[10]

But in France, where the term had originated and which still provided the impetus for its international diffusion, Balzac's novels had popularized it in the 1830s in its reduced, secondary meaning of *bureaucratism.* This is clear from the little essay on bureaucracy toward the beginning of his *Les Employés,* the main source. Three months later John Stuart Mill published an article on France using the term (probably its first appearance in an English magazine) with exactly the same limited meaning.[11] A similarly limited meaning was also dominant in

---

susceptible to control from below, are found in all levels below the state machine—for example, in corporations, sociologists' associations, charity foundations, large organizations of many kinds. Marx's views on the trade-union bureaucracy are reserved for another volume.—For the confused multiplicity of meanings of "bureaucracy" in contemporary thought, see the introduction to Albrow, who illustrates the sad state of affairs by writing a section on Marx which is factually inaccurate in virtually every sentence.[7]

German academia up to a "short time ago," according to a contemporary authority writing in 1846.*

When Marx first discussed bureaucracy in his Hegel critique of 1843, then, there was a choice. But in Marx's critique, *bureaucracy* definitely denotes a ruling bureaucracy as a basic social formation.

The present chapter will begin the discussion of how Marx regarded the role of the state bureaucracy in the context of class society. There is a present-day tendency, unfortunately, to concentrate this subject under the narrow issue *Is the bureaucracy a class?* While taking account of this current approach, it must be emphasized that the question did not exist in this form for Marx's milieu or for Marx himself; and we shall see that this formulation of the question violates some fundamentals of Marx's method.

If the question *Is the bureaucracy a class?* were asked in the society in which Marx came to political consciousness, it would have been as frivolous as asking whether Prussia was a monarchy. In the Prussian absolutist regime, in which the bourgeoisie was only commencing to aspire to participation in political life, the classes usually meant the *Stände,* the estates of the realm. These were the official classes of society: social formations recognized as having a formal-juridical relationship to the state even though rooted in civil society—represented as such in the Rhenish Diet, for example, as we saw in Chapter 1.[14]

* Though published three years after Marx's notebook on Hegel was written, this essay by Robert von Mohl provides the nearest thing to a report on the meaning of *bureaucracy* in serious literature at the time Marx first used it. In a footnote added later, the author stated that to his knowledge his 1846 article was the first attempt at an analysis of this "new term," this "new favorite expression." Mohl's article began: "Since a relatively short time ago, talk about 'bureaucracy' has been cropping up everywhere and under the most various circumstances. As a rule, not in a favorable and fair sense. . . . Now what is the precise conception of this term which is condemned as barbarous by philologists?" For some years, relates Mohl, the term was sparsely applied, under the influence of Malchus' *Politik der Staatsverwaltung,* to government departmental organization in which "business is not discussed collectively by the staff" but ordered by hierarchic authority. "But nowadays," he complains, "the bureaucracy is spoken of as a social power or a governmental system. . . . It is in any case something bigger and broader [than Malchus' sense] . . . ."[12] This broader usage in German circles, decried by the influential professor of political science, is attested indirectly by one of the first English-language articles to use the term analytically: J. S. Blackie's "Prussia and the Prussian System," a review of recent German books (1842). The magazine's editor appended a note treating the term as Blackie's.[13]

It was a Hegelian tenet, previously discussed,[15] that not only was the bureaucracy a class, it was *the* Universal Class (*allgemeine Stand*), the one that represented the interests of society as a communal whole as against particularistic interests. Even when Marx set out to refute Hegel's view in his first theoretical exploration of state concepts, in 1843, it did not even occur to him to question the plain fact that the bureaucracy was *a* class: he sought only to prove that it was a particularist class like all the others, that it did not deserve the "universal class" badge which Hegel pinned on it in order to raise it above the ruck of the other social classes.

This view had incubated while he was still a *Rheinische Zeitung* left democrat. After all, the Cologne paper was not simply a business enterprise: it was the mouthpiece of an embattled political tendency, whose direct enemy was precisely the existing state bureaucracy. Writing for it, and then taking over its editorship, meant a day-to-day collision with the agencies of that bureaucracy. In the foreground, as The Enemy, was not merely the monarchy in the abstract but the *Beamtenstaat* (functionary state). The power of the bureaucracy had to be clipped, Marx wrote.[16] The state arrogantly demands that the people put "unlimited trust in the officialdom" while the state itself holds "unlimited distrust of all nonofficials": this is the "basic defect" of "all our institutions."[17]

His article on the wood-theft law anticipated his critique of Hegel: the Diet debases the state officialdom into "material instruments of private interest."[18] His article on the Moselle peasants emphasized the narrowmindedness of the bureaucratic mentality: the government official is guilty of "demeaning the state [that is, communal] interests into his private affair," and of regarding "the domain of governmental authority" as the one and only "official reality."[19] In another passage this article pushed the insight a little further. The obtuseness of the bureaucratic mind is no personal or adventitious characteristic but inherent in the *"bureaucratic* essence" of the government administrative machine, which is not *able* (Marx's emphasis) to see that the trouble lies within itself, not only "in the sphere of nature and the private citizen." He continued:

> *With the best will in the world,* the keenest humanitarianism and the strongest intelligence, the administrative authorities are *unable* to do more than resolve temporary and transitory conflicts,

and are unable to resolve a continual conflict between reality and administrative precepts; for neither is this a task covered by their position, nor is the best will in the world capable of breaking out of an *essential relationship* or *fatality,* if you will. This *essential relationship* is the bureaucratic relationship, inside the administrative body as well as in its *connection with the body administered.* [20]

The last sentence drew a necessary distinction between bureaucratism as a characteristic of the internal life of the administration itself (hierarchy, and so on) and bureaucracy as a characteristic of the government's relationship to society at large. For it was the second that defined the bureaucracy as a social stratum.

Then Marx's 1843 notebook on Hegel's state theory spelled out a hard position—demoting Hegel's Universal Class to just another class with selfish (particular) class interests, which were falsely identified with those of the state (society). The bureaucracy holds "the essence of the state . . . in its possession; it is its *private property*"—that is, for the bureaucracy state power plays the same role, in terms of the material basis of its ascendancy (posts, career, and so on), as private property does for the property-owning classes. [21] "*Class* in the medieval sense [*Stand*]," writes Marx, "remained only within the bureaucracy itself, where the civil status and political status are directly identical." [22] That is: the fusion of economic and political position which characterized society as a whole in the Middle Ages, [23] holds true today *only for the bureaucracy;* only for the bureaucracy is its economic position directly based on its political.

Furthermore, the bureaucracy generates typical bureaucratic symptoms. Thus the state exists as "various bureau-mentalities connected by relations of subordination and passive obedience." The "chief abuse" becomes "hierarchy." Nor is this bureaucracy a mere institutional abstraction: it is *certain people.* "The affairs and operations of the state are bound up with individuals (the state operates only through individuals). . . ." Hegel forgets "that the state affairs and operations are human functions," incarnated in "human beings" called bureaucrats (officials, functionaries, and so on), [24] because Hegel made the state an abstract category.

This is Marx's first reminder that, while customary language spoke in shorthand of the state (or the monarchy or the Crown) doing thus and so, it was not merely one royal individual that was in question, but the whole class (*Stand*) which corporately governed under the aegis of the Crown-holder.

2. THE ABSOLUTIST BUREAUCRACY
BEFORE 1848

When Marx wrote down the first clear exposition of a Marxist view of social development in *The German Ideology,* he did not suddenly suffer amnesia about something previously accepted as part of the ABC of politics.

In this work Marx is no less aware than before of the role of the bureaucracy, but now he also points to the *difference* in the socio-political role of the state bureaucracy before and after the bourgeoisie acquires dominance in the state. Let us first examine the exposition in Marx and Engels of the "before" role of the bureaucracy—its role in the epoch of absolute monarchy before the bourgeois assumption of political power.

In *The German Ideology,* to illustrate the epoch-making thesis there first formulated that "The ideas of the ruling class are in every epoch the ruling ideas," the immediate example given by Marx is not a period with *a* ruling class. He starts with the harder case:

> For example, in a period and in a country in which royal power, aristocracy, and bourgeoisie are contending for [political] rule, and where the rule is therefore shared, the separation-of-powers doctrine manifests itself as the ruling idea and is now expressed as an "eternal law." [25]

This, then, is a three-sided contest, still unresolved; there is not *a* ruling class, but a pattern of shared rule.

In this type of situation, in which the prebourgeois estate system has not yet been decisively replaced by social class divisions, "in which no one section of the population can achieve dominance over the others," one still finds "the independence of the state"—Germany being given as the case in point—as distinct from the "more advanced countries" (France, England, and America) where the modern state has become subordinated to bourgeois private property. This "independence of the state" clearly refers to its relative autonomy from control by any of the contending classes, not the basic independence of any state from society as such.[26] Later in the same work, this autonomy is concretized as the "abnormal independence" of the *bureaucracy* under the royal power, not simply of the state. For there was no question but that operationally the state manifested itself as the state bureaucracy.[27]

As the manuscript of *The German Ideology* was being finished, Engels wrote an article in which he carried this line of thought further. His subject was the persistence of the absolute monarchy in Germany, the current form of which he viewed as "a new system, which has been peculiar to Germany." His explanation was in terms of a class equilibrium which would later apply much more widely:

°°The aristocracy was willing to govern, but too weak; the middle classes were neither willing to govern nor strong enough—both, however, were strong enough to induce the government to some concessions. The form of government, therefore, was a sort of mongrel monarchy. A constitution, in some [German] states, gave an appearance of guarantee to the aristocracy and the middle classes; for the remainder there was everywhere a *bureaucratic* government—that is, a monarchy which pretends to take care of the interests of the middle class by a good administration, which administration is, however, directed by the aristocrats. . . . The consequence is, the formation of a separate class of administrative government officers, in whose hands the chief power is concentrated, and which stands in opposition against all other classes.[28]

This article illustrates the prevalent view of the absolutist bureaucracy as a classlike formation. However, the relation of class forces is not yet clear in this 1846 article: the "separate class" of administrators in this "bureaucratic government" holds the "chief power" as against all other classes, yet the government is "directed by the aristocrats." Into the bargain, the next sentence is: "It is the barbarian form of middle-class rule"—meaning a form *preparatory* to bourgeois rule, as barbarism is preparatory to civilization. At this point Engels had just begun his intellectual association with Marx. The following year he wrote more clearly of the balancing of classes—nobility versus bourgeoisie— by "the king, representing the central power of the state, and supported by the numerous class of government officers, civil and military. . . ."[29]

It was also in 1847, as we saw in the previous chapter, that Marx presented the same bureaucracy in quite as autonomous a light, without actually using the class label. The absolute monarchy, which did not act as the instrument of the feudal aristocracy, was still farther from acting as if it had become a bourgeois state. On the contrary, from previously encouraging the development of commerce and industry, it now stood in the way, positively resisting bourgeoisification. Why? "Besides their personal prejudices, the Princes have their hands tied by a whole civil, military, and clerical bureaucracy—components of the absolute monarchy which by no means want to change their status as rulers for one as servants with respect to the bourgeoisie." (The attitude of the feudal orders is given as an additional reason.) The royal power now sees its interests as allied with the feudality, not with the bourgeoisie.[30] Clearly this state power involves so autonomous a social formation at its heart that the class label becomes a mere matter of terminology.

Outside the triangle of contending forces there is a new class growing up, the proletariat. It confronts alternatives:

> It asks whether it is the present political state of affairs, the rule of the bureaucracy, or the one which the liberals strive for, the rule of the bourgeoisie, that will offer it more means to attain its own ends.[31]

This "rule of the bureaucracy" referred concretely to the Prussia of 1847, still cramped and clogged by absolutism. More summarily, Marx indicated the same line of thought for absolutist France, in retrospect. In his *Eighteenth Brumaire* he explained that the enormous over-bureaucratization of the French state—"embracing wide strata, with a host of officials numbering half a million,"—had arisen under the old absolute monarchy, but had continued on through and after the bourgeois revolution. The privileges of the former ruling class, the land-owning nobility, had been transmuted by absolutism into the bureaucratic power of the new rulers:

> The seignorial privileges of the landowners and towns became transformed into so many attributes of the state power, the feudal dignitaries into paid officials, and the motley pattern of conflicting medieval plenary powers into the regulated plan of a state authority whose work is divided and centralized as in a factory.[32]

This description of the transference of political power from the feudal lords to the state bureaucracy was somewhat revised by Marx in 1871 for his work on the Paris Commune.*

Objectively, this autonomized state incubated the bourgeois economy and thereby a new class rule, but the state itself did not become the instrument of any ruling class of civil society except as it was eventually mastered by either the old feudals or the new bourgeois:

> ... under the absolute monarchy, during the first Revolution, under Napoleon, bureaucracy was only** the means of preparing the class rule of the bourgeoisie. Under the Restoration, under Louis Philippe, under the parliamentary republic [of 1848], it was the instrument of the ruling class, however much it strove for power of its own.[35]

This makes the interesting statement that until 1814–1815 the autonomized state, under various leaderships, could *not* be considered "the instrument of the ruling class," either of the former ruling class (the feudal aristocracy) or of the upcoming ruling class (the bourgeoisie).

3. THE TEST CASE OF FRIEDRICH WILHELM IV

Marx spelled the point out even more bluntly in connection with the problem posed by the reign of the current Prussian king, Friedrich Wilhelm IV.

---

* The final version of *The Civil War in France* followed *The Eighteenth Brumaire* in tracing back to the period of absolute monarchy the "centralized state power, with its ubiquitous organs of standing army, police, bureaucracy, clergy, and judicature—organs wrought after the plan of a systematic and hierarchic division of labour. . . ."[33] The first draft added some detail here, subsequently condensed out, about the "ubiquitous and complicated military, bureaucratic, clerical and judiciary organs" of the "centralised state machinery." This passage is plainly a rewrite direct from *The Eighteenth Brumaire:* "The seignorial privileges of the medieval lords and cities and clergy were transformed into the attributes of a unitary state power, displacing the feudal dignitaries by salaried state functionaries. . . ."[34]

** This *only* (*nur*) is an intensive, as previously explained in Chapter 11, page 257 fn. The very same passage makes clear that bureaucracy was a quite different means from the standpoint of the absolute monarchy itself; it is from an *objective* historical overview that it was "the means of preparing the class rule of the bourgeoisie," in the same sense that capitalist development is objectively the means of preparing socialist society.

We have already touched on this king's inclination to turn the clock back in social conditions.[36] As Marx explained in 1843, the king "who burbled about a great past full of priests, knights, and bondsmen," a feudal past to which he dreamed of returning, found that even the Crown could not transfer power back to the old feudality: for "the servants of the old despotism soon put an end to these un-German activities." These servants were the bureaucracy, whom the Crown could not control (so Marx argues). For while the young king had illusions about the omnipotence of the royal power, thinking it was *"his* state," the actual outcome was a return to the "servants' state" (*Dienerstaat*).[37] Here was a test of strength, a test of the realities of state power, and—Marx insists—it was the bureaucracy that wielded the power of decision, not the Crown.

In 1850 Engels, in his series on *Revolution and Counter-Revolution in Germany* (which, remember, was reviewed by Marx and published as his own work), gave an account of the same interesting class struggle. After describing the pre-1848 Prussian regime as "a half-feudal, half-bureaucratic monarchism,"* he writes that Friedrich Wilhelm IV "was known to be no supporter of the predominantly bureaucratic and military monarchy of his father," Friedrich Wilhelm III. Rather,

°°He hated and despised the bureaucratic element of the Prussian Monarchy, but only because all his sympathies were with the feudal element. . . . he aimed at the restoration, as complete as possible, of the predominant social position of the nobility.

And this aspiration was combined with the concept of a class equilibrium: the king's ideal was to rule over "a complete hierarchy of social ranks or castes" fixed rigidly by birth and social position, "the whole of these castes or 'estates of the realm' balancing each other, at the same time, so nicely in power and influence, that a complete independence of action should remain to the King. . . ."[39]

Finally, in 1859 Marx presented this test case in even greater detail, for there was now more evidence to go on. "The King with the brainless head" wished a return to medieval relations, with an "independent aristocracy" while at the same time retaining "an omnipotent bureaucratic administration."[40] Up to 1848 he was unable to satisfy the class aspirations of the Junkers, despite his preachment of "the necessity of

---

* The *Neue Rheinische Zeitung* had used to refer to the Prussian regime typically as "the bureaucratic-feudal-military despotism."[38]

engrafting the poetical rule of aristocracy upon the Prussian prosaic rule by the schoolmaster, the drill-sergeant, the policeman, the tax-gatherer, and the learned mandarin"—that is, rule by the bureaucracy—and so the Junker aristocracy "were forced to accept the King's secret sympathies in lieu of real concessions." The weak bourgeoisie was still unable to move. And—

> °°Finally, the romantic King himself was, after all, like all his predecessors, but the visible hand of a common-place bureaucratic Government which he tried in vain to embellish with the fine sentiments of by-gone ages.[41]

The "absolute" monarch was typically only the visible agency of the bureaucracy, which was the real ruler.

This remained, during the 1848–1849 revolution, the viewpoint from which Marx and Engels wrote voluminously in the *Neue Rheinische Zeitung.* Perhaps its most general expression came in Marx's speech at his Cologne trial in February 1849. All through this period, as before and after, the *Crown* and similar shorthand labels were freely used in writing in the usual way; but in this political lecture to the jury Marx differentiated the relationships. The Crown is viewed alongside the bureaucracy in specifying the "political expression" of the regime.[42] And:

> The *political* expression corresponding to the old society was the Crown-by-the-grace-of-God, the domineering bureaucracy, the autonomous army. The *social* foundation corresponding to this old political power was the privileged aristocratic landed property. . . . The old political power—heaven-annointed Crown, domineering bureaucracy, autonomous army—saw that its actual material foundation would disappear from under its feet as soon as there was any infringement on the foundation of the old society, the privileged aristocratic landed property, the aristocracy itself. . . . On the other hand, that old society saw that political power would be torn out of its hands as soon as the Crown, the bureaucracy, and the army lost their feudal privileges.[43]

So the bureaucracy (which term properly covers the military bureaucracy too) joined with the aristocracy in impelling the Crown to counter-revolution. In any case, it is made repetitively clear that the label *Crown* does not denote the rule of one man: "The rule of the Crown-by-the-grace-of-God is precisely the rule of the antiquated social elements."[44]

Then, after 1849, Junkerdom utilized the victorious counter-revolution to implement the king's medievalizing dreams for a few years (1850–1857), turning the clock back to pre-1807 conditions. Marx's summary of this short-lived Restoration shows he saw it in terms of a power struggle in which the state bureaucracy was temporarily subordinated to the old feudal class:

> °°There was an end of coy, romantic aspirations; but in their place there sprang up a Prussian House of Lords; mortmain was restored, the private jurisdiction of the manor flourished more than ever, exemption from taxation became again a sign of nobility, the policemen and the Government men had to stoop to the noblemen, all places of power were surrendered to the scions of the landed aristocracy and gentry, the enlightened bureaucrats of the old school were swept away, to be supplanted by the servile sycophants of rent-rolls and landlords, and all the liberties won by the revolution—liberty of the press, liberty of meeting, liberty of speech, constitutional representation—all these liberties were not broken up, but maintained as the privileges of the aristocratic class.[45]

This describes a more thorough purging and recasting of the bureaucratic state by the restored aristocracy than was effected by the bourgeoisie during its temporary ascendancy in 1848. Marx sums it up this way: "The police and administrative machinery were not destroyed, but converted into the mere tools of the ruling class." That is, of the ruling class in civil society, the landed aristocracy. The bureaucratic monarchic state, then, had *not* been the tool of this ruling class.

Marx's article continues with an explanation of how the bustling bourgeois economy grew and spread, until even the "aristocrat became converted into a profit-loving, money-mongering stockjobber," and price rises brought about "the general fall of the fixed incomes of their [the bourgeoisie's] bureaucratic rulers."* In short, the struggle for dominance between the old feudal class and the "bureaucratic rulers" was finally superseded by the common bourgeoisification of the contending classes.

---

* A second, continuation article is promised, but it did not appear; the survey ended at this point.

4. THE BUREAUCRACY
IN BOURGEOIS SOCIETY

It is this basic process of social bourgeoisification which, in Marx's view, changes the autonomous role played by the state bureaucracy. The new bourgeois society had to subordinate the state bureaucracy to itself, to the new ruling class of civil society; it had to break the tradition of autonomy established by the special conditions of absolutism. The bourgeoisification of the bureaucrats was a means toward the political subordination of the bureaucracy.

The change can be summarized as follows: In the highly autonomized state of the absolute monarchy, the bureaucracy had been in position to act as a class element in terms of the specific structure of *that* society. But insofar as the bourgeoisie gained more and more social and political power in its own name, thereby taking over direct command of the state, the bureaucracy was reduced more and more to the status of a social stratum acting merely as the agent of the ruling class. This is the status it tends to be restricted to, as a rule, wherever the ruling class of a given society is still robust enough to exercise unchallenged socioeconomic *and* political sway. In this sense, it is its *normal* status.* In the United States, which had started on a more or less bourgeois basis without evolving through feudalism, Marx noted that "the state, in contradistinction from all earlier national formations, was subordinated from the first to bourgeois society and bourgeois production, and could never make the claim of being an end in itself."[46]

For Marx, this new relationship under bourgeois conditions, in the "modern state," first came to the fore in *The German Ideology,* as we saw in Chapter 8. There Marx's exposition of the class nature of the state was already applied to a social order taken (by anticipation) as already bourgeois in essentials, even though the retarded actuality in Germany was fully recognized in other sections of the same book.

The thesis about the change in the role of the bureaucracy was set

* This suggests why the class status of the bureaucracy has again become a moot question in the contemporary world, which sees the down phase of bourgeois society and the increasing prevalence of autonomized state phenomena. It is this phase that is prefigured in the Bonapartist elements discussed in Chapters 14–19. The above formulation of the "normal" status of the bureaucracy was later turned into a suprahistorical law by "Marxist" dogma.

down by Marx in so many words in his 1849 speech to the Cologne jury, in the midst of the passage already cited. The Crown had been linked with "the old feudal-bureaucratic society" and represented "the feudal-aristocratic society" as against "modern bourgeois society."

> It inheres in the conditions of existence of the latter [modern bourgeois society] that bureaucracy and army, instead of being masters of commerce and industry, be reduced to their tools, and be *made* into mere organs of bourgeois business relations [*Verkehr*]. It cannot be tolerated that agriculture be restricted by feudal privileges or industry by bureaucratic tutelage. . . . It must subordinate the Treasury administration to the needs of production, while the old state had to subordinate production to the needs of the Crown-by-the-grace-of-God and to shoring up the pillars of royalty, the social props of this Crown. . . . In modern society there are still *classes* but no longer *estates.*[47]

We have seen that the thesis was repeated, in passing, in Marx's *Eighteenth Brumaire:* until 1814–1815 the bureaucracy was historically a means of "preparing" bourgeois class rule, but with the bourgeois monarchy born in July 1830, and still more with the Second Republic in 1848, the bureaucracy became the "instrument" of the ruling class.[48]

To be sure, this downgraded bureaucracy still "strove for power of its own," adds Marx in the same work. This reminder is necessary, since the bureaucrats' *strivings* by no means disappear from history. Caliban continues to mutter, "I must obey: his art is of such power . . ." but adds, "And yet I needs must curse . . . sometime am I / All wound with adders, who with cloven tongues / Do hiss me into madness." The servant-monster cries throughout the subsequent history of the bourgeoisie: "A plague upon the tyrant that I serve!" while he dreams of riches and a return to power. Caliban drunk seeks a new master; and in the next *Tempest,* the Caliban-state did find a new god to worship in the form of Louis Bonaparte.

With this new master, the state machine took off at a zigzag angle away from that straight course which history rarely follows. The bureaucracy was conjuncturally able to tear itself free again: "Only under the second Bonaparte," wrote Marx, "does the state seem to have made itself completely independent."[49] With this contrast Marx asserted that under the regime of Louis Bonaparte the state was *more* autonomous than ever before, more so even than under the absolute monarchy. It was not dominated by any ruling class of civil society.

But even in this case "the state power is not suspended in mid-air," Marx cautions in the next paragraph. This power *rests* on the support of the peasantry, the support or toleration of sectors of the bourgeoisie, and above all, on the precarious equilibrium of the bourgeois–proletarian antagonism, the frozen class struggle. This highly autonomized state is not the "instrument" of any one of the propertied classes contending for political power; *but it is still the resultant of class society taken as a whole* in its current constellation of countervailing powers. We thus get behind the formula version of Marx's theory, to find that even in this abnormal situation the class conception of the state is as central as ever.*

Furthermore, the Bonapartist state power "is not suspended in mid-air" in terms of its own social orientation: it does not set itself against the ruling socioeconomic powers of civil society; on the contrary, it strives to be accepted by the latter, to be accepted as the managing committee of class society taken as a whole. And one of the decisive issues of the period will be whether it can impose itself in this capacity on the reluctant bourgeoisie.

It should then be clear that, in terms of Marx's historical method, the abstract question *Is the bureaucracy a class?* is little better than "How high is up?" An answer can be considered only in terms of a specific social order at a given historical stage. If Marx had no trouble explaining that the state bureaucracy of Friedrich Wilhelm III functioned as a class in the framework of the estates structure of the Prussian absolute monarchy, he also had no doubt that the triumph of the bourgeoisie normally produced social relations in which the state bureaucracy was demoted to a status too amorphous and ancillary to claim a class role.

This same conclusion about the role of the bureaucracy *under capitalism* was approached from the economic side in Marx's manuscripts for the fourth volume of *Capital*. Here Marx is concerned with

---

* This is the conception that Engels more than once presented as being the *basic* formulation of the theory of the state, a more all-embracing formulation than the narrower sort of "normal" case where the state acts as the managing committee of *a* ruling class in a more or less stable situation. We saw Engels make the same point in explaining the complex class basis of Bismarckian Bonapartism: "In reality however the state as it exists in Germany is likewise the necessary product of the social basis out of which it has developed."[50] He made the point even more sharply in connection with a similar test case, a nonbourgeois government in process of forcing the development of capitalism—absolutist Russia. This case is reserved for fuller discussion in Chapter 22.[51]

the state officialdom as one of those social strata that consist of people who do unproductive labor but are nevertheless useful to the ruling class in some way. (These strata are collectively labeled "the ideological, etc. classes" in one of the passages to be cited, and the "ideological *Stände*" in another.) The question under discussion in this context is the revenue devoted by the bourgeoisie to maintaining these strata, hence the bourgeoisie's original objection to the expense of maintaining them, and its subsequent reconciliation to this expense.

> Political economy in its classical period, just like the bourgeoisie itself in its parvenu period, took a severe and critical attitude toward the state machinery, etc. Later it saw and—as was also shown in practice—learned by experience that it was out of its own organization that the necessity arose for the inherited societal combination of all these classes which were in part quite unproductive.[52]

With this realization the bourgeoisie became willing to justify even "the exaggerated demands" of its defenders, and "The *dependence* of the ideological, etc. classes on the *capitalists* was in fact proclaimed." [53]

Marx then quotes a notable passage from Adam Smith lumping the whole state officialdom among the unproductive laborers along with the men of the church and the intellectual professions as well as "players, buffoons," and so on. He explains:

> This is the language of the still revolutionary bourgeoisie which has not yet subjected the whole of society, state, etc. to itself. These illustrious and time-honored occupations—sovereign, judges, officers, priests, etc., the aggregate of all the old ideological strata [*Stände*] arising out of them, their men of learning, teachers and priests—are *economically speaking* put on a par with the swarm of their own lackeys and jesters. . . . They are mere °servants° of the °public,° just as the others are their °servants°. . . . State, church, etc. are justified only insofar as they are committees for the management or administration of the common interests of the productive bourgeoisie. . . .
>
> But as soon as the bourgeoisie has conquered the terrain, in part itself taking over the state and in part making a compromise with its former possessors; as soon as it has acknowledged the ideological strata [*Stände*] to be flesh of its flesh, and has everywhere transformed them into its functionaries in accordance with its own nature . . . as soon as the intellectual tasks them-

selves are more and more carried out in its *service,* entering into the service of capitalist production: then, taking a new tack, the bourgeoisie seeks to justify "economically" from its own stand-point what it previously had critically opposed.[54]

Even where, in other cases, Marx emphasizes the autonomous impor-tance of the bureaucratic apparatus, he does not forget that, under bourgeois relationships, its power after all is limited to a subordinate sphere. We saw such a case in Marx's apparently sweeping identification of "the permanent and irresponsible *bureaucracy"* of "creatures of the desk" and "obstinate old clerks" staffing India House as "the real Home Government" of British India. But before the end of this tirade against bureaucratism, it is made clear that the power of the state is wielded by the British "oligarchy" and "moneyocracy," and it is under their aegis that "a subordinate Bureaucracy paralyze its [India's] administration and perpetuate its abuses as the vital condition of their own perpetuation." [55] The "abject" bureaucratic "odd fellows" reigned over the administration, but did not rule. The same view is implicit in a sketch of the British bureaucracy in India itself, written a few years later.[56]

5. THE QUESTION OF CLASS PROVENANCE

The autonomized hierarchy "is not suspended in mid-air" in another respect: with regard to its class composition. This important question of the class provenance of the bureaucracy was first discussed at some length in an important manuscript (of an unfinished educational pamphlet) by Engels in 1847. Let us follow its line of thought.

German backwardness is shown by the dominance of agriculture; on the land dominance is held by the aristocracy; below the aristocracy and dependent on it is the petty-bourgeoisie (small property-owners, artisans, and so on); the poorly developed bourgeoisie still counts officially only alongside the petty-bourgeoisie. What political structure results?

The present constitution of Germany is nothing more than a compromise between the aristocrats and the petty-bourgeois, which is tantamount to turning over governmental administration to the hands of a third class: the bureaucracy. The two high-contracting parties share in the makeup of this class in accordance with their mutual position: the aristocrats, who represent the more important branch of production, reserve for themselves the higher positions, the petty-bourgeoisie is content with the lower ones and gets only exceptional candidates into the higher echelons of administration. Where the bureaucracy is subjected to a direct control, as in the constitutional states of Germany, the aristocrats and petty-bourgeois share in it in the same way; and it is easy to understand that here too the aristocracy reserves the lion's share for itself.[57]

Engels then asks: "Now, how does the German bourgeoisie stand in relation to the two classes that share in the political rule?"[58] It would seem that the aristocracy and the petty-bourgeoisie "share in the political rule" in proportion to their contribution to the formation of the bureaucracy, which however functions as "a third class," the one that runs the government. Is this bureaucratic class merely derived from the two classes dominant in civil society, or is it more basically conditioned by its derivation? How autonomous is this peculiar class with respect to the other two? Engels' pamphlet is concerned with quite other problems, not these; but his picture of Germany clearly expresses the conception that no single class has managed to achieve ruling status as yet:

> The wretchedness of the German status quo consists principally in the fact that no single class has so far been strong enough to put its own sector of production forward as the national one *par excellence,* and thereby put itself forward as the representative of the interests of the whole nation. . . . This regime represented by the bureaucracy is the political compendium of the general impotence and contemptible meanness, the stuffy tediousness and the filth, of German society.[59]

The thrust is, in hindsight, plainly toward the view, more clearly formulated later, of the "bureaucratic monarchy"[60] as the result of an equilibrium of class forces, producing a highly autonomized bureaucracy.

As Marx did in his article of the same year, Engels proceeds to emphasize strongly that this bureaucratic state power is a fetter on the development of the progressive class, the bourgeoisie, whose decisive section is the manufacturing capitalists:

The manufacturers, however, are hampered in the full utilization of their capital not only by inadequate tariffs but also by the *bureaucracy.* If they are confronted with indifference in the matter of tariff legislation, they are here, in their relationship to the bureaucracy, confronted with the very direct hostility of the government.

The bureaucracy has been established to rule petty-bourgeois and peasants. . . . The petty-bourgeois and peasants therefore cannot do without a powerful and numerous bureaucracy. They must let themselves be kept in tutelage in order to avoid the greatest confusion, in order not to be ruined by hundreds and thousands of lawsuits.

But the bureaucracy, which is a necessity for the petty-bourgeois, very soon becomes an intolerable fetter on the bourgeois. The officialdom's surveillance and interference become very irksome already in manufacturing; the manufacturing industry is hardly possible under such supervision. Up to now the German manufacturers have kept the bureaucracy off their necks as much as possible by bribery, for which they certainly cannot be blamed.[61]

There is more about "the bureaucratic hatred of the bourgeoisie." Then comes an important statement about the change in the status of the bureaucracy that would result from bourgeois political victory:

The bourgeoisie is therefore compelled to break the power of this arrogant and double-dealing bureaucracy. From the moment that the running of the state and legislation come under the control of the bourgeoisie, the independence of the bureaucracy collapses; indeed, from that moment the tormentors of the bourgeois turn into their submissive servitors.[62]

All this ties in with the main argument of Engels' pamphlet, which was directed against the "feudal socialists" whose antibourgeois fervor pushed them to look with favor on the monarchical regime. In the course of this argument, it is the state bureaucracy that emerges as the main political obstacle to social progress at the given point in history.

After the revolution, Engels had another go at the question of the class provenance of an absolutist bureaucracy and its relation to civil society. The subject is Austria; and perhaps this exposition is clearest because the situation described is starkest.

In *Revolution and Counter-Revolution in Germany* Engels explains that the Hapsburg absolutism balanced the feudal landlords and the "large stockjobbing capitalists" against each other while keeping both tied to the state power by class economic interests.

°°Thus, Metternich was sure of the support of the two most powerful and influential classes of the empire, and he possessed, besides, an army and a bureaucracy which, for all purposes of absolutism, could not be better constituted. The civil and military officers in the Austrian service form a race of their own; their fathers have been in the service of the Kaiser, and so will their sons be; they belong to none of the multifarious nationalities congregated under the wing of the double-headed eagle; they are, and ever have been, removed from one end of the empire to the other . . .; they have no nationality, or rather they alone make up the really Austrian nation. It is evident what a pliable and at the same time powerful instrument, in the hands of an intelligent and energetic chief, such a civil and military hierarchy must be.[63]

Here it is emphasized that the state bureaucracy, however derived originally, has been torn from its roots in civil society—both class roots and national roots—and turned into an order of Janissaries beholden only to the state power. It is an extreme form taken by autonomization.

If Engels used the conveniently vague *race* (in the old meaning of any classification of people)[64] for this social formation, we also find resort to the elastic word *caste.* In an 1858 article Marx discussed the class position of the Prussian *Landräte,* landowners appointed as Crown officials, the highest government representatives in their districts. "These *Landräte* combine, therefore, in their persons the quality of the *Krautjunker* (fox-hunter)* and the Bureaucrat." They do not live on their state salaries. "Generally, therefore, their interests are more strictly bound up with the class and party interests of the landed aristocracy than with the caste interests of the Bureaucracy."[66]

Here the case is farthest away from that of the Austrian Janissaries: this Prussian part-time "bureaucrat" not only has his provenance in the aristocracy, he still lives primarily as an integral part of the class milieu based on land ownership, not state ownership. And by this time, as we have seen, even the central bureaucracy was well on the way to

---

* In this jocular definition, Marx, writing in English, is equating the Prussian rural aristocrat ("cabbage-Junker") with the English country squire. It is an approximation, of course, as he noted elsewhere.[65]

bourgeoisification. This bureaucracy was *déclassé*—displaced from its class role—as a whole. While it was increasingly difficult to think of it as a class, it was still a *something*.

6. CASTE OR CLASS?

Again we must deal with a terminological aspect not because it was important to Marx but for the contrary reason: he was so indifferent to the finicky choice between *class* or *caste* that he left plenty of room for latter-day marxology to blow the matter up to huge proportions. As against a modern propensity to consider Marx's terminology, often taken anachronistically, as the key to his conception, we must emphasize it is only his conception that explains his terminology.

Another element too often ignored is the usage of the times. Since the late Enlightenment brought a vogue for things Indian, *caste*—including its combinations like *caste spirit, caste mentality,* and so on—had come into wide currency as a swear-word directed especially against Old Regime strata seen as fossilized, such as the old nobility, officer élite, and so on, as well as the bureaucracy.[67] This pop-sociological or journalistic usage existed alongside the technical or narrow meaning of caste in Hindu society. As in other cases, both meanings are to be found in Marx. In addition, there is a third aspect to the imported term that is important to understand.

The underlying problem is that, while Marx could and did apply his own conception of social class (taken objectively) to any period of history, the drawing of *class* lines of demarcation through civil society does not at all exclude other lines of demarcation within the same society. Thus at various times Marx considers color lines, other racial or ethnic lines, occupational lines, and so on, as lines of demarcation, and these have a certain relationship to the basic class lines. But history shows another and very important way of drawing lines of demarcation through a given civil society: namely, the way in which a society officially establishes such divisions *for itself*. In various social systems, these divisions have been called estates (*Stände, états*), orders (for example, Equestrian Order), castes, and so on.

Three points may usefully be made about this terminological problem.

1. As distinct from the Marxian category of class, the contemporaneous labels (estates, and so on) typically denoted social divisions *whose boundaries were fixed or recognized juridically,* established or enforced by political-legal means with openly accepted sanctions. Whatever the means or the degree of rigidity, the boundaries thus demarcated were a refraction, but not necessarily a reproduction, of the objective lines of social division that underlay the society's consciousness. They were conditioned by the class divisions, possibly related ethnic divisions (for example, conqueror and conquered), sometimes occupational divisions, and so on. The contemporaneous labels marked a pattern of *juridical orders* which lay athwart the pattern of social classes.

Capitalism finally does away with this duality. "Bourgeois society knows only *classes,"* Engels noted when he had to explain in 1885 the meaning of a passage written by Marx in 1847, about estates and classes. He was echoing Marx's words of 1849.[68] Bourgeois society as such involves no class-like formations or privileged orders that are *juridically* established with relation to the production process and the appropriation of the surplus product, exceptions being recognizable as prebourgeois survivals.

If bourgeois society knows only classes, prebourgeois societies knew the duality. The famous roll call of classes at the beginning of the *Communist Manifesto* is not, in fact, a list of classes only: it loosely mixes classes in the Marxist sense with juridical orders in the contemporaneous sense. For example, patrician and plebeian were recognized orders of Roman society; and the plebeian order incubated more than one class. This same freedom in mixing the two terminologies characterizes the next paragraph too.

2. In Marx's and Engels' writings, social formations that are classes in the Marxist sense are also freely given the other label, the one which is specific or indigenous to the social system in question.

The most common case in point involves *class* and *estate* (*Stand*) with respect to feudalism. Thus, from the standpoint of Marx's historical analysis, the landed aristocracy was a class under feudalism; it was also a feudal *Stand* or estate, from the standpoint of the contemporaneous social structure. Marx freely calls it one or the other depending on the context, without risk of being misunderstood. It would be quite senseless to ask whether Marx thought the aristocracy was a class *or* an estate.

The relation between class and estate has its complications but they offer little difficulty. For example, before 1789 the young French bourgeoisie ranked as *part* of a feudal estate, the Third Estate; on the other hand, the First Estate of the realm, the high clergy, was part of a class in social reality. The estates system was rooted in the objective class structure, but the two patterns of division were not necessarily congruent. Marx, writing for contemporaries who did not need to have this explained, sometimes used one framework, sometimes the other—like everyone else. Hence what seem to be loose usages to us were often merely idioms of the day.

3. Under the absolutist regime the state bureaucracy was seen as one of the estates of the realm. But it was also seen as a social class. This depends not on some suprahistorical definition of class, but on the concrete nature of the social system involved.

The way in which a given society divides up into classes is specific to its own social relations. Thus, there are warlord elements in many societies, but a warlord becomes a *feudal* lord or baron only when specific social relationships become dominant. There is no rule-of-thumb definition which decides whether the chief of an armed band who resides in a stronghold and lives off the surplus labor of unfree producers, etc. is or is not a member of a *feudal* class. The point can be settled not by a glossary but only by a concrete examination of the overall social relations of the society. Similarly, merchants become a separate *class* not simply because they buy and sell, but only when buying and selling begins to play a certain role in a given society.*

Likewise, *state bureaucracy* always describes a formation of government officials, of course; but an officialdom enters into differing social relations depending on what societal whole it functions in. We have already explained that to ask whether the bureaucracy is a class in some suprahistorical sense—that is, apart from the social relations of a specific system—is quite as pointless as to ask whether the aristocracy was a class or an estate.

It should now be possible to understand what is implicit in a passage

* This point is closely related to Marx's explanation of how other socio-economic categories take on class character only in the context of a given social system. Thus: "A Negro is a Negro. He only becomes a slave in certain relations. A cotton-spinning jenny is a machine for spinning cotton. It becomes *capital* only in certain relations. Torn from these relationships it is no more capital than gold in itself is *money* or sugar the price of sugar."[69]

Marx wrote in 1849. A progovernment writer, expounding a supra-historical view of classes as fixed for all time, had argued that wherever there was "labor and division of labor" there were necessarily class differences, for which reason the worker–bourgeois relationship could never be abolished. Marx replied:

> In Egypt there was labor and division of labor—and *castes;* in Greece and Rome, labor and division of labor—and *freemen* and *slaves;* in the Middle Ages, labor and division of labor—and *feudal lords* and *serfs, corporations, estates* and the like. In our era there is labor and division of labor—and *classes,* one of them being in possession of all the instruments of production and means of livelihood, while the other lives only by selling its labor. . . .[70]

Here *caste* is used coordinately with *class* and *estate. Caste is to ancient Egypt what the estate is to feudalism:* it is the juridically demarcated social formation that is specific to the society—one of the contemporaneous social divisions that lie athwart the underlying class division.

Marx did not have available any agreed-on generic term to denote this family of social formations, no umbrella term marking what is common to *estate, caste, order,* and so on. There is still none in common acceptance today. In addition, the word *estate* is specially ambiguous in English: for example, when Engels wanted to refer to the estates of pre-1848 Prussia for American readers, his solution in one article was to call them "social ranks or castes" and "these castes or 'estates of the realm.' "[71] Does this mean he thought the feudal estates were *castes?* Not at all; as often, *caste* was simply a stand-in for something without a tag of its own. Contrariwise, in *Anti-Dühring* Engels referred in passing to the "system of social estates" (*Stände-gliederung*) in the "heroic epoch" of ancient Greece.[72] Does this mean he thought there were feudal estates in the Homeric age? Of course not, as Engels' accounts of this society show elsewhere.[73] *Ständegliederung* should be translated as any ordered arrangement of social ranks; for *Stände* then and today often has this broader generic meaning.*

---

* It is interesting that in his *Historical Materialism,* realizing the need, Bukharin adopted *caste* as his generic term for a juridically established legal-political category, hence inclusive of *estate.*[74] He wrote *inter alia:*

In ancient Egypt, the administration of production was practically identi-

Estate and *caste*, as well as *rank, order*, and the like, have occasionally functioned as generics pointing to any kind of class-like formation, leaving open the specifics. The kind of exegesis, therefore, that stresses how frequently Marx and Engels called a bureaucracy a class or a caste is not very helpful. By and large these usages followed the circumstances of the time. Consider the following three passages in Engels:

1. In 1850 Engels remarked of the 1849 campaign in Germany that "The reactionary classes, aristocracy, bureaucracy, and big bourgeoisie, were few in number."[79] The bureaucracy—specifically, the bureaucracy of the absolutist monarchy—is called one of the classes without inhibition.

2. In 1872, as we have already quoted, he wrote that "both in the old absolute monarchy and in the modern Bonapartist monarchy the real governmental authority lies in the hands of a special caste of army officers and state officials."[80]

3. In 1884, describing the 1848 revolution, he listed "the absolute monarchy, feudal land ownership, the bureaucracy, and the cowardly petty-bourgeoisie" as adversaries of the German bourgeoisie.[81] The bureaucracy is here implicitly regarded as part of the class structure of 1848—and separate from the monarchy as a social force, at that—but no labels are applied.

These usages do not involve a change in Engels' *conception* of the sociopolitical role played by the autonomized state bureaucracy in the recent past. But something else did change during the decades between the first and the last of the above statements. As Germany developed with rapid strides from the semiabsolutist, semi-Bonapartist monarchy

---

cal with that of the state, the great landlords heading both. An important fraction of production was that turned out by the landlord state. The role of the social groups in production coincided with their caste, with whether they were higher, middle, or lower officials of the state, or slaves. . . .[75]

This is one of many cases where *caste* has been detached from the narrow meaning based on its Hindu form, and more or less arbitrarily invested with some broader meaning for purposes of sociological analysis. More often than not, however, Marx himself used *caste* with some relation to the narrow sense, especially in his scientific economic writings.[76] (Since Marx refers to Egypt more than to India in this connection, it should be mentioned that later Egyptologists rejected the earlier view of "the Egyptian system of castes," as Marx called it in *Capital*.)[77] On the other hand, for example, in his *Eighteenth Brumaire*, Marx applied the *caste* label to Louis Bonaparte's inflated bureaucracy: as an "artificial caste" which was *created* by the head of the state, it is contrasted with "the actual classes of society."[78] Here the term *caste* is obviously a stand-in, as often, and has no relation to the Indian social formation.

to a modern bourgeois society, then (as we have discussed) the bureaucracy was accordingly subordinated to bourgeois power, hence downgraded from its previous height of autonomization as a class, caste, or estate, becoming a subaltern "social stratum." It certainly was still visible as a distinctive social category, but it could no longer be viewed as playing an autonomous class role. By 1884, calling the *old* bureaucracy of the absolutist period a class in a historical sense would have required an explanation for the contemporaneous reader. Back in 1850 no explanation had been necessary as a matter of course.

7. BUREAUCRATIC HYPERTROPHY

There is another question that has to be put in its place. It concerns the distinction already mentioned between bureaucratization as the necessary accompaniment of a state in class society, and *over*bureaucratization as a pathological symptom.

The phenomenon of bureaucratic hypertrophy is, of course, very old, antedating even the swollen state machine of the later Roman Empire, and is in no way limited to any one type of class society. It is especially typical of the fatty-degeneration stage of any class society, and reached a new peak in the ancien régime, as the feudal class lay in its death throes and the young bourgeoisie grew to adolescence. Thus bourgeois political consciousness, arising amidst the rank overgrowths of the absolute monarchies, grew up with a certain hostility to "statism," a frame of mind which produced the laissez-faire ideology in its moderate form and bourgeois anarchism in its extreme form. (It is interesting that the same Frenchman, Vincent de Gournay, is credited with inventing both the term bureaucracy and the phrase *laissez faire, laissez passer* in the eighteenth century.)[82]

However, the tendency to state gigantism tended to reproduce itself in the bourgeois state too, just as in previous class societies. This is a tendency which worked itself out at different rates and in more or less offensive forms, depending on country and period. Above all, it is necessary to keep in mind that even where a tendency is itself inevitable given certain social developments, the particular manifestations in which it takes form are *not* inevitable as individual phenomena, and indeed usually seem to be highly avoidable and remediable—*if only* the leaders were wiser, or whatever—especially in small-scale cases. If, therefore, one asks whether a particular problem of bureaucratism or overbureaucratization is rooted in the system or merely adventitious, the question may be ambiguous. Any given case of bureaucratic excess may be avoidable, but not so the tendency that some such phenomena will be generated.

Cases of bureaucratism naturally attracted Marx's and Engels' pens. The army bureaucracy provided examples galore for Engels' military writings. The Crimean War was a rich source, perhaps the most notorious case being the disastrous administration and logistics of the British forces, topped by the famous blunder that launched the Charge of the Light Brigade at Balaklava (which Engels wrote up at the time).[83] More important than the fact that "someone had blundered" was the decimation of the British army by the incompetence of its own bureaucracy. The scapegoat, wrote Engels, is Lord Raglan,

> but this is not just. We are no admirers of his Lordship's military conduct, and have criticized his blunders with freedom, but truth requires us to say that the terrible evils amid which the soldiers in the Crimea are perishing are not his fault, but that of the system on which the British war establishment is administered.[84]

This introduces an article which details "this beautiful system of administration . . . this machinery so well adapted to fetter generals and to ruin armies." Marx followed, after a British investigating commission had reported, with a more comprehensive study of the fossilized routinism of bureaucratism. A typical passage:

> The regulations were so beautifully arranged that . . . nobody knew where his authority began nor where it ceased, nor to whom to apply for anything; and thus, from a wholesome fear of responsibility, everybody shifted everything from his own shoulders to those of somebody else. Under this system, the hospitals were scenes of infamous brutality. . . . And the authors of all these horrors and abominations are no hard-hearted barbarians. They are, every one of them, British gentlemen of good extraction, well-educated, and of mild, philanthropic, and religious dispositions. In their individual capacity, they no doubt were ready and willing to do anything; in their official capacity, their duty was to look coolly and with folded arms upon all these infamies, conscious that the case was not provided for in any part of Her Majesty's regulations affecting themselves. . . .

Not a man on the spot had the energy to break through the network of routine, to act upon his own responsibility as the necessities of the case demanded, and in the teeth of the regulations. The only party who has dared to do this is a woman, Miss Nightingale.[85]

Raglan Marx dismissed as "all his life a head-office-clerk to Wellington . . . a man bred to do just as he was bid." Other high officers "are well bred, good-looking gentlemen, whose elegance of manner and refinement of feeling do not permit them to handle a thing roughly, or to act with even a show of decision. . . ."

But we must now note that Marx did *not* draw the conclusion that these particular bureaucratic horrors flowed inevitably from the social system, though a connection was obvious. On the contrary, he predicted flatly (and accurately) that, since the system could not afford these indulgences to its inherent tendencies, "it is impossible that there should not be a reform in the system and administration of the British Army."[86]

For this situation can be taken as a classic example of a bureaucratic foul-up which, while visibly the outcome of tendencies inherent in the class structure, yet had to be and could be remedied in the short run—even if plugging a hole in one place meant that the same tendency would burst out elsewhere. The same can be said of instances of the bureaucratic mentality, which are usually removable in retail and inescapable in wholesale.*

---

* Perhaps the purest case of a reaction to bureaucratic mentality and tone *alone* is provided by the tale of Engels and the librarian. In the 1860s Engels became active in the German cultural center of Manchester, the Schiller Institute; in fact, he became president 1864–1868 and remained on its executive till he moved to London.[87] One day in 1861 he received a curt form letter from the institute librarian about returning a book. Its form and tone (the request itself not being in question) ignited him and he fired a missive at the executive protesting the brutal style of the communication: "In fact, when I read the document I thought I had been suddenly translated back to the homeland." It was like "a peremptory summons from some German police commissioner. . . ." He then looked back at one of the founding documents of the institute (1859) and flared up again:

It said the Schiller Institute should serve to make "the young German . . . feel immediately *at home* here . . . be better *taken care of and provided for,* morally and spiritually . . . and above all return home *unestranged from the fatherland.*" Beyond question, the bureaucratic style of this sort of official communication is quite calculated to make the recipient feel immediately on *home* soil, and forced to believe that he is as well if not "better taken care of *and provided for*" than at home in his beloved

We have seen other instances of Marx's attention to the development of bureaucratization in England, particularly in the form of British colonial machinery for the control of India.[89]

Still, it was not England that was the hearth of state bureaucratism; indeed, well past the middle of the century, the islanders regarded the new word *bureaucracy* as the name of a foreign phenomenon known to be rife on the Continent. The visible vanguard of bureaucratization in Western Europe was constituted by France and Prussia. The two went together: when Marx refers to the Prussian bureaucracy as "that omnipotent, all-meddling parasitic body," the context is a comparison with "the France of Louis Philippe."[90] Elsewhere, comparing the state expenditures of France with England's, Marx notes that "in a bureaucratic country, like France, the cost of collecting the revenue grows at a rate disproportionate to the amount of the revenue itself."[91]

It was mainly in connection with this bureaucratic country par excellence, especially under Bonapartism, that Marx uses the catchword *state parasite* and similar expressions. The reference above to the "parasitic" Prussian bureaucracy is an exception; it is significant that it was written in 1858, that is, well past the heyday of the old absolutist bureaucracy, when this social holdover was taking on an anachronistic look in critical eyes.

To be sure, Marx's occasional use of the epithet or metaphor *parasite* is always made offhand, and never becomes a statement on the subject, let alone a theory. For the most part it underlines the unproductiveness of overbureaucratized sectors of the state machinery. Later, in *The Civil War in France* and its drafts, where the elimination of the state as such

---

patriarchal police state, that great institution for the care of little children; and as long as this sort of official communication flourishes, there is certainly not the least danger that any member of the Schiller Institute will be *estranged from the fatherland.* Yes indeed, if by exception some member had not yet had occasion at home to get acquainted with the forms of the bureaucratic civil service and the peremptory way of speaking of the authorities, the Schiller Institute would seem to offer him the best opportunity to do so; . . .

To be sure, many members have hardly allowed themselves to suppose that "the German spirit in the fullest sense of the word," for whose cultivation the Schiller Institute is to be the center, also comprises that spirit of bureaucratism which at home unfortunately still holds almost all political power, which all Germany is fighting, winning victory after victory just at this time. This tone of direct command, these peremptory summonses to restore order within twenty-four hours, are out of place here anyway. . . .[88]

is under discussion, it may also suggest the dispensability of *any* state as an instrument of class oppression.*

But what is mainly wrong with a sober-sided effort to read portentous theoretical conceptions into a phrase like *state parasite* is that it misses the main point. Marx's critics usually like to point out that he not only had a theory about capitalism, he was so deficient in academic objectivity that he hated it with a passionate detestation. When, therefore, they read in Marx about "capitalist vermin" and bourgeois "bloodsuckers," and so on, these phrases do not move them to break out with the discovery that Marx held a Theory of the Increasing Verminosis of Capitalism. Instead, they cry shame at such blatantly unscientific language, for everyone knows the said critics have a perfectly unemotional detachment about the social powers they live under.

Likewise with *state parasite* as an imprecation against the bureaucracy: Marx labored under the complication of feeling passionate hostility to everything the state bureaucracy represented. It was not merely an institution to be studied, but an enemy to be fought. The two aims were not contradictory: it had to be studied in order to be fought effectively.

In the hour when hatred of the bureaucracy was not merely a political idea but a matter of day-to-day agitation, that is, in the 1848–1849 revolution, Marx's articles were already studded with castigation of "the ox-heads of the arrogant bureaucracy with upturned noses," and the like, and a call to an active "distrust of the executive bureaucrats" on generalized grounds.[92] In short: in Marx, the bureaucracy as a social formation (not simply bureaucratism) is a dirty word from very early on.

* In Special Note D, a closer examination is given to Marx's use of the phrase *state parasite*.

21 | ORIENTAL DESPOTISM: THE SOCIAL BASIS

If bureaucracy was an enemy to be fought, it was also a mid-nineteenth-century commonplace that "the most stupendous bureaucracy in existence" was to be found in the Oriental empires, especially China.[1]

By this time, Europe was long past the cult of admiration for Chinese despotism which had reached its zenith in the Sinomania of the Enlightenment; state bureaucratization had become notorious on the Continent as a burgeoning evil; the imperialist aims of the European powers in China and India dictated derogation, not admiration, of Oriental society. The climate of thought was no longer as hospitable to the formerly widespread idealization of bureaucratic despotism as a model state. This idealization persisted, to be sure, in other forms, as in the rife illusions about the "progressiveness" of the czarist regime in Russia—a notion that lived on among liberals and leftists in proportion to the belief that the czarist state was *not* merely a bureaucratic despotism any more than it was bourgeois or feudal.

Marx did not become interested in the nature of Oriental society because of the problem of its bureaucracy, which held no puzzle for his day.* His attention was first drawn eastward at the beginning of the 1850s by the growing possibility that the East might provide a new force for a revolution in the West, perhaps even a decisive force for

---

* In our time, this version of Marx's relation to the problem has been promoted by the writings of K. Wittfogel, and has sterilized much of the discussion of the issue. Special Note E sketches the nature of this diversion and traces the career of the Oriental despotism concept before Marx, as against the Wittfogel fable. Perhaps this Special Note should be read as an introduction to the present chapter. It explains why the idea of a bureaucratically ruled state was "perfectly conventional, if not downright platitudinous" in Marx's milieu.

initiating the overthrow of a European capitalism which, having become colonialist, was exploiting not only workers at home but peoples abroad. From this standpoint the problem that required elucidation was the interaction between Western society, that is, capitalism, and Far Eastern society, mainly Chinese and Indian; and the basic dimension of this interaction was naturally the socioeconomic. Therefore Marx's and Engels' main interest in understanding Oriental history became, and remained, an understanding of the socioeconomic relations that were being shaken by the Western impact. As far as the political structure of Oriental society was concerned—Oriental despotism proper—this always remained a subordinate issue and an apparently simple one at the time.

In the following pages, given the subject of this volume, we shall try to treat summarily that side of Oriental society which is actually of major importance to Marxist theory, its place in Marx's theory of social evolution, in order to concentrate on the nature of the political structure and its bureaucracy. However, because of the specific nature of this society, these two aspects can be disentangled less easily than in most others.

1. MARX STARTS WITH STATE PROPERTY

The various "Eastern questions" did not arise in Marx's and Engels' writings until they were quite through with elaborating their theory in general (up to 1848) and then with testing their politics in the revolutionary proving grounds of 1848-1849. Their first attempt at an overall sketch of social evolution in Part I of *The German Ideology* had made only passing references to the East.* This sketch was implicitly or explicitly based on the experience of the ancient world and the Middle Ages,[3] therefore on classical and European history; it certainly did not follow Hegel's example in starting with the Orient as the "childhood of history."

The noteworthy feature of this first historical sketch is that *it posits state property, not private property, as the basis of the earliest class societies.* To be sure, Marx's researches in social history had barely begun; his exposition is rather vaguely formulated and can scarcely be

* As far as we know: for there are four missing pages of the manuscript which, judging by the context, take up early social evolution.[2]

taken as a contribution to scholarship. The importance of this early presentation, outside its use to explain the historical-materialist method, is simply that the concept of a state-dominated economy was ordinary enough to be mentioned without fanfare. It was not a concept Marx had to come to, but one that he started with.

Two forms of property* preceding feudalism are put forward. The first is "tribal property," corresponding to "the undeveloped stage of production, at which a people lives by hunting and fishing, by animal breeding, or, at most, by agriculture." The tribe is an extended family headed by a patriarchal chief, and eventually has slaves (at least in higher stages).[4]

> In the case of the ancient peoples, since several tribes live together in one town, the tribal property appears as state property, and the right of the individual to it as mere "possession," which however, like tribal property as a whole, is confined to landed property only.[5]

"The slavery latent in the family" continues to develop to a more important level, but even the second form is not primarily based on private property:

> The second form is the ancient communal and state property which proceeds especially from the union of several tribes into a *city* by agreement or by conquest, and which is still accompanied by slavery. Beside communal property, we already find movable, and later also immovable [landed], private property developing, but as an abnormal form subordinate to communal property. The citizens hold power over their laboring slaves only in their community, and on this account alone are therefore bound to the form of communal property.[6]

A summary statement says that by the time tribal property has evolved through its several stages up to modern capital, which is "pure private property," it "has cast off all semblance of a communal institution and has shut out the state from any influence on the development of property."[7]

At this point Marx is using *communal property* and *state property*

---

* *Property* is used here, and in other translations, for *Eigentum,* which can be, and often is, also translated *ownership.* In most cases the two translations can be considered interchangeable.

interchangeably, thereby blurring the difference seen later between primitive communalism *before* the rise of a state and statified property *after* the breakup of society into classes. No doubt the Hegelian amalgam of state with communality is still a conditioning influence. For other reasons too, this sketch cannot be taken as a mature "Marxist" formulation of social evolution. What it testifies to, however, is the matter-of-fact lack of inhibition about societies based on state property, typical of Marx's development from the earliest.

2. LOOKING TO CHINA—1850

The German Ideology was written between the British victory in the First Opium War, which opened up Chinese ports as a Western bridgehead, and the outbreak of the main Taiping Rebellion in 1850, a peasant-powered uprising against the Manchu dynasty. As Marx was preparing the first issue of his London magazine, the *Neue Rheinische Zeitung/Revue [&c.]*, in January 1850, a German missionary brought initial reports about the first large-scale revolutionary upsurge in three centuries in the "imperturbable" Oriental empire.[8]

In writing up the good news, Marx emphasized the "gratifying fact that the bales of calico of the English bourgeoisie have in eight years [since the opening of the ports] brought the oldest and most imperturbable empire on earth to the threshold of a social upheaval, one that will in any case hold most significant consequences for civilization." The uprising was rooted in economic privation. On top of long-standing oppressive conditions due to overpopulation, the forceful imposition of British free trade soon flooded the country with cheap machine-made goods.

> Chinese industry, reposing as it did on hand labor, succumbed to the competition of the machine. The imperturbable Celestial Empire went through a social crisis. The taxes ceased coming in, the state was on the brink of bankruptcy, the population was pauperized *en masse,* revolts broke out, the people went out of hand, mishandled and killed the Emperor's mandarins and the Fohist [Buddhist] bonzes.[9]

The news was gratifying because it augured "a violent revolution" in this previously static corner. What constituted "social crisis" in China? The breakdown of the state's economic machinery and the attack on the imperial officialdom.*

The missionary's report was also gratifying because he complained that socialistic talk had been heard from the Chinese "mob." Marx gives the socialistic quality of the talk short shrift (it "may stand in the same relation to the European variety as Chinese philosophy stands to the Hegelian"—that is, as the primitive stands to the advanced), but he does project the possibility that a revolution might establish at least a republican form of government in that "stronghold of arch-reaction and arch-conservatism," by the time the approaching revolution in Europe sends "our European reactionaries" fleeing across Asia.[10] This hopeful prospect is put in terms of the international interaction between revolution in the East and in the West. The same note will be struck as soon as Marx returns to the Chinese revolution in 1853.

In the same article Marx also proposed a sort of "orientation to the Pacific," including its Asian coast. His view was that California gold, and the immense tilt of world trade toward the west it had already induced, was making the Pacific what the Mediterranean and the Atlantic had once been, the central sea; the Asian as well as the American coast of the Pacific was seen as the new arena of economic expansion.[11]

3. SCOTS AND TAIPINGS—1853

The Taiping rebels continued to gain ground through 1853 and after. In the articles which Marx had begun to write the preceding year for the *New York Tribune*, European issues predominated, but Marx's attention must already have recurred to the Chinese potential. An article written in January 1853 indicated in passing a new familiarity with the history of Asian society. Its subject was not the East but the

---

* Here, and throughout this chapter, some readers may be interested in following Marx's frequent references to the Chinese bureaucracy and other Oriental bureaucracies, since the Wittfogel fable (as discussed in Special Note E) suggests that Marx was inhibited about discussing the existence of the officialdom under the Oriental regimes.

Scottish enclosures movement in the early nineteenth century replacing farmers with sheep-walks and the old forms of clan property with modern private property for the aristocracy. (Marx recalled this bit of history in order to pillory the Duchess of Sutherland as she posed before the women's movement as a philanthropist.)

This is the first time that Marx analyzed social forms founded on the absence of private property in land. The old Scottish clan system, he explains, represented a stage before feudalism, that of patriarchal society. The land belonged to no individual but to the clan, an extended family organized militarily, just as in the Russian "community of peasants" there is also no question of "private property in the modern sense of the word." But there was a hierarchy of officers: the imposts levied on the producing families, though small, represented "a tribute by which the supremacy of the 'great man' and of his officers was acknowledged."

> The officers directly subordinate to the *"great man"* were called *"Taksmen"* . . . Under them were placed inferior officers, at the head of every hamlet, and under these stood the peasantry.
> . . . But the land is the *property of the family*, in the midst of which differences of rank, in spite of consanguinity, do prevail as well as in all the ancient Asiatic family communities.[12]

Thus Marx connected the clan form not only with the contemporary Russian village community but also with that of Asiatic society. The forms based on communal property in land, which he often called Asiatic or Oriental in accordance with the common language of the day, were forms which he knew from the beginning of his investigation were not historically limited to the East. Furthermore, in this very first consideration there was much emphasis that the clan was organized under a hierarchy of officers in a military manner, and that the relations of consanguinity did not gainsay the fact that differences of rank prevailed. Indeed it is this latter feature which immediately produced his comparison with Asiatic society. Finally: the relationship between the peasantry and the magnate's power was already described as *tributary;* later this will be given a fuller content.*

---

* The first volume of *Capital* quoted another part of this article dealing with the enclosures movement.[13] James Mill, in his *History of British India,* had suggested that there were "curious strokes of resemblance" between the Indian village community and certain Celtic manners in parts of Scotland, but his footnote was not pointed.[14]

In the course of 1853 the Taipings took Nanking and made it their capital. In the course of this year Marx also returned to the theme which became the title of his first *Tribune* article on China: "Revolution in China and in Europe." It repeatedly made the point that the European revolution "may depend more probably on what is now passing in the Celestial Empire—the very opposite of Europe—than on any other political cause that now exists." [15]

His demonstration of this thesis traces the economic and political impact of British intervention on China's "barbarous and hermetic isolation from the civilized world," via the cotton industry, movement of silver, and so on. One of the consequences was the breakdown of the imperial administrative cadres; opium-connected corruption "has entirely demoralized the Chinese state officers in the southern provinces." These imperial officers were regarded as sustaining the Emperor's paternal authority. "But this patriarchal authority, the only moral link embracing the vast machinery of the state, has gradually been corroded by the corruption of those officers. . . ." In proportion as "opium has obtained the sovereignty over the Chinese, the emperor and his staff of pedantic mandarins have become dispossessed of their own sovereignty." The force of "all these dissolving agencies acting together on the finances, the morals, the industry, and political structure of China" underlines the question: "Now, England having brought about the revolution of China, the question is how that revolution will in time react on England, and through England on Europe." Marx argues, as in previous articles on England, that this country is heading for an economic slump; and if a Chinese revolution withdraws the Eastern market for British goods, then

> it may safely be augured that the Chinese revolution will throw the spark into the overloaded mine of the present industrial system and cause the explosion of the long-prepared general crisis, which, spreading abroad, will be closely followed by political revolutions on the Continent. It would be a curious spectacle, that of China sending disorder into the Western World while the Western powers, by English, French, and American war-steamers, are conveying "order" to Shanghai, Nanking, and the mouths of the Grand Canal. [16]

In this reciprocating interaction, Marx traces another element. The Manchus' effort to exclude foreigners was largely due to "the fear of the new dynasty, lest the foreigners might favor the discontent existing among a large proportion of the Chinese during the first half century or thereabouts of their subjection to the [Manchu] Tartars. . . . In any case an interference on the part of the Western governments at this time can only serve to render the revolution more violent, and protract the stagnation of trade."[17] In fact, as the rebellion continued to mount, Britain abandoned its benign attitude toward a struggle that was weakening China, and moved openly to crush the rebels militarily.

Later, *Capital* (in a footnote omitted from all English translations) remarked that revolutionary convulsions began in China in 1853—*"pour encourager les autres"*—at a time "when the rest of the world seemed to be remaining quiet."[18] No wonder it engaged Marx's attention.

4. LOOKING TO INDIA—1853

In the spring of the same year, 1853, another Eastern problem faced the British government as the charter of the East India Company came up for renewal: how to deflect the cry for reforms in Indian administration into a means of continuing "the privilege of plundering India for the space of [the next] twenty years."[19] The Indian people were giving trouble, and expensive wars were frequent: the First and Second Sikh Wars had been fought since the writing of *The German Ideology;* the Second Burmese War had just been ended; in less than six years the East India Company was going to be abolished in the midst of the Sepoy Revolt. Here was another front of the revolution, an impulse that might ricochet from East to West and back again. Marx's attention turned decisively to India, and his research on Indian history continued into his last years.[20]

Marx's course of reading on India turned up a gem in François Bernier's accounts of his travels through the Mogul empire in the seventeenth century; he reported on it to Engels, who had just written him about his own study of Arab and Biblical history. Marx put this question: "Why does the history of the Orient *appear* as a history of religions?"—why does it take this form?

Bernier had made clear that even a capital city like Delhi was basically a big military camp economically dependent on supplying the court and the army. (That is to say, it was not an urban concentration of private property.) "The king," wrote Bernier in a statement quoted and underlined by Marx, "is the sole and exclusive owner of all the lands in the kingdom." [21] Marx concludes

> Bernier rightly finds the basic form of all phenomena in the Orient—he speaks of Turkey, Persia, Hindustan—in the fact that *no private property in land* exists. This is the real key even to the Oriental heaven. [22]

Engels took up the thesis and went on:

> The absence of [private] property in land is in fact the key to the whole Orient. Herein lies its political and religious history. But why did it come about that the Orientals did not arrive at property in land, not even the feudal kind? [23]

As Marx and Engels discussed this question, it merged with the problem of the static character of Oriental society, which Hegel and others had long emphasized. Marx and Engels are equally free with generalizations about "the unchanging character of Asiatic societies," particularly with regard to China, "that living fossil," whose "fossil social existence" and "rotting semicivilization" are "vegetating in the teeth of time, insulated by the forced exclusion of general intercourse." [24] (These are phrases from four articles.) But as they went on, this conception became something more definite. Marx formulated it particularly with regard to India:

> . . . the whole of her past history, if it be anything, is a history of the successive conquests she has undergone. Indian society has no history at all, at least no known history. What we call its history, is but the history of the successive intruders who founded their empires on the passive basis of that unresisting and unchanging society. [25]

It is Indian *society* that has "no history," that is, has not evolved,* even though it has plenty of political history:

---

* Compare Marx's similar use of *world history* in *Grundrisse* notes: "World history did not always exist," he jots down in a telegraphic memo listing points to be made about the materialist conception of history as a method. The context makes the meaning clear: the subject is "Influence of means of communication," and he wants to argue that "history as world history" is a *result* of the development of means of communication. [26]

However changing the political aspect of India's past must appear, its social condition has remained unaltered since its remotest antiquity, until the first decennium of the nineteenth century. [That is, until the establishment of the ryotwari system by Sir Thomas Munro.] [27]

Marx applied this conception to China and the Orient in general:

... the Oriental empires show us a picture of steadfast immobility in the social substructure and restless change in the persons and peoples [*Stämme*] that get control of the political superstructure. [28]

The thesis, then, is that political history in the Orient is superficial— literally the history of the surface of society; this superficies also tends to take a religious guise ("appears as a history of religions"). In the margin of Irwin's *The Garden of India,* Marx jotted a note contrasting "a modern centralized gouvernement" with "the much more 'fluid' Asiatic despotism or feudal anarchy." [29] Fluid, not static? It is the political surface which is fluid, while the social deeps remain frozen. The reference made above to "the unchanging character of Asiatic societies" can now be filled out:

... the unchanging character of Asiatic societies, which is in such striking contrast with the constant dissolution and reconstitution of Asiatic states and incessant dynastic changes. The structure of the basic economic elements of the society remains untouched by the storms in the political skies. [30]

We will shortly note a basic socioeconomic reason for this socially static quality (the "self-sustaining unity of manufacture and agriculture") but in any case the duality exists. In the same passage last cited, from *Capital,* Marx presents the key to this dual character of Oriental society. Let us go back a bit and pick up the course of his thinking.

5. THE KEY TO THE ORIENT

We have seen that the inquiry started with the thought that the absence of private property in land (the basic and dominant form of private property in any agricultural society) was the "real key" to

Oriental society,* leading to the question why private property in land had not arisen. Engels began by giving a geographical-materialist explanation: the climate makes artificial irrigation necessary, and this can be accomplished only by government, central or local. This in turn conditioned the nature of Oriental governmental machinery: "Government in the Orient always had no more than three departments: finance (plundering at home), war (plundering at home and abroad), and public works—provision for reproduction."[32] Wars and dislocations could therefore turn whole regions into wastelands, with accompanying cultural retrogression that might obliterate knowledge even of writing and foster the rise of myths.

Marx expanded this explanation for his article in the *Tribune* on "The British Rule in India":

There have been in Asia, generally, from immemorial times, but three departments of Government: that of Finance, or the plunder of the interior; that of War, or the plunder of the exterior; and, finally, the department of Public Works. Climate and territorial conditions, especially the vast tracts of desert, extending from the Sahara, through Arabia, Persia, India and Tartary, to the most elevated Asiatic highlands, constituted artificial irrigation by canals and waterworks the basis of Oriental agriculture. As in Egypt and India, inundations are used for fertilizing the soil of Mesopotamia, Persia, etc.; advantage is taken of a high level for feeding irrigative canals. This prime necessity of an economical and common use of water, which, in the Occident, drove private enterprise to voluntary association, as in Flanders and Italy, necessitated, in the Orient where civilization was too low and the

---

* Marx had written that it was the "real key even to the Oriental heaven," that is, to Oriental religion, which played such a large part in Hegel's discussions. In his *Grundrisse* notebooks, as explained below (pp. 531-533), Marx's discussion of the "Unity" of the primitive tribal society ties up the roots of religious ideas with the social and political development; but the religious side is not developed. He did not come back systematically to a demonstration of how Oriental religious ideas reflected the socioeconomic pattern. There is a general passage in *Capital* on how religious ideas in very early societies (including specifically the Asiatic) reflect their conditions, in comparison with Christianity. An interesting remark is made at the beginning of his article "The British Rule in India," regarding the Hindu religious amalgam of sensuousness and asceticism. The fact that popular movements in the Orient tended to have "a religious coloration," noted in 1862, is also true of much of Western history. Engels' later references to the subject are made in passing, as was an early mention in *The German Ideology*. Among later Western Marxists, Thalheimer dealt with the question.[31]

territorial extent too vast to call into life voluntary association, the interference of the centralizing power of Government. Hence an economical function devolved upon all Asiatic Governments, the function of providing public works. This artificial fertilization of the soil, dependent on a Central Government, and immediately decaying with the neglect of irrigation and drainage, explains [barren lands, ruins, depopulation by war, and so on].[33]

In *Capital*, Marx developed the thesis that, where the soil is fertile and nature is lavish, there is a large amount of surplus labor that is freely disposable (for use by the authorities, for example) and less need of a drive toward economic development; hence it is not the tropics but the temperate zone "that is the mother-country of capital." More generally, "It is the necessity of bringing a natural force under the control of society, of economizing, of appropriating or subduing it on a large scale by the work of man's hand, that first plays the decisive part in the history of industry." It is in this context that he mentions the irrigation works developed in Europe and in the Orient, and footnotes: "One of the material bases of the power of the state over the small disconnected producing organisms in India was the regulation of the water supply."[34]

Contrariwise it follows that where the state failed to perform this function (because of war, for example), the small producing organisms were blighted, and retrogression could set in.

But Marx did not believe that this geographical factor could by itself account for the lack of socioeconomic development in the Orient. In his reply to Engels' letter suggesting the irrigation factor, he accepted it as only the first part of the answer. Interrelated with it was the nature of the basic socioeconomic unit of Oriental life, the village community, which was self-sufficient with respect to other villages, being dependent only on the far-off central state power for the water supply. Atomized, it was an atom detached from any mass, in orbit around a distant sun.

What fully explains the stationary character of this part of Asia [India], despite all aimless movement on the political surface, are two circumstances mutually bolstering each other: (1) The public works were the concern of the central government. (2) Alongside this fact, the whole empire, apart from the few larger towns, was atomized [*aufgelöst,* dissolved] in °*villages*° each possessing a completely distinct organization and forming a little world of its own.[35]

6. THE VILLAGE COMMUNITY AS BEEHIVE

This societal pattern was found by Marx in a number of recent works on India, and was best described by a much-quoted passage in an 1812 report of a House of Commons committee. (Marx cites this 1812 report three times: in his letters to Engels, in "The British Rule in India," and later in *Capital.*)[36] The parliamentary report, discussing one of the northern districts, mentioned "those petty communities, into which the whole country is divided," and described this village community in some detail, particularly "its proper establishment of officers and servants," who are maintained by allotments from the common produce. Wearing British spectacles, it states of the community that "politically viewed, it resembles a corporation or township." Marx interpolates at this point: "Every village is, and appears always to have been, in fact, a separate community or republic."*

The kernel of the 1812 description goes as follows:

Under this simple form of municipal government, the inhabitants of the country have lived, from time immemorial. The boundaries of the village have been but seldom altered; and though the villages themselves, have been sometimes injured, and even desolated, by war, famine, and disease; the same name, the same limits, the same interests, and even the same families, have continued for ages. The inhabitants give themselves no trouble about the breaking-up and division of kingdoms; while the village remains entire, they care not to what power it is transferred, or to what sovereign it devolves; its internal economy remains unchanged; the Potail is still the head inhabitant, and still acts as the petty judge and magistrate, and collector or renter of the village.[37] [Punctuation in original]

In his letter to Engels, Marx added the remark:

These idyllic republics, which jealously guard only the *boundaries of their villages* against the neighboring village, still exist in fairly °perfect° fashion in the northwestern parts of India only recently acquired by the English. I believe that no one could think of any more solid foundation for Asiatic despotism and stagnation.[38]

---

* In all texts of Marx's letter to Engels (presumably in accordance with the manuscript), this sentence appears as a part of the quotation from the 1812 report. It is not in that passage. Inserted by Marx, it is no doubt a paraphrase from one of his readings.

In Marx's opinion, this village-community form had long been the dominant one in India and in at least the early history of China. To be sure, "These small stereotype forms of social organism have been to the greater part dissolved, and are disappearing," as a result of the impact of English goods as well as English forcible intervention.[39] Also, Marx was entirely aware of pockets or patches of other economic forms in various parts of India.* But it was the once-dominant village-community economy that accounted for the main lines of India's social past.

Besides the characteristics of this form already mentioned, there was another aspect which Marx saw as basic to its operation and to its static character:

> Those family-communities were based on domestic industry, in that peculiar combination of hand-weaving, hand-spinning and hand-tilling agriculture which gave them self-supporting power.[44]

> The broad basis of the mode of production here [India and China] is formed by the unity of small-scale agriculture and home industry, to which in India we should add the form of village communities built upon the common ownership of land, which, incidentally, was the original form in China as well.[45]

This "unity of small-scale agriculture and home industry" was important because it underpinned the self-sufficiency of the community and thereby its atomization—"their worst feature, the dissolution of society into stereotype and disconnected atoms."[46]

The atom metaphor might be replaced by a comparison with the spore form of organism, which has the advantage of being resistant to dissolving forces. Marx pointed out that even "usury" (loaning at

---

* In the above-quoted letter to Engels, Marx cautions that landed property did seem to have existed in at least one part of India. Campbell, like others studied by Marx, included considerable attention to forms of slavery and "feudal" relations occurring in the subcontinent; he reported that the village-community form was dominant in the north and frequent in the south, not that it was universal. Marx mentioned the existence of forms of slavery in his articles, and referred to the native princes as feudal landholders and the Indian aristocracy.[40] But the village community was not a feudal form.[41] In *Capital* Marx mentioned the subordinate role of commodity production and trading in "the ancient Asiatic, ancient classical, etc. modes of production" and the interstitial place of trading organisms. The "question of property," Marx warned in his letter to Engels, "constitutes a big *controversial question* among the English writers on India." In a *Tribune* article he discussed the various views in this field, pointing out how the Europocentric slant of the writers, together with the pressure of

interest), which "has a revolutionary effect in all precapitalist modes of production only insofar as it destroys and dissolves those forms of property on whose solid foundation and continual reproduction in the same form the political organization is based," has a dim effect on *this* precapitalist form: "Under Asian forms, usury can continue a long time, without producing anything more than economic decay and political corruption."[47] Even trade, with its increased use of money, "scarcely shook the ancient Indian communities and Asiatic relations in general."[48] After all: in the plant kingdom, fungi, one of the most primitive divisions, can produce highly resistant spores, but have not changed much "since time immemorial."

To Marx, then, the village community that lay at the root of India's history was a specific form of primitive communalism (if taken in terms of its own little world). As he explained in *Capital:* cooperative labor among producers "at the dawn of human development . . . or, say, in the agriculture of Indian communities," is based on two things: (1) "ownership in common of the means of production," and (2) on the fact that "each individual has no more torn himself off from the navel-string of his tribe or community than each bee has freed himself from connection with the hive."[49] This beehive relationship is very important to an understanding of the primitive community. In later forms of exchange, the private owners of the things exchanged treat each other as independent individuals—"But such a relationship of mutual alienness [*Fremdheit*] does not exist for the members of a primitive community [*Gemeinwesen*],* whether it has the form of a patriarchal family, an ancient Indian community, an Inca state, etc."[50] In the margin of Irwin's book on India, Marx jotted down an observation on the big difference between the beehive relationship and *security* in the modern world:

°°It seems very difficult for the English mind—having always present before itself the examples of the small British and the

---

material interest, distorted their understanding of a non-European society.[42] As he said of a European anthropologist: "these civilized asses cannot free themselves of their own conventionalities."[43] In this connection, see also Marx's marginal note in Irwin's book, cited below, p. 529f. Perhaps it goes without saying that the historical question of property is as controversial now as then.

* In the standard translation, *Fremdheit* is de-Hegelianized into *independence;* *Gemeinwesen* is expanded into "society based on property in common."

diminutive Irish *tenant at will*—to understand that *fixity of tenure* may be considered a *pest* [pestilence] by the *cultivator* himself; even the *fugitive slave* or *serf* presupposes a society where, to get free, you have only to escape, to get rid of *a man*, but to get rid, to escape *from social interdependence*, à s'échapper des rapports sociaux [escape from social relationships], is quite another thing.[51]

7. THEORY OF PRECAPITALIST FORMS

Marx had a brief summary on the nature of the Indian village-community form of society in *Capital*, but it is only a fragment of the analysis that reposed in his notebook drafts. The passage in *Capital* is the one, already mentioned, which gives "the key to the secret of the unchanging character of Asiatic societies." Here now is the rest of this passage. The context is the subject of various forms of division of labor.

For example, those very ancient small Indian communities which still continue to exist in part are based on common possession of the land, direct union of agriculture and handicraft, and a fixed division of labor, serving as a pre-set ground-plan for founding new communities. Each forms a self-sufficient production unit. . . . The main bulk of the products is produced for direct use by the community itself, not as commodities, and even these in part only if in the hands of the state, which from time immemorial receives a certain quantity of them as rent in kind. Different parts of India have different forms of these communities. In the simplest form, the community tills the land in common and divides the products among its members, while each family carries on spinning, weaving, etc. as an accessory domestic industry. Along with this body of people engaged in the same work, we find [a number of community officers are here listed] . . . . These dozen persons are maintained at the expense of the whole community. . . . The law regulating the division of communal labor operates here with the inviolable authority of a natural law. . . . The simple productive organism of these self-sufficient communities, which constantly reproduce themselves in the same form and, if they happen to be destroyed, reconstitute themselves in the same place with the same name—this supplies the key to the secret of the unchanging character of Asiatic societies. . . .[52]

It is in his notebooks of 1857–1858 (the *Grundrisse*), written during the height of the Sepoy Revolt in India and while the Taiping rebellion was still going forward in China, that Marx put together his fullest analysis of the "Asiatic" mode of production and its relationship to its political structure, the "Oriental despotism." Far from being in finished form, these notes are rough "reminders to myself" jotted down under difficult personal circumstances. The line of thought is partly a summary of some ideas he had already written about and partly a supplement and elaboration.

Marx begins this section, "Forms Preceding Capitalist Production . . . ," by taking up the forms of property in land before the separation of the worker from the means of labor, which in the first place was land. One such early form was free small-holding; another was "collective landed property based on the Oriental commune [*Kommune*]."

> In the first form of this landed property: there figures, to begin with, a naturally evolved [*naturwüchsiges**] community as the first precondition. [There is the] family and the tribe formed by an extended family, or by intermarriage among families, or by a combination of tribes. . . . [T]he *tribal collectivity*, the natural community, appears not as the *result* but as the *precondition for the collective appropriation* (temporary) and *use of the soil*. . . . The naturally evolved tribal collectivity, or, if you will, the herd order, is the first precondition. . . . They naively relate to the land as to the *property of the community*—that community which produces and reproduces itself in living labor. Each individual relates to it, as *owner or possessor*, only as a member of this community. . . . This form can be realized in very varied ways on the basis of the same fundamental relationship.[53]

One of these ways is encountered where, "as in most *Asiatic* fundamental forms," there is an all-encompassing "Unity" above the communities. (Marx is here using Hegel's *Einheit,* or Unifying Entity, for the relationship that holds the community together.) This *Oneness* of the

---

* *Naturwüchsig*—then a relatively recent term—is often translated *primitive*; it means developed directly out of a state of nature. We shall meet it again. In the translation of *Capital* by Moore-Aveling-Engels, it is translated *spontaneously developed* as well as *primitive*. In general, *community* translates *Gemeinwesen* or *Gemeinde* (and their forms), while *collectivity* is used for *Gemeinschaft*; but the nuance is not usually significant.

community may be embodied in various ways as the development proceeds: at first religious-social, then also identified with the person of the sovereign or despot. However conceived, this unity stands above all the small, separate communities and figures as the owner of all the land, while the communities under it figure only as the *possessors* of the land by tradition. No individual holds property in land. The property relation is understood as a grant from above, made *to* the individual land-tillers *via* the local communities *by* the entity that represents the Overall Unity (*Gesamteinheit*) of society in their eyes.[54]

This Overall Unity

> is embodied in the despot as the father of the many [local] communities. . . . The surplus product . . . therefore belongs to this supreme Unity. Therefore, at the core of the Oriental despotism and of the propertylessness which it juridically seems to entail, there exists this tribal or communal property which is in fact its foundation. This property is created mostly through a combination of [hand-] manufacture and agriculture inside the small community, which thus becomes thoroughly °self-sustaining° and contains within itself all conditions for reproduction and surplus production. A part of its surplus labor belongs to the higher [that is, overall] collectivity, which finally takes on existence as a *person* and this surplus labor shows up both as tribute, etc., and as labor in common for the glorification of the Unity—in part, of the actual despot; in part, of the imaginary tribal entity, the god.[55]

This kind of common property can develop in two ways. In one, "small communities independently vegetate alongside each other, while the individual works, with his family, independently on his allotted portion of land"; there are also certain kinds of common labor for economic purposes as well as for war, religious worship, and so on. This form is the source of the original rise of dominion by lords, and may form a transition point to serf-labor. In another form, "the Unity can extend to collectivity in labor itself, which can be a formal system, as in Mexico, in Peru especially, among the ancient Celts, and some tribes in India."*

---

* A later passage elaborates: "Communal production and common property such as is found in Peru, for example, is evidently a *secondary* [that is, second-stage] form, introduced and transmitted by conquering tribes which in their own

In addition, the collectivity of the tribe may take the form of a Unity represented by the head of the tribal group or of a relationship among the heads of families:

> Accordingly, therefore, either a more despotic or democratic form of this community. The collective conditions for actual appropriation through labor, *water supply systems* (very important among the Asian peoples), means of communication, etc., appear then as the work of the higher Unity, the despotic government which looms over the small communities.

In this connection, Marx makes the point, which he originally found in Bernier, about the character of the towns as an appendage to the sovereign and his satraps:

> Real towns are established here alongside these villages only at points specially favorable for trade with the outside, or where the head of the state and his satraps exchange their revenue (surplus product) for labor, which they expend as °labour-funds.° [57]

This special character of the towns—"nothing but roving encampments *au fond*"—is one of the consequences of the fact that "in Asiatic societies . . . the monarch figures as the exclusive owner of the land's surplus product." [58] For the peripatetic towns are essentially centers where the state functionaries ("the head of the state and his satraps") distribute this revenue to camp-followers. The Oriental city was shaped by the mode of production.*

Of the social forms, the Asiatic is the longest-lived:

---

areas were acquainted with common property and communal production in the old simpler form found in India and among the Slavs. Likewise, the form we find among the Celts in Wales, for example, seems to be one that was transmitted there, that is, to be *secondary,* introduced by conquerors among less advanced tribes they conquered." [56]

* This also conditions the distinction which Marx later makes between the nature of cities in different societies. "Commercial wealth as an independent economic form" has existed at a variety of economic stages, including "the ancient Asiatic city" among others. Primitive Germanic society did not have concentrated centers in the form of towns at all; classical civilization was *based* on the city. But the Asiatic form was different from both: "Asiatic history is a kind of indifferent unity of town and country (the really large towns are to be considered here simply princely camps, excrescences on the economic structure proper). . . ." [59]

The Asiatic form necessarily holds out longest and most tena-
ciously. This fact is rooted in its very presupposition: that the
individual does not become autonomous vis-à-vis the community;
that the production cycle is self-sustaining; unity of agriculture
and hand-manufacture, etc.[60]

The latter part of this presupposition is connected with a typical lack of
roads: on the one hand, there is little need for them between self-
sustaining communities; on the other, their absence locks the communities into isolation.[61] Whenever slavery and serfdom develop, they necessarily modify the property relations of tribal communalism, but they
are least successful in doing so in the case of the Asiatic form, where
"the self-sustaining unity of manufacture and agriculture" resists
conquest by these rivals.[62] In the Oriental form it is hardly possible
for the individual member of the community to lose his fixed relationship to property (the community property) "except through
entirely external influences"; for he "never enters into a free relationship to it such that he could lose his (objective, economic) tie
with it. He has taken root."[63]

8. THE "GENERAL SLAVERY"

To take root is to be bound to the soil. In *Capital,* as previously
mentioned, Marx uses the more traditional and more accurate beehive
metaphor. If the individual "never enters into a free relationship" to
this communal beehive, then his condition can be called a sort of
slavery—at least metaphorically, just as Marx freely uses *wage-slavery*
for an entirely different social system. Some Europeans had called the
Asiatic state of affairs slavery *tout court.*[64] Marx proceeded to a
differentiation, to separate the Asiatic form from the slaveholding
mode of production familiar to Europeans. Thus we get his phrase "the
general [*allgemeine*] slavery of the Orient."*

* It will be useful to remember, from earlier chapters, that *allgemein* (as in
Hegel's *allgemeine Stand,* the civil service or bureaucracy) is often best translated
universal, and with a Hegelian cast, suggests the communal rather than the
particular or individualist. It is this connotation that allows it to carry the thought
that the producer is the slave not of an individual but of the community. The
English *general slavery* does not convey this connotation, which is suggested by
the *gemein* common to *allgemein* and *Gemeinde, Gemeinwesen.* Much later

This exposition starts with the following course of analysis. In tribal society in general, an individual's relationship to property is based on the fact that he is a member of a tribe. It is the tribe that holds property (primarily land). Therefore, if one tribe is conquered by another and made subject to the conquerors, it becomes *propertyless* (Marx's emphasis). Instead of having its own property, it itself becomes the tribal property of the conquerors. Marx draws the conclusion: "Slavery and serfdom, therefore, are [*understand:* begin as] only further developments of property based on tribalism. They necessarily modify all forms of the latter." This is true of tribalism in general, but "They can do this to the least extent in the Asiatic form." Why? Due to "the self-sustaining unity of manufacture and agriculture on which this form is based," the Asiatic form is more resistant to the effects of conquest than where agriculture (alone) and private-property forms of landholding predominate exclusively. So on the one hand, the Asiatic form resists the encroachments of slaveholding as a private-property-holding mode of production; but on the other hand it is true that a sort of slavery already characterizes the internal life of this Asiatic community. In Marx's words:

... since in this [Asiatic] form the individual never becomes owner [of land] but only possessor, he is at bottom himself the property, the slave, of that in which the unity of the community exists; and here slavery neither abolishes the conditions of labor nor modifies the essential relationship.[66]

The point recurs a little further on, as Marx reminds us that property takes different forms in accordance with different conditions of production. When, in early societies including the Asiatic, property involves the relationship between a working producer and the conditions of *his own* production and reproduction (his own livelihood), then we must assume that the individual producer is "a member of a tribal or communal organism (whose property he himself is, up to a certain point)."

(1887) Engels referred to slavery in both "Asiatic and classical antiquity" as "the predominant form of class oppression" in a polemic against the single-taxer Henry George, in which Engels wanted to refute the proposition that the root cause of class divisions is "the expropriation of the mass of the people from the land." It is rather, he argued, "the appropriation of their persons."[65] It is this feature which apparently led him to blur classical slavery and Asiatic "slavery" together. Under the best interpretation Engels' formulation of this argument is unbuttoned. For the claim that Engels abandoned or rejected the Asiatic concept at this time, see Special Note F.

The individual is the "property" of the tribal community? Then he is its "slave"? Marx proceeds to make a distinction in order to avoid misunderstanding. There is the kind of "slavery, serfdom, etc. where the worker himself figures as one of the natural conditions of production for another individual or community," but "this is *not* the case with (*e.g.*) the general slavery of the Orient"; it is so "*only* from the European point of view."

That is: to European eyes the rootedness and unfree condition of the producer might seem like slavery, but in point of fact a basically different mode of production is involved. (We may remark that this mode could just as well have been called the *general serfdom* of the Oriental community form.)

Where the real slave relationship does occur in this Asiatic society, Marx adds, it is "always secondary, never the original form," that is, it is a second-stage development out of the original communal form.*

In another place Marx likewise carefully distinguished chattel slavery from the Asiatic form, in much the same terms:

> The original unity of laborer and conditions of labor (leaving out the slave relationship in which the laborer himself is one of the objective conditions of labor) has two main forms: the Asiatic community (primitive [*naturwüchsigen*] communism) and small-scale family agriculture (combined with domestic industry °in one or the other form.° Both forms are infantile forms, and are alike unsuitable to develop labor as *social* labor and develop the productive power of social labor.[68]

One important difference is this: in the Asiatic form the individual himself is not a slave; he does not live in a slave relationship either to another individual or to the community as a slavemaster. The slave-like

---

* The passage here explained is an involuted, stream-of-consciousness sentence that owes more to carbuncles and insomnia than to grammar. The phrase about "general slavery" occurs as a parenthetical insert with a close reference. A literal translation of this monster sentence might read:

> Slavery, serfdom, etc., where the worker himself figures as one of the natural conditions of production for another individual or community (this is *not* the case with, *e.g.*, the general slavery of the Orient; [it is so] *only* from the European °point of view°)—hence property is no longer the relationship of the individual working for himself to the objective conditions of labor—is always secondary, never the original form, even though it is the necessary and consistent result of property based on the community and labor in the community.[67]

Note that "Slavery, serfdom, etc." is the subject of "is always secondary . . ."

relationship that does exist is generalized or universalized—to apply to the community itself, which is exploited *as an organism* by the despotic Unity (organizing entity) above it.

9. THE MEANING OF THE ASIATIC MODE

The form of society, or mode of production, we have been discussing had impinged on European consciousness from the Far East, and hence first appeared to Europeans with the geographic label *Asiatic* or *Oriental*. It was Marx who first stated that the mode of production which Europeans had discovered in Asia in modern times had also existed in the prehistory of European society, that the Asiatic mode of production had to be considered a more or less world-wide development, even though it had taken different paths in different regions and had fossilized in one of them.

It is the terminology which has been confusing, not the conception; and the terminology is confusing today only if it is lifted out of its contemporaneous context (as is usually done). In fact, this social form discovered in Asia was treated by contemporaries much the same as other fossils being unearthed in far-flung places. It was (and is) standard procedure to use geographic terms as universal designations in a number of sciences then young, including geology, anthropology, and paleontology. Thus Peking man, Java man, and Mousterian culture were named after the places of first discovery. Nor was the formation of social forms exempt from being metaphorically compared with the process of geological formation, by Marx as well as others.[69]

We have seen that already in 1853 Marx had an idea of the historical connection between the Asian and European forms.[70] He worked it out in his notebooks during 1857–1858.

In Marx's exposition, the starting point is the "naturally evolved community" of primitive tribal society, which, in the course of time, develops its property relations in two different forms, along two different paths. These are summarized (on the first page of the section "Forms Preceding Capitalist Production") as: "free smallholdings" and "collective [*or* communal] landed property based on the Oriental commune." Further on, a little more fully, the two ways are described as independent cultivation by families, which may lead to the rise of lords and serf labor, and a unified organization of labor whose collectivity is embodied in a Unity as previously discussed.[71]

Of these two main forks, Marx summarizes: "Accordingly, therefore, either a more despotic or democratic form of this community."[72] Clearly, the more despotic form is the second of the main forks, the village community based on a unified organization of labor, which leads toward the concretization of the Unity of the community in a despotic regime—the Oriental form. It is this form that became dominant in the Orient. The "more democratic form" was typical of the European development.*

It would have been convenient if, from here, Marx had applied the label *Asiatic* (or *Oriental*) form only to the "more despotic" form which actually dominated in Asia, rather than to both and either indifferently. This would have required the invention of a new overall term for the type of society which was bifurcating along these two paths. But, as mentioned, it was the Asiatic label that was retained for both—for a time. (We will see a new overall term in 1881.)

Therefore, in 1859, writing the preface for his *Critique of Political Economy,* which was carved out of the *Grundrisse* notebooks, Marx summed up the outline of societal evolution in a sentence just as concise as the other formulations given in this preface about his

---

* Why did a particular society take one or the other fork in the road leading out from the naturally evolved community? In the *Grundrisse* notebooks Marx comments on this question briefly in three separate passages, no doubt written at various intervals; he discusses or mentions factors of geography, climate, physical conditions like soil, tribal character, effect of historical movements like migrations, relation to other tribes. Marx's classification is not altogether clear. At one point, examples of the first fork are given as the Slavic and Rumanian communes; but further on, the second fork is described as based on the *"directly communal property"* and is equated with the "Oriental form, modified in the Slavic form" and further developed in the classical and Germanic forms. This indicates that the second fork branches off in four subdivisions, and would be neat enough except that the Slavic form appears to be listed under both forks. Apart from this inconsistency (if it is one), it is clear that the main forking roads are presented as two, not four. Where Marx describes the communities of the second fork, as based on "a unified organization of labor," he gives as examples "Mexico, Peru especially, among the ancient Celts, some tribes in India." The second-fork communities, therefore, are not Oriental ones only, though the Oriental commune is taken as the type. When in one place Marx wants to specify the "Oriental community" in the Orient itself, he uses the phrase "the specifically Oriental form."[73] A somewhat different pattern which Marx wrote down in 1881, in connection with Europe, will be discussed in the next section.

historical method. "In broad outlines, Asiatic, ancient [classical], feudal, and modern bourgeois modes of production can be designated as progressive* epochs in the economic formation of society." [75]

The only way to interpret this terse formulation is in terms of the notebook (*Grundrisse*) material which it sums up. Understood this way, there can be little doubt that by the "Asiatic" mode of production here Marx designated the general form of naturally evolved community which took different courses of development in different historical contexts, starting from primitive common property. It is an umbrella name, in terms of a social development known to the educated public, for the several forms of primitive communal society which Marx discussed in these notes. The notebooks themselves do not contain any other overall term for this mode of production which would mean something to readers without considerable explanation.

The line of thought in the *Grundrisse* which we have already set out should be enough to indicate this. But in addition, there is no lack of direct statements, all making this much clear: that the underlying village-community form based on common property was not peculiar to Asia but rather was a more or less universal development in the beginning of man's society. Just as the discovery of Peking man did not mean that only the Chinese had prehuman ancestors, so too the survival of living-fossil social forms in Asia did not mean that the "Asiatic" mode of production was an Oriental monopoly. This can be found in the main body of the *Grundrisse* notes from the first pages to the last, literally. In the first pages we read that "History . . . shows common property (*e.g.* among the Indians, Slavs, ancient Celts, etc.) to be the

---

* The German is *progressiv* (not *fortschrittlich*), hence tends to reinforce the idea of succession in time to some degree. Writing in French, Marx later used *phases d'évolution successives* for the types of primitive communities—this in his drafts for a letter to V. Zasulich which is full of expressions of temporal succession in connection with early social forms.[74] At the same time these drafts strongly reinforce the caution implied in the conditioning phrase *in broad outlines*. It is unquestionable that Marx conceived the "progressive" epochs (stages or types) within the framework of a broad time series; but it is equally clear that the time relationships involved no rigid linear sequence. On the contrary, there was plenty of room (as always in history) for overlapping forms, fossil leftovers, lateral diffusion of cultures, reciprocal influences, and a host of other complications in the ordinary pattern of historical inquiry. The idea that Marx meant that each "progressive" epoch had to come to an end before the next in line of destiny could begin, or that everywhere the epochs goosestepped in fixed sequence like a parade, is simply grotesque. But this is really an issue in Marx's historical method, which is outside our scope here.

original form, a form which long plays an important role in the shape of community property." And a little earlier Marx had referred to "the decline of common property, as among Oriental and Slavic peoples." The view is broadened in what is the very last paragraph of the manuscript:

> Common property has recently been rediscovered as a special Slavic curiosity. But in point of fact India offers us a sample-case of the most multifarious forms of such economic communities, more or less in dissolution but still entirely recognizable; and a more thoroughgoing historical research finds in turn that it was the starting point with all civilized peoples.[76]

This passage was in turn expanded to become a part of the *Critique of Political Economy* itself, for publication. New emphasis is put on the universal application of this social form. In the course of an economic argument, the book reads: "Let us take collective labor in its naturally evolved [*naturwüchsigen*] form, as we find it on the threshold of history among all civilized peoples." A footnote at this point makes the following statement:

> In recent times a ridiculous prejudice has become widespread, to the effect that the *naturally evolved* [*naturwüchsigen*] form of common property is a specifically Slavic or even exclusively Russian form. It is the original form, which we can point to among the Romans, Teutons, and Celts; of this form, however, a whole showcaseful, with diverse specimens, is still to be found among the Indians [of Asia], even though partly in ruins. A closer study of the Asiatic, especially the Indian, forms of common property would show how different forms of naturally evolved common property gave rise to different forms of its dissolution. Thus, for example, the various original types of Roman and Teutonic private property can be traced back to various forms of Indian common property.[77]

Capital later quoted this in full, as a footnote to a similar statement.[78]

The scope of "the Asiatic . . . forms of common property" in this passage would be ambiguous perhaps, were it not introduced by the reference to the "history among all civilized peoples." There is no question, however, about a later letter by Marx to Engels, written after reading Maurer's books on the constitution of the old German mark and village community:

... he demonstrates in detail that private property in land developed only later. . . . Precisely now it's interesting that the *Russian* way of redistributing the soil at definite times (in Germany at first annually) was maintained in Germany here and there up into the eighteenth and even the nineteenth century. The view which I put forward [in the *Critique of Political Economy*], that everywhere the Asiatic, or Indian, property forms constitute the starting point in Europe, here receives a new proof (although Maurer does not know about it). For the Russians, however, even the last trace of a claim °of originality° disappears, even °in this line.° What's left them is that they are still stuck in forms that their neighbors cast off long ago. [79]

If "Asiatic" property forms "constitute the starting point in Europe," it is plain that Marx was quite willing to apply the Asiatic label to the communal forms of primitive Europe or any other continent. *Asiatic* is used as a type-label; and "the Asiatic mode of production" was the generic designation for the primitive community in any or all of the various forms discussed in the *Grundrisse* notebooks, from the earliest community taken as it is evolving out of natural conditions, up through its transition to a state-organized class society, and, with a certain additional looseness, including the final stage where, in the "specifically Oriental form," this mode of production becomes subordinated as the economic foundation of a developed Oriental despotism.

In subsequent references by Marx, there is strong affirmation that the village-community economy based on common property (whatever the label pinned on it) was once the general case in Europe as well as in Asia. A few days after the last-mentioned letter, Marx again wrote Engels about Maurer's works:

His books are exceptionally important. . . . Even the best minds fail to see—on principle, owing to °a certain judicial blindness°— things that are right in front of their noses. Later, when the moment has arrived, one is surprised to find traces everywhere of what one has failed to see. . . .

To show how much we all labor under this °judicial blindness°: Right in *my own* neighborhood [near Trier], in the *Hunsrück* mountains, the old German system survived up till the *last few years.* I now remember my father talking to me about it from a *lawyer's* point of view! [80]

In another letter two years later:

It is, furthermore, a historical lie to say that this [Russian] *common property* is *Mongolian*. As I have repeatedly indicated in my writings, it is of *Indian* origin and therefore is found among all civilized European peoples at the beginning of their development. Its specifically *Slavic* (not Mongolian) form in Russia (which also recurs among *non-Russian South Slavs*) indeed has the greatest similarity *mutatis mutandis* to the *old German* modification of Indian common property.[81]

There is an especially interesting passage where Marx used the very term *Oriental* for the primitive economic form in the development of classical society (Greece and Rome). A footnote in *Capital* remarks that the small peasant economy and handicrafts in combination not only form the basis of the feudal mode of production but "likewise form the economic foundation of the classical communities in their best period, after the original Oriental common property ownership had disintegrated and before slavery had taken over production in earnest."[82] Obviously, *Oriental* is used here purely as a typological label meaning "common property as found in the Orient," or "Oriental-type common property." The English translation by Moore-Aveling-Engels in 1887 struck the word *Oriental* out of this passage (though it remained in the German editions of *Capital*).

If Marx could publish this statement in 1867, without realizing that it might be confusing to readers, there should be no difficulty in accepting the fact that, in 1859, he intended "Asiatic mode of production" to have the same scope, that is, to apply to a general stage in social evolution, not one limited geographically to Asia.

10. THE "ARCHAIC FORMATION"

The next step in the development of Marx's view of early social evolution, as he continued to study the problem, is mainly known to us from his drafts for a letter to V. Zasulich about the Russian village commune, in 1881 (two years before his death).

Here he was addressing himself more to the European past than to the Asian. His comments are incidental to the main point of the letter, hence not intended to be systematic; in addition, the exposition was left unfinished. For present purposes, it is triply fragmentary, but still suggestive. He is thoroughly aware of the inadequacy of the historical material at his disposal: "The history of the decadence of the primitive communities still remains to be done. . . . Up to now only meager outlines have been provided."[83]

The former predominance of the primitive communal form in Europe is the basis of the whole discussion.

> Go back to the origins of Western societies and everywhere you will find common property in the soil; in the course of social progress this has everywhere disappeared in the face of private property. . . .[84]

The general label used throughout these drafts for the early epoch, anterior to the development of slavery and serfdom and the breakup of the communal land system, is "the archaic formation of society."[85] (In one place, "the primitive formation of society" is also used,[86] and in another "common property of a more or less archaic type."[87])

This archaic formation is our previous acquaintance, the naturally evolved community. It is divided into two main stages: the "community of the more archaic type," that is, the earliest stage, and its successor, the "agricultural commune" or "rural commune" (so called "by common agreement," writes Marx). The latter stage was no longer based on kinship, gave more scope to private property, and had periodic redivisions of the communal land for individual cultivation. It is "the *last expression* or last period of the archaic formation"—"the *most recent type* and, so to speak, the last word in the *archaic formation* of societies."[88] The contemporaneous Russian commune was of this later type.

This agricultural-commune form is, in turn, the transition to the class societies based on private property (in Europe):

> As the last phase in the primitive formation of society, the agricultural commune is at the same time the phase of transition to the secondary formation, hence transition from society based on common property to society based on private property. The secondary formation, of course, embraces the series of societies based on slavery and serfdom.[89]

In short, this archaic formation, which Marx specifically sees as the generally early form in both Europe and Asia (and elsewhere), represents exactly the same rung in the ladder of social evolution that had been labeled the Asiatic mode of production twenty-two years previously.

Even the difference in the label can be easily understood. In 1859 Marx had gone through a study of the village community mainly in its Asian forms, which at that time were relatively well known, while there were only intimations of a similar development in Europe. The label "Asiatic mode of production" could be used *faute de mieux*, in the same sense as the anthropologists and geologists were using geographic labels for time periods. By 1881 Marx had gone through an exciting study of Maurer and other works on Europe's past, and the letter he was drafting specifically dealt mainly with Europe. Using "Asiatic mode of production" as generic label was out of the question in this new context. But the change in label should not obscure the identity of substance.*

With the 1881 letter drafts before us, we have as full an idea as we can get of Marx's conception of the social basis of Asiatic society. Now: what was the nature of the *political* structure associated with this form?

---

* Also identical in substance is Engels' linking of the common-land institutions of early Europe with those in India and Java, in 1875 in an article doubtless discussed with Marx: "In reality communal ownership of land is an institution which is to be found among all Indo-Germanic peoples on a low level of development, from India to Ireland, and even among the Malays, who are developing under Indian influence, for instance, in Java." And so on.[90] As in the case of Marx's letter drafts to Zasulich, the background target was the Russian Narodnik claim that the village-community pattern was peculiar to the Russian soul.

22 | ORIENTAL DESPOTISM: STATE AND BUREAUCRACY

If the societal form represented by the Asiatic village community was based on a mode of production different from those familiar to Europeans from their own class history, that is, from classical slavery and medieval feudalism, then can it be considered an example of primitive communism? If so, does this mean it was classless and stateless like the earliest tribal communities?

Indeed, in a passage we cited on page 536—from Marx's notes for the fourth volume of *Capital*—he does label the Asiatic community, in passing, as primitive [*naturwüchsigen*] communism, that is, a primitive communal form that has developed directly out of the state of nature.* In this case, where does the Oriental despotism come in?

1. THE TRANSITION TO THE STATE

This question arises because so far, in summarizing Marx's notebooks and his line of thought, we have been largely bypassing what is half the problem. So far the spotlight has been mainly on the underlying village-community economy. If an ancient Indian village community

---

* The same idea is behind an interesting passage in a little-known work by Marx's follower J. G. Eccarius (secretary of the International 1867–1871), a work "which was written with mighty assistance and coaching by Marx," according to Engels. Chapter 1 gives a bird's-eye view of the succession of social epochs, after quoting Marx's summary statement on this from his preface to the *Critique of Political Economy*. Then comes a substantial passage on the Asiatic mode of production, beginning:

> The leading characteristic of the Asiatic, as contradistinguished from any other mode of production, is a species of *communism*, with a political

were transposed to another planet as an isolated colony, then its character as a primitive communism would stand out in relief. But if we consider the village community as it existed in historical Asia, not on Mars, then we must take account of the fact that it did not exist as an isolate.

It should be apparent that, in the *Grundrisse* notebooks, Marx inextricably fused the nature of the village-community economy with the role of the "higher Unity" towering over it. Marx's resort to the seemingly vague term *unity*, in the sense of something that unites or embodies the collectivity of the social unit, is not simply a Hegelian reminiscence. The Hegelianizing term is useful because its vagueness, or indeterminacy of content, allows this unifying entity to be seen as a historical process as its content changes. The concept has an algebraic character: the x changes, but the equation (the social relationship) remains.* The Unity *ends* by being embodied in, and identified with, the supreme power of the sovereign or despot; it *begins* with the earliest forms of collectivity, or the sense of Oneness, in the tribal extended family, in the institutions of communality developing out of primitive natural conditions (the *naturwüchsiges Gemeinwesen*).

Underlying this conception is the view of the state's origin which was explained in Chapter 11: the state does not arise as an institution that descends on society out of the blue; it develops out of the overall unifying institutions of the primitive community, out of the already existing organizing authority of the originally stateless society. It follows that this could have taken place only in the course of transitional

---

superstructure of "caste." The *soil* is the common possession of the people . . . every village was in itself a *whole*, insulated and secluded from the rest of the land and produced all that was necessary to the satisfaction of human needs.

Eccarius' book goes on to stress that the monarch was the controller of the economy, assisted by "the public officers." Outlining the composition of the population, it lists first "the higher officers of state, the dignitaries of religion, the standing army" and then the "artists [sic] and artisans" and their domestics—and no other classes. While this is Eccarius writing, not Marx, there can be little doubt that this is Eccarius' version of what he had gathered from Marx's coaching.[1]

* The same x is used elsewhere in these notebooks for a different relation. From the outset of capitalist development, says Marx, "capital stands as One or Unity vis-à-vis the workers as Many . . . as a Unity that is external to the workers,"[2] for capital is by nature the concentration of many units of living labor. In this case, capital is viewed as the unifying entity over the separate atoms of labor.

epochs and in transitional forms. Inevitably (given the paucity of positive knowledge of prehistory) a given transitional form will appear to us as a a puzzling phenomenon: it seems to be neither this nor that. One task of theory is to aid investigation by suggesting what it is transitional *from* and *to*.

Marx's exposition in the notebooks assumed such a process of transition, the historical process in which one variant of the naturally evolved community arose under Asiatic conditions and eventually fossilized. The general process of transition was most clearly sketched by Engels in *Anti-Dühring,* as presented in Chapter 11. Now, in addition, let us see how Engels specifically discusses this transition in terms of Asiatic society.

To refute the notion that the state comes into being simply as an imposition by force from outside the social structure, Engels develops the following argument (in his preparatory draft for the book):

> But state and force are precisely what all hitherto existing forms of society [after primitive times] had had *in common,* and if I should try to explain, for instance, the Oriental despotisms, the republics of antiquity, the Macedonian monarchies, the Roman Empire and the feudalism of the Middle Ages by stating that they were all based on *force,* I have explained nothing as yet.

The explanation has to be made in terms of what the force is used to take, namely, the products and productive forces of the time, and so on.

> It would then appear that Oriental despotism was founded on common property, the antique republic on the cities engaged in agriculture, the Roman Empire on the latifundia, feudalism on the domination of the country over the town, which had its material causes, etc.[3]

The rough summary statement that "Oriental despotism was founded on common property" did not get into the finished work, though this rough formula had been written down by Marx more than once. In what sense could a *state,* which is the outcome of class divisions, be "founded on common property"? In *Anti-Dühring* itself, the matter is put in terms of historical process. Engels brings up the role of the Oriental water works, for example, precisely in connection with the process of class differentiation:

> Society divides into classes: the privileged and the dispossessed,

the exploiters and the exploited, the rulers and the ruled; and the state,[4] which the primitive groups of communities of the same tribe had at first arrived at only in order to safeguard their common interests (*e.g.* irrigation in the East) and for protection against external enemies, from this stage onwards acquires just as much the function of maintaining by force the conditions of existence and domination of the ruling class against the subject class.[5]

The protostate institution arises in order to safeguard "common interests"—in the Orient, irrigation—and then evolves its class function. This is what it means to say that it was founded on common property. To complete this picture, let us see how a *ruling class* arises out of the same foundation of common property.

2. THE TRANSITION TO A RULING CLASS

Pointing to the Asiatic village communities, Engels recalls that "For thousands of years Oriental despotism and the changing rule of conquering nomad people were unable to injure these old communities," whereas the importation of European goods started to dissolve them, not primarily by the use of force.

... the peasants simply find it to their advantage that the private ownership of land should take the place of common ownership. Even the formation of a primitive aristocracy, as in the case of the Celts, the Germans and the Indian Punjab, took place on the basis of common ownership of the land, and at first was not based in any way on force, but on voluntariness and custom.[6]

This primitive aristocracy which was formed on the basis of common ownership of the land: was it a ruling class? We can raise the same question about the primitive aristocracy that Marx had first described in his article on the Duchess of Sutherland and the Scottish clan. We are dealing with transitions; in this case it is clear that we are dealing with a social formation which is in transition. In general, we are dealing with a ruling class in the process of becoming, an embryonic ruling class, that is, not yet a (finished) ruling class; or merely—depending on what point in the transition is in question—an officialdom with the potentiality of becoming a ruling class. Marx gave thought to the same problem in his anthropological studies.[7] It is in the nature of transitions that a definite answer is possible only after concrete factual investigation of a particular case. There is still a controversy over when fertilized ova become persons, and how many hairs must be lost before one is officially bald.

The Scottish clan officialdom described by Marx was needed to safeguard communal interests. Likewise, Engels writes of the need for offices even in classless communities to safeguard certain common interests, including control of water supplies, and adds:

> Such offices are found in aboriginal communities of every period —in the oldest German marks and even today [the 1870s] in India. They are naturally endowed with a certain measure of authority and are the beginnings of state power.

These beginnings of state power, which naturally do not begin by quite being a state power, tend to become increasingly independent of the community as a whole as class differentiation proceeds.

> It is not necessary for us to examine here how this independence of social functions in relation to society increased with time until it developed into domination over society; how he who was originally the servant, where conditions were favorable, changed gradually into the lord; how this lord, depending on the conditions, emerged as an Oriental despot or satrap, the dynast of a Greek tribe, chieftain of a Celtic clan, and so on; to what extent he subsequently had recourse to force in the course of this transformation; and how finally the individual rulers united into a ruling class.[8]

"It is not necessary for us," wrote Engels in this notable example of apophasis, "to examine here how" this potential, embryonic, unfinished, proto-ruling class, comprising all these lords, chieftains, satraps, Oriental despots and whatnots, moulted into such a ruling class as could be recognized by a textbook; or united (crystallized, amalgamated, clotted, or synthesized) out of class elements into a certifiable class. At any rate, if the *how* of it was not further examined, it is still quite clear that the individual rulers *did* unite into a ruling class, including the individual big and little despots and satraps of the Orient, emerging out of the community infrastructure with independent powers that could be transferred, by conquest or otherwise, to bigger

Oriental despots. Engels, like Marx, saw no puzzling problem in this process.*

When a state power did crystallize, continued Engels' exposition, its basis was always "the exercise of a social function." And "However great the number of despotisms which rose and fell in Persia and India, each was fully aware that above all it was the entrepreneur responsible for the collective maintenance of irrigation throughout the river valleys, without which no agriculture was possible there." This reflected the "common interests" side of the political power, which continued alongside the class function. It really was in the common interest of the despot or state to keep the communities flourishing; for how else could state revenue be collected? On the other hand, if the amalgamated ruling class of despots and satraps could maintain themselves only in constant warfare, which devastated the villages and undermined the maintenance of the state's social function, this was an internal contradiction of the system.**

3. THE TRIBUTE-COLLECTING STATE

If a distinctive type of class society developed out of the village-community economy and produced individual rulers who finally united into a ruling class (with a characteristic type of state, the Oriental despotism), there are more questions raised about the relationship between the mode of production and the political power.

The key point was the "question of property"—the dominant type, landed property. *Who owned the land?* The answer is duplex, reflecting two sides of the reality. On the one hand, Marx made clear often enough, as we have seen, that in this mode of production it was the village community that owned the soil. On the other hand, he wrote

---

* All this describes, according to Engels, *one* "process of formation of classes," alongside which "another was also taking place." This was the emergence of slavery.[9] It is clear that class society based on slavery is regarded as qualitatively different from the type of class differentiation described above, even though both might proceed in conjunction.

** A modern account, starting with Marx's views, of the development of a ruling class out of village-community society may be found in an important work by F. Tökei.[10]

more than once that it was the state (Oriental despot, etc.) that owned the land. In a *Tribune* article he referred quite in passing to "the Asiatic system making the state the real landlord." In *Capital,* emphasizing that the appropriation of ground rent presupposes the ownership of landed property "by certain individuals," he gave examples beginning with: "The owner may be an individual representing the community, as in Asia, Egypt, etc.," that is, the state sovereign or despot. The context is a warning against "confusing the various forms of rent pertaining to different stages of development. . . ." In other notes, he wrote that most of the surplus product in the precapitalist modes of production goes to "the landowner (the state in Asia)." In *Anti-Dühring* Engels combined the two formulations to make the point that "In the whole of the Orient, where the village community or the state owns the land, the very term *landlord* is not to be found in the various languages. . . ."[11]

If we are considering the naturally evolved community before the institution of the state separates out, that is, while the Unity is located within the life of the tribal community itself, then there is no problem. The land is communal property. But a special feature of the Asiatic mode of production in the Orient is not simply the existence of the village-community form but the continued existence of this form after the communal Unity has become embodied in a "higher" power, one that has risen *above* the local communities, that has separated itself from the producers as a collectivity and now towers above them with a separate body of armed men and special institutions to extract the surplus product. This is the village-community form taken after it has given birth to a class differentiation, which in turn has taken on a life of its own as a state power—*while the village-community infrastructure persists,* "vegetating in the teeth of time."

Within the framework of its own little world, the village community may remain relatively unchanged for a long time; and within this framework it is still the owner of the soil *as against the individual.* But there is now a new relationship between it, as a little world, and the larger world outside its sporelike walls. The essential feature of the new relationship is the appropriation of its surplus product by the state power, which is the real owner of the soil *as against the local community.*

The form in which this surplus product is extracted, the form in which this ground rent is paid, is *tribute.* The characteristic relationship between the Oriental state and the underlying village community is *the tributary relationship.*

Thus, Marx writes in *Capital* that

Under the slave relationship, serf relationship, tributary relationship (insofar as primitive communities are concerned), it is the slaveholder, the feudal lord, the tribute-collecting state that is the owner and hence the seller of the product.[12]

Further on, there is a similar remark that specifies the state as the economic ruler (owner of the surplus product) taken parallel to the slaveholder and the feudal lord. Marx mentions

under those earlier modes of production the principal owners of the surplus product with whom the merchant dealt, namely, the slaveholder, the feudal lord, and the state (for instance, the Oriental despot). . . .[13]

The tribute-collecting state is the specific political structure corresponding to the Asiatic mode of production in its Oriental form.* There are three features of this type of state that may usefully be reviewed here:

1. This state extracts tribute not from the individual producer, not from a slave or serf, but from the community of producers as a whole. In general, the tributary relationship did not primarily regulate the relations of the state with individuals; it was the form in which the surplus product (or surplus labor) was extracted from the local community as a collectivity.

2. The relationship of this state to its economic infrastructure more nearly resembles symbiosis than in any other society; for it appears as a relationship between two organisms that seem to be more or less autonomous. The Mogul power can be imagined conquering Afghanistan or Turkey instead of India (though not necessarily with the same socioeconomic result, of course); and the village communities did in fact get along much the same under a variety of conquerors. The

---

* See also the passage in *Capital* that speaks of the greater amount of freedom for the worker under the "tributary relationship" than under "serfdom with compulsory labor."[14] The tribute-collecting nature of this state was not yet developed when Marx was jotting down his *Grundrisse* notes, though it is suggested in passing in the passage quoted above, p. 532. Elsewhere Marx mentions the ordinary tribute relationship between a conquering state and subjugated peoples, with a reference to the Turks and Romans;[15] but Roman society was not built around tribute-collection any more than around merchant capital.

communities felt the effect of changes in state composition in terms of the "three departments of government" that Engels and Marx had described as characteristic of the Oriental state: more or less tribute extracted, more or less devastation by war, more or less attention to the necessary public works (especially water works). Otherwise, the "restless change in the persons and peoples that get control of the political superstructure" merely changed the hands that collected the tribute. The conquests, the "storms in the political skies," replaced one centralized power with a similar one, this centralization being the other face of the atomization that reigned below, in "a society whose framework was based on a sort of equilibrium, resulting from a general repulsion and constitutional exclusiveness between all its members [components]." [16]

3. The tributary relationship—unlike the slave relationship, serf relationship, or wage-labor relationship—is scarcely conceivable except as a relationship between the producers on the one hand and the ruling *political* power on the other. In the case of the other three, the relationship of exploitation appears as a relationship between two classes of civil society, between a class of producers and a class of private-property owners.* In these cases, the state normally arises as the instrument or guardian of the economic rulers, the owning class. But in the tributary relationship, the relationship of exploitation is between the producers and *the state itself, directly.* Put another way: in the case of the other three modes of exploitation, economic exploitation and political rule are *related* in a certain way; but in the tributary mode, economic exploitation and political rule are *fused* in the same hands.

---

* With the qualification that the feudal ruling class tends to have the dual character of property-owner and political power-wielder, a point that has already been made in several connections.[17] Therefore serfdom partly shares the characteristic of the tributary mode explained above. But in the tribute-collecting state of the Orient, it was the *ruling* political power (the summit) that owned the land and the surplus product, intermediaries being merely its agents. Under feudalism, the serf relationship could and did exist formally between direct producers (serfs) and landowners quite low in the feudal hierarchy, each of whom was one member of the ruling class.

4. SYMBIOSIS: LOCALISM
AND ORIENTAL DESPOTISM

The disconnected local autonomy of the communities, then, was the complement of the over-all state centralization. "I believe that no one could think of any more solid foundation for Asiatic despotism and stagnation," Marx told Engels.[18] When he sent this letter, Marx had already written his first article on "The British Rule in India," which closed with a powerful passage along these lines. "Sickening as it must be to human feeling" to see what British imperialism is doing to these "inoffensive social organizations," the village communities, still "we must not forget that these idyllic village communities, inoffensive though they may appear, had always been the solid foundation of Oriental despotism. . . ."

It is worth reading the rest of this indictment of an outlived and retrograde society, set alongside his invective against the vileness and stupidity of the British masters. We must not forget, continued Marx,

> that they restrained the human mind within the smallest possible compass, making it the unresisting tool of superstition, enslaving it beneath traditional rules, depriving it of all grandeur and historical energies. We must not forget the barbarian egotism which, concentrating on some miserable patch of land, had quietly witnessed the ruin of empires, the perpetration of un-speakable cruelties, the massacre of the population of large towns, with no other consideration bestowed upon them than on natural events, itself the helpless prey of any aggressor who deigned to notice it at all. We must not forget that this undig-nified, stagnatory, and vegetative life, that this passive sort of existence evoked on the other part, in contradistinction, wild, aimless, unbounded forces of destruction and rendered murder itself a religious rite in Hindostan. We must not forget that these little communities were contaminated by distinctions of caste and by slavery, that they subjugated man to external circumstances instead of elevating man to be the sovereign of circumstances, that they transformed a self-developing social state into never-changing natural destiny, and thus brought about a brutalizing worship of nature, exhibiting its degradation in the fact that man, the sovereign of nature, fell down on his knees in adoration of *Kanuman,* the monkey, and *Sabbala,* the cow.[19]

Turned around, from an indictment to a program, this is also a statement about the grand socialist alternative as against both the "inoffensive" victims stuck in the past and the "vile" exploiters of the present.*

Marx also applied this insight into the symbiotic union of atomized localism with despotism to the obvious case of Russia. The Russian village community has a self-weakening characteristic:

> This is its isolation, the lack of liaison between the life of one commune and the others'—this *localized microcosm*,** which is not found everywhere as an inherent characteristic of this type but which, wherever it is found, has given rise to a more or less central despotism over the communes.[21]

Engels echoed the point more than once, usually with an eye on Russian czarism:

> Such a complete isolation of the individual communities from one another, which creates throughout the country similar, but the very opposite of common, interests, is the natural basis for *Oriental despotism,* and from India to Russia this form of society, wherever it prevailed, has always produced it and always found its complement in it.[22]

> This common ownership [of land] quietly persisted in India and Russia under the most diverse forcible conquests and despotisms, and formed their basis.[23]

> Where the ancient communes have continued to exist, they have for thousands of years formed the basis of the cruelest form of state, Oriental despotism, from India to Russia. It was only where these communities dissolved that the peoples made progress of themselves.[24]

---

* Marx ended this article (a sure sign that he regarded it as an important piece of writing) with a flourish from the literary classics, in this case from Goethe:

> Since their pain has swelled our pleasure,
> Should we too not feel this pain?
> Have not souls beyond all measure
> Been consumed by Tamerlane?

** Elsewhere in this draft letter, the phrase becomes: "its *localized microcosm,* which deprives it of historical initiative."[20] For another reference (by Engels) to this insight, see the passage about Dutch state-socialism in Java, page 559f (letter to Kautsky).

We shall take up the case of Russia in the next chapter. It is more unexpected that Marx saw the Oriental despotism element in a European country at the western end of the continent: Spain.

5. THE CASE OF SPAIN

On plunging deep into Spanish history for his series of articles on the Spanish revolution in 1854, Marx was struck by the occurrence of the localism–despotism pattern in the peculiar development of absolutism on the peninsula.

On the one hand, Spain was "the very country, where of all the feudal states absolute monarchy first arose in its most unmitigated form"; yet here "centralization has never succeeded in taking root"— that is, centralization of the social infrastructure as distinct from the political centralization represented by the absolute monarchy. Marx asked: "How are we to account for the singular phenomenon"?[25]

Marx's answer (which he announced was "not difficult") does not concern us here in detail; it sought to explain historically why the absolute monarchy in this country did not play the same civilizing (modernizing) and centralizing role as elsewhere in Europe, and hence why the towns and bourgeoisie vegetated in decay.

°°And while the absolute monarchy found in Spain material in its very nature repulsive to centralization, it did all in its power to prevent the growth of common interests . . . the very basis on which alone a uniform system of administration and the rule of general laws can be created. Thus the absolute monarchy in Spain, bearing but a superficial resemblance to the absolute monarchies of Europe in general, is rather to be ranged in a class with Asiatic forms of government.

What was "Asiatic" about this form of government? It is the localism–despotism relationship that Marx has in mind.

°°Spain, like Turkey, remained an agglomeration of mismanaged republics with a nominal sovereign at their head. Despotism changed character in the different provinces with the arbitrary interpretation of the general laws by viceroys and governors; but despotic as was the government it did not prevent the provinces from subsisting with different laws and customs, different coins, military banners of different colors, and with their respective systems of taxation. The oriental despotism attacks municipal self-government only when opposed to its direct interests, but is very glad to allow those institutions to continue so long as they take off its shoulders the duty of doing something and spare it the trouble of regular administration.[26]

In presenting this observation on a Spanish peculiarity, Marx is *detaching* the pattern of Oriental despotism as a form of government from the Asiatic mode of production. There is no question here of a primitive village-community economy, only municipal self-government.* This usefully underlines the fact that Marx uses *Oriental despotism* to mean a form of government, like *republic* (which, remember, he metaphorically applied even to the Indian village community itself) or *monarchy*.

Furthermore, the element of Oriental despotism is only one strand in the political character of this peculiar Western state. It is that aspect of Spain's history which differentiates it from other European countries; but it does not negate the area of likeness. The background is not the village community but feudalism; and "Charles I attempted to transform that still feudal monarchy into an absolute one," by destroying the power of the nobles and restraining the power of the Cortes. The royal power won out in civil war: "it was, above all, the bitter antagonism between the classes of the nobles and the citizens of the towns which Charles employed for the degradation of both."[28]

This class pattern is similar to the rise of other absolutisms, as we saw in Chapter 19. But for specific historical reasons in Spain it led to economic stagnation and a decaying infrastructure, instead of industrial development and a burgeoning bourgeoisie: hence to retrograde political forms. We may add: hence also to retrograde political ideologies, such as anarchism, which flourished in Spain longer than elsewhere—its localism being the natural complement of despotism.

---

* In this study Marx does not mention the role of water works in Spain's economic past. He does in *Capital:* "The secret of the flourishing state of industry in Spain and Sicily under the domination of the Arabs lay in their irrigation works."[27] A footnote at this point makes a connection with India but not with Spanish history.

6. THE TRIBUTE-COLLECTING CLASS

Let us now take a closer look at the nature of the tribute-collecting state. Specifically, we are interested in the class at the receiving end of this relationship. For Marx the ruling class was defined, socio-economically speaking, as the class possessing control over the appropriation of the surplus product. Under the Oriental despotisms—as under feudalism, but not capitalism—the answer to this basic question was visible to the naked eye of the most untutored peasant: it was acted out in front of him every day. He could see the physical hands that reached out to take away his surplus product, and he was solemnly made aware of—not deceived about—the hierarchy of power that lay behind those hands. We are, in fact, asking one of the easiest questions in all social history.

That is, it is an easy question as long as we are dealing with Marx's tribute-collecting state, and not with the views of others who claim that the dominant forms of Asiatic history have been chattel-slavery or feudalism, that is, forms familiar to the Europocentric mind.

An illuminating light on the nature of the tribute-collecting state is cast, from another direction, by an inquiry of Engels'—unwittingly, for he was not thinking about Oriental despotism in this connection. Soon after Marx's death, Engels, reading about the Dutch colonial system in Java, saw an important point in the difference between Dutch and British colonial policy in Asia. J. W. B. Money's *Java* made clear to him that, whereas the British in Java (1811–1836) as well as in India had tried to introduce private property in land for peasants, the Dutch refrained from such a westernizing effort in Java. The Dutch maintained the old village-community system, and channeled their control and exploitation through the native chiefs and village heads without changing the age-old economic forms of the infrastructure. They merely put *themselves* at the receiving end. The villages paid their tribute as usual to their higher-ups, who in turn were milked by the Dutch.

To Engels, preoccupied at the time (1884) with the problems of Bismarckian Germany and its homegrown "Bonapartist socialists," the pattern had a familiar look. He wrote the German party to examine this case of state-socialism in order to use it as a means of educationally exposing the exploitive meaning of the Bismarckian state-socialism then making a stir.*

In terms of our present subject, the case of the Dutch in Java showed how a modern imperialist power could step into the role of the Oriental despot just like any other conquering tribe—*and maintain the same mode of production as the underpinning of its exploitation and rule.* There were two officialdoms, not one, involved in this political system. Standing between the direct producers and the Dutch rulers was the native aristocracy (Money's term) of chiefs and village heads, equivalent to the "primitive aristocracy" discussed above on pages 548-549; and standing above this native communal hierarchy was the Dutch colonial bureaucracy, which appropriated the surplus product, allowing part to stay with the native chiefs. In the case of the old despotisms, this would be the complete pattern; in the case of the Dutch, of course, there was an extra step up, for above the colonial bureaucracy was its ruling class back home. But (to run a hypothetical test mentioned before) if Java with its colonial masters were transported to Mars, it would be detached from the overseas capitalist class. Only the Dutch settlers (immediate colonial exploiters) would remain at the head of the society. To be sure, this transmogrification could not actually be worked on the Dutch; but *it serves to illustrate the exact pattern of the traditional Oriental despotism* with modern imperialists at the summit.

---

* Engels wrote to Bebel:

> If you want a model of state-socialism, then take *Java*. Here, on the basis of the old communistic village communities, the Dutch government has organized all production in so beautifully socialistic a fashion, and has so nicely taken the sale of all products in hand, that, aside from about 100 million marks in stipends for officials and the army, there is still another sum of about 70 million marks in net proceeds that accrues annually.... In comparison Bismarck is a mere child indeed![29]

The explanation to editor Kautsky was longer:

> It would be good if someone took the trouble to lay bare the state-socialism now rife, through an example that is in full-blooming practice in *Java*. All the material is contained in [Money's book].... Here one sees how, on the basis of the old community communism [*Gemeindekommunismus*], the Dutch organized production under the aegis of the state, and secured for the people their idea of a quite comfortable existence. Result: the people are kept at the stage of primitive stupidity and 70 million marks a year (very likely more now) are raked in for the Dutch treasury. The case is highly interesting, and the practical applications can easily be seen. Besides, it is proof how primitive communism [*Ur-*

Engels had leaped the gap between two apparently unrelated social forms: the updated Oriental despotism of the Dutch in Java (subordinated to an overseas capitalism), and the up-to-date state-socialism of Bonapartism in its Bismarckian version, the class content of which was discussed in Chapter 16.[31] What the two had in common, amidst a host of differences, was the autonomous role of the state power with respect to the class structure of civil society: this was what linked Java to state socialism.

In Java as in Germany, the executor of this autonomous role was the bureaucracy.

It is ironic, in view of the contemporary intimations that Marx was reluctant to recognize the existence of the Oriental bureaucracy, that Marx—so far as I have been able to discover—was the very first writer to do exactly that: apply the still new-fangled term *bureaucracy* to the Chinese state apparatus (in 1858).* More than today, the very use of the word had overtones. As we have pointed out, Marx wrote about the highly visible officialdom of the Chinese state with about the same relative frequency as he did of the Prussian, and with about the same division of labor between terms treating the sovereign power as a *Gesamteinheit* (king, emperor, Crown, throne, monarchy) and terms referring to the inside of the state apparatus. And as in the case of Prussia, he assumed everyone knew that "The *existence* of the sovereign power is, indeed, precisely its *officials,* army, administration, judges. Apart from this its body, it is a shadow, a figment of the imagination, a [mere] name."[34]

kommunismus] there, as in India and Russia today, provides the finest and broadest foundation for exploitation and despotism (as long as no modern communist element stirs it up), and how it shows itself to be as much of a crying anachronism in the midst of modern society (one to be removed or else well-nigh reversed in course) as were the independent mark associations of the original Swiss cantons.[30]

* Marx's 1858 articles on the British-imposed opium trade dealt with one of the consequences for China: "[t]he corruption that ate into the heart of the Celestial bureaucracy, and destroyed the bulwark of the patriarchal constitution."[32] (It would seem that it was *not* the emperor that was the bulwark of this political system.) The sovereign power was powerless to control its officialdom in its efforts to suppress the opium trade, efforts which (Marx points out) were decided on by the deliberations of "all the high officers of the Empire." Among other interesting glimpses of the Chinese bureaucracy in Marx's articles, there is the role of the mandarinate in meeting the Taiping rebels' attacks, which can be read in an interesting if neglected article entitled "Chinese Affairs."[33] I do not mean to exclude the possibility that a search might turn up other writers who applied the neologism *bureaucracy* to China earlier than Marx.

It is certainly true that it never occurred to Marx to reassure future marxologists about a question no one was yet asking, since his unsophisticated era knew no special inhibition about the concept of a bureaucratic ruling power. For two centuries writers on China had again and again routinely described the locus of all power in the hands of the state apparatus, whether this was considered to be the emperor operating through his far-flung administrative machine or the apparatus with the emperor at its head. In the case of Russia, the Marquis de Custine* had taken some time to conclude that the state power was in the hands of an *apparat* that was no longer effectively controlled by the czar, but the one theory that Custine never entertained was that the power was in the hands of the nobility or any other property-holding class. In Marx's lifetime, it would have been a puzzling innovation if anyone had claimed that the ruling power under Oriental despotism was in any hands *other* than the state apparatus.

Another reminder is necessary, if only as background: as in the case of many other subjects, Marx's political writings about China and India were usually keyed to current issues, like British policy, movements of revolt, and so on. He never got around to writing his planned volume on the state, nor did he set pen to paper to wrap up the political scene in scientific formulas. He did not do this even with a long list of far more important issues—unfortunately. Nowhere did he ask, in good catechetical fashion, *What is the ruling class under the absolute monarchy?* and set down the answer for the textbooks of the future. Several scores of marxologists have written learnedly of his failure to promulgate a canonical definition of class.**

The fact is that Marx took it for granted that everyone and his or her mother knew who ruled under Oriental despotism and similar regimes. It was an easy question, not a difficulty. In *Capital,* one of his first remarks about "the ancient Asiatic and other ancient modes of production" is this: "Those ancient social organisms of production are, as compared with bourgeois society, much more simple and transparent, to an extraordinary degree."[36] In contrast, Marx has amply explained that "bourgeois society is the most highly developed and most multi-

---

* The Marquis de Custine's observations are reported in Special Note E.

** It remained for Wittfogel to claim that Marx's alleged reticence about a ruling class under Oriental despotism "was a strange formulation for a man who ordinarily was eager to define social classes. . . ."[35]

plex historical organization of production."[37] On the economic level, the simple peasant understood about his own society what the simple professor disputes in ours, namely the fact and mode of exploitation, the appropriation of the surplus product. *Simple and transparent.*

7. THE "POLITICAL DEPENDENCY RELATIONSHIP"

Most important is the common failure to understand the significance of Marx's repeated insistence on what was *basic* to the inquiry: the contention, which he put forward aggressively time and again as the key to everything, that this Oriental society was founded on "common property"; that is, that *there was no private-property-holding class in existence.* Only today do we have to spell out that there could be no ruling class based on private property if the social scene contained not a single candidate for this honor. To be sure, private-property-holding elements existed in the pores of this society; but they were not such candidates. It was therefore no problem for Engels—writing in *Anti-Dühring,* in intellectual collaboration with Marx, the sole work in which they undertook a more or less systematic presentation of Marx's ideas —to speak of the amalgamation "into a ruling class" of ruling elements *not* based on private-property power.[38]

In *Capital* Marx used an appropriate term for the stratum of economic exploiters in the Asiatic mode of production: referring specifically to the old village-community system, he wrote of the nonagricultural laborers that they

> are directly employed by the magnates [*den Grossen*], to whom a portion of the agricultural surplus product is rendered in the shape of tribute or rent. One portion of this product is consumed by the magnates in kind. . . .[39]

Die Grossen—the Great Ones, magnates, or grandees—is a term used globally for the appropriators of the surplus product, the identity of whom we know from Marx's explanations. It may remind us of Marx's use of *the great man* for the head of the hierarchy of officers in the Scottish clan.[40] Later Marx used *rural magnates* (in English) to refer to the landed aristocracy in the French provinces.[41]

In 1881–1882 Engels resorted to the same algebraic term *die*

Grossen in describing the transition to the feudal ruling class out of the Germanic communities that had melded in the invasions of Rome and gone over to private property in land. But this ruling class-in-formation did not begin simply out of land ownership.

> When, during and by means of the civil wars, the beginnings of a ruling class of the great men [*Grossen*] and the powerful— landowners, officials, and military chiefs—were already being formed, their support was bought by the princelings with gifts of land.[42]

Thus the "officials and military chiefs" who entered into the formation of this ruling class were homogenized with the landowners—eventually. So it was in the European, not the Asiatic, course of development. In the Asiatic pattern, they could not be so homogenized because a private landowning class did not arise.

In *Capital* Marx's use of the *Great Ones* for the ruling magnates who received the tribute or rent (the distinctive revenue of rulers under Oriental despotism) occurs in the course of a favorable summary of Richard Jones's analysis of the Indian system. In his economic notebooks Marx had copious notes on and excerpts from Jones regarding this point among others. These notes show Jones referring only to "the sovereign" as the controller of the general labor fund for the non-agricultural laborers.[43] It was Marx who introduced the *Great Ones*. In another book Jones referred incidentally to "the state and its officers" as the receivers and dispensers of this fund; and Marx excerpts this passage for quotation in his work.[44]

Most interesting is a statement that occurs as Marx's conclusion from Jones's material on the history of rent:

> In all earlier forms it is the landowner, not the capitalist, who figures as the direct appropriator of the *surplus labor* of others. *Rent* . . . appears historically (on the biggest scale among the Asiatic peoples) as the general form of *surplus labor,* of labor performed gratis. Here the appropriation of this surplus labor is not mediated through exchange, as in the case of capital, but its basis is the forcible rule of one section of society by another (hence also direct slavery, serfdom, or political dependency relationship).[45]

"The forcible rule of one section of society by another," which provides the basis for the appropriation of the producers' surplus labor, "on the biggest scale among the Asiatic peoples": what else did this mean to Marx than the pattern of the state in socioeconomic terms?

This is immediately followed by a list of three modes of production presented as exemplifying different forms of the preceding pattern. Two of these three are well known: direct slavery and serfdom, both of which we know Marx ruled out as descriptions of the dominant Asiatic mode of production. The Asiatic form is termed the political dependency relationship (*politisches Abhängigkeitsverhältnis*). This is *not* a designation for the political superstructure of this mode of production: it is the term for the central relationship of the mode of production itself.

What is the political dependency relationship which is set coordinately alongside slavery and serfdom? Why is it a *political* dependency relationship? Because of the specific characteristic of this mode of production which was explained in a previous section:[46] the direct dependence of the producer on the political power. It is the political power that is the *socioeconomic* exploiter, that section of society which exercises its forcible rule over another.

When the state apparatus is taken as a ruling "section of society," it is idle to believe that some crowned head is the total content. If, further on, Marx remarks that in precapitalist modes of production most of the surplus labor and surplus product goes to "the landowner (the state in Asia),"[47] it is as disingenuous to believe that he means a single landowner in the first case as that he knows only a single person in the second.*

Let us put this passage alongside the previously cited one in which the same three modes of production were listed in their double aspect:

> Under the slave relationship, serf relationship, tributary relationship (insofar as primitive communities are concerned), it is the slaveholder, the feudal lord, the tribute-collecting state that is the owner and hence the seller of the product.[49]

The threefold division is identical, for the tributary relationship is the

---

* A similar remark occurs in *Capital* under "Rent in Kind," where Marx again discusses characteristics common to precapitalist societies. Even when rent in kind replaces labor rent, he writes, it is still usually accompanied by survivals of the earlier form (rent paid in compulsory labor), "no matter whether the landlord is a private person or the state." Rent in kind as a form "is quite suitable for serving as the basis for stationary social conditions, as we see *e.g.* in Asia."[48]

same as the political dependency relationship. It is *political* because it is the tribute-collecting *state* which is the owner of the products of labor as well as of the land itself, that is, owner of the economic infrastructure as well as ruler of the political structure, thereby fusing economics and politics in this form of society. It is this fusion which makes the political dependency relationship central to the mode of production.

The importance of the designation *political* dependency relation for the Asiatic mode of production may be better gauged if we get acquainted with the role played in Marx's thinking by the basic concept of *dependency relations* (*Abhängigkeitsverhältnisse*). Marx worked this out in the *Grundrisse* notebooks; *Capital* reflects the results.

Well known is Marx's periodization of history in terms of modes of production characteristic of different societies. In his notebooks Marx proposes a related periodization of history in terms of the dependency relations characteristic of three great stages of society. In these terms, *all* precapitalist societies become the first stage; capitalism represents a second stage; and the future socialist society will be the third stage. An interesting feature of this synoptic view is the basis on which all precapitalist forms are subsumed under a single head: this common content is called *"personal* dependency relations."

Following is a résumé of Marx's exposition which follows his language fairly closely, with added explanations:

• The mutual interdependence of everybody with everybody else in production is a characteristic of all societies and always remains true, but this "all-around dependency of the producers on each other" may be organized in different forms. In modern bourgeois society, where all products and activities tend to become exchange values (commodities), the necessary interdependence of everybody in production is brought about for the first time by a *social* bond, not a personal one.

• This social bond, the binding force that keeps people working in concert, is represented by bourgeois exchange value (commodity relations, production for the market), and is objectified as money. Thus the social bond, which embodies the social character of production, confronts the individual producer as something alien to him *which has become a thing* (in this case, money), not simply a relation.

• But in precapitalist societies, money (wherever it existed) had nothing like this social power. It could not be, and it was not, this *thing* which acted as the social bond enforcing the necessary interdependence in production. Rather, this function—the function of binding individuals together for production—was performed by the *power of the community* over the individual, whether this community was the old patriarchal community, the community of ancient classical society, or of the feudal and guild system.

• Today, in bourgeois society, the thing—the social bond standing outside the individual—has an impersonal power over him. In a society where no *thing* has this social power, the same job has to be done by people, that is, by personal relations. Thus Marx writes:

> Every individual [today] possesses this social power in the form of a thing [money]. Rob the thing of this social power and you must give it to [certain] people [to exercise] over [other] people. Personal dependency relations (quite spontaneously developed from nature, to begin with) are the first forms of society in which human productivity develops, [if] only to a slight extent and at isolated points. Personal independence based on dependence on *things* is the second great form, one in which for the first time there takes shape a system of general social metabolism, a system of universal interrelations, multifarious needs, and universal [social] wealth. Free individuality, based on the universal development of individuals and on gaining mastery over their communal, social productivity as well as over their social wealth, is the third stage. The second stage creates the preconditions for the third.[50]

Or in bare outline: (1) The societies based on personal dependency relations. (2) The society, capitalism, in which the personal bond in dependency relations is replaced by a social bond, alien to or external to the individual's personal relations. This is summarized as "personal *in*dependence based on dependence on *things."* (3) The coming replacement of all dependency relations by "free individuality."

This sets the framework in which to understand Marx's treatment of the Asiatic form. All the social forms of the precapitalist stage are based on *personal* dependency relations in one way or another; but in the Asiatic form these personal dependency relations are *political:* that is, the binding force in production is the relationship to the state. This is why Marx can write "direct slavery, serfdom, or political dependency relationship" as a quick rollcall of precapitalist societies. Under all three, the power that enforces the interdependence of production is wielded by "people over people." Under slavery, it is wielded by certain people called slaveowners; under serfdom, it is wielded by certain people called feudal lords; under the political dependency relation, it is wielded by certain people called the state.

8. THEOCRATS AND PRIEST RULE

Before coming to the main passage in *Capital* where this political dependency relationship is expounded somewhat systematically if briefly, it is worth noting a place where it appears in passing.

Discussing "the colossal effects of simple cooperation" in labor, Marx presents a passage from Jones about the gigantic structures erected by Oriental states, out of the surplus, through prodigal use of massed human labor. Jones remarks that what makes this possible is the "confinement of the revenues which feed them [the laborers] to one or a few hands." This does not sound as if he is aware of a ruling class; but in the same passage (still as quoted by Marx) he had also remarked of Egyptian food production: "this food, belonging to the monarch and the priesthood, afforded the means of erecting the mighty monuments. . . ."[51] In Egypt he is aware of the priesthood as a social element which is an integral part of the state structure.

Marx then adds the following comment of his own:

> This power of Asiatic and Egyptian kings or Etruscan theocrats, etc., has in modern society passed over to the capitalist, whether he figures as an isolated capitalist or, as in joint-stock companies, a collective capitalist.[52]

The reference to the Etruscan theocrats is not in Jones, who was discussing Oriental states. Etruscan society, of course, is a dark subject, now as then; but whatever Marx had in mind by Etruscan theocrats— presumably either early priest-kings or the later aristocracy that assumed religious sanctions (called the "Etruscan priest-nobles" elsewhere by Marx)[53]—the term plainly pointed to a class or classlike formation. Moreover, the power over the disposal of the social surplus—the basic socioeconomic power in any society—is regarded as held by the Asiatic sovereigns in the same sense as the Etruscan ruling class and the modern capitalist ruling class.

The reference to the Etruscan theocrats as a ruling class has its near-counterpart in an equally casual reference by Marx to Egypt, which is however far more specific than Jones's "the monarch and the priesthood," though it derives from the same historical sources. Marx writes: "The necessity for calculating the periods of the Nile's overflow created Egyptian astronomy, and with it the rule of the priest caste as the director [*Leiterin*] of agriculture."[54] Typically, Marx is not here posing the question *What is the ruling class in Egypt?* but making a different point, whose very formulation reveals what he is taking for granted.* The control by the priest "caste" over the technological essential of the conditions of production led to their control over economic life not by means of private-property ownership but rather by means of their control over the state apparatus—a *political* control exercised through religious sanctions much like the Etruscan theocrats. What was established was a political dependency relationship, basically different from direct slavery or serfdom as Marx had explained. (Whether and when slavery *also* existed within the framework of this system, as in India, is an entirely separate issue.)

9. THE "INNERMOST SECRET" OF
SOCIETY AND STATE

It is in the section on "Labor Rent" included in the third volume of *Capital* that Marx comes closest to a direct discussion of the political dependency relationship. It begins with labor rent under serfdom (ground rent in the form of unpaid labor for the feudal lord's estate). Marx then generalizes that in all forms of society in which the direct producer does not own his land but is only its "possessor,"

---

* Equally typically, Wittfogel disposes of this passage by a diversion. Besides objecting that Marx gives him caste and not class, he throws it out on the ground that Marx uses "a most peculiar determinant of economic dominance," namely "making astronomy the basis for economic leadership" instead of "control over the means of production."[55] But astronomy did not begin as an intellectual pursuit by professors. Marx's point is precisely that the *technology* involved (astronomy) was the economic necessity (condition of production) essential for "control over the means of production." Furthermore: if this inept objection were indeed justified, then it would mean that Marx departed from his own theory in order to nominate a *nonprivate-property-holding* stratum as the ruling power of Egyptian society. A most peculiar insistence for a man "paralyzed" by fear of just such a conclusion!

the property relationship must likewise show itself as a direct relationship of rulers and ruled [*or* lordship and servitude], and therefore show that the direct producer is not a free man—a lack of freedom which can soften from serfdom with compulsory labor down to a mere obligation to pay tribute [*Tributpflichtigkeit*].[56]

The latter, we know, is the central feature of the Asiatic mode of production, or better, tributary mode of production based on the village community. The direct producer independently carries on his cultivation and handicrafts.

This independence is not negated by the fact that, much as they do in India, these small peasants may form themselves into a more or less naturally evolved community of production, since involved here is merely their independence from the nominal landlord. Under these conditions, surplus labor for the nominal landowner can be squeezed out of them only by noneconomic coercion, whatever form this may take.

One should keep in mind that, for the worker under capitalism, the normal form of pressure involves *economic* coercion, coercion not directly mediated through the state. Basically the same is true of serfdom, which normally involved a *mutual* dependency relationship—the direct land-tiller receiving protection and other services from his lord. But slavery involved noneconomic coercion (forceful compulsion at least implied). Therefore in the next sentence Marx makes the distinction: "What differentiates this from the slave or plantation economy is that the slave works with another's conditions of production, and not independently." He then continues on the village-community form: "Hence a personal dependency relationship is necessary, personal unfreedom to one degree or another, and the condition of being tied to the soil as an appurtenance, bondage in the true sense." This characteristic applies to both the serf relationship and the tributary relationship. The next sentence narrows it down:

If it is not a private landowner but rather, as in Asia, the state which confronts them [the direct producers] directly as their landowner and their sovereign at one and the same time, then rent and taxes coincide; or rather, there then exists no tax other than this form of ground rent.

To paraphrase: if the state, vis-à-vis the direct producers, is both economic and political overlord rolled into one, then ground rent and taxes are also rolled into one package (the tribute in this case); and it is this amalgamated levy which is the source of the social surplus collected by the rulers. Marx continues:

> Under these conditions, the dependency relationship* politically as well as economically need not take harsher form than what is common to any subjection to that state. Here the state is the supreme landlord. Here sovereignty is concentrated land ownership on a national scale. It follows, however, that private land ownership does not exist, although there is both private and collective ownership and usufruct in the soil.[58]

In this system, "sovereignty," that is, political rule, "is concentrated land ownership," writes Marx. This is not merely another form of the aphorism that politics is concentrated economics, which merely points to a relationship between the two. What we have here is an identity, a fusion. Here the state is not the managing committee of the landlords; "here the state is the supreme landlord."

Is this view somehow out of line with Marx's theory of the state? As if to answer this in advance even at the expense of an intrusive digression,** at this very point we get the most generalized statement in *Capital* on the nature of the state in terms of its socioeconomic underpinnings. In line with the context, the formulation is *not* pitched in terms of class—which provides only a mediating definition—but rather *in terms of that which defines class too.* This rock-bottom determinant is the "sovereignty-dependency relationship" which derives from "the specific economic form in which unpaid surplus labor is pumped out of the direct producers."

> The specific economic form in which unpaid surplus labor is pumped out of the direct producers determines the relationship of rulers and ruled, as it grows directly out of production itself and in turn reacts upon it as a determinant. But on it is based the entire formation of the economic community growing out of the

---

* This key term (*Abhängigkeitsverhältnis*) has disappeared from extant English translations. Not quite as bad is the fact that, in the first volume of *Capital*, where Marx remarks that the Asiatic mode of production is based on "direct ruler–ruled relationships," the translations blur this into: "direct relations of subjection."[57]

** The order was possibly determined by Engels' editing; the original manuscripts would have to be checked to determine this.

productive relations themselves, and therewith its specific polit-ical form likewise. It is always the direct relationship of the owners of the conditions of production to the direct producers—a relationship whose actual form always naturally corresponds to a definite stage of development in the ways and means of labor and hence its social productive power—which holds the innermost secret, the hidden foundation of the entire social structure and hence also of the political form of the sovereignty-dependency relationship, in short, of the specific form of the state in each case.[59]

These three sentences* present the most concentrated statement by Marx of his theory of the state in relation to his theory of social structure and change, pitched in terms applicable to all class societies without exception. If one had to select from Marx's writing a single statement which contains the main body of his theoretical work *in ovo,* this would be it.

---

* A fourth sentence completed the paragraph:

This does not gainsay the fact that, due to innumerable different empirical circumstances, natural conditions, relationships among races [tribes, &c.], outside historical influences, etc., the same economic basis—same in terms of the main conditions—can show endless variations and gradations in the phenomenon, which can be made out only by analysis of these empirically given circumstances.[60]

This was a caution to the coming generations of marxologists who were going to repeat endlessly that Marx reduced all history to unilinear, one-factor, rigidified uniformity. *"How long wilt thou speak these things? and how long shall the words of thy mouth be like a strong wind?"* said Bildad the Shuhite in an Eastern land.

23 | RUSSIAN CZARISM: STATE AND BUREAUCRACY

It is now possible to take up Marx's views on the nature of the Russian czarist political superstructure, and, finally, come to a statement of his general theory of the state.

The case of the Russian state has already been mentioned in connection with Oriental despotism. What exactly was the connection? By its nature the connection was not exact at all. To Marx as to everyone else, Russia was the "semi" country: semi-Asiatic, semi-Occidental, semi-civilized, semi-Byzantine, semi-Mongolian. While every country has an admixture of influences, Russia was an extreme case for obvious historical reasons; and moreover the problem of what was, or was becoming, its dominant line of development changed even while Marx and Engels were considering it during their lifetime. The challenge was to disentangle the separate interacting factors, evaluate their relationship to each other at any given time, and estimate their direction and rate of change.

There are, of course, a number of questions clustering about Russian history, but for present purposes we are interested in Marx's views on the nature of the state power.

1. THE ASIATIC SIDE

The economic forms that the Russian state encompassed were as conglomerate as the historical influences on the country. A letter by Engels to a Russian socialist in 1885 sums up an important aspect:

There [in Russia] where the situation is so strained, where the revolutionary elements have accumulated to such a degree, where the economic conditions of the enormous mass of the people become daily more impossible, where every stage of social development is represented, from the primitive commune to modern large-scale industry and high finance, and where all these contradictions are violently held in check by an unexampled despotism, a despotism which is becoming more and more unbearable to a youth in whom the dignity and intelligence of the nation are united—there, when 1789 has once been launched, 1793 will not be long in following.[1]

We want to focus not on the nature of the coming Russian revolution which is adumbrated here and elsewhere in Marx and Engels* but on the peculiarity of this society "where every stage of social development is represented": a living museum of precapitalist economic forms alongside the latest capitalist formations—the "combined" aspect of the Russian development. The two extreme ends of this spectrum, mentioned by Engels, represented different features: on one side, the still primitive peasant village community (*obshchina, mir*); on the other, the modern industrial works in the big cities. In between there were the surviving feudal forms represented by the privileges of the aristocracy, though serfdom had been formally abolished in 1861.

In this potpourri, *who ruled?* What class wielded the state power? This now-standard question assumes that *a* class wielded the state power: an assumption without a shadow of justification within the framework of Marx's conceptions. In any case, this is not how the Russian reality looked to Marx. While the state was tied to the interests of the socioeconomic infrastructure as always, it was not acting as the tool of any one of the classes of civil society. As we have seen in the case of Western Bonapartism, this means we are dealing with a state characterized by a high degree of autonomy.

The Asiatic component of this "semi" country was represented socially by the village-community economy in which the bulk of the peasantry still lived. When Marx found evidence in Maurer that the

---

* Marx's and Engels' views on the coming Russian revolution are reserved for another volume. In the above passage, 1789 stands for the bourgeois-democratic revolution; 1793 was the high point in the domination of the French Revolution by the plebeian left wing, pushing beyond the bourgeois boundaries of the revolution.

Russian village commune (which the Narodniks, or Populists, vaunted as a Russian originality) had arisen in Asia and elsewhere in Europe, he commented that "the very last vestige of a title to originality disappears for the Russians. . . . What remains true of them is that they are still to this day stuck fast in forms that their neighbors cast off long ago."[2] Later that year, Marx specified further:

> The whole thing [the Russian community], *down to the smallest detail,* is absolutely identical with *the primitive Germanic community.* What must be added in the case of the Russians (and this is also found in a section *of the Indian community,* not just in the Punjab but in the South) is (1) the *nondemocratic* but *patriarchal* character of the commune executive, and (2) the *collective responsibility* for taxes to the state, etc. It follows from the second point that the more industrious a Russian peasant is, the more he is exploited on behalf of the state, not only for taxes but for supplying produce, horses, etc. during the continual troop movements, for government couriers, etc. The whole pile of crap is in process of collapse.[3]

In another connection we have also seen some of Engels' references to the link between the Russian community and Oriental despotism.[4]

This provides the economic underpinning of Marx's (and others') view of Russia's Asiatic heritage: the village-community economy represents "the economic groundwork of Asiatic production" in Russia.* In another place Marx linked the institutions of "common property of the Russian peasants" to their "Asiatic barbarism," the same Asiatic barbarism being also regarded as a general characteristic of the Russian power vis-à-vis Europe. Indeed, Marx and Engels were free with characterizations of the Russian power as Asiatic, "semi-Asiatic in her condition, manners, traditions, and institutions"; "semi-Eastern" (whereas China was "completely eastern"), a "Byzantine offspring" in religion and civilization, Mongolian-Tartar especially in the aristocracy.[6]

In short, the "Oriental despotism" aspect of the Russian complex referred to the symbiotic relationship between the disconnected "localized microcosms" of the old village communities in which the peasantry lived, on the one hand, and the autocratically centralized despotism on top, on the other.

---

* This remark in *Capital*[5] refers to the impact of Russian commerce, and no doubt refers not only to "Asiatic production" in Russia itself but also to the "neighboring Asiatic market" (so in Engels' appended footnote).

2. THE REVOLUTION FROM ABOVE

But this Asiatic side represented the past, which still weighed on Russia's development. The European side, or the side which looked to Europe, depended on the economic modernization of the country in order to maintain it as a power among the other great powers.

On this side the Russian state resembled the absolute monarchies of the West rather than the Oriental despotisms. In Chapter 19 we saw that the absolute monarchies, no matter how great their initial feudal sympathies, were compelled to encourage the development of capitalist commerce and industry, that is to stimulate the growth of the new class that was to destroy them. This was easy to understand in England and France *before* the first bourgeois revolutions, when the feudal power simply regarded the bourgeois as moneybags to be exploited or cows to be pastured for milking. But even in the nineteenth century, when Europe was already part bourgeois and part prebourgeois, the old regimes were not scared off this course by the suspicion they might be digging their own graves. On the contrary, the remaining absolutisms intensified efforts to *bourgeoisify their own social orders* while still holding tightly onto the reins of state power. They accepted social bourgeoisification (development of capitalist industry, and so on) as necessary and inevitable, and set out to carry out this revolutionization of society under the auspices of the absolutist state power precisely in order to avoid seeing it carried out under a bourgeois state power; that is, in order to avoid a revolution from below. This was what Marx called the revolution from above, which was characteristic of the Bismarck regime.

> ... then came the new period [wrote Engels], ushered in by Germany, a period of revolutions from the top ... Russia took part in this general movement.[7]

Russia was under even greater strains than Germany; for Russian society was very obsolete, the state was very autocratic (autonomous), the aristocracy was very dinosaurian, the liberal bourgeoisie was very spineless, and the peasantry was very resentful and restive. The dislocation between state and civil society was the greatest in Europe. It meant: a social order *in extremis*, and a state power autonomized *ad extremum*.

This course worked itself out under various pressures. As Marx wrote in a somewhat different connection, "Russia exists in a modern historical milieu; it is contemporaneous with a superior culture; it is tied to a world market in which capitalist production predominates."[8] The form in which this economic imperative manifested itself most imperiously was, as often, the problem of military might, with war as the court of judgment. Not only were the Russian nobles paupers (in their own eyes) as compared with the Western capitalist nabobs; not only did they habitually speak French instead of Russian as their link to a higher culture; but Russia was sliding down to a third-rate power, as the Crimean War showed. Five years after the Treaty of Paris came the "emancipation" of the Russian serfs as a step toward modernization. As Engels wrote to a Russian correspondent in 1892:

°°From the moment warfare became a branch of the *grande industrie* (ironclad ships, rifled artillery, quickfiring and repeating cannons, repeating rifles, steel covered bullets, smokeless powder, etc.), *la grande industrie*, without which all these things cannot be made, became a political necessity.

A political necessity: that is, the economic modernization of the country was required by the *state*'s interests. Engels' letter continued:

All these things cannot be had without a highly developed metal manufacture. And that manufacture cannot be had without a corresponding development in all other branches of manufacture, especially textile.

I quite agree with you in fixing the beginning of the new industrial era of your country about 1861. It was the hopeless struggle of a nation, with primitive forms of production, against nations with modern production, which characterised the American [Civil] War. The Russian people understood this perfectly; hence their transition to modern forms, a transition rendered irrevocable by the emancipation act of 1861. . . .

Another thing is certain: if Russia required after the Crimean War a *grande industrie* of her own, she could have it in one form only: the *capitalistic form.*[9]

The low level of culture in general meant that Russia, like Austria, "lacks the numerically large educated class that alone can supply a sufficient number of competent officers for so large an army," hence the Russian mishaps in the 1878 war with Turkey.[10] During the fighting with Turkey, Engels explained to Marx why neither side could carry on a modern war:

> The immobility of the Turks lies essentially in the lack of supplies organization. It seems impossible for any barbarians and semi-barbarians to make an army fit not merely for fighting but also for free mobility; their army, organized by dint of great exertions to approximate a modern one (for fighting), has to carry out movements by means of the °appliances° of an old-time barbarian army. Modern weapons are introduced, but the ammunition for them is left to take care of itself. Brigades, divisions, and army corps are organized and massed in accordance with the rules of modern strategy but they forget that they are then unable to forage for their own upkeep like a horde of Janissaries, Spahis, or nomads. This is already visible with the Russians, still more with the Turks. . . .[11]

Result? In an encyclopedia article, "Infantry," Engels compared the Russian situation with the bureaucratization of the Byzantine army. In Byzantium

> °°The hierarchic and administrative organization of the troops was perfected to an almost ideal state of bureaucracy, but with the result that we now see in Russia: a perfect organization of embezzlement and fraud at the expense of the state, with armies costing enormous sums and existing in part only on paper.[12]

The Russian state power undertook a "social revolution"—the revolution from above. So Engels summarized it, from the perspective of 1890:

> °°The internal development of Russia since 1856, furthered by the Government itself, has done its work. The social revolution has made giant strides; Russia is daily becoming more and more Occidentalised; modern manufactures, steam, railways, the transformation of all payments in kind into money payments, and with this the crumbling of the old foundations of society, are developing with ever accelerated speed. But in the same degree is also evolving the incompatibility of despotic Tsardom with the new society in course of formation. . . . The Revolution that in

1848 halted on the Polish frontier, is now knocking at the door of Russia. . . .[13]

Russia, Engels argued, could not have "held its own in the world" without industrialization. "A nation of 100 million that play an important part in the history of the world could not, under the present economic and industrial conditions, continue in the state in which Russia was up to the Crimean War." The "domestic patriarchal industry" would have been smashed by the West's cheap goods, and Russia would have wound up like "India, a country economically subject to the great Central Workshop, England," that is, with a semicolonial status.[14]

3. THE STATE BREEDS A CAPITALIST CLASS

Looking back in 1894 over the changes in Russia in the past two decades, Engels again insisted that, after the Crimean defeats of the old czarist despotism, "there was only one way out: the swiftest possible changeover to capitalist industry." But one change had to lead to another in an inexorable chain. The vast expanses of the empire

> had to be spanned by a network of strategic railways. But railways implied a capitalist industry and a revolutionizing of the primitive agriculture. On the one hand, agricultural produce even from the remotest part of the country come into direct contact with the world market; on the other, an extensive network of railways cannot be built and run without a domestic industry supplying rails, locomotives, railway cars, etc. But it is impossible to create *one* branch of large-scale industry without also introducing the whole system; the relatively modern textile industry . . . was given a fresh impetus. The construction of railways and factories was followed by the enlargement of the existing banks and the establishment of new ones; the emancipation of the peasants from serfdom led to freedom of movement, and it was only to be expected that this would naturally be followed by the emancipation of a sizable part of these peasants from landownership as well. In this way, all the foundations of the capitalist mode of production were laid in Russia in a short time.[15]

This precipitate growth of modern industry in Russia "has been brought about only through artificial means, protective tariffs, state subsidies, etc."[16] To be sure, industrialization had been furthered by state policy and action in Western Europe too.* But Russia's case, as seen by Marx and Engels, showed a qualitative difference. The English and French monarchies acted largely under the pressure of an objective economic impulsion (the rise of money, for example) and an expanding bourgeoisie; but by the time this wave of the future hit Russia, the relationship had to be reversed. The Russian state, under the impress of the socioeconomic forces that gripped the modern world to which it was tied, set out to *create* in Russia the modern economy which it lacked, hence also the class and the bourgeois conditions which alone could produce this result.

°°The [Crimean] war had proved [wrote Engels in 1890] that Russia needed railways, steam engines, modern industry, even on purely military grounds. And thus the government set about breeding a Russian capitalist class.

In "breeding a Russian capitalist class," the state bred another class too, continued Engels:

But such a class cannot exist without a proletariat, a class of wage-workers, and in order to procure the elements for this, the so-called emancipation of the peasants had to be taken in hand; his personal freedom the peasant paid for by the transference of the better part of his landed property to the nobility. What of it was left to him was too much for dying, too little for living. While the Russian peasant Obshtchina [village community] was attacked thus at the very root, the new development of the bourgeoisie was artificially forced as in a hot-house, by means of railway concessions, protective duties, and other privileges; and thus a complete social revolution was initiated in town and country. . . .[18]

* Even to furthering the creation of classes, for example in the creation of the class of free laborers by freeing them of all property. Marx's *Grundrisse* notebooks put it:

It has been historically established that they [the free laborers] first tried the latter alternative [begging, vagabondage, and robbery], but were driven off this road, onto the strait and narrow path leading to the labor market, by means of gallows, pillory, and whip—from which [it follows] therefore that the *governments*, for instance Henry VII, VIII, etc., figure as conditions for the existence of capital.[17]

Marx had written before this about a case of the deliberate *creation* of social classes by a political power: by the British in India.* With regard to Russia, he too had used the image of the czarist state's hothouse-forcing the growth of capitalism:

> At the expense of the peasants the state has hothouse-forced the growth of branches of the Western capitalist system which are best fit to facilitate and stimulate the robbery of agricultural products through unproductive intermediaries. . . . It has thus collaborated in the enrichment of a new capitalist vermin sucking the blood of the already debilitated "rural commune." [21]

Marx saw the big industries as "placed under governmental tutelage." [22] "A certain kind of capitalism, nourished at the expense of the peasants through the intermediary of the state, has been erected vis-à-vis the commune." [23]

4. THE ROLE OF THE
CZARIST BUREAUCRACY

There is an interesting passage in which Engels discusses possible class alternatives before Russia at the crossroads following the Crimean War. What actually happened, he had explained, was the changeover to capitalist production and the chopping down of the Russian village community.

> To lament over this now is useless. Had the czarist despotism been replaced after the Crimean War by the direct rule of nobles

---

* Marx wrote that Campbell was right, from the English standpoint, in his assertion that "it is necessary to create a fresh class" in India, an intermediate privileged class. [19] In fact, the British did call into being a new class of pseudo-landowners in the shape of the "zemindars," replacing "the original class of zemindars," and the new class "have introduced a variety of the zemindari tenure called *patni*"—who "have created in their turn a class of 'hereditary' middlemen called *patnidars*, who created again their subpatnidars, etc., so that a perfect scale of hierarchy of middlemen has sprung up. . . ." Again: "From the Indian natives, reluctantly and sparingly educated at Calcutta, under English superintendence, a fresh class is springing up, endowed with the requirements for government and imbued with European science." [20] Obviously Marx was not as finicky in using the appellation *class* as his epigones.

and bureaucrats, the process [of the commune's destruction] would perhaps have been somewhat slowed down; had the budding bourgeoisie come to the helm, it would certainly have been accelerated still more. The way things were, there was no other choice. With the Second Empire in France and the most dazzling upswing of capitalist industry in England, Russia could not really be expected to plunge into state-socialist experiments from above on the basis of the peasant commune.* Something had to happen. What was possible under the circumstances did happen, as is always and everywhere true in countries of commodity production, for the most part only half consciously, or quite mechanically without knowing what one was doing.[24]

There was no other choice? Certainly each of the classes named had its own choice. It was the autonomized state that decided. But who exactly made the decision?

In this connection, there is special interest in the casual reference to "the direct rule of nobles *and bureaucrats*" as one of the alternatives proposed (even if unrealistically). This course being counterposed to the maintenance of the despotism, it means that the bureaucracy and the state were not always synonymous in terms of political reality.** In fact, there was (and is) a tendency in political literature to speak of the bureaucracy as an independent reality *only* insofar as it escapes from complete subordination to the sovereign. As long as it remains an inert tool of the central Unity, it does not impose itself on observers as a social force and does not provoke separate identification.

In the Russian case, the talk about a parliament of nobles and bureaucrats meant, in the second member, a decisive sector of the bureaucracy; it did not imply that the czar would be left with only his valet. But after all, such splits are inevitable in the case of any social stratum. What is important is that the despotism (the central state power around the czar, therefore including a sector of the bureaucracy) pushed in one direction while an important sector of the bureaucracy pressed in another. The latter acted as an independent class element.

---

* For such state-socialist experiments, compare this with Engels on state-socialism in Java under the Dutch, above, p. 559f.

** An earlier glimpse of this reality played a key role in the estimate of the state by Custine, discussed in Special Note E. The next sentence above applies to Custine particularly.

As in the classic case of France under Richelieu, the creation of the czarist bureaucracy had begun as part of the necessity for freeing the central state power from the pressure of the landed aristocracy. The emancipation of 1861 was another step in this direction: "First of all," said Marx, "the emancipation of the serfs had emancipated the supreme government from the obstacles the nobles were in a position to place in opposition to its centralized action."[25] This pattern—balancing the peasants against the nobility in order to free the hand of the central state—went back at least to Ivan the Terrible and the sixteenth century: "While enraged against the boyars and also against the rabble in Moscow, he sought, and had to seek, to present himself as *representative* of the *peasants' interests*," wrote Marx.[26] More positively, the bureaucracy was the indispensable instrument of the czarist state for the execution of the long revolution from above. So wrote Marx:

> °°If the Muscovite Czars . . . were obliged to *tartarize* Muscovy, Peter the Great, who resolved upon working through the agency of the west, was obliged to *civilize* Russia. In grasping upon the Baltic provinces, he seized at once the tools necessary for this process. They afforded him not only the diplomatists and the generals, the brains with which to execute his system of political and military action on the west, they yielded him, at the same time, a crop of bureaucrats, schoolmasters, and drill-sergeants, who were to drill Russians into that varnish of civilization that adapts them to the technical appliances of the Western peoples, without imbuing them with their ideas.[27]

Diplomatists, generals, bureaucrats, schoolmasters, drill-sergeants—all of these elements belong to the state bureaucracy in reality, though the word *bureaucrats* appears as only one item.

These are the human components of the state machine, which, when they act as one, seem to merge into one visage. This was the bureaucratic army—civil and military, for the military is included in the bureaucracy—of the long revolution of the czarist despotism. In the first place, as mentioned, it was an army mobilized against the landed nobility, to subordinate them to the central state power; that is, to shear them of power to control it. In the second place, it was an army of taskmasters to modernize the leading elements of the population, including the brood of bourgeois in the aforementioned hothouse. The state's need of the bourgeoisie gave the latter a hold on the former's economic policy, just as the bourgeoisie's fear of change from below kept it under the state's tutelage.*

This bureaucracy, acting out not a conjunctural but a long-term historical role, could not seriously be regarded as the instrument of any of the extant classes of civil society.

Now what is the Russian system of government, wherever it is not mixed up with feudal institutions, but a military occupation, in which the civil and judicial hierarchy are organized in a military manner, and where the people have to pay for the whole?[29]

This was an attempt by Engels, even before the Crimean War and the emancipation of the serfs, to find a label for "the Russian autocratic system, accompanied with its concomitant corruption, half-military bureaucracy, and pasha-like exertion."[30] When talk of the coming emancipation arose in Russia as it staggered under the Crimean War, Engels noted that the country was stirring, but

°°Still, with the existing political state of the country, no other system of administration was possible than the exclusive and exaggerated bureaucratic system which existed. To lay a foundation for a better system, Alexander II. had to recur to the idea of emancipating the serfs. He had two formidable opponents to contend with, the nobility and the very bureaucracy which he intended to reform against its own will, and which at the same time was to serve as the instrument of his designs.[31]

In effect, this pointed to a contest inside the bureaucratic system.** In any case, it assumes the most extreme condition of autonomization on the part of the state.

In 1875 Engels published an essay we have had occasion to cite more than once: a polemic against the views of a Populist-Jacobin-confusionist named Tkachov, who maintained that the Russian state

---

* As Engels put it:

In all important economic questions, the state must comply with its [the bourgeoisie's] wishes. If meanwhile the bourgeoisie still puts up with the despotic autocracy of the czar and his officials, it does so only because this autocracy, which in any case is mitigated by the corruption of the bureaucracy, offers it more guarantees than do changes—even bourgeois-liberal ones—whose consequences for Russia's internal situation no one can foresee.[28]

** This passage continues with the discussion of countervailing social forces in Russia quoted in Chapter 12, p. 278f.

was an "imaginary power," a state "hanging in the air, so to speak, one that has nothing in common with the existing social order," and which "does not embody the interests of any particular estate [*Stand*]."[32] The kernel of rationality in this we have already seen; but Engels has little difficulty showing how the interests of the various classes (he uses *Stand* and *Klasse* interchangeably) are the material bases on which the state rests, instead of hanging in the air. After listing the interests of the noble landowners, the peasantry, the usurers and traders, he winds up with the big bourgeois elements, and finally asks:

> . . . have all these important and rapidly growing elements of the population no interest in the existence of the Russian state? To say nothing of the countless army of officials, which swarms over Russia and plunders it and here constitutes a real social estate [*Stand*].[33]

The term *a real Stand* would ordinarily be translated *a real class,* not only in 1875 but even today for the most part. In using *Stand* here instead of *Klasse,* Engels is merely echoing the text of Tkachov's statement, which he is engaged in refuting. Insofar as there was formerly a historical distinction, it has no present bearing on the case. True, it runs into the consideration previously explained in the case of *caste.*[34] But the sterile question of terminological refinement is unimportant compared to the plain reality of the special social role played by the czarist bureaucracy, as seen by Marx as by Engels. For it is here—in Russia, says Engels, not in bourgeois Western Europe—that the bureaucracy constitutes a real class-like formation.

5. THE GENERAL THEORY OF THE STATE

Let us now put the question *Who ruled?* in the following form: What class was it that pushed through the long "social revolution" in Russia? The state was the executive or managing committee of what class as it set about breeding a bourgeoisie and bourgeois industry as in a hothouse? Certainly not of the bourgeoisie that first had to be bred up; not of the aristocracy which fought it every step, tooth and nail; not of the peasantry which was being ruined in the process. That does not leave very many classes as candidates for the post.

It is in this connection that Engels presented the basic formularization of the socioeconomic foundation of the state structure. It is expressed in terms broad enough to include the normal class interpretation of the normal state; that is, it underlies the class formula. Like the latter, it is put in terms of executors. Writing specifically of the complex role of the Russian state absolutism, Engels stated:

> °°All governments, be they ever so absolute, are *en dernier lieu* [in the last analysis] but the executors of the economic necessities of the national situation. They may do this in various ways, good, bad and indifferent; they may accelerate or retard the economic development and its political and juridical consequences, but in the long run they must follow it.[35]

This, Engels continued, was why the industrial revolution in Russia was unavoidable.

This was no new thought for Engels, even in this aphoristic form. He had met the same problem in a similar way, if from another direction, in 1875. In the essay against Tkachov, as mentioned, Engels showed how the interests of the various classes are the material bases on which the state stands, instead of hanging in the air. But he does not turn the Tkachov fantasy over on its other side by trying to prove that this Russian state is simply the instrument of *a* particular class. The conclusion he comes to is put as follows:

> Not only the Russian state in general but even its specific form, the czarist despotism, instead of hanging in the air, is the necessary and logical product of the Russian social conditions with which, according to Mr. Tkachov, it has "nothing in common"![36]

This is a formula for the nature of the state which cuts behind—or deeper than—the normal class formula.*

The relation between these two formulas can now be understood to state the full content of Marx's theory of the state:

Under normal conditions—conditions of relative stability in society— the necessary product of the social conditions is the accession of *a*

---

* At this point it would be useful to look back to Chapter 20, where the same conception is arrived at from another direction, the nature of the Bismarckian state. Compare Engels' conclusion that "In reality however the state as it exists in Germany is likewise the necessary product of the social basis out of which it has developed."[37] Also related is the passage by Marx on the "innermost secret" of the state (p. 571f).

particular class to the unshared domination of the state power. But this
can hardly be the product in a period when a societal transition is still
unresolved. It cannot be the product when classes are still struggling for
dominion in an undecided contest; in such a flux the state's class
content will reflect the state of the war. Nor can it be the necessary
product in a situation such as Russia's, driven into the maelstrom of
social revolution from above, where no class of civil society was capable
of acting as "executors of the economic necessities of the national
situation."

In this Russian case, what was needed was a class whose own
interests impelled it to act as the instrument to save the real interests of
all the social strata that had a stake in the ongoing society, to save them
*by saving the society itself from the collapse which was the only
alternative to the social transformation.* This is what defines "the
economic necessities of the national situation," not in terms of the
interests of any single class, but in terms of the class constellation as a
whole.

The only social power that could perform this function was the state
apparatus. In this way the state acts as the *Gesamteinheit*—the overall
Unity—not simply of "society" in the abstract, but of all class elements
whose real interests rest on the maintenance of social exploitation in
one form or another.

And the maintenance of social exploitation in one form or another,
in the midst of the Russian transmogrification, had a very concrete
meaning, capable of being figured in rubles. In general, we here meet a
phenomenon that was also important in Western Europe in the eventual
bourgeoisification of the feudal aristocracy itself, insofar as the latter
reconciled itself to the inevitability of change instead of inviting a 1789
type of revolutionary convulsion. Both the old and the new ruling
class—the landowning nobles and the bourgeois—were equally property-
owning, exploitive classes. The revolution from above was a shift from
one mode of extracting surplus labor to another. *This was also the
reason why a revolution from above was possible.* The old ruling class in
crisis learns that, at any rate, this sort of revolution offers them some
very comforting mitigations of the indignity forced upon them:
namely, continued economic privileges to one degree or another. (We
had occasion to make this point in Chapter 14 regarding the Bismarckian development.)[38]

But this consolation prize depends on channeling the inescapable revolution into a form that maintains social exploitation in one form or another. It is not usually just one of the contending classes themselves that can undertake the organization of this redistribution of power; as we have pointed out elsewhere, it is difficult for one sector of the capitalist class, for example, to referee the internecine struggles of competing capitalists to make sure that the system is not shaken apart by the melee. In the Russian case, it is the state that acted as the executor for the interests of class society as a whole. Autonomous from any particular class of civil society, it could embody what the contenders had in common: the need to ensure the conditions under which to continue the extraction of surplus labor from the mass of people.

This spells out the class content of Engels' formulation of the theory of the state: the state, "necessary and logical product of the [given] social conditions," is always in the last analysis "the executor of the economic necessities of the national situation." Thus it is always the organizer of society in the interests of the class (exploitive) structure taken as a whole.

This is the general theory of the state in Marx and Engels.

Within its framework lies the special theory of the state which applies to normal times and conditions in roughly the same way as Euclidean geometry applies to normal space. It is the view of the state as the managing committee of a ruling class with which we started in Chapter 11.

Normality here is a function of the process of change. The more rapid the change—the more revolutionary the times, the more history is caught in the flux of becoming—the more does the special theory begin to warp away from a close match with reality, and the more does the general theory of the state become applicable in order to explain the pattern of political power in the process of social transformation.

APPENDICES

MARX AND THE
ECONOMIC-JEW STEREOTYPE

There is a bulky output of literature alleging that Marx's essay "On the Jewish Question" is anti-Semitic because it equates Jewry with the spirit of money-making, the merchant-huckster, preoccupation with self-interest and egoism—that is, with the .commercialism of the new bourgeois order. The charge has been furthered in various ways, including forgery: one honest critic renamed the essay "A World Without Jews" as if this were Marx's title.[1] Few discussions of the essay explain clearly its political purpose and content in connection with the Jewish emancipation question, or even accurately present the views of its target, Bauer. Mainly, the allegation is supported by reading the attitudes of the second half of the twentieth century back into the language of the 1840s. More than that, it is supported only if the whole course of German and European anti-Jewish sentiment is whitewashed, so as to make Marx's essay stand out as a black spot. This note will take up only the 1843 essay and its background.

The general method was memorably illustrated in C. B. Kelland's 1936 novel *Mr. Deeds Goes to Town,* which some may know as a Gary Cooper film. In an attempt to have a hearing declare Mr. Deeds of unsound mind, two little old ladies are brought in from his home town to testify. It's well known, one explains, that he is pixillated—balmy in the head. The honest woman's evidence seems damning. But the case blows up later when she is asked one more question: "Who else in your town is pixillated?" She answers: "Why, *everybody!*"

As soon as the question is raised, it is not difficult or even controversial to show that virtually the entire population of Germany (and the rest of Europe, too) was pixillated—that is, habitually used and accepted the words *Jew* and *Jewry* in the manner of Marx's essay whether they were favorable to the Jews' cause or not, whether they were anti-Semitic or not, whether they were Jews or not. In this they were only following the very old, if now discredited, practice of using national and ethnic names as epithets, usually derogatory, for people showing a trait supposedly characteristic of the nation or ethnic group. This practice, which began to be suppressed in self-consciously polite society only a few decades ago, was as common in English as in any other language, and some of it still hangs on. Consider a few: *wild Indian* (active child), *apache* (Paris criminal), *Hottentot* (as in *Hottentot morality*), *street arab, gypsy, bohemian, Cossack, blackamoor, Turk;* or, as an adjective: *Dutch courage, Mexican general, French leave*. Another of this group, for centuries, has been *Jew*.

1. THE PATTERN IN GERMANY

Marx's essay represents a very attenuated form of the general pattern, for most commonly *Jew* was a synonym for *usurer,* whereas by this time mere money-making was eminently respectable.[2] Bauer's writing assumed that *Jew* meant usurer—quite in passing, for he was not interested in the economic Jew but in the "Sabbath Jew."[3] The same economic stereotype of the Jew can be found in Arnold Ruge,[4] who remained a liberal and never became a communist, as well as in Max Stirner,[5] whose book *The Ego and Its Own* heralded anarchism. These names already cover the spectrum of the Young Hegelian milieu, whose philosophic mentor Feuerbach provided the immediate example for this language about the role of Jewry.[6]

A special case, near if not in the Young Hegelian tendency, was Moses Hess: conscientiously Jewish himself, Hess had been brought up in an orthodox household and later became the progenitor of Zionism. It is well known that the language of Marx's Part II of "On the Jewish Question" followed the view of the Jews' role given in an essay "On the Money System" just written by none other than Hess, and just read by Marx.[7]

Hess's thesis was that present-day society was a "huckster world," a "social animal-world," in which people become fully developed "egoists," beasts of prey and bloodsuckers. "The *Jews,*" wrote the father of Zionism, "who in the natural history of the social animal-world had the *world-historic* mission of developing the *beast of prey* out of humanity have now finally completed *their mission's work.*" It was in the "Judeo-Christian huckster world" that "the mystery of the *blood of*

more verbiage, going back to the "blood-cult" of ancient Judaism as the prototype of modern society, and on to a condemnation of priests as the "hyenas of the social animal-world" who are as bad as the other animal-people by virtue of their "common quality as beasts of prey, as bloodsuckers, as Jews, as financial wolves."[8] Earlier in 1843 Hess had published an important article on "The Philosophy of Action," which only incidentally remarked that "The Christian God is an imitation of the Jewish Moloch-Jehovah, to whom the first-born were sacrificed to 'propitiate' him, and whom the *juste-milieu* age of Jewry bought off with money. . . ."[9] Hess intended no special anti-Jewish animus in any of this stuff, compared to which Marx's approach is complimentary and drily economic. Note that Judaism is criticized as part of the Judeo-Christian complex, and not in order to praise Christianity—this being the same pattern as Voltaire's; although Hess saw no contradiction between his own continued Jewish faith and loyalties and his opinion, expounded in his writings, that Christianity was the more advanced, modern and "pure" religion—all in the Feuerbachian groove.[10]

It is relevant to add that much of the economic-Jew stereotype had at this time gained general *Jewish* acceptance, at least as applied to rich Jews: so one can learn from the best German historian of anti-Semitism, Eleonore Sterling.[11]

If we move outside Young Hegelian circles, we may note that two other famous Jews of the period are no exception to the rule: Lassalle[12] and Heine. Heine is especially interesting, as always. His article on the Damascus affair of 1840—one of the famous frameups of Jews on the "blood" accusation—is full of bitter indignation against the French Jews for lack of concern over their victimized brethren abroad. "Among the French Jews, as with other Frenchmen," wrote Heine (in France), "gold is the god of the time, and industry is the prevailing religion." Baron Rothschild and the noted Jewish plutocrat Fould are called "two distinguished rabbis of finance." Heine says caustically, "I do not believe that Israel ever gave money, save when its teeth were drawn by force. . . . There are, of course, now and then examples that vanity can open the obdurate pockets of Jews, but then their liberality is more repulsive than their meanness."[13] (At this point the American translator was moved to apologize for Heine's language, for by this time, 1891, the modern racist type of anti-Semitism was over a decade old; in 1840 it had no such significance or motivation.) An excellent study by William Rose gives the context of Heine's aphorism that "The Jews were the Germans of the Orient, and now the Protestants in the Germanic countries . . . are nothing else than old-oriental Jews."[14] Rose naturally makes clear Heine's polyvalence about Jewry (*ambivalence* would be too weak).

As for other products of the Hegelian school, farther right, D. F. Strauss[15] was *more* virulently anti-Jewish than those mentioned; and the famous Hegelian scholar Eduard Gans, whose lectures Marx attended at the university, was another Jewish case in point. Indeed, Gans's case can be considered a symbol. When Marx came to the University of Berlin in 1836, Gans (in jurisprudence) was the big Hegelian influence on the faculty. Seventeen years before, Gans had helped Leopold Zunz found the first society for Jewish studies in the world, of which he became president. The project bogged down because the rich Jews whom they had counted on refused to dip into their pockets. Zunz cried that Jewry was beyond reform, "the prey of barbarians, fools, moneylenders, and *parnasim,"* (synogogue moneymen), "slaves of mere self-interest . . . a pap of praying, bank notes, and charity." But he plugged on. President Gans reported: "The only link which unites the Jews is fear; the only interest for which they are willing to part with some of their worldly goods is charity"—whereupon he went through the baptism route from the *cheder* to the *Katheder.* But even earlier, in the society's journal, Gans had had no inhibition against remarking that "Jewish life" reflected a "double aristocracy whose component parts . . . are . . . money and rabbis."[16]

Hegel himself had written along the same lines mainly in early works, that is, before his Prussian conservatization.[17] This was no paradox. It was the conservative right that usually expressed antipathy to Jewry in religious and racialist terms; it was the left-of-center that put the spotlight on the *economic* role of Jewry, the economic Jews; and both stereotypes flourished among peasants and other poor victims of the system. Fichte, another source of philosophic radicalism, deserved the name of systematic anti-Semite more than any so far mentioned.[18]

If we move to anti-Establishment dissent to the right of the Young Hegelians and their circle, we find that the Young Germany movement, through the pens of its leader Karl Gutzkow and prominent literary light Heinrich Laube, wrote no differently about the Jews, and at some length.[19]

2. THE UNIVERSALITY OF PIXILLATION

In the 1840s both sides, for and against political emancipation, held the economic image of the Jew as common ground. The strong bourgeois-liberal movement pressing for Jewish rights was quite vocal in arguing that civil emancipation was necessary in order to solve the Jewish question by dissolving Jewry as a recognizable entity into the general pool of Germanness and thus eventually eliminating it. Hess himself had presented this viewpoint in his most successful book, in 1841.[20] Says Gustav Mayer of the pro-Jewish liberals: "Only through full and equal rights, they believed, would it be possible to wean away the Prussian Jews from their un-German customs and from their one-sided preference for petty trade."[21]

Glickson, in the course of an indignant harangue against Marx, lets slip the following statement: "It is a well-known fact that the contemporary masters of philosophy and literature, with the single exception of Lessing, had no sympathy for Jews or Judaism. The greatest of them taught that the Jews were foreign and different, and drew definite political conclusions from these teachings. Goethe, the great world-citizen, strongly opposed the liberation of the Jews; he saw in them heretics who deny 'the source of our high culture.' "[22] Goethe had worse and stupider things to say about the Jews than this, including of course the commercial stereotype.[23] Lessing, the alleged "single exception," had been dead for sixty-two years and was hardly a contemporary; we will come back to this mythical exception. (*Why, everybody's pixillated!*)

Silberner, who writes as a prosecuting attorney, eventually makes the following remark: "The most various writers could indeed have reinforced Marx's prejudice against the Jews. Many representatives of German classical literature and philosophy were not precisely fond of the Jews, and since he read much of them, they could have contributed to his Judeophobia."[24] Silberner does not mention any who *were* "fond of the Jews," including Jews. All of German history exists, for him, only as an influence on Marx. This bizarre approach is due to the understandable reluctance, shown by him and similar writers, to inform the modern reader that so many great men either disliked the Jews or thought of them in terms of the economic stereotype, for fear of reinforcing contemporary anti-Semitic currents by giving them respectable sanction. It is only Marx who is to be accused of being pixillated.

As Roman Rosdolsky said of this modus operandi, "In this manner one could very easily assign to the camp of anti-Semitism three-quarters of the thinkers, writers, and politicians of the past."[25] If we consider only left-of-center circles, the proportion would be closer to 100 percent, since it is on the left, rather than on the right, that the *economic* structure and role of Jewry was the main operative factor.

All this was not only true of Germany. In France and England the economic stereotype of the Jew and its expression in leftish circles was similar; we are not dealing with a phenomenon of the German soul. France was worse.

An essay by Z. Szajkowski is illuminating on the subject of France. It reports at the end that it is impossible to find *any* "sympathetic reference to the Jews in the French socialist literature, from Saint-Simon to the date of Drumont's first appearance [1886]." For the most part, what this involved was the stereotyped identification of Jews with money values and economic exploitation. More virulent attitudes existed among the Fourierists especially. The tradition of dislike for Jewish economic activities goes back in France not simply to Voltaire but to the history of Jewry in the later Middle Ages and the Enlightenment.[26]

In France, indeed, one first finds a new note: here Jew-hatred took a proto-Nazi form in the express desire of Proudhon (father of anarchist "libertarianism") for the physical extermination of all Jews. Bakunin, the other father of anarchism, was almost as virulently anti-Semitic in the modern sense as Proudhon.[27] But in this period, this proto-Nazi anti-Semitism is found only among these anarchist liberty-shouters, as far as I know.

England was by no means as bad as France. But routine equation of the economic Jew with money-bags, financial overlords, commercial exploitation, and the rest, cropped up in the Chartist press, including the best of the left Chartists,[28] in the manner of Marx's essay. To take another part of the political spectrum: Macaulay can be viewed as an English example of the liberal *supporter* of Jewish civil emancipation who expressed as much aversion to Jewish economic activities as many an opponent.[29] The jibes at the economic Jew stereotype are not at all peculiar to socialist writings: they are found wherever there is expression of antagonism to the bourgeois or financial world. The reactionary antibourgeois critic Thomas Carlyle was not only virulently anti-Jewish but also opposed the granting of greater legal rights to the Jews.[30]

But it would be a complete misunderstanding of the economic-Jew stereotype if it is identified with an *anti*-Jewish context only. Leaving aside the advocates of Jewish emancipation who used language similar to Marx's essay just as automatically as its opponents, it is instructive to look at the first *Jewish* socialist movement which began stirring in the latter 1870s.

This is three decades later than the period of Marx's essay; the whole basis of awareness of the Jewish question has been transformed by the rise of a systematically racist anti-Semitic movement for the first time; we are dealing with Jewish-conscious socialists reacting to a *real* anti-Semitic threat; and by this time there is something of a Jewish proletariat in existence. Everything is different; but still, consider the terms of the first socialist manifesto issued to Jewry, by Aaron Lieberman, the historic pioneer of this movement. His *Call to the Jewish Youth* reverberated with the tones of Isaiah (as in Isaiah 2:7–9, for example). It said: "Emancipate yourselves from the power-lust that lies at the bottom of your privileges. Stop praying to gold and might." Lieberman blames the Jewish bankers and merchants for the plight of his people:

> We have had to pay for your sins! The race hatred, the religious hatred, with all their terrors have fallen mostly upon us [the poor Jews]. You kindled the fire that devours us. We have you to thank for it that the name Israel has become a curse. The entire Jewish people, suffering and astray, must suffer more than all other peoples because of your greed. It is your fault that we have been exposed to calumny. International speculators, who have dragged our name through the mud, you do not belong to us![31]

The power of the traditional stereotype is recognized here precisely by the justified fervor of the plea to repudiate it, to emphasize the class struggle *within* Jewry in order to exorcize it. There is a historical background to this.

3. ROOTS OF THE ECONOMIC JEW

We have assumed up to now that the reader has a general conception of the economic history behind the stereotype—at any rate, how Jews were forced into a lopsided economic structure by Christendom's prohibition on their entrance into agriculture, guild occupations, and professions. Three myths about the economic Jew are easy to refute but not germane here; they are: (1) that Jews *controlled* finance or any part of economic life; (2) that *all* Jews were rich; and (3) that it was the Jews that created, or invented, capitalism. After these myths are disposed of, however, the real historical basis of the economic Jew can be broached. Something else was involved beyond these exaggerations, and may be summarized as follows:

1. The important role that the (upper stratum of) Jews did play in the development of postfeudal society, especially considering the tiny proportion of the population they constituted.

2. The great tilt in the economic structure of Jewry toward middleman and financial occupations, including the bulk of *poor* Jews in huckstering occupations, for example, peddlers, petty merchants.

3. The relatively high visibility of the Jews' economic role—as, for example, when Junkers employed Jews as loan collectors and mortgage foreclosers, thus gaining the profits while the Jews gained the onus as "bloodsuckers."

In 1843 little was known, even to those aware of the question, about the economic or sociohistorical development of the Jewish people. The very concept of a *Wissenschaft des Judentums* (Jewish studies) had arisen only in the first quarter of the nineteenth century. Today there is a considerable literature on the question,[32] but it is ahistorical to predate its acquisition. A portion of that history which is important background for our present subject is well summarized in Sterling's *Judenhass,* which deals precisely with Germany in the years 1815–1850:

> The enlightened officials recognized, already in the middle of the eighteenth century, the useful and progressive function of the Jews in the development of commerce and industry, which tended to transform the still seminatural-economy state into a modern money- and credit-economy state. The princes summoned Jews to their courts in order to carry out the financing of their provinces independently of the Estates, in order to obtain moneys for raising and maintaining their armies, and to make possible the operation of new businesses. In this way was formed a small rich and politically privileged upper stratum within the Jewish population. Jewish court agents, bankers, and army contractors assumed an important position in finance, in commerce and in the industry of the mercantilist-oriented states. When the economic upswing set in after the Napoleonic war, many Christians as well as Jews found themselves in an advantageous position because they had large amounts of liquid capital at their disposal. Still their number must have been slight. . . .
>
> In the course of time arose a new but also not numerous group of Jews who became well-to-do through the new economic development. Unhindered by old traditions and guild regulations, they quickly adopted the methods of the modern English credit

system and stock speculation. They understood how to turn out large quantities of goods produced in the new factories for the market, got in position to give state loans, and participated in railroad construction and built factories.

In that way the real security of the Jews essentially depended on their usefulness to others and on the good will of the governments; all their enterprises, indeed their very existence, remained always in jeopardy. They therefore attempted with great energy to compensate with economic power for the legal and social security they lacked. In this way the Jewish financiers who had grown rich in the new capitalist order, in which money was all-powerful, achieved a "privileged" position. . . .

In the sections where capitalist commerce and industry had already made important progress even without Jews, the Christian population by no means felt that the success of the Jewish upper stratum was a handicap for themselves. Thus, already in 1817 the *Gewerbepolizei* in Aachen said that Jewish business in the Prussian Rhineland could no longer be considered "usury" but a synonym for free trade and the profit system.[33]

Such favorable attitudes were not taken, however, by merchants' corporative guilds and the patrician order in the smaller German states and backward areas, not to speak of the peasantry and artisanry.

It is clear why the spearhead of the Jewish emancipation drive, the petition campaign,

> came mostly from the big-bourgeois circles of the cities in which industrial development was already far advanced and in which the Jews of the bourgeois upper stratum already played an integrating function in the economy. It was Christian and Jewish great merchants, factory owners, bankers, and insurance directors who drafted the petitions and submitted them with numerous signatures.[34]

This was the nature of the emancipation campaign which Marx supported and Bauer attacked.

But it would be a mistake to believe that the economic-Jew stereotype among the population was merely a reflection of this upper stratum, of the Rothschilds and Foulds. Many or most of the *poor* Jews also functioned as middlemen—peddlers, hawkers, hand-to-mouth traders and merchants, petty money-lenders—in very direct contact with the poor Christian population, caught in the classic pattern of having to squeeze those below as they were squeezed from above. Jews were associated with "financial exploitation" on levels far below Rothschild: "Recent happenings in the Rhineland and Alsace," relates

Solomon Bloom, "strengthened this popular suspicion; Jewish money-lenders broke up properties of landlords and farmers at the end of the eighteenth and the beginning of the nineteenth century. The Western radical community was not unaffected by the resulting animosities." Gustav Mayer says, of anyone brought up in the young Marx's place and time: " 'The Jews' to him meant mainly the Jewish cattle dealers in the Rhineland, those who bought from, and sold to the small peasants, taking advantage of their own superior business abilities."[35]

For our present purposes it is not necessary to settle the controversy over just how important the Jews were in the rise of capitalism. The identification of Jewry with commercialism, which was everybody's pixillation in the 1840s, was elaborated in great detail as late as 1911 by Werner Sombart's *The Jews and Modern Capitalism;* and after all the nonsense in that erudite opus is discounted, there is more than enough left to explain the mind of a generation that existed before economic history had even been invented.

4. EX POST FACTO ANTI-SEMITISM

After the rise of Hitlerism, it became *de rigueur* to play down the Jews' significance for capitalism, since the Nazis used it for their own purposes.[36] But eminent Jewish historians have proudly lauded their role. In his introduction to Ruppin's *The Jews in the Modern World*, for example, Professor L. B. Namier, writing militantly as a Zionist Jew and a true-blue Englishman, boasted: "Two races [*sic*] headed the movement [of progress in the capitalist system] though under vastly different conditions—the British and the Jews; they were the pioneers of capitalism, and its first, and perhaps chief, beneficiaries." For others, that picture was considered to hold only until about the middle of the nineteenth century, which thoroughly covers Marx's essay.[37]

A. Léon has argued, against Sombart and others, that Jewry played such a role in *pre*capitalist society:

> Judaism was an indispensable factor in precapitalist society. It was a fundamental organism within it. That is what explains the two-thousand year existence of Judaism in the Diaspora. The Jew was as characteristic a personage in feudal society as the lord and the serf. It was no accident that a foreign element played the role of "capital" in feudal society. . . . The "capital" of precapitalist society existed outside of its economic system.[38]

But, continues Léon's thesis, the rise of capitalism to dominance in the social system went hand in hand with the *decline* of Jewry in this function. Thereupon the Jews were pushed more and more into the interstices of the system, especially in a capacity as distribution middlemen and as usurers dealing more with the poor than with kings, as formerly. "In the measure that usury became the principal occupation of Jews, they entered increasingly into relations with the popular masses, and these relations worsened all the time." The peasant who lost his land or stock, or the artisan who lost his tools, to the Jewish money-lender, was incapable of seeing the upper-bourgeois Christians behind the usurer; hatreds were let loose on the highly visible intermediaries.[39] Léon's term for Jewry, the *people-class*, is an attempt to give scientific form to the social basis of what we have been calling the economic-Jew stereotype.*

Léon aimed at a Marxist analysis; but we can turn to a leading theoretician of Socialist Zionism for confirmation, from an entirely different angle, of the effective universality of the old equation for which Marx's essay gets denounced. Hayim Greenberg, writing in 1942, was disturbed about the use made by Nazi anti-Semitism of the *facts* of the Jews' economic role. He denies "the old charge that Jews are parasites in the world's economic order" by arguing that the economic role which Jewry was forced into was in fact useful, honorable, and nothing to apologize for. He concludes that "There is nothing wicked in being a middleman, but it is not sound for a whole people to consist of middlemen." What Greenberg is trying to say is that it is no more wicked to be a Jewish middleman than a Christian one. All of which was true, of course, as Marx had demonstrated in his own way by transforming the issue from the *contrast* of Jews to Christians into the *economic equivalence* of Jews and Christians. In the course of this defense, however, Greenberg testifies to the universality of pixillation— in queasy terms which, it must be remembered, are being written by a Zionist champion a hundred years after Marx's essay and over a decade after the rise of Nazism:

> Jews also have been considerably influenced by the notion that
> they constitute an unproductive, or even a destructive force, in
> the world's economy. We speak of Jews as essentially a people of

* Léon's term *people-class*, which marks the conjuncture of an ethnic group with a collective economic role, is similar to Marx's repeated references to the "merchant-peoples" (or trading peoples, *Handelsvölker*) of antiquity and the Middle Ages. Among these he mentioned the Phoenicians, Carthaginians, Lombards, and Normans, as well as the Jews, all of them operating in the "interstices" or "pores" of a society not itself based on commerce.[40]

... individuals whose occupations are unsubstantial, who are exploiters, speculators and traffickers in the labor of others.

Signs of this self-condemnation first appear in the literature of our "enlightenment." Jews who felt spiritually emancipated from the civilization of the ghetto even before they were emancipated from its legal disabilities, developed a great admiration for European culture and were in no small degree affected by its anti-Jewish prejudices. Certainly they shared the European's disdain for the Jew as a trader.

By 1942 all this had become anti-Semitic by ex post facto determination; but note that Greenberg was not so ignorant or hypocritical as to pretend that he had Marx in mind:

The views of many Jewish socialists in regard to the economic role of the Jews have also been tinged by a certain anti-Semitic bias. . . .

Non-Jewish socialists, and not necessarily Marxian socialists, have tended to look down on the Jew in the world's economy.

He cites the Russian Narodnaya Volya, the peasant-oriented populist-terrorist movement of the late nineteenth century, which was even known to encourage peasant pogroms as one activity in their struggle. The Populists, he explains, held "the idea that the Jew was essentially a 'bloodsucker,' " and adds: "This also explains Tolstoy's rather unfriendly attitude towards the Jews, an attitude most eloquently expressed by his repeated failure to speak up on behalf of the persecuted Jews." There goes another pixillated "libertarian." But Greenberg goes further: to the Zionist socialists themselves *and* their left wing:

Nor is Zionism free from its share of responsibility. There was a time when it used to be the fashion for Zionist speakers (including the writer) to declare from the platform that "to be a good Zionist one must first be somewhat of an anti-Semite."[41]

Greenberg states that this attitude can be found in Pinsker, Syrkin, Borochov, A. D. Gordon, and others—all of them the leaders and founders of the Labor Zionist movement. "To this day," he adds, "Labor Zionist circles are under the influence of the idea that the Return to Zion involves a process of purification from our economic uncleanness."[42] It should be added that the movement's social-democratic theoretician, Ber Borochov, based his whole theory of Socialist Zionism on a class analysis of the Jewish people along the now-interdicted ("anti-Semitic") lines, and that his fundamental "Marxist" argument for Zionism was that it was the only road to changing the class composition of the Jews. The same goes for his successor as the theoretician of Socialist Zionism, Nachman Syrkin.[43]

It cannot be overemphasized that all of this, for which Greenberg beats his breast, was a matter of contrasting the economic Jew with the Christian world to the Jews' *discredit;* for this bolstered the Zionist aim of making the Jews "a people like other people." None of this sort of thing was in Marx's 1843 essay, which repudiated such a derogatory contrast by already *identifying* modern (bourgeois) Christendom with the commercial role of what Léon called the people-class.

While we have shown that this identification was in no way peculiar to Marx but was the common coin of the time—and it was precisely for this reason that Marx could turn it to account in order to make his political point—we must now go a little further along these lines. This identification was not merely generally accepted, but had been built into the language. McLellan goes so far as to put it this way:

> *Judentum,* the German word for Judaism, had the derivative meaning of "commerce," and it is this meaning which is upper-most in Marx's mind throughout the article. "Judaism" has very little religious, and still less racial, content for Marx and it would be little exaggeration to say that this latter part of Marx's review [Part II of "On the Jewish Question"] is an extended pun at Bauer's expense.[44]

This pun was not a jest but a play on words. Such word-play was indeed a favorite literary pattern of the young Marx, as it was of Hegel. In both it was not a humorous but an explicatory device: a means of developing, out of the different aspects of meaning packed into one word, various aspects of the reality which the word reflected.

Ruppin states that "in the Middle Ages the conceptions of Jew and trader became well-nigh synonymous." Gustav Mayer makes a similar statement: "to the average German, Judaism and capitalism came pretty close to being synonymous." Sterling quotes the economist Friedrich Harkort at the time, on the fact that behind the Jewish money-lenders and mortgage collectors stood the Junkers, who made the profit. These Junkers Harkort called "the Jews with boots and spurs" who constituted the real speculators and grasping creditors.[45] The synonymy of Jew and some form of commercialism was taken for granted not only by those who threw epithets at the Jews but equally by those who defended them.

With this background in mind, one can go back to Marx's "On the Jewish Question" to read it as it was written, not as it is refracted through the dark glass of contemporary ignorance and malice.

It was a contribution to a hotly fought campaign in favor of Jewish political emancipation—not however on behalf of the "Christian and Jewish great merchants, factory owners, bankers, and insurance directors who drafted the petitions," but to show how to link this current battle up with the eventual struggle *against* these very gentlemen. Its aim was to support political emancipation today in order to make possible social emancipation tomorrow. Hence its last words: "The *social* emancipation of the Jew is the *emancipation of society from Judaism.*"

These compact words do in fact sum up the entire burden of the argument: It is wrong to make the political emancipation of the Jew wait on his social emancipation (as Bauer wanted); for we are dealing with the economic Jew, and economic Judaism is now one with bourgeois society as a whole.

5. HOW TO MANUFACTURE ANTI-SEMITES

It should be clear now that there were two quite different issues involved in attitude toward the Jews, from the period of the Enlightenment to at least the 1870s (when anti-Semitism first became a racialist social and political movement and indeed the term itself was invented—by anti-Semites). One issue involved an opinion about *das Judentum** (like or dislike); the other, a position on the status of Jews in the state and society (abolition of civic, legal, political disabilities). As we have seen, a dim view of Jewry was well-nigh universal, in some not-always-clear sense and for varying reasons, but with clear roots in the nature of "economic Judaism." The division in public opinion occurred on the second issue, the question of political emancipation and equal rights.

As a result there is a curious system common among historians, not to speak of marxologists. Historical figures are made into "philo-

---

* This, in turn, divides into two subquestions: one's opinion of the religion (Judaism) or of the people. The first problem was consciousness of the distinction. Marx had distinguished between the two with unusual clarity in his letter of 13 March 1843 (see p. 111 fn), in which he mentioned his repugnance to the religion as against supporting the demand for Jewish emancipation. It must be recalled that at this point Judaism meant mainly the orthodox faith as it had emerged from the Middle Ages; Reform Judaism had just taken shape but would not have determined the public discussion. The rise of Reform Judaism was itself a symptom of the widespread repugnance felt by those modernized Jews who were not willing to be hypocritically orthodox à la Rothschild.

Semites" or "anti-Semites" at will by referring only to one or the other issue, with the same obtuse lack of distinction that was so characteristic of the people of that benighted era itself. A couple of examples will give a proper perspective on the treatment of Marx's essay.

We saw that Glickson (p. 595) had looked for a single exception among the contemporary masters to the general lack of sympathy for Jews, and had gone back to the previous century to turn one up: G. E. Lessing, whose poetic drama *Nathan the Wise* (1779) was the most renowned "philo-Semitic" production in Germany, perhaps in European history. This reputation is based on the sympathetic portrayal of Nathan as *Edeljude,* the noble Jew, good and wise. This reputation brought down on Lessing's head the vituperation of generations of anti-Semites—for example, Nazi-like ravings by E. Dühring in 1881.[46] Without derogating Lessing's contribution for its time, a closer look at the play produces a strange result if it is counterposed to Marx's essay.

1. Lessing's play does not raise the question of equal rights for Jews; to the contrary, it takes their inferior status for granted. For the setting is Saladin's Jerusalem, where both Jews and Christians exist on the sufferance of Saladin, who is portrayed as being just as noble as Nathan.

2. Lessing's chosen model, Nathan, is a rich Jewish merchant who has just returned from a debt-collecting trip, bringing back a fabulous wealth of goods. He is so rich that he is capable of playing the part of Rothschild to the sultan. In short, he is the worse of the two stereotypes of the economic Jew, not the poor-huckster model but the financial-plutocrat model. Lessing does not challenge the stereotype; he gilds it. He glorifies his rich Jew by painting him in pleasing colors.

3. Nathan is a Jew by birth but not by belief in Judaism, being in fact a Deist, like Lessing himself. He explains in a parable (which is the ideological centerpiece of the play and was its starting point in Lessing's mind) that the three religions are as like as identical rings; the only difference is that one happens to inherit one rather than the other. The repugnance the wise Nathan would feel for Jewish orthodoxy is left implicit but is unquestionable.

4. The point is repeatedly made that Nathan is an *exceptional* Jew. Repeatedly "Jew" is used generically to refer to the usual mean, miserly, money-mad Jew of the popular language. The noble Sittah twice wonders whether Nathan is a Jew like other Jews or whether he is good as reported; the noble Templar wonders whether Nathan has really unlearned "to be a Jew"; and the noble Nathan himself, wondering at one point what game the sultan is playing with him, soliloquizes, "Who here is really the Jew—he or I?" (To be sure, Lessing does not refer to "the dirty Jews"; instead, he refers just as routinely to "the

dirty Moors," the contemporaneous equivalent of "dirty niggers.")[47]

In short, the great "philo-Semitic" message of the play is the equivalent of "Some of my best friends are Jews," or even "You would hardly believe he's a Jew, my dear!" In fact, Lessing had written it down himself, in an early (1749) "philo-Semitic" comedy called "The Jews": "Truly there are Jews who aren't Jews at all."[48] Replying to a critic who urged that the noble-Jew figure was so great an improbability as to invalidate the play, Lessing vigorously agreed the case was rare, but argued that, since the Jews' unfortunate condition was due to their necessity for "living purely and simply from trade," it would cease with the cause, when the Jews no longer "maintain a wretched existence through base small trade." Hence, he explained, he chose a rich man as his figure.[49] Lessing's views revolved around the economic-Jew stereotype as completely as anyone's.

The single exception in a hundred years, Lessing, turns out to have used *Jude* as the same generic cuss-word as every other pixillated German and European. In contrast, Marx used *Judentum* as an impersonal historic-economic category, to make the point that Jewry and Christendom had been homogenized in our huckster society.

There is a second example, mentioned earlier: the case of "Voltaire's anti-Semitism," as reported by Peter Gay.[50] Voltaire's derogatory remarks about the Jews, including the inevitable economic stereotype, are exhibited. But we are told in addition that Voltaire's transgression is so much the less forgivable because the very same period held a live option for "philo-Semitism" which was taken by other men.

John Locke is cited as the philo-Semite, against Voltaire the anti-Semite. The evidence is Locke's *Letter on Toleration* (1689), where he indubitably comes out in favor of religious worship for Jews: "The Jews are permitted to have dwellings and private houses; why are they denied synogogues?" If Locke was also in favor of equal rights for Jews across the board, as Gay seems to imply, Locke neglected to say so in this essay. He goes so far as to state that "neither Pagan nor Mahometan nor Jew should be excluded from the commonwealth because of his religion."

Gay did not mention, however, that in this very same passage Locke makes clear that *he* considers Judaism to be "abominable."[51] This is said only in passing; but then the other statements are in passing too; for Locke's essay is a closely reasoned argumentation, not a discursive article, and the reference to the Jews is a hurried one. We know of no reason to believe that Locke had any greater liking than Voltaire for the practitioners of this "abominable" cult: he was arguing in the spirit of the civil-liberties lawyer who battles for equal rights even for known criminals.

But was not Voltaire also for religious toleration in the same sense? Yes, he was; and in fact in 1764 a French translation of Locke's essay was joined to Voltaire's treatise on toleration to make one book, with a preface (which Professor Klibansky believes was written by Voltaire himself) praising Locke's argument.[52]

We can now see how to create (or appoint) philo-Semites and anti-Semites at will. Granted that both Locke and Voltaire were for toleration of the Jewish religion, and that both disliked the Jews themselves, you quote Locke on the first and Voltaire on the second— *voilà!* The system is an infallible recipe.*

There is a further complication about the "anti-Semite" Voltaire, which Gay does set forth. It seems, argues Gay, that in these excursions Voltaire was interested in striking not so much at Judaism as at Christianity, for he wanted to reinforce his hostile view of Christianity by also discrediting the source (Judaism) from which this pernicious religion derived. Hence his "dislike of the Jews . . . was a partly unconscious, partly conscious cloak for his anti-Christian sentiments."[54] In fact, Voltaire was interested in attacking all religions from his Deist standpoint—just as, from the same Deist standpoint, Lessing wanted to represent all religions as equally meaningless as far as differences were concerned. Where Lessing portrayed the noble Jew, Moslem, and Christian with equable brush in a paroxysm of reconciliation, Voltaire painted all the devout as fools, knaves, and miscellaneous miscreants—also fairly impartially. In his century there was no reason to let the Jews off the hook; that makes him an "anti-Semite" in this century—for historians who project themselves back into history as undercover agents of the Anti-Defamation League.

Lastly: we mentioned earlier that the "Young Germany" movement (Gutzkow, Laube) has been cited for anti-Semitic treatment of Jewish figures—like everybody else. Gutzkow, for example, wrote a novel involving this sort of anti-Semitism. But when the young Engels, not yet nineteen, became enthusiastic about Young Germany's liberal and democratic tendency, the figure he admired most was Ludwig Börne.

* Gay does the same with Montesquieu, but with an open contradiction. He cites Montesquieu as his second example of philo-Semitism as against Voltaire, since Montesquieu deplored persecution of the Jews. But Gay also mentions, before closing the matter, that Montesquieu was so misguided as to note "the Jews' affinity for commerce and banking," and that he even wrote: "You ask me if there are Jews in France. Know that wherever there is money, there are Jews."[53] Everybody is pixillated.

Indeed his letters of this time to a boyhood friend are filled with encomiums on this German Jewish publicist.[55] In this young man's eyes, Young Germany stood not only for political freedom in general but in particular for Jewish emancipation—"Who can have anything against this?"* For him, the "distress of the Jews" is part of the liberal indictment of the status quo. He tells his friend about his literary hero: You call for a faithful Eckart? "See, there he is already, a small chap with a sharp Jewish profile—his name is Börne. . . ." He mentions the liberal poet Creizenach twice with warm praise, and both times prominently identifies Creizenach as a Jew. He brings up the "Wandering Jew" (in German, the "Eternal Jew") as one of the models for freedom of the spirit about which he dreams of writing a second *Faust*. He lists "the emancipation of the Israelites" as the first of three positive achievements of Napoleon.[57]

Is this young man a philo-Semite like Lessing? Yes, like Lessing: for, in this same correspondence with his friend, one also finds the routine use of the economic-Jew stereotype as a jibe, as also in later life. Quoted by itself, this would make him an anti-Semite—like all the other pixillated people.

The real issue of the time had nothing to do with the use of language about Judaism based on the universally accepted economic-Jew stereotype. The real Jewish question was: *For or against the political emancipation of the Jews? For or against equal rights for Jews?*

This was the Jewish question that Marx discussed, not the one that dominated the minds of a sick society a century later.

---

* See page 200 for two citations from Engels' letters of 1839 mentioning the Jewish emancipation issue. The emancipation of the Jews, as a political issue, continued to play the same role for Engels in later years.[56]

RHYME AND REASON:
THE CONTENT OF MARX'S
JUVENILE VERSE

Comments on the verse that Marx wrote in 1836–1837, when he was about 18 or 19, usually echo Franz Mehring's negative opinions.[1] This would seem a safe procedure, in view of Mehring's status as a Marxist, historian, and literary critic. Besides, there is the scornful view of his own poetic productions which Marx himself expressed by late 1837 and in later years.[2] Since Mehring, any serious independent evaluations of these poems can be counted on the fingers of one hand.[3]

This much remains uncontroversial: most of the poems are amatory effusions of a personal sort; the themes were common in recent German romantic poetry, going back at least a couple of decades; and esthetically speaking they are not notable as poetry. "However," Mehring added, "something that has no esthetic value can nevertheless have a biographical and psychological value."[4] This is our present concern: what features of interest do the poems show in the context of our discussion in Chapter 9?

Precisely on this point Mehring is of limited use as a guide, for a reason that is usually overlooked. The poems he discussed are not the ones that have been available to us. He saw the poetry notebooks of 1836, which were later lost; the poetry notebook of 1837, the only one extant until recently, had not been discovered when Mehring wrote. But the latter is substantially more interesting than the former with regard to the "biographical and psychological value" of the material.*

To begin with, there is no doubt that many of the poems breathe a spirit of passionate energy; but the trouble with making much of this

---

* Here is a summary of the facts about the various poetry notebooks. (1) *Poems of 1836:* in three notebooks, dedicated to Jenny von Westphalen (to whom Marx had become secretly engaged earlier that year) and given to her as a Christmas present; some poems may have been written before 1836. Two of the notebooks are titled *Buch der Liebe* (Book of Love); Part I, compiled in October–November, was dated "Berlin, 1836, end of autumn"; Part II, compiled in

fact is that it is just in this respect that they are most plainly echoes of romantic clichés. Byronic and Heinesque heroes with emotions that are tearing them apart had long been a drug on the market. This has never prevented young apprentices to poetry from feeling the old emotions anew, but the forms into which the passions are poured have to be seen in their contemporaneous context. Thus, if in a "Song to the Stars"[7] the young Marx denounces the tranquillity of his subject—

> But ah! you shine forever
> With calm ethereal rays;
> The gods will fill you never
> With burning brands that blaze—

one must recognize that the sentiment was in a rut, though it is illogical to conclude that it was insincere.

In this body of verse, the most often mentioned examples of tearing a passion to tatters are the two—the only two—that Marx published, four years later, under the joint title "Wild Songs."[8] The very first products of Marx's pen to see print, they are as good examples as any of this genre. The first is "The Minstrel":

November, was dated "November 1836." The third notebook, titled *Buch der Lieder* (Book of Songs), was compiled in November–December and dated simply "1836." This set of notebooks had disappeared by 1925 when D. Ryazanov of the Marx-Engels Institute searched for them, and were not published in *MEGA*. A handful of stanzas had been quoted in print—for example, by Mehring and in John Spargo's *Karl Marx* of 1910. But in 1954 and 1960 members of the Longuet family turned them over to the Moscow institute. Their reappearance was mentioned in a note in *MEW*, which however published only one of the newly recovered poems; others appeared in translation in the new English edition of the *Collected Works.*[5] (2) *Poems of 1836:* a single notebook which Marx compiled for his father's sixtieth birthday in April 1837. Although previously known from Marx's description in his letter to his father of 10 November 1837, it was discovered through Ryazanov's efforts, and is the only notebook reprinted in *MEGA.*[6] Postscript: As this volume is prepared for the press, the first volume of the new *Marx-Engels Gesamtausgabe* has just appeared with the full contents of the above-listed notebooks, plus more early poems by Marx from two notebooks compiled by his sister Sophie.

"Minstrel, Minstrel, how savage you sound!
Minstrel, why look so wildly around?
     What inner storm is so heart-rending?
     Look, your very bow is bending!"

—"You ask me why? Why does Ocean roar?
To shatter waves on its rocky shore,
     Till eyes go blind and hearts rebel,
     And the soul goes roaring down to hell!"

—"Minstrel, though scorn tears at your heart,
A shining God sent the healer, Art,
     To draw you on high to rhythms entrancing
     Till you mount the sky where stars are dancing!"

—"What's that! I'll thrust, beyond control,
This blood-black saber into your soul;*
     God knows not of Art, and less does he care;
     Art rises as fumes from the Devil's own lair,

Till it addles the brain and transmutes the heart:
I got it from Old Nick himself, this Art.
     'Tis he beats the time, he tells me how
     I must play the dead-march wildly now,

Must play a-darkling, must play a-glow,
Till the heart is broken by strings and bow."

The Minstrel's viol is singing;
His light-brown hair out-flinging
     He wears a saber at his side,
     His pleated cloak is flaring wide.

The companion poem, entitled "Love in the Night,"[10] is somewhat darker:

          His arms round her strain,
          His eyes dark and stormy:
          —"Love, hot burns your pain,
          You, you tremble before me.

---

* At this point there is an additional couplet in Marx's original (notebook) version of the poem; it was omitted on publication in 1841. This couplet continues the threat: "Get out with you, get out of my sight, / Or children will play o'er your head tonight!" The other lines move down accordingly, till the next-to-last stanza is filled out to a quatrain like the rest. There were some other small changes.[9]

"You drank of my soul,
From me took fire!
Blaze out, aureole,
Young blood, blaze higher!"

—"Sweet, whitely you stare,
Speak so strangely, my love;
Look, singing up there
High the worlds spin above!"

—"High, darling, high!
Burn, stars, O burn!
Up! up to the sky
Let our souls flash in turn!"

His voice low and frightening,
Despair in his sighs,
His glances dart lightning,
Burn a void in his eyes.

—"It was poison you drank,
We must go—come away!
Night's host, rank on rank,
Comes to banish the day."

His arms round her strain,
Death stands at the door;
And stabs of deep pain
Close her eyes evermore.

Perhaps the maximum that can be read into these juvenile effusions, this side of common sense, has been set down by W. M. Johnston in connection with "The Minstrel." He sees it as an "expression of the artist's isolation"; the artist is "a victim of alienation"; he "knows no restraint in his calling."

Indeed, at first glance it may seem that here Marx is expressing a whole series of romantic commonplaces. The artist as a man in league with the powers of darkness, the musician as the supreme artist, the power of music to intoxicate the soul, the scorn of the artist for the restraints of the social order—these themes are familiar in Germany from Wackenroder, Tieck, and Novalis in the 1790's on down to Platen, Lenau, and Heine in the 1830's. Marx, however, voices these sentiments with a fury that suggests rebellion of a starker sort than mere poetic *Weltschmerz.*

Why is this "of a starker sort"? Because this artist carries a saber and threatens to commit mayhem. This effort to endow the becloaked minstrel with originality assumes that Heine and the others always expressed "mere poetic *Weltschmerz*" rather than fury with the way of the world: an assumption which is simply not true. But why must the poetical sentiments be established as original before they can be taken to reflect Marx's temperament? Johnston also writes:

> While it may be going too far to say that this minstrel is an incipient revolutionary, it is plain that his estrangement from society is total. He lives uniquely for his art, as a dedicated revolutionary lives uniquely for his cause. In temperament, Marx's minstrel is a born despiser of the social order. It is not far-fetched to say that out of this minstrel a revolutionary is waiting to be born. And even if we ignore Marx's post-1846 vocation as a revolutionary, his portrait of the artist as the alienated individual *par excellence* suggests that his own sense of alienation may have deepened enormously during 1836 and 1837.[11]

Maybe. The trouble with this kind of case is that too many adolescents and youths of idealistic temperament have gone through stages of rebellion and estrangement without becoming revolutionaries; the revolutionary that waits to be born is aborted by the despised society. Plainly Marx's case went deeper than anything visible in the juvenile verse.

Obviously more self-revealing was the poem which Mehring selected for quoting from the notebook that was later lost.[12]

> I ne'er can treat with calm dispassion
> What grips my soul the mightiest,
> Ne'er repose in easeful fashion—
> On I dash, without a rest.

> *   *   *

> I would compass all, attaining
> Every boon the gods impart:
> Dare to crave all knowledge, straining
> To embrace all song and art.

> *   *   *

> So let's dare all things to seek out,
> Never resting, never through,
> Not so dead as not to speak out,
> Not to want, and not to do.

Only never, meekly standing,
Bear a yoke in fear and pain;
For the yearning, the demanding,
And the deed—all these remain.

There are quite a number of poems in the 1837 notebook that deal directly with ideas, though none is overtly political.* Some reflect the youth's idealistic indignation against sordidly materialistic attitudes. Among a group directed at the medical profession, perhaps best is one entitled "To Physicians." [14]

You philistine physicians, cursèd pack,
To you the world's a bone-heap in a sack.
If once you've cooled the blood with hydrogen,
And felt the pulse begin to throb, why then
You think: "I've done what can be done for these:
Now one can live in tolerable ease;
The Lord God is a clever one, I see,
To be so well-versed in anatomy;
And every flower is useful, it is true,
When once it's made into an herbal brew."

The same spirit is evident in several of the "epigrams," taking the side of the high-minded, loftily spiritual, and idealistic against the mundane. Goethe and Schiller are taken as representing the former. There is a philosophical quartet of "epigrams" entitled "Hegel," which reflects Marx's first antagonistic reaction to that thinker. In the following example, the third of the quartet, [15] it must be understood that the "I" refers to Hegel, and the whole thing was intended as a needle-thrust against him:

* There is a possible exception in the prose piece, *Scorpion und Felix,* subtitled a Humorous Novel, of which Marx included some chapters in the 1837 notebook. Its style is something like *Tristram Shandy* but written with more deliberate incoherence. Chapter 27, the whole of which follows, [13] can be interpreted as a cry of political confusion. Or perhaps not. I quote it with fingers crossed:

"Ignorance, boundless ignorance."
"Because (referring to a previous chapter) his knees bent too much to one particular side!" but there is nothing definite, and who can define or fathom which side is right and which is left?
Tell me, mortal, where the wind comes from, or whether God's face has a nose, and I will tell you what right and left are.
Nothing but relative concepts are they, in order for folly and madness to drink themselves into wisdom!
Oh, vain is all our striving, illusory our yearning, until we fathom what right and left are, for the goats will be put on the left but the sheep on the right.
Turning around, he takes a different direction, since he dreamed at

> Kant and Fichte like to roam the ethereal blue,
>   Where they sought a distant shore;
> But I seek only to grasp through and through
>   What I found—right outside my door!

A year later, this sarcastic jab was going to 'change from derogatory to honorific, as Marx found that Hegel's concern with the real world (which is mundane by definition) was his strong side as compared with previous idealist philosophy. Indeed, the same reversal would affect Schiller later: Marx used "Schillerizing," counterposed to "Shakespearizing," to connote abstraction-mongering in literature.[16]

But in other "epigrams" of the 1837 notebook, Schiller and Goethe were put on a pedestal. In the following two examples,[17] the assumed speaker is a despised critic of the Olympians:

V

> This is the trouble with Schiller, I'd say:
> He can't entertain in a human-like way;
>   He drives things so far they take off and soar,
>   But won't put his hand to a workaday chore.
> He's good at the thunder-and-lightning bit,
> But entirely lacks plain everyday wit.

VI

> There's Goethe now, too precious a man:
>   He'd rather view Venus than Raggedy Ann;
> Right stoutly he'd grasp things from below,
> Yet if soaring on high one is forced to go,
>   Don't make the form too sublime, on the whole:
>
>   It leaves no footing for the soul.
> Now Schiller was right to a greater extent:
> With him the ideas were evident,
>   You could say they were down in black-and-white,
>   Even if you didn't quite grasp them aright.

---

night that the goats are to the right and the pious to the left in accordance with our wretched views.

Therefore settle for me what right and left are, and the whole riddle of creation is solved, *Acheronta movebo* . . . if Mephistopheles appeared, I would become Faust, for it is clear, everyone of us, everyone is a Faust, in that we know not which side is right, which side is left, our life is therefore a circus, we run around and search for the sides, till we fall on the sand and the gladiator, namely Life, slays us, we must have a new Redeemer, for—tormenting thought, you rob me of slumber, you rob me of health, you destroy my life—we cannot distinguish the left side from the right, we do not know where they lie——

There is a group of "epigrams" under the collective title "Pust-kuchen," defending Goethe and Schiller against the Lutheran pastor of that name who became notorious when he attacked Goethe as the "most typical representative of the licentious and depraved tendencies in modern literature" and published a moralizing parody of *Wilhelm Meister.* Here are three of the Pustkuchen "epigrams."[18]

1

Schiller, he thinks, might have been all right
Had he only read more in the Bible at night;
His poem "The Bell" would be fine if a section
Were added to expound the Resurrection,
    Or how on his little ass
    Christ rode into town, alas.
And his "Wallenstein" needs additional scenes
On how David defeated the Philistines.

2

For the ladies Goethe is pure Hades,
A horror above all to old ladies;
All he has grasped is nature's totality
But hasn't polished it up with morality.
    Let him study Luther's book a bit
    And manufacture verses out of *it.*
On beauty, indeed, he'd sometimes call
But forget to say, "God made it all."

7

On the wings of sin this Faust would soar;
He lived for himself and nothing more.
    He doubted in God, in the world no less,
    Forgot Moses thought it a smashing success.
And Maggie that goose, she loved him instead
Of stuffing the fear of the Lord in his head
    By reminding him he was the Fiend's own prey
    As he soon would find out on Judgment Day.

"How David defeated the Philistines" is indeed the keynote. The sensitive youth sees the "apathetic throng" and the dead weight of philistinedom flattening all public life, and reacts with scorn. The first and third of the "epigrams"[19] express this most clearly:

I

In snug armchairs, dull and dumb,
The German public all keep mum.
What if the storms rage nimbus-shrouded,
What if the sky grows dark and clouded,
   What if the lightnings writhe and hiss—
   They are not stirred by things like this.
But when the sun comes out of hiding,
The breezes rustle, the storm's subsiding,
   Then forth they come and crow at last,
   And write a book: "The danger is past."
They spin out fancies, fabrications,
Would trace the thing to its foundations,
   Claim the correct way wasn't pressed,
   It just was heaven's peculiar jest,
Life needs a more systematic model—
First rub your feet and *then* your noddle—
   They act like children, babble on,
   Chase after things long dead and gone—
Meanwhile, let them only seize the day,
Let earth and heaven go their own way,
   Things would go on as they did before
   And the wave roll calmly along the shore.

III

If the Germans had ever got under way,
The people would surely have won the day;
   And when it all was over, indeed,
   On every wall here's what you would read:
"Marvels have happened! Will wonders ne'er cease?
All men will soon have three legs apiece."
   Thereupon everybody would fidget and fret
   And begin to be covered with shame and regret:
"Too much all at once has happened, we vow—
Let's all become quiet as mice for now;
   That sort of thing belongs in a book—
   And it won't lack for buyers, the way things look."

If Johnston saw the "incipient revolutionary" in the alienated artist-figure, D. Ryazanov pointed to the last-cited epigrams as "the germinal form of rebellion":

It is against philistinism that the idealist concentrates the whole bitterness of his scorn and the sharpness of his ridicule. But it is not a question of the traditional antithesis between the gay life of students kicking over the traces and the orderly, comfortable everyday life of the good burgher: *this* "Sturm und Drang" period Marx had already gone through in Bonn [the university]. He appears here, rather, as a youth filled with philosophical and political aspirations that come into contradiction with the insipid realism and inertia of the "public." . . . This protest against the intellectual domination of the philistine is, however, nothing but the germinal form of rebellion against the dominant state of things in society.[20]

There are many kinds of germs, and from this undifferentiated form one does not always know what the germ will grow up to be. What we have at this point is a leaning in character and temperament.

| # THE STATE AS POLITICAL SUPERSTRUCTURE: MARX ON MAZZINI

In 1858 Marx's attention was focused on what he thought were the last gasps of the Bonaparte regime in France. The political temperature had heated up with the attempt by the Italian nationalist Felice Orsini to assassinate the emperor on January 14, in protest against the French designs on Italy. In brief, Bonaparte wanted to "liberate" Italy from Austrian domination in order to impose French control. In Italy, Cavour was playing the cat-and-mouse game of alliance with France, aiming to use Bonaparte's imperial ambitions for the purposes of the House of Savoy, without being swallowed up by the French "liberator." In this situation the émigré leader of the republican wing of the Risorgimento, Giuseppe Mazzini, called on the "people" to forge Italian national unity against both Cavour and the foreigners.

Mazzini took the Orsini attentat as an occasion for issuing an open letter denouncing Bonaparte.[1] Now in general Mazzini represented about everything Marx detested in the self-styled radical: he was as bitterly antisocialist as he was antidemocratic; a much admired rhetorician who substituted empty moralizing abstractions for political ideas; a bourgeois nationalist who sought a following among the working classes with social elocution rather than a social program; a conspiratorialist who preferred plots to mass organization. Six years after this episode, it was going to be a knot of Mazzinians in London, headed by Mazzini's secretary Luigi Wolf, who presented one of the first obstacles to putting the International on its feet.

But Mazzini's open letter to Bonaparte impressed Marx as striking a new note, in its awareness of the relationship of socioeconomic development to political problems in general, and in its attention in particular to the interests of working people. In consequence Marx wrote an article for the *New York Tribune* on the Mazzini letter which greeted it with pleasure and quoted from it extensively and approvingly.

The longest Mazzini passage quoted indicted the Bonaparte regime in terms of the economic conditions of the peasantry and working class as well as of the "dissatisfied bourgeoisie." It is also made clear that Mazzini was pronouncing the doom of the Second Empire: "The fullness of time approaches; the Imperial tide is visibly rolling back," he wrote. ". . . From this moment, your fate is sealed. You may now live months; years you cannot."

Written on March 30, 1858, Marx's piece was published on May 11 under the title "Mazzini and Napoleon," as a leading article (editorial), hence unsigned. We reproduce the first part of the article, up to the point where Marx starts quoting and summarizing the content of the Mazzini letter.

So much for the context. Its interest for us here lies in its remarks on the relation between the political superstructure and the "economic realities."

MAZZINI AND NAPOLEON

M. Mazzini has recently addressed a letter to the French Emperor, which, in a literary point of view, must hold, perhaps, the first place among his productions. There are but few traces left of that false sublimity, puffy grandeur, verbosity and prophetic mysticism so characteristic of many of his writings, and almost forming the distinctive features of that school of Italian literature of which he is the founder. An enlargement of views is also perceptible. He has, till now, figured as the chief of the Republican formalists of Europe. Exclusively bent on the political forms of the State, they have had no eye for the organization of society on which the political superstructure rests. Boasting of a false idealism, they have considered it beneath their dignity to become acquainted with economical realities. Nothing is easier than to be an idealist on behalf of other people. A surfeited man may easily sneer at the materialism of hungry people asking for vulgar bread instead of sublime ideas. The Triumvirs of the Roman Republic of 1848*, leaving the peasants of the Campagna in a state of slavery more exasperating than that of their ancestors of the times of imperial Rome, were quite welcome to descant on the degraded state of the rural mind.

All real progress in the writing of modern history has been effected by descending from the political surface into the depths of social life. Dureau de Lamalle,[2] in tracing the different phases

* On March 29, 1849 (not 1848), upon the Italian defeat at Novara and the abdication of the king, the nationalist forces in Rome set up a triumvirate to keep order; Mazzini was one of the three triumvirs.

of the development of landed property in ancient Rome, has afforded a key to the destinies of that world-conquering city, beside which Montesquieu's considerations[3] on its greatness and decline appear almost like a schoolboy's declamation. The venerable Lelewel[4], by his laborious research into the economical circumstances which transformed the Polish peasant from a free man into a serf, has done more to shed light on the subjugation of his country than the whole host of writers whose stock in trade is simple denunciation of Russia. M. Mazzini, too, does not now disdain to dwell on social realities, the interests of the different classes, the exports and imports, the prices of necessaries, houserent, and other such vulgar things, being struck, perhaps, by the great if not fatal shock given to the second Empire, not by the manifestoes of Democratic Committees, but by the commercial convulsion which started from New York to encompass the world. It is only to be hoped that he will not stop at this point, but, unbiased by a false pride, will proceed to reform his whole political catechism by the light of economical science.

The hope that Marx expressed in this article was not to be fulfilled. In September of the same year, Marx devoted another *Tribune* article to Mazzini, "Mazzini's New Manifesto."[5] Most of the article is given over to a translation of his "historical document enabling the reader to judge for himself of the vitality and the propects of that part of the revolutionary emigration marshaled under the banner of the Roman triumvir." Marx limits himself to a brief comment:

Instead of inquiring into the social agencies on which the Revolution of 1848–1849 foundered, and of trying to delineate the real conditions that, during the last ten years, have silently grown up and combined to prepare a new and more powerful movement, Mazzini, relapsing, as it appears to us, into his antiquated crotchets, puts to himself an imaginary problem which, of course, cannot but lead to a delusive solution.

The "imaginary problem" is why the *émigrés* have failed "at renovating the world"; Mazzini "busies himself with advertising nostrums for the cure of their political palsy." The long excerpts from the manifesto show Mazzini appealing for "action" regardless of views, with the People "writing upon its banner the signal: God, People, Justice, Truth, Virtue."

Still, the following year Marx had occasion to write another *Tribune* article complimentary to Mazzini, for by that time the expected war had broken out, with France ostensibly allied with Piedmont against Austria. Marx's article on "Mazzini's Manifesto" welcomed the republican leader's position of intransigent opposition to Bonaparte's schemes.[6]

THE "STATE PARASITE" AND THE "CAPITALIST VERMIN"

A number of different theories of the state have been assigned to Marx posthumously, since it is easier to deal with a Marxian theory if one has first invented it oneself. One of these is "the 'independent parasite' theory" of the state, fabricated by an ingenious marxologist by putting together two words to form a phrase which Marx never used and which makes no sense in his framework.[1] It is done with rare economy, by quoting a sentence from *The Eighteenth Brumaire* without wasting words on analysis.

While none of Marx's passing mentions of *state parasite* constitutes a theory, there is a certain interest in examining the train of thought behind its use.

1. IN *THE EIGHTEENTH BRUMAIRE*

The use of the metaphor state parasite (or similar term) is concentrated in, though not limited to, two of Marx's historical works written about two decades apart, *The Eighteenth Brumaire of Louis Bonaparte* and *The Civil War in France* (especially the drafts of the latter), representing respectively the beginning and end of Bonaparte's Second Empire. Since it is found mostly in connection with a denunciation of the grossly overinflated bureaucratic machine of the Bonapartist state, the question arises whether, in the thought behind the phrase, it is the state as such which is being impugned as parasitic, or only the Bonapartist overgrowth.

The second interpretation is certainly in the forefront, for the context overwhelmingly emphasizes the *dispensability* of the characteristically Bonapartist expansion of the government apparatus. We meet the epithet in a key passage of *The Eighteenth Brumaire,* describing the overbureaucratization of the French state. It says that "in a country like France," where the state has swollen to such immense and all-pervading proportions, "where through the most extraordinary centralization this parasitic body acquires a ubiquity . . ." one of the National Assembly's tasks was to "simplify the administration of the state, reduce the army of officials as far as possible. . . ."*

This is also the interpretation we would expect from everything else that, we have seen, Marx wrote about Bonaparte's regime, with its superstructure of praetorians, stockjobbers, swindlers, functionless functionaries, and lumpen adventurers, piled on top of the normal state superstructure.

But it is evident that to point to a parasitic element as dispensable does not mean it is useless to the ruling class. On the contrary, not only was the inflated bureaucracy obviously useful to Bonaparte: in the very next sentence Marx points out it became useful also to the French bourgeoisie. The fact that the Bonapartist freebooters sponge off the social revenue does not in the least prevent them from playing a role as instruments of the rulers: indeed, the first is requisite to the second *from the standpoint of the rulers,* though not from the standpoint of society's objective interests. These elements are certainly parasites from a basic social point of view, but pillars of the state from the point of view of their patrons.

A second key passage in *The Eighteenth Brumaire* elaborates the description of the French bureaucratic tradition, and again the "parasite" epithet crops up in the indictment.** But this time we are clearly told that "This executive power . . . this appalling parasitic body . . . sprang up in the days of the absolute monarchy, with the decay of the feudal system. . . ."[2] It was not the state that sprang up at this time, only a particular type of state or state apparatus. Unquestionably the reference is not to the state as such but to the special phenomenon of the heavily overbureaucratized state structure.

A similar remark six years later also refers specifically to the Bonapartist regime: "the Administration, that ubiquitous parasite feeding on the vitals of France. . . ."[3]

---

* For the whole passage, see pp. 395-396.
** The context of this passage is given on p. 401.

2. IN *THE CIVIL WAR IN FRANCE*

When we get to *The Civil War in France* there is a certain ambivalence built into the relevant passages. The reason for this is the great and repeated emphasis in this work, particularly in its drafts, on the Commune's replacement of the state as such.* This pervades the work so thoroughly that the two possible interpretations under discussion appear to be telescoped.

To be sure, the second draft of the essay repeats the statement, from *The Eighteenth Brumaire,* that "The huge governmental parasite . . . dates its birth from the days of absolute monarchy."[6] Again, it is clear at this point that the parasite is the overinflated bureaucratization of the state, and not the state as such. But in a dozen other passages—mainly by juxtaposition of ideas, never by direct statement—the attribution of parasitism could just as well be an epithet hurled against the state as such, and not only against the particular French leviathan.

The final version of *The Civil War in France* says that the organization of national unity by the Commune constitution would become a reality "by the destruction of the State power which claimed to be the embodiment of that unity independent of, and superior to, the nation itself, from which it was but a parasitic excrescence." But this is followed immediately by the clearest of all statements that there was no question of abolishing the state *tout court:* the "legitimate functions" of the state would be exercised by "the responsible agents of society." Further: "The Communal Constitution would have restored to the social body all the forces hitherto absorbed by the State parasite feeding upon, and clogging the free movement of, society." The argument is made that the Commune would have provided "cheap government . . . by destroying the two greatest sources of expenditures—the standing army and State functionarism [bureaucracy]."[7] In short,

---

* This question of the Commune state (or nonstate) is reserved for another volume. Suffice to say that the meaning is concisely explained in the second draft: the old state is replaced by

> the central functions, not of governmental authority over the people, but [those] necessitated by the general and common wants of the country. . . . These functions would exist, but the functionaries themselves could not, as in the old governmental machinery, raise themselves over real society, because the functions were to be executed by *communal agents,* and, therefore, always under real control.[4]

I have reviewed part of this question in a special article.[5]

parasitic excrescences are to be eliminated, legitimate functions retained in a new form—the concept of the smashing and recasting of the state machine. Further along, we read that "The Commune would have ... transformed his [the peasant's] present bloodsuckers, the notary, advocate [lawyer], executor, and other judicial vampires, into salaried communal agents. . . ."[8]

In the first draft of this work, where Marx—along with an unusual number of other cuss-words, please note[9]—uses the "parasite" epithet very freely, the passing mentions are equally casual. None in the least resembles a statement on the idea.*

But we may well pause at the remark that the Commune does away "with the unproductive and mischievous [that is, harmful] work of the state parasites. . . ."[14] This links the charge of parasitism with the fact that, economically speaking, state officials are unproductive laborers. This is a significant ingredient in the connotation of the phrase.

The economics of unproductive labor had already been thoroughly explored by Marx in his manuscripts for *Capital*, particularly the fourth volume, and we will take this subject up in some detail in Volume 2 of this work, dealing with the role of intellectuals in society. One connection has already been made in the passage which we had occasion to quote about the subordination of the bureaucracy to bourgeois society.[15] Here the subject is the social stratum of unproductive laborers such as "state officials, military people, artists, doctors, priests, judges, lawyers, etc." All of them find it unpleasant

---

* Some samples: "official France, the France of Louis Bonaparte, the France of the ruling classes and their state-parasites—a putrescent cadaver" ... "the exploiting classes, their retainers and their state parasites" ... "a mere state parasite, like Thiers, a mere talker" ... "the state parasite received only its last [i.e., latest] development during the second Empire" ... the state bureaucracy is "a trained caste—state parasites, richly paid sycophants and sinecurists, in the higher posts" ... The Commune means "the army of state parasites removed."[10] The main passage on state gigantism in France is followed by this: "This parasitical [excrescence upon] civil society . . . grew to its full development under the sway of the first Bonaparte."[11] The bracketed words were apparently added by the original Russian editors under Ryazanov, but it is not clear whether as an interpolation or reconstruction. This draft also refers to the "state vermin" and the "state monster," and, just as we have read of bloodsuckers and vampires, it denounces "the bourgeois spiders that suck its blood," meaning the state's judiciary functionaries who dip into the people's pockets.[12] The word *excrescence* did not by itself mean *parasitic* to Marx; he used it in the sense of any outgrowth, not a dispensable morbid growth; as in his remark that "in all its forms it [the state] is an *excrescence of society.*"[13]

to be relegated [by Adam Smith] *economically* to the same class
as clowns and menial servants and to appear merely as people
partaking in the consumption, parasites on the actual producers
(or rather agents of production).[16]

The bourgeoisie originally objected to the expense of keeping such
unproductive laborers, but changed back insofar as state power came
under its own control.*

Bourgeois society reproduces in its own form everything against
which it had fought in feudal or absolutist form. In the first place
therefore it becomes a principal task for the sycophants of this
society, and especially of the upper classes, to restore in theoretical terms even the simply parasitic section of these "unproductive laborers," or to justify even the exaggerated demands
of the section which is indispensable.[18]

It is seen on closer examination, then, that Marx does not say that
all unproductive laborers are also parasitic. There is a "parasitic
section," but others are indispensable. And if the parasitic elements are
dispensable, they may still be useful in a class sense. In any case, while
unproductiveness is a scientific category and not a value judgment
(poets and socialist theoreticians are just as unproductive as policemen),
it would be a mistake to treat the "parasite" epithet as if it aspired to
be the same sort of scientific term. That is why we never meet it except
as an incidental sideswipe.

If this is understood, then it may well be that in *The Civil War in
France* Marx pinned the "parasite" label on the state as such in one
definite sense: namely that the best interests of society no longer need
a state at all any longer, and that it will be the task of socialism (as it
was the orientation of the Commune) to get rid of this *no longer
indispensable institution.*** This points to the well-known prospect of
the withering away of the state, but not to any innovation in Marxist
theory.

---

* Thomas Jefferson, like Adam Smith reflecting "the still revolutionary bourgeoisie" on this point, likewise linked overbureaucratization with parasitism: "I
think we have more machinery of government than is necessary, too many parasites living on the labor of the industrious."[17]
** This is the interpretation seen by Lenin, in *State and Revolution*, of the
two Marx passages he quotes on the state as parasite. The context is his argument
against "Kautskyite opportunism" (social-democratic view of the state) which
"considers the view that the state is a *parasitic organism* to be the peculiar and
exclusive attribute of anarchism."[19] This argument, in which Lenin was unquestionably correct, involves only that aspect of the "parasite" epithet which
points to the "withering away of the state."

3. "PARASITIC" CAPITALISM

Insofar as *parasitic* simply connotes *dispensable,* then Marx should be just as complaisant about applying it to capitalism itself, not only the state. And that is exactly what he does—in exactly the same way, as a passing expletive. It crops up particularly in notes and drafts rather than in finished and published writings, as an expression of antipathy rather than analysis. Thus, in the notes for the fourth volume of *Capital,* Marx discusses just how much the productivity of labor must rise "before a °profitmonger,° a parasite, can come into being. . . ."[20] This certainly reflects Marx's feelings about the role of capitalists, but it hardly constitutes a new theory of capitalism.

Some profit-mongers are more parasitic than others: this is applied, with or without the epithet, especially to usury and commerce as distinct from manufacturing.[21] It applies redoubled to special situations, like that of the czarist state, which has "collaborated in the enrichment of a new capitalist vermin, sucking the blood of the already debilitated 'rural commune.' "[22]

Besides the "capitalist vermin," we also find Marx denouncing the English factory owners as °°"These vampyres [*sic*], fattening on the lifeblood of the young working generation of their own country. . . ."[23] because of their sweatshop use of child labor. And in a draft of *The Civil War in France* he refers to the "financial swindler[s]" as "the most parasite fraction" of the reactionary classes.[24]

Like Marx, Engels pointed to Russia as the country where "capitalistic parasitism" was most developed, referring to elements less advanced than the big bourgeoisie.[25] More important, Engels flatly called the merchant class in general "a class of parasites." The context shows that this label referred to its character as an unproductive class,

> . . . a class that took no part in production, but engaged exclusively in exchanging products—the *merchants.* . . . Here a class appears for the first time which, without taking any part in production, captures the management of production as a whole and economically subjugates the producers to its rule; a class that makes itself the indispensable intermediary between any two producers and exploits them both. . . . [Thus] a class of parasites arises, real social spongers, who, as a reward for very slight real services, skim the cream off production at home and abroad.[26]

Here the use of *parasite* is clearly rhetorical, especially since it is simultaneously acknowledged that this parasite is indispensable under the given historical circumstances. It is not used as a scientific economic term, any more than *state parasite* is a rigorous political term. One might as well try to read something into Marx's note that "Capital . . . constantly sucks in living labor as [its] soul, like a vampire."[27] But any marxologist who is beating the brush for new and profound Marxian "theories" can spin the Theory of Vampire Capitalism into a fresh discovery without any more difficulty than heretofore.

ORIENTAL DESPOTISM
BEFORE MARX:
THE WITTFOGEL FABLE

Today, discussions of Oriental despotism have mainly become a surrogate form of discussing the contemporary "Communist" social system—that is, a society ruled by a state bureaucracy. As such, the subject is outside our purview, but a word about its genesis may help to clarify our own inquiry.

1. THE CONTEMPORARY ISSUE

Just as the literati of the Enlightenment praised Chinese despotism as a means of criticizing the society they lived under, Voltaire being the type, so now theories of Oriental despotism tend to be—and to be regarded as—predated judgments on the type of society developed in Stalin's Russia. This approach was first adopted by the Stalin bureaucracy itself, when a Leningrad conference in February 1931 decreed a new party line, a departure from views expressed in the 1920s by D. Ryazanov and others, and even from the views embodied in the 1928 Program of the Communist International.[1] The new pronouncement by the scholastic establishment was that henceforth Marx's views on the Asiatic mode of production, if mentioned at all, were to be interpreted to mean that the Asiatic societies were essentially feudal.

The political motivation behind this decision was not hidden: it was specifically directed against the menace of "Trotskyism," after the disaster of Stalin's China policy of 1925-1927. What was required from scholars was a theory justifying Stalin's popular-front type of policy, which in turn involved the notion that *the* enemy in China was the "remnants of feudalism" and imperialism—at any rate, precapitalist social forces familiar to European political thought. Supporters of any other view were decreed to be Trotskyites, and a number of them were sent to their ancestors for instruction on this point.

The party line was later amended by 1934 to make the Asiatic societies slavery-based instead of feudal; later, loosened up to allow other versions mixing slavery or feudalism as ingredients, as long as interpretations stayed inside the framework of European classical and medieval society. The Chinese Communists (Maoists) continued to enforce this policy after their accession to power, as before. Even dissidents who persisted in emphasizing the uniqueness of Chinese society relative to the two European patterns had to do so in terms of the "slaveholding" or "feudal" labels. The crux was the proposition that the ruling class had to be one of these two private-property-holding classes, so that the possibility of the mandarinate bureaucracy was excluded.[2]

The contribution by Wittfogel on this issue, especially through the publication of his book *Oriental Despotism* in 1957, was to rouse a hue and cry in the Western marxological enterprise, which widely accepted Wittfogel's claim that here was a new handle by which to administer a beating to Marx's reputation. As it happened, this coincided with the intellectual thaw touching Eastern Europe after the death of Stalin and after the Twentieth Congress in 1956. It was clear that refutation of Wittfogelism on the basis of the Stalinist dogma on Oriental society was impossible for anyone striving for a modicum of intellectual honesty. There arose a strong thrust in some intellectual circles of the Communist world for a change in the party line, or at least a loosening to allow deviationist opinions, namely Marx's.

One of the prominent spokesmen of this tendency was the Hungarian Sinologist Ferenc Tökei, who first published his views in his own country and then participated in discussions that bubbled up in French Communist circles of Orientalists and others who respected scholarship more than political dogma. During the 1960s the French discussion became the main international sounding-board for dissident opinion on this issue from scholars in various Communist countries, at any rate in print.[3]

A discussion opened in Russia in December 1964, sparked by E. Varga. In May 1965 the Russian academic establishment organized a conference on the issue in Moscow, where variants of the Asiatic mode of production view were permitted to be expressed in a careful form (one that indicated no political conclusions) as *one* dissident theory. At its close the reporter, V. Nikiforov, laid down the line again with full force. The very term *Asiatic mode of production* was still to be rejected (the official pretense being that Marx and Engels had abandoned it themselves) but, Nikiforov emphasized, the crux was not the term itself but this:

> When it is said that there is no Asiatic form [of society], what is meant is that there is not, and there could not arise, a society characterized by antagonisms without a class of private owners of the means of production; that the state could not arise in a society where classes have not formed—in any case up to now we do not know any facts attesting such a development.[4]

The crucial word is *private:* no class society can exist except under a ruling class of *private*-property owners—so goes the decree for the past, present, and future. The concept of a state bureaucracy functioning as a ruling class in any conceivable society is outlawed. In the international discussion there was somewhat more leeway for analyses of Oriental society as a mode of production, but much less for any political conclusions, that is, implications for the theory of the state.

2. WITTFOGEL'S CLAIMS

With respect to this issue, Wittfogel represented the opposite side of the coin.

Karl Wittfogel came out of the matrix we have just sketched. A former Comintern theoretician, he had been one of those whose views were scotched in Leningrad in 1931. By 1957 he was one of the many ex-Communists reconciled to Western capitalism and specializing in exposing his ex-colleagues. However, by the time of the cold-war period of the 1950s, anti-Communist expositions were neither new nor scarce. Wittfogel's novelty consisted primarily in three allegations:

1. Marx refused to take the obvious step of designating the ruling class of Oriental despotism to be the state bureaucracy.

2. He did this because he was "paralyzed" by the precognition that his socialism had to lead to a bureaucratic despotism like Stalin's.

3. This was embedded in a grandiose theory about a world-historical pattern of "hydraulic society" (based on water works), which purported also to offer a historical explanation for the rise of the Stalinist regime in Russia.*

* Wittfogel's theories are mainly presented in his book *Oriental Despotism* (1957) and the article which heralded it, "The Ruling Bureaucracy of Oriental Despotism: A Phenomenon That Paralyzed Marx" (1953). Other articles added

Not all of these propositions had equal success. The hydraulic-society theory on its Wittfogelian scale soon began petering out, as an over-watered exaggeration of the water-works factor. The second proposition—the paralysis thesis in its most psychiatric form—has not been taken up with a will by most of the marxological industry; apparently it required too much of the instant-Freudian psychoanalysis seen mainly in movie plots and the works of L. S. Feuer. The deposit that was left behind by Wittfogel's contributions has worn down mainly to one theorem: Marx failed to "solve the problem of the ruling class" under Oriental despotism because he could not accept a bureaucracy in this role; and this shows that his theory cannot account for historical reality.

We have seen in Chapter 21 that, along with everyone else, Marx was unaware of an unsolved problem of this sort in connection with Asiatic society, and that he had no difficulty working with the then commonly accepted view of the nature of this Oriental state and society. But this is exactly what had to be expunged from the picture if Wittfogel's thesis was to have verisimilitude. If Marx was to be depicted as *refusing* to see what was so clearly before his eyes that his blindness could be explained only by mental "paralysis," then there must have been contemporaries of his who did make the discovery that he closed his eyes to. Wittfogel entered his nominees for this service: "the classical economists," mainly Richard Jones and John Stuart Mill, also Adam Smith and James Mill.

Hence Wittfogel solved his problem with the following two propositions, essential to his case:

1. Marx learned about Oriental despotism (or Asiatic society) from these classical economists, who—in the Wittfogel story—were the first to use these concepts, indeed the first to use these labels or their similars.

2. "Jones, Mill, and others" did "indicate the character of the ruling class in Oriental society," thereby providing Marx with the answer which he refused to adopt. Therefore the excuse cannot be made for

---

little of interest. The originator of the Oriental-despotism theory of post-1917 Russia was Karl Kautsky, as far as I know: "Some forms of government are incompatible with a prosperous capitalist development. One of them is Oriental despotism, and another is its most modern prototype, which masquerades in the garb of the dictatorship of the proletariat."[5] Wittfogel's own obsessions go beyond the propositions listed above. He actually proposed, for example, that Marx's "paralysis" was at least in part over the following worrisome question: "Would state ownership of the means of production work as well in an industrial socialist society [as envisaged by Marx] as in Asiatic agrarian society?"[6]—that is, as in ancient China!

Marx that the idea was unheard of. If Marx has to be depicted as rejecting it, then someone has to be discovered who proposed it. These claims are a farrago of misinformation in a double-barreled way. The classical economists did *not* do what Wittfogel claims; but, far from the concept of Asiatic society being otherwise unknown, it had been spread over Europe on a massive scale for two centuries and had become ideological platitudes. Far from the British classical economists being innovators of these ideas, they were relatively silent about—perhaps uninterested in—Continental views about the Oriental state and bureaucracy which were part of an educated person's baggage when Marx was a mere student, frequently encountered in the literature on which he was educated.

But before we review this Continental furor over Oriental society, let us see what it is Wittfogel tries to extract from the writings of Jones, Mill, and others.

3. THE CLASSICAL ECONOMISTS

Wittfogel scoured the writings of Smith, Jones, and Mill, and came up with a meager handful of phrases which went little further than *to refer to the existence of state officials* under the power of the Oriental emperor. Naturally this material, if clearly presented, would not have set the Potomac on fire. Their phrases had to be puffed up into the semblance of a theory, or at least a serious conception, about the Oriental state structure and bureaucracy. This job is accomplished by Wittfogel indirectly.

To begin with, how are these writers represented as innovators? We are told that Marx, on reading them, "accepted . . . their conviction that . . . there existed a specific institutional conformation, which they [*they*, presumably not others before them] called Asiatic or Oriental society." When the *Communist Manifesto* was written, Marx and Engels "seemed unaware of a specific Asiatic society."[7] It was in the early 1850s that Marx began to use the concept "following Richard Jones and John Stuart Mill. . . ." He had found "the 'Asiatic' concept . . . ready-made in the writings of the classical economists." Again: "Marx's concept of Asiatic society was built largely on the views of such classical economists as Richard Jones and John Stuart Mill. . . ."[8] The invention of the term *Oriental society* is assigned to Mill in 1848, and of *Asiatic society* to Jones. (We shall see that the picture implied by these claims is pure fantasy.)

How does Wittfogel know that Marx learned about Asiatic society only from Jones and Mill? The factual basis is solely that Marx *read* them, as he did indeed. There is no question of evidence that he so much as jotted down a note about the discovery claimed by Wittfogel. But Wittfogel embroiders freehand:

> In the 1850s the notion of a specific Asiatic society struck Marx with the force of discovery. Temporarily abandoning party politics, he applied himself intensely to the study of industrial capitalism. . . .[9]

This is pure fiction. No attempt is made to confuse by citing a fact. But we know quite well, from the Marx–Engels correspondence, why Marx temporarily "abandoned" party politics (organizational life) after the revolution; and we know that it had nothing whatsoever to do with the unrecorded moment when the discovery of Asiatic society burst on Marx as he read the classical economists. The historical method here is vintage Hollywood, the script being modeled after the dramatic moment when Don Ameche invented the telephone.

What exactly was the innovative political theory allegedly put forward by the classical economists? In his original article on the subject, Wittfogel went close to the edge of outright falsification: "In contrast to Jones, Mill, and others, Marx failed to indicate the character of the ruling class in Oriental society."[10] Ordinary people would take this to mean that Jones, Mill, and others *did* designate the ruling class in Oriental society; and furthermore the context would leave no doubt that the ruling class they nominated was the state bureaucracy. But Wittfogel cannot cite a line or word where Jones or Mill did this service; in fact, no such statement exists in Jones or Mill to account for Marx's "discovery"; in fact, neither of these men even raised the question of what the ruling class was in Oriental society, or "indicated" that such a question existed.

A couple of pages after this dangerous juggle, the claim is stated more carefully:

> . . . Marx should have had no real difficulty in determining the ruling class in Asiatic society. Moreover, Jones and Mill had already volunteered important suggestions. Jones had viewed, as the representatives of the Asiatic state, the monarch "and his officers"; at times he omitted the sovereign altogether and spoke only of "the king's officers" or "the state and its officers." John Stuart Mill listed among the "many" persons who benefited from the revenue of the Asiatic state "the immediate household of the

sovereign," and particularly "the various functionaries of government" and "the objects of the sovereign's favor or caprice."[11]

The inquiring reader who turns to the actual passages in Jones and Mill indicated by Wittfogel will find that these passages are not at all concerned with any political exposition or theory about the state officials mentioned, let alone about a ruling class.* The great "discovery" is that these state officials *exist* and consume revenue, that the state does not consist solely of the person of the monarch. We are to assume that somehow Europe had believed, before Jones and Mill uncovered the truth, that the Oriental state had no officers, that perhaps the monarch had no household, or that the officers and household were not maintained by state revenue, or some other remarkable notion which would mean that Jones and Mill were preceded in Europe exclusively by simpleminded witlings.

The "important suggestions" about the nature of the ruling class which Jones and Mill made, then, turn out to be the fact that they reveal the existence of state officials and such. It was on coming across this revelation one day that Marx threw up his hands and abandoned party politics. Moreover, according to Wittfogel, upon learning the crucial fact that an officialdom existed, "Marx should have had no real difficulty in determining the ruling class in Asiatic society." On this a provisional comment: it becomes very puzzling why, three quarters of a century and several revolutions later, after everybody and his brother had raised the question of the bureaucratic ruling power all over the world press, Wittfogel himself had such agonizing difficulty in determining the ruling class in a society right in front of his eyes, where state officials not only obviously existed, but in fact ordered him what to think—about state officials.

In his main opus published four years later, Wittfogel was more discreet. At the very beginning he even stated some of the damaging

---

* Neither Jones nor Mill used the term *bureaucracy* in connection with the Oriental state, in the works cited by Wittfogel, that is, up to 1848. It was only in 1861 that Mill's *Representative Government* referred to "The Chinese Government, a bureaucracy of Mandarins." The same 1861 essay contained formulations about the "oligarchies of officials" in several European countries and in past governments.[12] By that time, *bureaucracy* had made its tour of the world, though the term was still regarded with suspicion in the academy. Furthermore, we have pointed out that the claims made for the classical economists by Wittfogel do not amount to much when these claims are given a hard look; but if, in addition, one bothers to look up the passages cited to back up the claims (when such passages *are* cited), things begin to dim out. This is entered as a general caveat without taking space for the textual demonstration.

facts about what his innovators had *not* done. True, Jones and Mill "indicated [a word that does not mean *said*] that in Oriental society the officials enjoyed advantages of income which in the West accrued to the private owners of land and capital." How this enjoyment of "advantages of income" differs from that by officials in any other society is not "indicated," nor is there any citation to explain it; nor is it mentioned that "advantages of income" is precisely what does *not* define a ruling class, or a class of any kind, from Marx's viewpoint.

But Wittfogel is very modest in making claims even for this minor accomplishment. For "they did so only in passing and without stating clearly that under agrodespotic conditions the managerial bureaucracy was the ruling class." (Did they come near stating it even unclearly? Wittfogel can't be caught stating this.) "They therefore did not challenge the widely accepted concept of class which takes as its main criterion diversities in (active) private property."[13] This means: their theoretical conceptions did not even raise the possibility of the bureaucracy being the ruling class. Perhaps Mill was "paralyzed" by the precognition that the coming aggrandizement of the state under liberal capitalism was going to lead to fascism—if Wittfogelian psychiatry is taken seriously.

In spite of this total lack of evidence for his central proposition, Wittfogel still manages to find words to contrast Marx's "paralysis" with the perspicacity of Jones and Mill, for he cannot do without some such ploy: "although Marx accepted the classical view in many important essentials, he failed to draw a conclusion," namely that his own theory required the designation of the bureaucracy as the ruling class.[14] The admission about the innovators leaves Wittfogel with remarkably little basis for claiming that Marx "should have had no real difficulty" in giving an answer to a question that no one had even asked as far as Wittfogel knows.

All he has is the indubitable fact that Jones and Mill had mentioned the *existence* of state officials in the Oriental society. To hint at a contrast, then, Wittfogel must actually suggest that Marx failed to note even the *existence* of anybody in the Oriental state except the individual monarch. How he manages this testifies to the advantages of being an ex-Comintern wrangler. The following statement appears:

> Marx established a ruling class as the main beneficiaries of economic privilege [in other societies], whereas with regard to government-dominated Oriental society he was satisfied to mention a single person, the ruler, or an institutional abstraction, "the state."[15]

A careful reexamination of this extraordinary statement turns up the possibility that this is not a summary statement (as it would appear to the ordinary literate reader) but that it applies only to certain previously mentioned passages in Marx. That is, in *these* passages Marx mentions only a single person or the state. If this were really all Wittfogel was saying, then it would be quite irrelevant. It is unquestionable that Marx—and everyone else, including Jones and Mill—*usually* referred to the political power by speaking of the sovereign, the Crown, and the like. It is likewise unquestionable that he usually did this not only in connection with Oriental society but in connection with the Prussian state and any other absolutism. Wittfogel's statement plays a crucial role in the argument only insofar as it is misleading.

We have seen in our last three chapters that Marx referred plentifully (more so than Jones and Mill) to the officialdom of the Oriental despotisms, when there was a reason for so doing. Wittfogel himself mentions that, in the fourth volume of *Capital,* Marx cites precisely the passage in Jones about the state and its officers, as well as a long passage by Bernier in his correspondence.[16] Does Marx get points for this? It is only another reason for denouncing him: with Wittfogel, it's Heads I win, tails you lose. About these two citations by Marx, Wittfogel complains they prove that Marx *did* "know of . . . persons who, in Asiatic society, shared the surplus with the sovereign"—and therefore presumably "should have had no difficulty." Then any officials who *share the surplus* with the sovereign power are thereby constituted as the ruling class? This foolishness is the only argument made on the subject.

In another place, a summary statement, Wittfogel asserts that Marx "crippled" the concept of an Asiatic society "by dropping the idea of a bureaucratic ruling class."[17] Whose idea was *dropped?* Not Marx's own, for Wittfogel denies he ever put it forward. Not that of Jones or Mill, for Wittfogel admits they never had it.

It remains now to emphasize that there *was* a special contribution made by Jones and Mill to the understanding of Oriental society, one that Marx repeatedly praised. It did not pertain to the political structure (state or bureaucracy), nor to innovating the concept of an Asiatic or Oriental society. Their positive contribution was to the economic analysis of these societies. This service is alluded to in Marx's remark in 1857, in praise of the classical economists, that "only when the self-criticism of bourgeois society had begun was bourgeois political economy able to understand the feudal, ancient, and Oriental economies." In this field Marx gave the palm to Jones, on the ground of his "sense of the *historical* differences in modes of production," and considered

Mill inferior in this respect as well as a mediocrity in general.[18] Both Jones and Mill were experts on India particularly, rather than China, for both were involved with the British administration of India in their working lives. *

4. THE DREAM OF ENLIGHTENED DESPOTISM

The real career of the Oriental-despotism concept dates back two centuries and more before Jones and Mill.

The European discovery of the wonders of Chinese society began with the merchant adventurers of the sixteenth century, and the first knowledgeable reports were brought by the missionaries who followed, especially the Jesuits. The latter, "the greatest trading company of Europe," were especially influential in arousing the interest and admiration of the European public. The praise heaped on Chinese society by Jesuit missionaries mounted up through the eighteenth century.[20]

The European intellectual and social world echoed this admiration (contrary to Wittfogel's assertion)[21] with few exceptions. There is a considerable literature on the wave of Sinophilism that gathered strength by the seventeenth century; and "It was in the following century—the Age of Enlightenment—that the spirit of Chinese culture reigned supreme. . . . Thus by the middle of the eighteenth century Sinomania had become one of the chief cults of the time." . . . "In religious, philosophical, political, and economic fields France turned to the East for enlightenment." The much-publicized portrait of Chinese institutions "afforded a rallying point for many advocates of reform" as the *"rêve chinois"* was popularized.[22]

This Chinese Dream had more than one source, but let us concentrate on its roots in an important sociopolitical development.

---

* Jones succeeded Malthus in the chair of political economy and history at the East India College at Haileybury, a training school for the Indian bureaucracy. Mill was a kingpin in that British Indian bureaucracy which Marx riddled with derisive denunciation. He became Chief Examiner at India House (head of the bureaucracy, in effect) shortly before dissolution was proposed in 1857, in time to take on the job of theorizing and composing the argument for the defense of the East India Company (as his father had done in 1833). In both cases, writes biographer Packe, "they were convinced that in India, as in primitive communities of the ancient world, despotism was the only possible system for the time, and in this sense they believed the Company to be unrivalled." Called radicals in England, "for India they were more tory than the Tories."[19]

The rise of the absolutist state out of polycentric feudalism established the idea that the general welfare could best be furthered by a firm state power based on a centralized bureaucracy, which subordinated the warring elements of civil society to overall control. But in practice, this new state power was accompanied by arbitrary injustice, harsh oppressions, corruption, and incompetence. If only the absolutist welfare state could be purged of its bad side! The notion of an idealized absolutism is familiar to us as the yearning for an enlightened despotism that filled the *philosophes* of the Enlightenment.

As H. Jacoby has pointed out, "These ideas were not at all put forward simply by apologists and propagandists for royal power, but no less by utopian visionaries, who were out to project the image of a better state." If for Hobbes the state (the absolute state) was an artificial contrivance to protect and benefit the people, then it was inevitable that advanced thinkers should look forward to an ideal Leviathan where the contrivance of society's welfare through a perfected bureaucracy was pushed to its furthest thinkable point. This represents the real root of the early (pre-1789) utopianism of Thomas More, Campanella, Morelly, and others.[23]

The conceptions of an enlightened despotism and the social idealism of the original utopianism were, then, of a piece. If Richelieu, the political engineer of the absolutist state, already put forward the essential concept of monolithism in his *"un roi, une foi, une loi,"* it is also true, as Tocqueville remarked in an analysis that should be read in its entirety, that "The modern [1856] idea of a single class of citizens on an equal footing would certainly have pleased Richelieu, since equality of this kind facilitates the exercise of power."[24] Or more generally: bureaucratic despotism tended to press in the direction of reducing everybody to the state of a mass of administered atoms, which it then celebrated as equality and fraternity.*

---

* The point is underlined by the fact that Tocqueville himself, who sees this clearly in 1856, is still imprisoned within the same conception. He writes of the French people that by 1789 "They had come to regard the ideal social system as one whose aristocracy consisted exclusively of government officials and in which an all-powerful bureaucracy not only took charge of affairs of state but controlled men's private lives." But he admits that his own objection is only to the plebeian cast of this development. He sighs for an autocratic revolution from above, rather than a destructive rebellion from below:

An absolute monarch would have been a far less dangerous innovator. Personally . . . I cannot help feeling that had this revolution, instead of being carried out by the masses on behalf of the sovereignty of the people, been the work of an enlightened autocrat, it might well have left us better fitted to develop in due course into a free nation.[25]

This is why the characteristic political attitude of the Enlightenment, as is well known, was a yearning for a *good* despotism (*enlightened* despotism)—whether in China, Egypt, Inca Peru, Jesuit Paraguay, or Catherine's Russia. This attitude was well known to Marx, of course, who mentions the phenomenon in connection with the Russophile cult of the period, which went hand in hand with the Sinophile dream. Of the Bonapartist Karl Vogt, who was also an admirer of Russian czarism, Marx wrote:

> Crying up phrases about Russia as the lord protector of liberalism and national aspirations is not new. Catharine II was celebrated as the banner-bearer of progress by a whole host of French and German Enlighteners. The "noble" Alexander I . . . in his time played the role of the hero of liberalism in all of Europe. Didn't he rejoice Finland with the blessings of Russian civilization? [And so on, until] Nicholas too was greeted before 1830 as a hero liberating nationalities, in every language with or without the help of rhyme.[26]

And just as we have interpreted More's Utopia as an idealized extrapolation of absolute despotism, so also Marx interpreted Plato's Republic (whose institutions were traditionally regarded as communistic) as an idealization of the Egyptian system as it appeared to Greek eyes:

> Plato's Republic, insofar as division of labor is treated in it as the formative principle of the state, is merely the Athenian idealization of the Egyptian system of castes, Egypt having served as the model of an industrial country to many of his contemporaries also. . . .[27]

It was the vogue of enlightened despotism among the Enlighteners that provided the real context for the career of Oriental despotism that flourished in the European intellectual and political world right up to Marx's day, in one form or another.

5. SINOMANIA IN GERMANY

The Sinophile cult of the Enlightenment meant that Oriental despotism was cried up as a model state and society. Two things must be kept clear that are blurred by Wittfogel: (1) This admiration was felt not *in spite of* the despotism of the regime but because it was viewed as a good despotism, the right kind of despotism; and (2) what was admired even more than the paternal beneficence of the emperor was the competence, efficiency, and effectiveness of the administrative apparatus, the mandarinate bureaucracy. One of the odd notions in Wittfogel is that the existence of the Oriental bureaucracy had to be discovered in the nineteenth century. On the contrary, from close to the beginning of the European infatuation with China, it was the performance of the state bureaucracy that was in the forefront.

The first great name in the Sinophile movement was, as it happens, a German, though the French later assumed leadership. Leibniz's *Novissima Sinica* ("Latest News from China") of 1697, based on the Jesuits' reports, called for Chinese missionaries to teach Europe the good life. It was Leibniz who gave the first strong impulse to both the French and German Enlighteners in presenting the Chinese despotism as a model.[28] Scholar, mathematician, and philosopher, Leibniz was also deeply concerned with politics and economic development. His Protestantism did not get in the way of his strong support of the Jesuit operation in China, which was in line with "the Leibnizian formula for missionary penetration through cultural and commercial exchange." The China cult was important in influencing the introduction of the merit system of civil-service examination for the state bureaucracies of France and Britain, perhaps also of Prussia, which began this system first in Europe. Leibniz may have stimulated this, as he did the establishment of at least one economic monopoly as a Prussian state enterprise.[29]

The positive value of Chinese despotism was very clear to Leibniz:

> For to win the mind of a single man, such as the czar or the monarch of China, and to turn it to good ends, by inspiring in him a zeal for the glory of God and for the perfection of mankind, this is more than winning a hundred battles, because on the will of such men several million others depend.

On the other hand, the Chinese system was equally effective in keeping the masses quiet while their "perfection" was being effected:

> Indeed, it is difficult to describe how beautifully all the laws of the Chinese, in contrast to those of other peoples, are directed to the achievement of public tranquillity and the establishment of social order, so that men shall be disrupted in their relations as little as possible.[30]

The autocrat, converted to "progress," octroys his reforms from above, while the people obey in silence and business is not disrupted: a real utopia.

Leibniz established the pattern for admiring this Oriental despotism, followed by other influential Germans including Christian Wolff and A. H. Francke. (Grimm was one of the exceptions in Germany as

Fénelon, Montesquieu, and Rousseau were in France.) Von Justi was a worthy successor among the Enlighteners. He "counterposed the European states, governed irrationally by their rulers and the latter's henchmen, to the well-ordered bureaucratic administration of China. In China there was not only one or two ministers with government authority but a whole administrative apparatus." In China, wrote von Justi, "a great mass of state servants" were organized into working ranks, their numbers running to 13,600:

> It is the special advantage of the Chinese monarchy that its principles, motives, conceptions, and ways have the aim of getting the state servants, or the mandarins who are so designated, to regard themselves in all matters as fathers of the people. . . .

He saw the despotic regime as an approach to a real welfare state, which would be perfected in proportion to the advance in *Polizeiwissenschaft* (the seventeenth-century term for social administration).[31]

Herder, while not uncritical of Asiatic despotism, recognized that the emperor of China was not simply an absolute despot but himself subordinate to the yoke of tradition—that is, the system. He was entirely aware of the mandarinate and state officialdom in general, and spoke of the people's "slavish service" to the "state machine."[32]

6. FRANCE: VOLTAIRE TO QUESNAY

The China cult reached its zenith in intensity and influence in the land of Voltaire, who became the leading encomiast of the Oriental despotism. In a play, in the *Dictionnaire Philosophique,* and particularly in his *Essai sur les Moeurs,* he portrayed China with uncritical enthusiasm as a social and political Eden of state wisdom and tolerance which put European institutions in an unflattering light. Previously, Voltaire had thought to find the ideal enlightened despot in Frederick the Great (that "inventor of patriarchal despotism," as Marx called him),[33] but he was disillusioned in Berlin; he did not make the mistake of trying to visit Peking.[34] Other *philosophes* and their admirers were no less involved in the apotheosis of the *rêve chinois,* such as Helvetius and Madame Pompadour.

In mid-eighteenth century, three series of "Chinese letters" with wide popular appeal reinforced the Sinomania. Alongside the Marquis d'Argens' *Lettres Chinoises* and Goldsmith's *A Citizen of the World,* it was Etienne de Silhouette's *La Balance Chinoise* that was most interesting. Silhouette's emphasis was on the perfection of the bureaucracy (which was the "balance" of the title, countervailing the sovereign power). The Chinese "recognize . . . no rank but that appertaining to a man's office"; promotion in government service is for virtue and ability only; the efficiency of the governmental machinery is lauded, the "perfect mandarin" being the ideal state official; hence the emperor, though a despot, cannot abuse his despotic power. "The state has regulated all things, even the most minute. . . ."[35]

Although, as mentioned, there was a minority among the Enlighteners who viewed the China cult with dubiety or reserve, it was the spokesmen for the old feudal aristocracy whose power had been curtailed by absolutism who strongly attacked the centralized bureaucratic state perfected by Richelieu and, in works published abroad, "pressed the similarity of the bureaucratic absolute monarchy with the bureaucratic despots of Oriental society."[36]

Bernier—whose *Travels*, read by Marx in 1853, was important in concretizing the latter's analysis of Oriental society—is chock-full of discussions and descriptions of the Mogul bureaucracies in India, including a long section detailing their numbers, varieties, hierarchical grades, and so on, as well as the great burden on the land and the people to satisfy their exactions. The French traveler, whose power of observation Marx lauded, notes more than once that the "tyranny" of the top bureuacrats is *stronger* than the sovereign power, and that the "reins of government" are often in the hands of viziers while the emperor remains "profoundly ignorant of the domestic and political condition of his empire." In another work, published 1688, Bernier took the usual contemporaneous view of China as a humane and enlightened despotism based not on force but on virtue, persuasion, and love.[37]

In all this adulatory literature, as well as in the writings of holdouts like Montesquieu,[38] the Chinese and Indian (Mogul) empires were freely and uninhibitedly labeled Oriental or Eastern *despotisms*, the word implying no necessary disapproval. Chronologically speaking, the apogee of the glorification of the Oriental despotisms as such came with that school of economists who first represented the bourgeois spirit in the absolutist state: the Physiocrats. Their head was Quesnay, a writer whose works Marx studied intensively. What has been called Quesnay's "political testament"[39] was his propaganda pamphlet *Le Despotisme de la Chine* (1767), unmatched in its eulogy of the Chinese despotism on the basis of the Jesuits' testimonials.

The eminent "Confucius of Europe" (so called by his admirers) begins his work with a straightforward defense of the term *despotism*, explaining that China is the good kind of despotism. Again and again, repetitiously, the bureaucratic machinery of the officialdom is described, for this emphasis on the countervailing power of the bureaucracy is part of his polemic against Montesquieu. Quesnay explains in some detail that the (formally) absolute power of the emperor is really tempered by the de facto power of the officialdom, and argues that an emperor who persisted in disregarding "remonstances" by the mandarins would eventually have to yield. The hierarchical organization of the bureaucracy is described in detail. A host and multitude of mandarins carry on administration, and "stamp out sects and errors at their inception, in order to preserve the true and solid doctrine in all its purity." (The last words of the booklet celebrate China's "inherently stable order.") Quesnay explains that the "nobility" is "no hereditary nobility," for he is using this European term to mean the actual ruling class: "Only two classes may be distinguished among the Chinese people, the nobility and the people; the first include the princes of the blood, those with titles, the mandarins, and the scholars; the second, the husbandmen, merchants, artisans, etc." He describes the various "classes of scholars," who are also the administrators, below the mandarinate, while the war mandarins "are divided into nine classes," and so on.[40]

Tocqueville, quite rightly if superficially, emphasized that the Physiocrats were not only principled supporters of enlightened despotism, but more, tended toward what we might today call totalitarianism: that is, they wished to destroy all centers of countervailing influence other than the central state power and to reduce all elements of the population to equally atomized individual fragments dependent on the beneficence of the bureaucratic state. Since Tocqueville's definition of *democracy* was equality of status, he accepted the contemporary label of democratic despotism for this political ideal of Quesnay's comrades.[41]

"The state . . . should be all-powerful," was the opinion of the Physiocrat Mercier de la Rivière. "We must see to it that the state rightly understands its duty and then give it a free hand," said another Physiocrat.

> Indeed, all thinkers of the period [continued Tocqueville], from Quesnay to the Abbé Baudeau, were of the same opinion . . . the new form of government contemplated by them was to be modeled to some extent on the monarchical government then in force, which bulked large in their vision of the ideal regime.
>   According to the Economists [Physiocrats] the function of the state was not merely one of ruling the nation, but also that of

recasting it in a given mold, of shaping the mentality of the population as a whole in accordance with a predetermined model. . . . In short, they set no limit to its rights and powers; its duty was not merely to reform but to transform the French nation—a task of which the central power alone was capable. "The state makes men exactly what it wishes them to be." This remark of Baudeau's sums up the Economists' approach to the subject. . . .

Being unable to find anything in contemporary Europe corresponding to this ideal state they dreamed of, our Economists turned their eyes to the Far East, and it is no exaggeration to say that not one of them fails, in some part of his writings, to voice an immense enthusiasm for China and all things Chinese.[42]

Tocqueville then links this Sinocultist movement with "the subversive theories of what today [1856] is known as socialism," referring to Morelly.[43] He is only half right, for he ignores the fact that the other prominent precursor of French socialism, Mably, was one of the few who publicly attacked the pro-Chinese views of Quesnay and Mercier de la Rivière.[44]

In his economic notebooks on the Physiocrats, Marx digressed to take passing cognizance of their political views too. He notes Quesnay's advocacy of absolutism and of the existence of "only one supreme power" in government. He quotes Mercier de la Rivière's saying that by nature man "is intended to live under a despotism." Yet, says Marx—

It was precisely this school, with its *laissez faire, laissez aller,* that overthrew Colbertism and all forms of government interference in the activities of bourgeois society. . . . The glorification of landed property [in Physiocratic theory] in practice turns into the demand that taxes should be put exclusively on ground rent . . . [and this implies] the virtual confiscation of landed property by the state. . . . For all their sham feudal pretences the Physiocrats were working hand in hand with the Encyclopedists![45]

Surely there has scarcely been a more mind-boggling contradiction, formally speaking, than the fact that the inventors of the very phrase *laissez faire* were also the first principled theoreticians of the all-encompassing despotic state in modern times. Coming in the dawn years of capitalism, this historical fact prefigures the combination, in its twilight period, of enthusiasm for authoritarian state controls in the name of free enterprise. The formal contradiction is easily resolved in terms of class interests: Let alone, to be sure, but let *whom* alone?

Marx analyzed the dawning contradiction with his thesis that the Physiocrats were the "first systematic spokesmen of capital" in reality,[46] while operating within the power context of the absolute monarchy. Intellectually, Quesnay's school heaped praise on an Oriental despotism which subordinated the rights of private property to the state, but in fact they had no desire to import *this* feature into Europe. The growing bourgeois system needed a bureaucratic despotism that could combine efficiency and virtue, for the purpose of "recasting [the nation] in a given mold," as required by the new class whose interests also molded the ideas of the Physiocratic school.

In short, a formal, scholastic case could be made out that the Sinocultist wave preceding the French Revolution was a movement for a social system and type of state basically different from the bourgeois as well as the feudal—one that we might anachronistically call bureaucratic collectivist of a sort; but this superficial case would be historically misleading in mistaking intellectual foreplay for social reality. The play of freefloating ideas, as always, revealed potentialities, but it was going to take the unwinding of a whole historical epoch before the intellectual potential was bodied forth.

It is also significant that the cult of Oriental despotism was relatively weak in bourgeoisified England, where it was mainly a literary echo from the Continent. One need only compare Goldsmith's use of the Chinese exemplar with Voltaire's to measure the great difference. In France and Germany, Sinomania started to fade soon after Quesnay's paean of praise, that is, after the 1760s, though its place was partly taken by a new faddist enthusiasm for Hindu marvels.[47] By 1789 it was no longer a popular cult or uncritical furor, to be sure, but the conception of Oriental despotism remained altogether familiar to the intellectual world.

7. HEGEL AND ORIENTAL DESPOTISM

It is therefore not surprising (except to readers of Wittfogel) that Hegel dealt with Oriental despotism time and again, using this term and similar ones. We are told that "preoccupation with the Orient was one of the most intensive, if not *the* most intensive, preoccupation of Hegel's in Berlin." He came to Berlin in the year Marx was born, and his interest in the Orient was at its height in 1826–1827.[48]

In his lectures on *The Philosophy of the Spirit* Hegel sought to differentiate "true monarchy" from Oriental despotism, since both seemed superficially to be cases where "the will of a single individual stands at the summit of the state." The difference he finds is in the "principles of right" on which the state power is based, namely "freedom of property ownership, at any rate personal freedom, freedom of civil society, its industry and the municipalities," plus the subordination of the authorities to law.[49] He thus assumed his readers understood that Oriental despotism was inimical to European (bourgeois) conceptions of property rights.

In China, noted Hegel's encyclopedic survey in the *Philosophy of History*, the soil came to be regarded as state property at some unspecified late epoch, after which time "it was established that a ninth part of what is produced goes to the emperor." Here he also mentions the existence of forms of slavery and serfdom as well as private property in land in certain times and circumstances, but stresses that these forms are all subordinate to the overall domination of the central power: "It is necessarily true in China that the difference between slavery and freedom is not great, since all are equal before the emperor, that is, all are equally degraded." In India, he mentions, the pre-British society was "organized in nearly feudal fashion," with various princes at the head of small realms,[50] but he is definitely not claiming that the society was feudal in some European sense. The remark is descriptive, not analytical, and the rest of the description is plainly alien to European feudalism.

In short, although Hegel does not pose the modern question of spotting social systems in time and space, he not only makes no effort to assimilate the Orient to familiar European forms, but, on the contrary, wishes to emphasize that Oriental social and political forms are fossil representatives of a first stage of human history that is long behind Europe.

For Hegel, of course, the stages of world history go hand in hand with corresponding steps in man's ascent to freedom, marked also by an ascent in political forms. "History begins" in China, and despotism in the Orient marks "the childhood of history." It is an inconvenience for his schema that, while despotism comes first in man's development, followed by the classical duo of aristocracy and democracy, it is monarchy that represents the culmination of progress;[51] yet he must admit that despotism is one variety of monarchy! The embarrassment is solved by dividing monarchy into despotism and monarchy proper, or "true monarchy," which is the blessed state of affairs that obtains when one-man rule is used only to effectuate whatever has become "necessary" in civil society and the state through the impact of Reason in history.[52] Unlike despotism, true monarchy does not atomize individuals into depersonalized fragments by the crushing force of the state but encourages individuality to flower (this being freedom). Hegel, therefore, is exercised to demonstrate the basic gulf between Oriental despotism, which represents political childhood, and the absolute monarchy of his day, which represents maturity. Far from wanting to assimilate Oriental society to European forms, Hegel's constant unspoken premise is that Oriental despotism must be shown to be as alien to modern Europe as a Manchu to a Hohenzollern.

Hegel has to distinguish despotism in general from the sovereign power which wields force, for state sovereignty is not *merely* a matter of force. "But despotism denotes in general the condition of lawlessness where a particular will as such—whether of a monarch or a people (ochlocracy [mob rule])—counts as law, or rather counts instead of law. . . ." Despotism is like "the purely feudal monarchies that formerly existed" in Europe and which were marked by constant revolts, wars, and outrages, "because under such conditions the division of the state's business is merely mechanical, since its sectors are handed over to vassals, pashas, etc." Despotism reduces the scene to a polarization of "the princes and the people" in which "the latter have an effect, if at all, merely as a destructive mass versus the organized structure." Given an organic role in the state system by the true monarchy, the masses will pursue their interests in a legal, orderly way; otherwise they run wild. "In despotic states, therefore, the despot goes easy on the people," who even pay little taxes! [53] It is clear that Hegel's criticism of despotism is not that this system oppresses the masses particularly: his objections focus on what despotism does to the upper strata who have to grovel before the emperor like everybody else. The ascent to freedom will be a boon mainly for the propertied magnates whom despotism represses. From this new direction it is implicit that there is a gulf between despotism and modern monarchy.

Hegel is also concerned about the way in which different societies determine division into classes (*Stände*).* If in modern Europe "free-

---

* In fact, Hegel went further: he was quite aware of the origin of the state in class divisions and property relations. This is indicated twice in the *Philosophy of History,* first in connection with the river-valley plains that saw the rise of the Oriental states:

> In these lands great empires arise and great states begin to be established. For agriculture, which predominates here as the prime principle of individuals' subsistence, is oriented around the regularity of the seasons and the operations so regulated: landed property begins, and the juridical relations connected with it; that is, the bases and foundations of the state, which becomes possible only under these conditions.

The second case concerns the United States and anticipates a slice of Turner's frontier thesis. The United States is "the land of the future" but its political present has not yet jelled, because the pressure of population is constantly relieved by the westward movement to open lands, which thereby provides an

dom" means that the arbitrary power of the sovereign is used to effectuate only what is Necessary and Rational, then by contrast, in the Orient as in the ancient world, the division into classes "was left to the governing class, as in the Platonic state [Plato's Republic] . . . or was simply a matter of *birth,* as in the Indian castes."[55] Or worse, class divisions may be virtually atomized as in China. Thus Hegel shows that the class system of Europe is not simply an arbitrary imposition from above as in the past, but the exercise of mature sovereignty within the framework of necessity and reason.

This conditions his class analyses of the despotisms. In Oriental society, "there is only a class of lords and thralls, it is the sphere of despotism," he remarks in his *History of Philosophy,*[56] and when he goes on to explain that "fear is the ruling category" there (a clear echo of Montesquieu's basic indictment) it is plain whose fear is meant concretely. His complaint is that despotism breaks up the class system in a bad way: "The [class] distinctions that develop in accordance with the various aspects of mores, government, and state, become . . . stodgy, complicated, and superstitious rituals, accidents of personal power and arbitrary domineering, and the arrangement into classes undergoes a natural rigidification into castes."[57] In this "patriarchal despotism" where the emperor's "fatherly solicitude" runs everything, even his upper-class subjects are legally minors, and "No independent categories or classes have interests to protect for themselves, as in India, for everything is managed and superintended from above." Thus "In China the people are dependent on the laws and moral will of the emperor without distinction of classes," but this is bad, for "this very equality is not a triumphant testimonial to a person's inner worth but to a low level of self-esteem that has not yet attained to recognizing distinctions."[58]

To put it somewhat anachronistically, Hegel seems to be complaining that this Oriental despotism is a classless society of equals: "Outside

---

outlet for the chief source of discontent and maintains the status quo in civil society. (The frontier thesis is also applied to Europe: "Had the old Teutonic forests still existed, then surely the French Revolution would not have taken place.") Hence no state is yet required in the United States, for besides the absence of internal pressure, there is no danger from the neighboring states. A "firm cohesion" is not yet needed,

> for a real state and a real government develop only if there is already a distinction in classes [*Stände*], if wealth and poverty have become very great and the situation arises where a big mass of the people can no longer satisfy their needs in the way they are used to.

Needless to say, Hegel does not conclude that the state comes in as a repressive or class force.[54]

of the emperor there is among the Chinese no specially distinguished class [or rank, *Stand*], no nobility. Only the princes of the imperial house and the sons of ministers enjoy any superior rank, more by their position than by their birth. Otherwise, all count as equals. Since in China equality rules, yet without freedom, despotism is necessarily the mode of government."[59] The point is very like the one that Tocqueville is going to make later. (But we shall have to mention that this passage is followed without a pause by his account of the wonderful Oriental bureaucracy.)

8. HEGEL TO MARX

Also like Tocqueville later, Hegel turns this criticism of Oriental despotism into a criticism of what we might nowadays call something like totalitarianism, that is, a society so rigidified by constraints from above that there is no allowance for the play of countervailing forces even in the upper strata, at least formally. He has to make do without the modern term. In his lectures on aesthetics, he remarks that the "unfree Oriental Unity"—that is, the monolithism of state power in the Oriental system—"results in religious and political despotism" because the individual has no rights as a person and therefore no footing of his own. Elsewhere: "Under the Asian despots, individuality is allowed no validity as such," whereas it is respected in modern Europe. "The Orient knew, and still knows, only that *One* is free," for all the freedom allocated by history to this toddler-society is concentrated in the one-man ruler who singly represented the Unity of society through the Fatherhood of all. "For outside the One Power, before which nothing can take independent form, there exists nothing but gruesome arbitrariness ranging at large to no one's good."[60]

In a comparison with the situation in India, he remarks that "China is all state" (as one would say an object is all steel); and in another comparison, that "the substantive totality [*Ganze*]" seen in China is not found in Persia. (Incidentally, for Hegel it is China that is "quite characteristically Oriental," while India and Persia compare with Greece and Rome.)[61]

It is instructive that it is as easy for Hegel to show that China is "all state" as that it is "no state," and that he does both, though not in the same book. In his *Philosophy of History:* "if China is all state, the Indian political system is only a people, not a state," since in India there is no principle of freedom located anywhere, not even in a monarch; it is merely the most arbitrary and evil despotism, not a true state. But in his *Philosophy of Right*, he wants to take a fall out of the advocates of church–state unity, and so argues: "Under Oriental despotism is found that oft-desired unity of church and state—but thereby the state does not exist: not the self-conscious formation based on lawfulness, free ethicality, and organic development which is alone worthy of the spirit." This elimination of the state's existence in Oriental despotism does not stop Hegel from writing (elsewhere) voluminously about the state in China, and even of its "perfected machinery" for "the unity of the state organization."[62]

This ambivalence, displayed over the question whether China is all state or no state, crops up also in Hegel's account of the Chinese bureaucracy. Here the realities of Prussian statism preserve the remnants of the Chinese Dream. The existence of a pervasive bureaucracy in this childhood-society can hardly be considered an infantile trait when it is found also in the state which crowns the ages, Prussia. To continue a passage already begun:

> . . . all count as equals, and only those take part in government administration who possess skill in it. Offices are thus filled by those most highly educated in a scholarly way [*wissenschaftlich*]. Therefore the Chinese state has often been put forward as an ideal that should serve as a model even for us.[63]

The praise is put forward secondhand but not negated, except for the caveats previously mentioned: equality minus freedom equals despotism. Explaining that "the government proceeds exclusively from the emperor, who carries it on as a hierarchy of officials or mandarins," Hegel lays in pages of detailed description of the bureaucracy: its numbers, varieties, gradations, classifications, and checks.[64] "The whole of this administration is thus covered with a network of officials. . . . Everything is arranged with the minutest precision. . . ."

This hierarchy of officials or mandarins—is it aristocracy? We have seen why Hegel denied that China had an aristocracy or nobility at least in the European sense. If modern jargon had existed, he would have been able to explain that it was a meritocracy, for he does explain it is "by the merit that anyone may acquire" that one attains to any high position in the state.[65] But, he would have to add, it is a meritocracy which is unfortunately lacking all autonomy with respect to the One Power above.

> From all this it is clear that the emperor is the central point around which everything revolves and to which everything refers

back, and it is on the emperor that thereby depends the welfare of the land and the people. The whole hierarchy of the administration works more or less according to a routine that becomes a convenient habit when things are quiet. It goes its own way first, last and always, with the uniformity and regularity of nature's course; only, the Emperor is supposed to be its alert, ever vigilant, and self-active soul.[66]

Now the importance to us of Hegel's portrayal of Oriental despotism does not depend on its accuracy in the light of later knowledge, which generally downgraded the emperor's unitary power and gave more emphasis to the power- or property-holding classes, which Hegel represented as thoroughly atomized under the thumb of the Imperial One. Its importance lies in the fact (1) that Hegel, who early absorbed the literature of the Enlightenment, takes his place in the long line of European thinkers and writers who since 1585 had published copious descriptions and analyses of Oriental despotism, its hierarchy, its bureaucracy, and its form of society; and (2) that Marx early absorbed, not only the literature of the Enlightenment like any other intelligent student of the 1830s, but in particular these writings of Hegel.

It would be supererogatory to explain that Marx absorbed Hegel, but it may be worth mentioning that most of our references to the *Philosophy of Right* come from the same part of that book that Marx dissected minutely in 1843; and that in *The German Ideology,* Marx refers repeatedly to Hegel's views on China as he ridicules Stirner for clumsily parroting Hegel's opinion of Chinese virtues, as expressed in the *Philosophy of History.*[67] In the discussion of precapitalist economic formations in the *Grundrisse* notes, Marx frequently makes use of Hegel's concept of Unity (*Einheit*) as underlining the role of the Oriental despot. While departing basically from Hegel's historical analysis, of course, Marx retains a number of other concepts, notably that of the Orient's static historical nature, so prominent in Hegel.[68]

9. HESS AND CUSTINE

Perhaps we can now appreciate the enormity of Wittfogel's claim that it took some incidental words in Jones and Mill to enlighten Marx (or any other well-informed literatus of the time) about the existence of a concept of Oriental society and its officialdom, so that he abandoned party politics in despair as the discovery pierced his soul. This after Hegel!*

Hegel was not the only one from whom Marx heard about Oriental despotism in his student days. The pioneer of comparative geography Karl Ritter was one of the live eminences at the University of Berlin in those days, and Marx took his course in General Geography in 1838.[70] Ritter gave considerable attention to Oriental society—with stress on material and social factors, too—in his works and doubtless in his lectures.

Then there was Moses Hess, whose collaboration with the young Marx has been noted in Part I. In a couple of articles in 1845 Hess made some revealing references to Oriental despotism. In one article, he charged that Weitling's type of communism would inevitably lead to "the destruction of all freedom, reversion to an Oriental despotism or some other already obsolete condition of lordship and servitude." In another essay he argued that if communism were really a system of forced labor, as painted by the bourgeoisie, it would run afoul of the sense of freedom of the Western peoples "who would not stand for any Oriental despotism."[71]

In these popular propaganda articles, Hess assumed general familiarity on the part of the educated public with the authoritarian features of Oriental despotism which already made it a bogy if regarded as the threatened outcome of communism. A similar reference to Oriental despotism as a bogy may be found in an early article by the young Engels.[72]

This familiar use of Oriental despotism by the German left was no doubt encouraged by the copious material on the Russian variety that pervaded the general press and the columns of the Paris *Vorwärts* in 1844. The *Vorwärts* was a semiweekly published for the German emigrants in France during that year; in the spring Marx and his friends began to collaborate with it closely and influence its politics in a radical direction.[73] Marx and Engels published material in fourteen issues of

* Of course Wittfogel knows Hegel's writings on China; in 1931 he published an article entitled "Hegel über China" in the Comintern's theoretical journal. A footnote in *Oriental Despotism* mentions cryptically that in 1931 he "pointed . . . to Hegel as possibly [!] having influenced Marx," adding: "but I did not then realize the fundamental dependence of Marx on the classical economists." That is all. Two pages before, Hegel had been listed as one of "the unilinealists of the nineteenth century" who "disregarded hydraulic society." This, the only statement made in the book about Hegel's views, is quite false, as Wittfogel's 1931 article made clear.[69]

the paper. The *Vorwärts* carried copious excerpts from a book just published by Marc Fournier in collaboration with the German radical Bornstedt, *Russie, Allemagne et France*. This in turn followed the sensational impact made about the same time by the book *La Russie en 1839*, by the Marquis de Custine, published in 1843 and immediately translated into German and English. Custine's book was of great importance in this period, and M. Rubel is probably right in claiming that Marx was much influenced by its formulations.[74]

The Marquis de Custine was a class-conscious feudal aristocrat whose travels not only made books but took him away from a France that alienated him. He was as hostile to absolutism as to democracy, hence sensitive to a despotism that made bondsmen out of the Russian nobility. During his sojourn in St. Petersburg he was dazzled by the czar's personal attentions though repelled by the regime, and at first his letters reflect the illusion that the Crown is the all-in-all of the state. Only after a sojourn in Moscow and the provinces does his realization come that the bureaucracy wields a collective power standing even above the czar's.

Nicholas himself tells him that the regime is a despotism: "it is the essence of my government." Custine adds that it is an *Oriental* despotism. Especially after Moscow, he repeats that the land lies between the Occident and the Orient, that Moscow is "between London and Peking."[75]

Custine's early view of the czar as the One Power resembles Hegel's of the Chinese emperor: "The empire is the emperor." It is his will "which alone animates the country," like "the patriarchal tyranny of the Asiatic governments." Acute observer in the tradition of Bernier, he early notes the shadowy background figures of the officialdom who seem to be saying, "Make way, I am one of the members of the grand machine of state." Yet in Petersburg he snorts at the ornate ministry buildings, "Temples erected to clerks!" In his first sketch of the "class of men" constituting the bureaucracy, he sees them only as instruments of the throne and a danger to the state.[76]

After traveling in the interior, he abandons his original notion that the czar's absolutism really means that equality reigns below him; he vaguely sees castes and mutually antagonistic secondary powers. The nobles can do what they please on their own estates "but the country is not governed by them." Where then is the power? He finally writes down, and elaborates, the thesis that it is the bureaucracy that really rules the vast state:

Russia is governed by a class of subaltern employés, transferred direct from the public schools to the public administration. . . . By virtue of their offices, these despots oppress the country with impunity, and incommode even the Emperor; who perceives, with astonishment, that he is not so powerful as he imagined, though he dares not complain or even confess it to himself. This is the bureaucracy, a power terrible everywhere, because its abuses are always made in the name of order, but more terrible in Russia than anywhere else. When we see administrative tyranny acting under Imperial despotism, we may tremble for a land. . . .[77]

Soon he concludes of this "class of subaltern employés, or secondary nobility":

This, indeed, is the class which, in spite of the Emperor, governs the empire. . . . These new men . . . are also masters of the supreme master; and are the preparers likewise of a revolution in Russia. . . .

These are old enemies created by the emperors themselves, in their distrust of the old nobility . . . a host of commissioners and deputies, the greater number of foreign origin. . . .[78]

10. THE IMAGE OF THE ORIENTAL BUREAUCRACY

The contemporaneous brouhaha over Custine's portrait of Russia was due to its exposé of the progressive pretensions of this despotism. It was not the notion of a bureaucratic ruling class that disturbed the readers.

An investigation of this corner of intellectual history would be interesting, though beyond the call of duty here. A couple of examples specially pertaining to Marx may be useful, with focus on the midpoint of the nineteenth century as Marx started writing about the subject.

1. We know that one of the important books Marx used and often quoted in his writings on India was George Campbell's knowledgeable *Modern India*, 1852. Campbell, an old India hand, shows constant interest in the varieties of social systems there. He notes areas of slavery, feudal forms, and so on, while stressing that these forms are not predominant. He describes the nature of the village organization as a stateless community (not his term). And as for the "centralized despotism" of the Mogul imperial power, he classifies it directly as an

Oriental despotism. Moreover, unlike Jones or Mill or Wittfogel's other stick-figures, Campbell takes up and answers the question of the ruling social power in this state: The "only aristocracy," he writes, is the officialdom, which is headed by the sovereign. There is "nothing feudal" in the composition of this empire, he avers. Naturally, he devotes detailed attention to the organization of the administrative cadres that make up the governing bureaucracy.[79]

None of these observations is made by Campbell as a discovery or revelation, nor even as a fresh or original thought.

2. Major encyclopedias of a period usually reflect thought about a decade behind. In all the leading encyclopedias at mid-century, it goes without saying, detailed attention was paid to the Oriental bureaucracies such as cannot be found in Jones or Mill. It was standard fare in such works as the *Britannica* or *Brockhaus.* Two others are especially interesting.

In the great *Larousse du XIXe Siècle* the article on China tells us quite matter-of-factly that, while the government is absolute, "As with all despotic governments, it is a eunuch . . . who, from behind the curtain, works the imperial puppet; hence one does not complain about the sovereign. . . . The imperial palace . . . is a veritable city, with its government and its people."[80]

In the *New American Cyclopaedia,* the leftish Dana-Ripley enterprise for which Marx and Engels ground out articles, one reads that the Chinese monarchy is *not* despotic, "since the emperor is bound by ancient laws and customs, and could scarcely without danger, if he would, disregard the advice or remonstrances of his ministers or the boards of administration." There is the usual devotion of great space to what is called "the most stupendous bureaucracy in existence." Indeed, of ancient Egypt we are told outright that "The priests were the ruling class," the monarchy being limited by "the powerful hereditary privileged classes of priests and soldiers." This was an interpretation very like what Hegel had written down.[81]

There is no awareness in these sober encyclopedia articles, any more than in Campbell, that one should be startled by these opinions, right or wrong. The idea that some states were, or could be, ruled by bureaucracies was perfectly conventional, if not downright platitudinous. The notion that this concept was ipso facto scandalous, sacrilegious, or sinful is a distinctly modern invention, which Marx never heard of.

ORIENTAL DESPOTISM
AND ENGELS

The statement has frequently been made that Engels eventually discarded or abandoned the concepts of the Asiatic mode of production and Oriental despotism.* The kernel of fact behind this claim is that neither term appears in Engels' writings after the death of Marx. More specifically, the main exhibit is Engels' *Origin of the Family,* written in 1884, only a year after Marx's death: not only does neither term appear, but it has been argued that some statements in that book exclude the concepts by making slavery, and only slavery, the first type of class society.

Certainly Engels never mentioned, or even hinted at, any change of view in this regard. There is not the slightest evidence that *he* was aware of it. The speculation about it, in my opinion, arises from a misunderstanding of Engels' relation to the question.

THE MISAPPREHENSION ABOUT ENGELS

The difference between Engels' relation to this issue before and after Marx's death is not as great as is made out. One must be struck by the relatively minor part that Engels played with respect to this question from the beginning, ever since 1853 when Marx first raised it. His part was even less than would be indicated by the few times that he has been quoted as using the terms under discussion.

In the original correspondence of June 1853, when Marx brought up the matter with his reference to Bernier's book, Engels duly made a

---

* The same claim is sometimes made with respect to Marx; in fact, this extended claim is part of the official Moscow line proscribing the concept. (See Special Note E, page 631.) But there is no case made for it that requires discussion.

useful suggestion in his reply [1]—and then immediately returned to the historical problem *he* had been working on (Arab and Middle East history) and his plans to learn Arabic or Persian. He never did comment on the interesting material that Marx included in his follow-up letter. [2] In fact, neither then nor at any subsequent time did Engels show much interest or initiative in studying or working out Asiatic social and economic history.

This was by no means an unusual facet of the division of labor, or division of interest, between the two men: on his part, Marx did not get involved in a number of the special enthusiasms developed by Engels, who pursued more than any one man could follow. Engels' attitude plainly was: "Marx is working up India and China, and that takes care of *that.*" His own journalistic articles on Indian and Asian events (mainly military, to be sure) never mentioned Oriental despotism.

In fact, for the thirty years before Marx's death in 1883, there was not one occasion on which Engels independently brought up or wrote on this subject—with a questionable exception in the 1870s. The exception, of course, is *Anti-Dühring;* what is questionable about the exception is whether Engels brought it up independently. We know that Marx closely reviewed the manuscript and wrote a part of it as explained in the foreword. It is difficult to ignore the coincidence that the only substantial references to these concepts ever made by Engels occurred in the work which was written in the closest collaboration with Marx.*

In short: with a prominent exception, Engels "failed" to mention Oriental despotism or the Asiatic mode of production for three decades *before* 1883. That hardly warrants much to-do over the fact that he did not mention it after 1883. But we know that this "failure" had nothing whatever to do with disagreement or doubt about Marx's views. It simply was not his bailiwick.

ENGELS' LINE OF INTEREST

On the positive side: if Engels never showed any initiative for independent work on Asian society, which Marx was covering, he was

---

* There is a minor exception of the same sort that was mentioned on p. 555 above: the reference to Oriental despotism in Engels' polemic against the Russian Tkachov in 1875. [3] This was exactly the sort of piece in which Marx would take detailed interest, and at Engels' behest. To be sure, Engels also used terms like "the despotic East" in referring to Russia. [4]

all the more involved in the early history of Europe. Unpublished manuscripts on the development of precapitalist society among the German tribes show his intensive work; he started on a history of Ireland; his letters show that he had done wide reading at various times on early history in a number of Scandinavian and Balkan countries—to mention a few of his projects.

It is therefore not to be wondered at that, after Marx had made him aware of Lewis Morgan's *Ancient Society,* Engels rounded out Morgan's material for his own purposes with the material that he knew best and could handle with some expertise. This is sufficient to explain why his *Origin of the Family* specifically restricted itself to filling out, or illustrating, the general thesis with material from Greek, Roman, and German history, remarks about other parts of the world being incidental.

In *The Origin of the Family* itself, Engels stated in so many words that he was leaving out consideration of Asia:

> Space prevents us from going into the gentile institutions still found in a more or less pure form among the most diverse savage and barbarian peoples of the present day; or into the traces of such institutions found in the ancient history of civilized nations in Asia. One or the other is met with everywhere.[5]

One may suspect that he exempted Asia from discussion not only because of space but also because it was not his field of knowledge. In any case, it is difficult to understand why this plain statement is ignored by those who make out a case for "abandonment" simply on the basis of what is *not* in the book.

When, therefore, Engels writes in his summary that "Slavery is the first form of exploitation, characteristic of the ancient [classical] world,"[6] he is summarizing the *European* material. It is not intended as a universal recipe, not only in view of what preceded it, but in the context of the qualification contained in the statement itself. Yet it is suggested that Engels wrote this sentence as a sort of secret repudiation of the form of exploitation which *Capital* called the tributary relationship: a manner of proceeding frequent in the academic world but not in Engels.

In any case, we have here another example of the marxologists' propensity for turning passing remarks, taken in one context, into theories about something else. The term *slavery* is an especially risky subject for this enterprise, for Marx's and Engels' writings are full of examples of the very common use of the word for any intensive or despotic exploitation, or for the whole range of master–subordinate relation in history. This broad use is not always signaled by a modifier, as in *wage-slavery,* and not confined to popular writings. For example, in the *Grundrisse* notebooks we find Marx writing, after a reference to capitalism: "All earlier forms of property condemn the greater part of humanity, the slaves, to be pure instruments of labor." [7] This "proves" that Marx saw slavery as the content of "all" social forms earlier than capitalism. . . .

Finally, we can point out that, in a real sense, the Asiatic mode of production is not absent from *The Origin of the Family,* though the term is not used. It depends on whether the term bears Karl Marx's meaning or someone else's. Marx's Asiatic mode of production, we have explained, is identical with the general social form of primitive tribal communalism which he termed the archaic formation in his 1881 letter drafts—a form which went through changes in time, and which took different aspects in Europe and Asia. In *The Origin of the Family* there are numerous mentions of the European examplars of this social form: the village community, the German Mark, the *naturwüchsiges Gemeinwesen,*[8] and many others.

In this book a point which Engels had explained in detail in *Anti-Dühring* now appears mainly as background: this is the process of class and state formation out of the proto-political institutions. For example, he writes about the outcome of the Athenian development:

> The class antagonism on which the social and political institutions rested was no longer that between the nobles and the common people, but that between slaves and freemen, dependents and citizens.[9]

It turns out, after all, that there *was* a kind of class antagonism which preceded slavery, even here. It is typical of this book's focus of concentration that the very existence of this primitive aristocracy (which arises out of the archaic formation, as we have seen) is referred to only in passing, though often enough.[10]

What this points to is a weak side of *The Origin of the Family;* the content derived from Morgan and other anthropologists, and filled out by Engels, is not well integrated with the approach taken in (say) *Anti-Dühring.* But this has nothing to do with the alleged rejection of Oriental despotism.

OTHER LATE WRITINGS BY ENGELS

As in *The Origin of the Family,* the primitive-communal mode of production gets mentioned in Engels' later writings under various designations, when he is writing about Europe. It would be rather wrongheaded to fault him for declining to pin the Asiatic or Oriental label on these European forms, to the confusion of readers.

Thus, *before* Marx's death, Engels had published a considerable essay on this early mode of production in "The Mark," without once using "Asiatic" terms or even linking this German form with other variations, as Marx might conceivably have done. Engels continued to approach the question this way after Marx's death, without any significant change in either his viewpoint or his terminological strategy. Take, for example, a letter to Sorge in his last year:

> The war in China has given the death-blow to the old China. Isolation has become impossible. . . . But with it the old economic system of small peasant agriculture, where the family also made its industrial products itself, falls to pieces too, and with it the whole old system which made relatively dense population possible.[11]

The description of this "old system" gets along without a label of any kind; there is none really available—none that even Marx stuck to in his private papers and notes. But by the same token this old system without a name is not any of the old systems that friend Sorge would recognize by name.

We have mentioned Engels' letters in 1884 about Java's "old communistic village communities." In line with our present point, we must be struck by the fact that, although dealing with an Asian primitive communism, Engels' mind made the operative connection with something going on in *Europe*—in this case Bismarck's state-socialism.

Finally, in 1894 Engels very clearly identified the Asian village-community system with the European, in his last polemic against the Russian Tkachov. Here he refers to "what soon [after Haxthausen] became common knowledge," and proceeds to summarize the views of Marx which are detailed in Chapter 21, sections 9-10.

> Namely, that communal ownership of land was a form of tenure which in the primitive epoch had been prevalent among the Germans, the Celts, and the Indians, in short, among all the

Indo-European peoples, which still exists in India, which was only recently forcibly destroyed in Ireland and Scotland and still occurs here and there in Germany even today, and that it is a disappearing form of tenure which is, in fact, a phenomenon common to all peoples at a definite stage of development.[12]

This is a general statement of Marx's view of the archaic formation.

It remains to be pointed out that in this last period there is one important work in which Engels continued to publish the view of Asiatic social formations and Oriental state forms as before: his editions of Marx's *Capital.* This bears on the English translation of Volume 1 as well as his construction of Volume 3 out of Marx's notes. Especially in the case of the third volume, where there was considerable room for choice in editing and arrangement, there is no indication that, after allegedly turning against and discarding Marx's views on this subject, he sought to save Marx's honor by leaving this erroneous material out. On the contrary, the material on this subject in Volume 3 is, if anything, more effective than in Volume 1.

KAUTSKY'S ARTICLE OF 1887

It is risky and speculative to cite anybody else's writings as a reflection of Marx's and Engels' views; certainly no firm conclusion can be founded on such evidence alone. With this warning, however, there is good reason to call attention to an article published by Karl Kautsky, editor of the party's theoretical organ *Die Neue Zeit* in 1887—the time of his closest collaboration with Engels, both being resident in London.

Entitled "Die moderne Nationalität," the article attempts to sketch the historical development of nationhood from the earliest times. A long section is devoted to the prehistoric crystallization of nations around economic needs, the first such formation discussed being that of the river-valley cultures of the Orient. The suggestions in Marx on the relation between water control (irrigation and so on) and the rise of the Oriental empires are developed here. The references to Marx's writings are only implicit but quite clear; for example, to the failure of the British to keep up Indian water works. Like Marx, Kautsky links the disconnected autonomies of the village communities with the anarchist ideal, and comments: "This ideal is not one of the future but of the hoariest past, as we have just seen. Its result, however, was not unbounded personal freedom but Oriental despotism."[13]

Kautsky evinces no paralysis about the ruling power in this Oriental despotism. He writes about the ruling aristocracies, "the holders of the central power—often with only a nominally personal head—the soldier and priest castes (as they have been called, not always very happily) . . ."

In fact, he digresses to polemize against the shallow historians who explain "the origin of class differences" purely and simply by conquest; and offers his own explanation for the origin of the ruling class (the aforementioned aristocracy). To be sure, he agrees, "There can be no doubt that the ruling aristocracy of the Oriental despotisms was and is often a foreign conquering tribe." But such a conquering tribe "could take over the central power only if it was already in existence."

> If it took over this central power and its functions, then the people would let it rule in peace, since actually nothing would be essentially changed. Both the rulers and the ruled class then blended into one nation, because both parts constituted a single economic organism.[14]

Further, of these conquerors-turned-rulers he adds:

> Far from feeling themselves to be foreigners, these aristocracies together with their retinue became, in the civilized states of the Orient, the bearers of all national life insofar as it developed at all. . . . But these beginnings of national life confined themselves always to a small fraction of the whole people, to the aristocracy, to the possessors of seats in the central power, to the free urban population.[15]

The article, it is true, is vague about the mode of production behind this national state development (although, on the other hand, this was not the subject). Clearly neither slavery nor feudalism is represented as dominant; the reference to the military and the priesthood as the ruling powers is not developed further, but certainly no private-property-holding class is on the scene. The term *aristocracy* is, as often, simply a generic term for a ruling stratum.

What is significant is that the concept of Oriental despotism as a historical state form is prominently put forward, and the class rulers are represented without visible inhibition in terms of those who held the central state power. In fact, one of the reasons for the lack of further detail along these lines appears to be the assumption that there is no great need for explanation.

Two queries:

1. Where did Kautsky get these concepts in 1887? It may safely be assumed that they did not arise in his own skull by spontaneous

generation. Certainly there were the suggestions in the first volume of *Capital* and in *Anti-Dühring,* already published. But the important third volume of *Capital* was not yet in being, nor were the *Grundrisse* notebooks known. If Kautsky read the seminal discussion in Marx's 1853 articles (not to speak of the letters) it was only because Marx or Engels made them specially available. Indeed, it is hardly conjectural that this was precisely the kind of historical subject that Kautsky would be eager to discuss with Marx in London before his death; no doubt also with Engels after that. In any case, the least doubtful proposition is that Kautsky wrote this in the belief he was giving currency to Marx's views.

2. What about his relations with Engels, who allegedly had now discarded the concept of Oriental despotism? If that allegation has any truth at all, we have a mystery. If it is baseless, all is clear.

For in this period Kautsky's intellectual association with Engels was close and dependent. That does not exclude disagreement, but it makes it overwhelmingly probable that such a disagreement would have left some traces.

As it happens, it was in just this year that we get the most far-reaching statement by Engels on his relations with Kautsky. A rumor was received—from America!—that Kautsky was becoming reserved in his association with Engels. Engels replied with a round denunciation of the rumor as a complete fiction.

> I rely on Kautsky as on myself; like most of the young people he can do something precocious at times, but if he had any doubts he would first let me know. In any case I'll ask him tonight what, if anything at all, the report may refer to.[16]

The close personal relations between Engels and Kautsky, indicated by this letter and abundant other testimony,[17] plus the nature of the subject on which Kautsky was writing, make it likely that Kautsky at least showed the article to Engels before publication.

REFERENCE NOTES

Titles are given in abbreviated form; full titles and publication data are provided in the Bibliography. Book and article titles are not distinguished in form. Page numbers apply to the edition cited in the Bibliography. Volume and page are usually separated by a colon: for example, 3:148 means Volume 3, page 148.

Some frequently used abbreviations are:

E = Engels
Ltr = Letter
M = Marx
ME = Marx and Engels
M/E = Marx or Engels
MEGA = Marx and Engels, *Gesamtausgabe*
ME:SC = Marx and Engels, *Selected Correspondence* (2nd ed., 1965)
ME:SW = Marx and Engels, *Selected Works in Three Volumes* (1969–1970)
MEW = Marx and Engels, *Werke*
NRZ = *Neue Rheinische Zeitung*
NRZ Revue = *Neue Rheinische Zeitung, Politisch-Ökonomische Revue*
Rev. after = Revised after the original text
Rev. from = Revised from an extant translation
RZ = *Rheinische Zeitung*
Tr. = Translation, translated in

The first source cited is the actual source of the quotation or statement; it is sometimes followed by a [bracketed] reference that cites an extant translation if the first reference is to the original, or vice versa. This second reference is given for the reader's convenience only; when it is to "Tr." with no title, it refers to the translation cited in the Bibliography.

15. THE BONAPARTE MODEL

1. See Ch. 14, p. 224.
2. Ltr, E to M, 3 Dec. 1851, in ME:SC, 60-63.
3. M: 18th Brum., in ME:SW 1:404.
4. Quoted in Cobban: *Hist. Mod. France,* 2:141.
5. M: 18th Brum., in ME:SW 1:404.
6. Ibid., 405.
7. Ibid., 406.
8. Ibid., 407.
9. Ibid., 408.
10. See Ch. 13, § 4, and Ch. 14, § 2.
11. M: 18th Brum., in ME:SW 1:412.
12. See Part II of M: Cl. Str. Fr., in ME:SW 1:239-256.
13. M: 18th Brum., in ME:SW 1:413-414.
14. Ibid., 414.
15. M: Civ. War Fr., in ME:SW 2:219.
16. M: 18th Brum., in ME:SW 1:417-418.
17. Ibid., 418-419.
18. Ibid., 421.
19. Ibid., 422.
20. Ibid., 422-423.
21. Ibid., 423-431, 438-440.
22. M: Cl. Str. Fr. in ME:SW 1:253-261.
23. M: 18th Brum., in ME:SW 1:432-433.
24. Ibid., 433.
25. Ibid., 434.
26. Ibid., 435.
27. Ibid., 436.
28. Ibid.
29. Ibid., 446-447, 449.
30. Ibid., 452.
31. Ibid., 454.
32. Ibid., 455-456.
33. Ibid., 464.
34. Ibid., 466; also 480.
35. Ibid., 468-469.
36. Ibid., 476-477.
37. Tocqueville: *Old Regime & Fr. Rev.* (III, 7), 202.
38. M: 18th Brum., in ME:SW 1:477.
39. Ibid., 478.
40. M: Civ. War Fr., 1st Draft, in ME: Wr. Par. Com., 151; cf. also 156.
41. M: 18th Brum., in ME:SW 1:479.
42. E: Notes on W., 46.
43. M: 18th Brum., in ME:SW 1:482-483.
44. Ibid., 484.
45. Ibid., 485.
46. E: Intro./Civ. War Fr., in ME:SW 2:181.
47. Ltr, E to M, 3 Dec. 1851, in ME:SC, 60-63.

48. M: 18th Brum., in ME:SW 1:398.
49. See ltr, M to Weydemeyer, 19 Dec. 1851, in ME: Ltrs Amer., 30 [MEW 27:594]. Ltr, M to E, 24 Jan. and 27 Feb. 1852, MEW 28:12 and 30, including the notes giving the editors' interpretation.
50. Ltr, M to E, 9 Dec. 1851, in ME: Sel. Corr. (55), 77. This letter is not included in ME:SC.
51. M: article (no title) in N. Y. Tribune, 22 Feb. 1858; E: Prosecution of Mont., N. Y. Tribune, 24 Nov. 1858.
52. M: French Cred. Mob. (Art. II), N. Y. Tribune, 24 June 1856.
53. E: Pruss. Mil. Qu., MEW 16:71-72.
54. E: Real Causes (Art. I), *Notes to the People,* 21 Feb. 1852.
55. Ibid. (Art. II), 27 Mar. 1852.
56. Ibid. (Art. III), 10 Apr. 1852.
57. ME: Com. Manif., in ME:SW 1:109.
58. ME: article (no title), N. Y. Tribune, 23 Dec. 1858. (Ascribed in MEW to E only.)
59. M: Civ. War Fr., in ME:SW 2:219.
60. M: Historic Par., N. Y. Tribune, 31 Mar. 1859.

16. BONAPARTISM: THE BISMARCKIAN EXTENSION

1. E: Orig. Fam., in ME:SW 3:328-329, rev. after MEW 21:167.
2. Ibid., 332.
3. M: Echoes of Erfurt, MEW 13:414.
4. Ltr, M to E, 17 Nov. 1862, MEW 30:301.
5. ME: Ltr to Brunswick Comm., in ME:SC, 247.
6. Ltr, E to Bernstein, 27 Aug. 1883, in ME:SC, 363; see also E: Pref./Peas. War Ger. (1874), in ME:SW 2:166.
7. E: Soc. Bismarck, II (*Egalité,* 24 Mar. 1880); cf. MEW 19:175.
8. M: Report of G. C. Hague Congr., in G.C.F.I. 71-72 [5], 457. M: Civ. War Fr., 2d Draft, in ME: Wr. Par. Com., 203.
9. Ltr, E to M, 29 Apr. 1864, MEW 30:393.
10. E: Pruss. Mil. Qu., MEW 16:71-73.
11. Ltr, E to M, 13 Apr. 1866, MEW 31:208 [tr. ME:SC, 177]; this passage previously quoted on p. 336.
12. Ltr, E to M, 11 June 1866, MEW 31:227.
13. Ltr, E to M, 9 July 1866, MEW 31:235.
14. Ltr, E to M, 25 July 1866, MEW 31:240-241.
15. E: Hous. Qu., in ME:SW 2:348, rev. after MEW 18:258.
16. Ltr, E to Pauli, 30 July 1878, MEW 34:335.
17. E: Hous. Qu., in ME:SW 2:348.
18. Ibid., 349.
19. Ibid., 350.
20. E: Crisis in Pruss., MEW 18:293.
21. Ibid., 294-295.
22. E: Pref./Peas. War Ger. (1874), in ME:SW 2:166, rev. after MEW 18:513.
23. Ibid., 166-167.
24. Ibid., 167.

25. This phrase is taken from E's outline for the chapter as a whole, MEW 21:463.
26. E: Role of Force, MEW 21:452-453 (cf. tr. in ME:SW 3:419).
27. Ibid., 453 (cf. tr., 420).
28. Ibid., 454 (cf. tr., 420-421).
29. Ltr, E to Bebel, 7 Mar. 1883, MEW 35:450.
30. E: Role of Force, in ME:SW 3:378, 380.
31. E: Role of Force, MEW 21:428, 431 [tr. 396, 398].
32. H.: *Karl Marx/Interview* (Dec. 1878), 22.
33. E: Role of Force, MEW 21:431 [tr. 398].
34. Ibid., 428 (cf. tr., 395-396).
35. Ibid., 428-429 (cf. tr., 396).
36. Ibid., 453 (cf. tr., 420).
37. Ibid., 460 (cf. tr., 426-427).
38. E: Ger. Soc. Dem., in Newcastle Daily Chronicle, 3 Mar. 1890 [MEW 22:5].
39. E: On Hist. Pruss. Peas., in E: Peas. War Ger., 191 [MEW 21:244f.].
40. E: Role of Force, MEW 21:426 (cf. tr., 394).
41. Ibid., 427 (cf. tr., 394).
42. Ibid., 428 (cf. tr., 395).
43. Ibid., 431 (cf. tr. 398-399).
44. For a comment on this point, see ltr, E to Bebel, 7 Mar. 1883, MEW 35:450.
45. Ltr, E to Bernstein, 27 Aug. 1883, MEW 36:54; cf. ME:SC, 363.
46. E: Role of Force, MEW 21:454 (cf. tr., 421).
47. Ibid., 456 (cf. tr., 423).
48. E: Role of Force—Outline of concluding section, MEW 21:464; my bracketed interpolations try to spell out the sense.
49. Ibid., 465.
50. This is from the last point in E's outline for the chapter as a whole, MEW 21:463.
51. E: Intro./Cl. Str. Fr., in ME:SW 1:193.
52. Ladendorf: *Hist. Schlagw.*, 271-272.
53. E: Debate on Poster Law, NRZ, 27 Apr. 1849, MEW 6:441.
54. E: Role of Force, MEW 21:433 (cf. tr., 400).
55. E: Intro./Cl. Str. Fr., in ME:SW 1:193.

17. BONAPARTISM AND THE "PROGRESSIVE DESPOT"

1. Ltr, H. Marx to Karl, 2 Mar. 1837, MEW Eb. 1:629.
2. M: Scorpion & Felix, in MEGA I, 1.2:85-86.
3. M: Ltrs from D. F. J.; no. 2 (May 1843), MEW 1:340; cf. tr., M: Early Texts, 76.
4. Esp. frequently in M: 18th Brum.; for another context, see e.g. ltr, M to Schweitzer, 24 Jan. 1865, in ME:SC, 158.
5. ME: Ger. Ideol. (64), 209.
6. M: Pruss. Press Bill, MEW 5:241; M: Bourgeois Doc., MEW 6:152; also cf. Marx's contrast of Napoleonic despotism with Prussian despotism, in ME: First Press Prosec., MEW 6:226.
7. ME: Holy Fam., MEW 2:130; cf. tr., 165.
8. M: 18th Brum., in ME:SW 1:399.

9. ME: Holy Fam., MEW 2:130-131; cf. tr., 166.
10. Ibid., 86; cf. tr., 110.
11. M: 18th Brum., in ME:SW 1:477-478.
12. E: Savoy, Nice & Rhine, MEW 13:598.
13. Ltr, E to L. Lafargue, 4 Feb. 1889, in E & Lafargue: Corr. 2:193.
14. Ltr, E to L. Lafargue, 16 Apr. 1890, in ibid., 371.
15. M: article (no title) in N. Y. Tribune, 13 Mar. 1854; repr. in M: East. Qu., 269; ltr, M to Lassalle, 23 Feb. 1852, MEW 28:498.
16. See Proudhon: Carnets, 1:286-288, 356-357; 2:333; 3:124, 134—these especially, among other passages. Disillusionment seems to set in with 3:200.
17. M: Cl. Str. Fr., in ME:SW 1:238; M: Pref./18th Brum., in ME:SW 1:395; M: Civ. War Fr., in ME:SW 2:207, 226; and 1st Draft, in ME: Wr. Par. Com., 157, 115.
18. Franzisca Kugelmann, in Reminisc. ME, 280-281; ltr, M to E, 10 Feb. 1870, MEW 32:436.
19. M: French Trials, N. Y. Tribune, 27 Apr. 1858.
20. Ltr, M to E, 14 Feb. 1858, MEW 29:281.
21. M: Ms. Poln. Fr., 187-188; see 181-188 for the whole case on Napoleon. For Marx's speeches on this question at the G.C. of the International, see G.C.F.I. 64–66 [1], 56, 61-62, 380 (n. 28); also Collins & Abramsky, 107-108. For Engels on Napoleon's betrayal of Poland, see E: Pref./On Soc. Rel. Russ., in ME: Russ. Men., 204, or MEW 18:585.
22. M: Herr Vogt, MEW 14:519-520 fn.
23. M: Revol. Spain, I (N. Y. Tribune, 9 Sept. 1854) and VI (24 Nov. 1854), in ME: Rev. in Spain, 27, 67.
24. M: Civ. War Fr., 1st Draft, in ME: Wr. Par. Com., 148-149; and final version of same, in ME:SW 2:218. The latter formulation already appeared in the 2nd Draft, for which see ME: Wr. Par. Com., 197.
25. Ltr, E to F. Graeber, Dec.–Feb. 1840, MEW Eb. 2:442; E: Immermann's Mem., MEW Eb. 2:146-147; E: E. M. Arndt, MEW Eb. 2:120, 122.
26. E: Imperial Cortege, MEW Eb. 2:139-140.
27. For the first side, cf. E: Progress Soc. Ref., MEGA I, 2:436; E: Cond. Eng./18th Cent., MEW 1:554 or ME: Art. Brit., 13. For the second, cf. esp. E: State of Ger./I, in MEGA I, 4:484-486; E: Ger. Socialism, MEW 4:233.
28. E: Status Quo in Ger., MEW 4:45.
29. E: Notes on Ger./Intro., in E: Peas. War Ger. (56), 231.
30. E: Mark, in E: Peas. War Ger. (56), 179; ltr, E to P. Lafargue, 19 Mar. 1888, in E & Lafargue: Corr. 2:107; E: Peas. Qu., in ME:SW 3:457.
31. E: To Span. Workers, MEW 22:405 (retranslated).
32. E: Intro./Civ. War Fr., in ME:SW 2:187; M: Civ. War Fr., 1st Draft, in ME: Wr. Par. Com., 149.
33. E: For. Pol. Russ. Cz./Time, Part III, 525. (This refers to the English translation overseen by Engels; for tr. from German, see ME: Russ. Men., 39.) The preceding citation came from the same, Part II, 365-369 (in ME: Russ. Men., 35-39).
34. Ltr, E to M, 25 July 1866, MEW 31:240; cf. ME:SC, 181-182.
35. Ltr, M to E, 27 July 1866, MEW 31:242.
36. M: Bolivar (see Bibliography).
37. Ltr, M to E, 14 Feb. 1858, MEW 29:280; see also Draper: K. Marx & Bolívar, 69.
38. M: Herr Vogt, MEW 14:685; see also 575 fn. for the equation of Bolívar with another shady Hungarian, Bangya.

18. BONAPARTISM IN EXTREMIS

1. Thompson: *L. Napoleon,* 227-254; for specific references, 227, 232-233, 236-241, 253.
2. M: Kossuth & L. Nap., N. Y. Tribune, 24 Sept. 1859.
3. For Proudhon's *La Révolution Sociale Démontrée par le Coup d'Etat du 2 Décembre* (Paris, 1852), see e.g., Schapiro: *Proudhon,* in his *Lib. & Challenge,* Ch. 14. (Woodcock's *Proudhon,* as usual whitewashes this episode; cf. 181-182.)
4. See ME: Alleged Schisms, in ME:SW 2:283-285.
5. M: Herr Vogt, MEW 14:548.
6. Leroy: *Hist. Id. Soc.* 3:262-268.
7. Quoted by Marx in ltr, M to Lassalle, 23 Feb. 1852, MEW 28:497, and then incorporated in M: 18th Brum., in ME:SW 1:476.
8. Ltr, E to M, 18 Mar. 1852, MEW 28:41.
9. Ltr, M to Cluss, bef. 26 June 1852, MEW 28:534.
10. Ltr, M to E, 2 June 1860, MEW 30:61; Silberner: *M. Hess,* 358ff., 377, 451, 463, 503f, 515, 520f, 537f; Hirsch: *Denker & Kämpfer,* 91-97.
11. M: French Cred. Mob.—I, N. Y. Tribune, 21 June 1856.
12. M: 18th Brum., in ME:SW 1:486; ltr, M to E, 7 Aug. 1855, MEW 28:455.
13. M: French Cred. Mob.—II, N. Y. Tribune, 24 June 1856.
14. M: New Treaty, N. Y. Tribune, 14 Feb. 1860.
15. M: French Cred. Mob.—II, N. Y. Tribune, 24 June 1856.
16. M: French Cred. Mob.—III, N. Y. Tribune, 11 July 1856.
17. Fourier: *Design f. Utop.,* 51 and (for mercantile feudalism) 100; also see Gide's introduction to this volume. Pankhurst: *Fourierism,* 427; Gurvitch: *Proudhon,* 51; Wilshire: *Socialism Inev.,* 149. Cuvillier: *Proudhon,* 10; for Ghent, see Bibliography.
18. E: Köln. Ztg. on Eng. Cond., MEW 5:287; cf. also E: True Soc., in ME: Ger. Ideol. (64), 609 (for feudalism of money).
19. Berle: *20th Cent. Cap. Rev.,* esp. Ch. 3, but it is the thesis of the whole book.
20. M: Brit. Com. & Fin., in N. Y. Tribune, 4 Oct. 1858.
21. M: article (no title) in N. Y. Tribune, 9 Oct. 1856.
22. Ltr, M to E, 11 Apr. 1868, MEW 32:58.
23. M: Monet. Crisis, N. Y. Tribune, 15 Oct. 1856.
24. Ltr, E to M, 17 Nov. 1856, MEW 29:86; M to E, 10 Jan. 1857, ibid., 93.
25. Ltr, M to E, 8 Dec. 1857, MEW 29:224.
26. Ltr, M to E, 25 Dec. 1857, MEW 29:238; E to M, 17 Mar. 1858, ibid., 303.
27. M: article (no title) in N. Y. Tribune, 15 Dec. 1858. Cf. also ltr, M to E, 29 Nov. 1858, MEW 29:371; M. to Lassalle, 4 Feb. 1859, ibid., 575.
28. Ltr, M to E, 18 Dec. 1857, MEW 29:233.
29. Ltr, E to M, 17 Mar. 1858, MEW 29:304.
30. E: Hous. Qu., in ME:SW 2:339f; E: Anti-Dühr. (59), 383 fn. (or Soc. Utop. Sci., in ME:SW 3:144 fn).
31. M: Grundrisse, 73.
32. M: Cap. 3:592.
33. Ibid., 594.

34. Ibid., 593-594.
35. See ltr, M to E, 2 Mar. 1858, MEW 29:291; Lassalle to Marx, 10 Feb. 1858, in Lassalle: *Nachgel. Br. & Schr.* 3:114.
36. E: Pruss. Mil. Qu., MEW 16:72; E: Intro./Cl. Str. Fr., in ME:SW 1:193.
37. M: Civ. War Fr., in ME:SW 2:219.
38. ME: article (no title) in N. Y. Tribune, 23 Dec. 1858 (ascribed in MEW to Engels only but I feel Marx's hand shows plainly).
39. M: Russ. Victory, N. Y. Tribune, 27 Dec. 1853; also M: Polit. Movements, ibid., 30 Sept. 1853.
40. Ltr, M to E, 29 Jan. 1858, MEW 29:269.
41. M: article (no title), N. Y. Tribune 22 Feb. 1858.
42. M: article (no title) in N. Y. Tribune, 12 Mar. 1858, pub. as a leading article.
43. M: Rule of the Pretorians, N. Y. Tribune, 12 Mar. 1858. (Not to be confused with the untitled article published on the same date, referred to in preceding note.)
44. See §6, p. 451.
45. M: Herr Vogt, MEW 14:472, 573.
46. M: Bonaparte's Pres. Pos., N. Y. Tribune, 1 Apr. 1858.
47. Ltr, M to Lassalle, 4 Feb. 1859, MEW 29:576.
48. M: Historic Par., N. Y. Tribune, 31 Mar. 1859.
49. E: Prosecution of Mont., N. Y. Tribune, 24 Nov. 1858.
50. M: article (no title) in N. Y. Tribune, 30 Apr. 1858; datelined 13 Apr.
51. From ltr, M to E, 31 May 1858, MEW 29:329.
52. M: article (no title) in N. Y. Tribune, 11 June 1858; datelined 27 May.
53. M: Bonaparte's Pres. Pos., N. Y. Tribune, 1 Apr. 1858.
54. M: Pelissier's Mission, N. Y. Tribune, 15 Apr. 1858.
55. M: article (no title) in N. Y. Tribune, 24 June 1858; written 11 June.
56. M: Peace or War, N. Y. Tribune, 25 Mar. 1859.
57. Rubel: *K. M. Devant le Bonap.*, 49-51; more generally all of Ch. 3-4.
58. M: 18th Brum., in ME:SW 1:478 [MEW 8:197].
59. M: Civ. War Fr., 1st Draft, in ME: Wr. Par. Com., 149-50.
60. Ibid., 150-151.
61. Same, 2d Draft, in ME: Wr. Par. Com., 196.
62. M: Civ. War Fr., in ME:SW 2:219.

19. STATE AUTONOMY IN PRECAPITALIST SOCIETY

1. Ltr, E to Bebel, 12 Apr. 1888, MEW 37:51.
2. ME: Com. Manif., in ME:SW 1:108-109.
3. E: Anti-Dühr. (59), 228.
4. Ibid., 386, or E: Soc. Utop. Sci., in ME:SW 3:146.
5. M: Pref./18th Brum., in ME:SW 1:395.
6. Ladendorf: *Hist. Schlagw.*, 40-41.
7. M: Aff. in Prussia, N. Y. Tribune, 14 June 1860, E: article (no title) in N. Y. Tribune, 23 Dec. 1858 (drafted by E but M sent the article in); M: War Prospect, N. Y. Tribune, 31 Jan. 1859.
8. Ltr, E to M, 3 Dec. 1851, in ME:SC, 62.

672 Notes to Pages 466–480

9. For ex., brief references in *Capital* and elsewhere, traceable through the subject or geographic index of most MEW volumes (but not 1–8, 26), most being to economic or military history only, in a technical connection. E: Orig. Fam., Ch. 6, which deals with Rome, focuses on the origin, not decline, of the state. Likewise M: Grundrisse, for ex. 378-82 (tr. 71-77); cf. also Hobsbawm intro to M: Pre-Cap. Ec. Form., 38-41.

10. Ltr, M. to Zasulich/1st Draft (final draft dated 8 Mar. 1881), in ME:SW 3:159.

11. E: Orig. Fam., in ME:SW 3:327-28.

12. M: Cap. 3:325.

13. M: Cap. 2, in MEW 24:113 (trans. *state enterprise* in M: Cap. 2:110).

14. M: Debates Wood-Theft, MEW 1:118.

15. See Ch. 3, §4, p. 87.

16. See Ch. 1, §1.

17. M: Crit. Heg. Ph. Law/Ms., MEW 1:233.

18. See Ch. 3, §3.

19. See Ch. 1, §3, p. 36 fn.

20. M: Crit. Heg. Ph. Law/Ms., MEW 1:275.

21. Ibid., 276, and more for another page.

22. See Ch. 5, §4, p. 118f.

23. M: Econ. Ph. Ms., MEW Eb. 1:505-506.

24. Ibid., 506.

25. Ibid., 507. Note also the passage quoted from Adam Smith, ibid., 484 (cf. tr. 78).

26. ME: Ger. Ideol. (64), 452.

27. Ibid., 90.

28. Ibid., 35.

29. E: Army, in ME: Art. N.A.C., 72.

30. ME: Ger. Ideol.(64), 77, 78, 79.

31. M: Cap. 1:332.

32. M: Cap. 3:603-604 rev. after MEW 25:631.

33. M: Grundrisse, 628.

34. E: Princ. Com., in ME:SW 1:88; E: Peas. War. Ger. (56), 40, and see also 41-42 in this connection; E: Rev. & C.R. Ger., in ME:SW 1:302.

35. M: Cap. 1:718; ME: Ger. Ideol. (64), 207.

36. Cf. E: Intro./Soc. Utop. Sci., in ME:SW 3:105; E: Notes on Ger./Intro., in E: Peas. War. Ger. (56), 224.

37. E: Status Quo in Ger., MEW 4:47.

38. ME: Ger. Ideol. (64), 458.

39. E: For 'Peas. War,' MEW 21:402; cf. tr. E: Peas. War Ger. (56), 222.

40. E: Decay of Feud., in E: Peas. War Ger. (56), 216-217.

41. ME: Ger. Ideol. (64), 78.

42. Ibid., 208-209 rev. after MEW 3:178. The basic idea is repeated ibid., 393-394 [MEW 3:345].

43. E: Pruss. Const., in MEGA I, 6:253-254.

44. ME: Com. Manif., in ME:SW 1:321.

45. E: Begin. End Austria, MEW 4:505.

46. E: Rev. & C.R. Ger., in ME:SW 1:321.

47. E: Hung. Strug., NRZ 13 Jan. 1849, MEW 6:167-168; cf. tr. in ME: Russ. Men., 58-59.

48. M: Cap. 1:718.

49. Ltr, E. to Kautsky, 20 Feb. 1889, in ME: Sel. Corr. (55), 481, rev. after MEW 37:154.
50. E: Anti-Dühr. (59), 252.
51. Ibid., 227.
52. M: Moral. Crit., MEW 4:339-340.
53. Ibid., 347.
54. Ibid., 353.
55. E: Hous. Qu., in ME:SW 2:348.
56. E. Bernstein: unsigned article "Zur Naturgeschichte der Volkspartei," in *Der Sozialdemokrat* (Zurich), 20 Mar. 1884. For E's comment, see his ltr, E to Bernstein, 24 Mar. 1884, in ME:SC, 371.
57. Ltr, E to Bernstein, 27 Aug. 1883, in ME:SC, 363.
58. E: Pref./Peas. War Ger./1874, in ME:SW 2:166.
59. E: Hous. Qu., in ME:SW 2:348-349. In this connection, E: Prussian *Schnaps*, MEW 19:37ff, is a spirited note on the bourgeoisification of Junkerdom.
60. E: Hous. Qu., in ME:SW 2:348.

20. STATE BUREAUCRACY AND CLASS

1. Ltr, E to C. Schmidt, 27 Oct. 1890, in ME:SC, 421; cited in Ch. 11, p. 246.
2. For this passage by Engels, see Ch. 11, p. 252.
3. M: Lassalle, in NRZ, 4 Mar. 1849, MEW 6:321.
4. Jacoby: *Bürok. d. Welt*, 251.
5. So says Dulaure: *Hist. Paris*, 438.
6. M: Notebk. on Maine, 329.
7. Albrow: *Bureaucracy*, intro., 13-15; on Marx, 68-72.
8. Ibid., 18f; this work, esp. Ch. 1, is also the source of other references to the early history of the term not otherwise ascribed. For the German press, see Schulz: *Deut. Fremdwb.*, 1:102.
9. For Marx in 1842-1843, see MEW 1:101, MEW Eb. 1:424. For Engels in 1839-1840, see MEW Eb. 2 name index.
10. Emge: *Bürokratisierung*, 179; Schulz: *Deut. Fremdwb.*, 1:102.
11. Mill: *Rev./A. Carrel*, 72.
12. Mohl: *Ueber Bur.*, 99-100; cf. also 101-102.
13. Blackie, in *Westminster Review*, v. 37, 1842, p. 134ff; edit. note on p. 170-171; most important passage is at p. 158-163; similarity with China invoked p. 156. Perhaps first use of the term in English was in *Popular Encyclopaedia* of 1837, based on Brockhaus. Albrow's ref. to *Blackwood's* for 1836 is misleading, the term occurring there as a purely French word.
14. Ch. 1, p. 36, incl. fn.
15. See Ch. 3, §3, esp. p. 82f; cf. also Ch. 6, p. 143, and Ch. 8, p. 169f.
16. See Ch. 1, p. 34.
17. See Ch. 1, p. 45f.
18. See Ch. 2, p. 72.
19. M: Vindication Moselle Corr., MEW 1:815; cited in Ch. 1, p. 65.
20. Ibid., 189.
21. M: Crit. Heg. Ph. Rt./Ms., MEW 1:248-249; cited in Ch. 3, p. 81.
22. Ibid., 284.
23. For this, see Ch. 19, §2.

24. M: Crit. Heg. Ph. Rt./Ms., MEW 1:249-255; cited in Ch. 3, pp. 81-84.
25. ME: Ger. Ideol., MEW 3:46, rev. from ME: Ger. Ideol. (64), 60-61.
26. This refers to the distinction made in Ch. 14, p. 312 fn.
27. These passages have already been cited in Ch. 19, pp. 477-478; see the references given there.
28. E: State of Ger./III, in MEGA I, 4:494-495.
29. E: Pruss. Const., in MEGA I, 6:253; this passage was quoted more fully in Ch. 19, p. 478.
30. M: Moral. Crit., MEW 4:353; this whole passage was quoted and discussed in Ch. 19, p. 481f.
31. M: Com. of Rh. B., MEW 4:193.
32. M: 18th Brum., in ME:SW 1:477; the whole passage was quoted and discussed in Ch. 15, p. 401.
33. M: Civ. War Fr., in ME:SW 2:217.
34. Same, 1st Draft, in ME: Wr. Par. Comm., 148.
35. M: 18th Brum., in ME:SW 1:477-478; this passage was referred to in Ch. 17, p. 431 fn.
36. See Ch. 9, p. 207f and its fn.; also Ch. 1, p. 36.
37. M: Ltrs from D.F.J., no. 2 (May 1843), MEW 1:341-342 [tr. M: Wr. Yg. M., 209-210]. *Dienerstaat* was trans. as *servile state* in Ch. 9, p. 208, where this passage was given in full.
38. M/E: Speech fr. Throne, NRZ, 2 Mar. 1849, MEW 6:319.
39. E: Rev. & C. R. Ger., in ME:SW 1:308, 310, 311.
40. This passage was given in Ch. 9, p. 208 fn., from M: Aff. in Prussia, N. Y. Tribune, 1 Feb. 1859.
41. From the same Tribune article.
42. M: K. M. bef. Cologne Jury, MEW 6:244 [tr. ME: Rev. 48-49, 232].
43. Ibid., 253 [tr. ibid., 241-242].
44. Ibid., 254 [tr. ibid., 243].
45. M: Aff. in Pruss., N. Y. Tribune, 1 Feb. 1859.
46. M: Grundrisse, 844.
47. M: K. M. bef. Cologne Jury, MEW 6:253 [tr. ME: Rev. 48-49, 242-243].
48. This passage was cited above, p. 493.
49. M: 18th Brum., in ME:SW 1:478. The larger context of this passage was given in Ch. 15, p. 401.
50. For context, see Ch. 16, p. 415; for source, ref. 15 in that chapter.
51. See Ch. 23, §5, esp. ltr, E to Danielson, 18 June 1892, there quoted.
52. MEW 26.1:145, rev. from M: Theor. S. V., 1:170.
53. M: Theor. S. V., 1:171 [MEW 26.1:145-146].
54. MEW 26.1:273-274, rev. from M: Theor. S. V., 1:291-292. Cf. also M: Grundrisse, 372.
55. Cited in Ch. 14, pp. 313-314, from a Tribune article by Marx (ME: On Colon. (68), 62-64).
56. M: Brit. Incomes, N. Y. Tribune, 21 Sept. 1857, in ME: On Colon. (68), 168-172.
57. E: Status Quo in Ger., MEW 4:44.
58. Ibid., 45.
59. Ibid., 50.
60. Ibid., 51.
61. Ibid., 53.
62. Ibid., 54.
63. E: Rev. & C. R. Ger., in ME:SW 1:322.

64. For ex., cf. "race of lawyers" in the same work, ibid., 308.
65. M: Morning Post, in M: Surveys fr. Exile, 286.
66. M: Aff. in Pruss., N. Y. Tribune, 3 Dec. 1858.
67. Ladendorf: *Hist. Schlagw.*, 162-163.
68. Footnote by E in M: Pov. Philo. (FLPH), 174; the whole passage illuminates this point. For M in 1849, see above, p. 498.
69. M: Wage-Lab. & Cap., in ME:SW 1:159.
70. M: Montesquieu LVI, in NRZ, 21 Jan. 1849, MEW 6:187-188.
71. E: Rev. & C. R. Ger., in ME:SW 1:311; passage cited above, p. 494.
72. E: Anti-Dühr. (59), 244, and MEW 20:164.
73. See esp. E: Orig. Fam., in ME:SW 3:275 (a summary); also ibid., 208, 237, 272.
74. Bukharin: *Hist. Mat.*, 279-281.
75. Ibid., 152.
76. ME: Ger. Ideol. (64), 51 [MEW 3:39] ; M: Pov. Philo. (FLPH), 127, 131, 135 [M: Misère, 135, 138, 143] —this passage being anticipated in ltr, M to Annenkov, 28 Dec. 1846, in ME:SC, 37; M: Cap. 1:339-340, 366; M: Grundrisse, 381, or M: Pre-Cap. Econ. Form., 76-77. Minor locus in ltr, M to E, 14 June 1853, in ME:SC, 86.
77. See "Caste," *Encyc. Brit.*, 11th ed., 5:468-469.
78. M: 18th Brum., in ME:SW 1:482-483; for context, see Ch. 15, p. 402.
79. E: Ger. Camp. Const., MEW 7:133.
80. E: Hous. Qu., in ME:SW 2:348; context given in Ch. 16, p. 415. (For a similar use of *caste* by Marx in 1871, see M: Civ. War Fr., 1st Draft, in ME: Wr. Par. Com., 153.)
81. E: M. & NRZ, in ME:SW 3:165.
82. Albrow: *Bureaucracy*, 16, 127.
83. E: War in East, N. Y. Tribune, 30 Nov. 1854.
84. E: Brit. Disaster, N. Y. Tribune, 22 Jan. 1855, in M: East. Qu., 506.
85. M: Brit. Army, N. Y. Tribune, 14 Apr. 1855.
86. Ibid.
87. Schiller: *F. E. & Schiller-Anstalt*, 486-489.
88. Ltr, E to Ex. Com. of Schiller Institute, ca. 3 May 1861, MEW 30:596-597.
89. See Ch. 15, pp. 312-314, and in this chapter p. 501.
90. M: Aff. in Pruss., N. Y. Tribune, 8 Nov. 1858.
91. M: Paper Tax, N. Y. Tribune, 22 Aug. 1860.
92. M/E: New Charter, NRZ 17 May 1849, MEW 6:497; ME: First Press Prosec., MEW 6:223.

21. ORIENTAL DESPOTISM: THE SOCIAL BASIS

1. The phrase is from the contemporary *New American Cyclopaedia*; see Special Note E, p. 656.
2. ME: Ger. Ideol. (64), 80 fn; the break is more accurately shown at MEW 3:65.
3. The explicit statement is made at ME: Ger. Ideol. (64), 77.
4. ME: Ger. Ideol., in MEW 3:22 [tr. 33] .
5. ME: Ger. Ideol. (64), 77 [MEW 3:61] .
6. Ibid., 33, rev. after MEW 3:22-23.

7. Ibid., 77 [MEW 3:62].
8. The ref. to three centuries is in M: Chinese Aff., MEW 15:514.
9. ME: Review/Jan.-Feb., in ME: On Colon., 18, 17.
10. Ibid., 18.
11. Same, in MEW 7:220-221.
12. M: Duchess of Sutherland, in ME: Art. Brit., 145.
13. M: Cap. 1:729-730.
14. Mill: Hist. Brit. India, 1:314.
15. M: Rev. in China, in ME: On Colon., 19
16. Ibid., 24.
17. Ibid., 25.
18. M: Cap. 1 in MEW 23:85 fn; the Eng. tr. omitted the ref. to "dancing tables," which would have needed explanation. (For the explanation, see "Tischrücken" in Ladendorf: Hist. Schlagwb., 314; cf. M: Chinese Aff., MEW 15:514.)
19. M: Aff. in Holland, in ME: On Colon., 29.
20. For M's later years, see his painstaking work in M: Notes on Ind. Hist. For his and E's reading in Oriental history, see Hobsbawm's intro to M: Pre-Cap. Econ. Form., 21-22.
21. For the passages in which Bernier stresses this, see Bernier: Travels, 5, 204, 220, 226, 232.
22. Ltr, M to E, 2 June 1853, MEW 28:252-254 [ME:SC, 80-81].
23. Ltr, E to M, 6 June 1853, MEW 28:259 [ME:SC, 82].
24. M: Cap. 1 in MEW 23:379 [tr. 1:358]; M: Chinese Aff., MEW 15:514, 516; E: Persia—China, N. Y. Tribune, 5 June 1857, in ME: On Colon. (68), 120; M: Opium Trade/I, N. Y. Tribune, 20 Sept. 1858, ibid., 216.
25. M: Future Res. Brit. Rule, N. Y. Tribune, 8 Aug. 1853, in ME:SW 1:494.
26. M: Grundrisse, 30.
27. M: Brit. Rule in Ind., N. Y. Tribune, 25 June 1853, in ME:SW 1:490. For Munro, see M: Notes on Ind. Hist., 138.
28. M: Chinese Aff., MEW 15:514.
29. Ex Lib. K. M., 103.
30. M: Cap. 1 in MEW 23:379 [tr. 1:358].
31. M: Cap. 1:79 [MEW 23:93-94]; M: Brit. Rule in India, N. Y. Tribune, 25 June 1853, in ME:SW 1:488; M: Chinese Aff., MEW 15:514; E: B. Bauer & Early Chr., in ME: On Relig., 201-203, and his On Hist. Early Chr., ibid., 314-315; ME: Ger. Ideol. (64), 51; Thalheimer: Intro. Dial. Mat., Ch. 14-15 (cf. also Ch. 1-2).
32. Ltr, E to M, 6 June 1853, MEW 28:259 [ME:SC, 82].
33. Brit. Rule in Ind., N. Y. Tribune, 25 June 1853, in ME:SW 1:489.
34. M: Cap. 1:513-514, 514 fn.
35. Ltr, M to E, 14 June 1853, MEW 28:267 [ME:SC, 85].
36. Same ltr, ibid.; M: Brit. Rule in Ind., in ME:SW 1:491f; M: Cap. 1:358 fn; in all three cases Marx is quoting from Raffles, not Campbell.
37. This passage is given here, punctuation and all, as it appears in the original report, not as transcribed by Raffles (from whom Marx cites it) or others. Source: Fifth Report of the Select Committee of the House of Commons on Indian Affairs, 1812. Part II, Presidency of Fort St. George, section on the "Northern Circars." In: I.U.P. Series of Brit. Parl. Papers, Colonies—East India, 3. East India Co. Affairs, 1812 (377) vol: VIII, p. 85.
38. Ltr, M to E, 14 June 1853, MEW 28:268 [ME:SC, 86].

39. M: Brit. Rule in Ind., in ME:SW 1:492.
40. Re slavery: e.g., same article, ibid.; re domestic slavery as a subordinate form, see E: Anti-Dühr. (59), 480. M: Lord Canning's Proc., N. Y. Tribune, 7 June 1858, in ME: On Colon., 192; ME: Russo-Turk. Difficulty, N. Y. Tribune, 25 July 1853, in ibid., 70-73.
41. For ex., see M: Notebk. on Phear, 256, 283.
42. M: Cap. 1 in MEW 23:93 [tr. 79]. Ltr, M to E, 14 June 1853, in ME:SC, 86. M: Lord Canning's Proc., in ME: On Colon., 190ff.
43. M: Notebk. on Lubbock, 340.
44. M: Brit. Rule in Ind., in ME:SW 1:492.
45. M: Cap. 3:328.
46. M: Future Results Brit. Rule, in ME:SW 1:496.
47. M: Cap. 3:583-584.
48. M: Grundrisse, 742.
49. M: Cap. 1:334.
50. M: Cap. 1 in MEW 23:102 [tr. 1:87].
51. *Ex Lib. K. M.,* 103.
52. M: Cap. 1 in MEW 23:378-379 [tr. 1:357-358]; the continuation of this passage was quoted on p. 524.
53. M: Grundrisse, 375-376 [tr. 68-69].
54. Ibid. (These ideas are repeated in other contexts later: p. 380, 383, 385 [tr. 75, 79, 82].)
55. Ibid., 377 [tr. 69-70]; cf. also 383 [tr. 79].
56. Ibid., 390 [tr. 88].
57. Ibid., 377 [tr. 70-71].
58. Ibid., 371.
59. Ibid., 742, 382.
60. Ibid., 386 [tr. 83].
61. Ibid., 423-424.
62. Ibid., 392-393 [tr. 91]; cf. also a brief repetition in 394 [tr. 93].
63. Ibid., 394 [tr. 94].
64. Cf. Marx's discussion of Linguet's "Asiatic slavery" in M. Theor. S. V., 1:335, 339.
65. E: Cond. Wkg. Cl. Eng./Pref. 87, in ME: On Brit., 10.
66. M: Grundrisse, 393 [tr. 91-92]; the preceding exposition began on 392.
67. Ibid., 395. (Tr. in M: Pre-Cap. Ec. Form., 95, garbles this.)
68. M: Theor. S. V. 3, in MEW 26.3:414 [tr. 3:422-423]; the first set of parentheses stand for brackets in Marx's ms.
69. M: Ltr to Zasulich, 8 Mar. 1881/2d Draft, in ME Archiv, 1:332; 1st Draft, ibid., 1:320 [ME:SW 3:154].
70. See §3, p. 520.
71. M: Grundrisse, 375, 377 [tr. 67, 70-71].
72. Ibid., 377 [tr. 70].
73. Ibid., 376, 378, 386 [tr. 68, 72, 82]; 377 [tr. 70]; 396-397 [tr. 97]. These four subdivisions are also listed at ibid., 395 [tr. 95]; 377 [tr. 70]; 380 [tr. 75].
74. In these drafts, see *passim,* 1st Draft, in ME Archiv, 1:318-322 [ME:SW 3:152-156]; 2d Draft, ibid., 332-333; 3d Draft, ibid., 335-338.
75. M: Crit. Pol. Ec./Pref., in ME:SW 1:504 [MEW 13:9].

76. M: Grundrisse, 9 (from Intro.; the corrected reading in MEW 13:619 is used here), 850-851 (from the earliest part), 764 (end); in addition cf. 628. See also 429-430 about governmental public works in Europe as well as Asia.
77. M: Crit. Pol. Ec., MEW 13:21 [tr. 33].
78. M: Cap. 1:77-78.
79. Ltr, M to E, 14 Mar. 1868, MEW 32:42.
80. Ltr, M to E, 25 Mar. 1868, in ME:SC, 201, rev. after MEW 32:51-52. For the same point, see M: Ltr to Zasulich, 8 Mar. 1881/1st Draft, in ME Archiv, 1:320 [ME:SW 3:154] and 3d Draft, ibid., 1:336. Re other survivals in Germany, see E: On Soc. Rel. Russ., in ME:SW 2:392, 393 [MEW 18:562, 563].
81. Ltr, M to Kugelmann, 17 Feb. 1870, MEW 32:650.
82. M: Cap. 1 in MEW 23:354 fn; cf. the editorial change in M: Cap. 1:334 fn; the difference was pointed out by R. Rosdolsky quoted in Thorner: *M on India*, 60 fn.
83. M: Ltr to Zasulich, 8 Mar. 1881/1st Draft, in ME Archiv, 1:320 [ME:SW 3:154].
84. Same, 3d Draft, ibid., 1:335; similar statement in 1st Draft, ibid., 1:318 [ME:SW 3:152].
85. Same, 1st Draft, ibid., 1:321, 322 [ME:SW 3:155, 156]; 2d Draft, ibid., 1:332; 3d Draft, ibid., 1:335, 336.
86. Same, 3d Draft, ibid., 1:337-338.
87. Same, 1st Draft, ibid., 1:318 [ME:SW 3:152].
88. Same, 3d Draft, ibid., 1:335, 336-337; 1st Draft, ibid., 1:321 [ME:SW 3:155].
89. Same, 3d Draft, ibid., 1:337-338; similar statement in 1st Draft, ibid., 1:322 [ME:SW 3:156].
90. E: On Soc. Rel. Russ., in ME:SW 2:393 [MEW 18:563].

22. ORIENTAL DESPOTISM: STATE AND BUREAUCRACY

1. The citations are from Eccarius' German version of this work, *Eines Arbeiters Widerlegung*, pp. 4-5. The translation is based on that in the *Labor Standard*, 20 Jan. 1877, p. 2 ("A Workingman's Refutation . . ."); the italicization does not appear in the German. For Engels on Eccarius' book, see ltr, E to Schlüter, 7 Dec. 1885, MEW 36:408. The quote from M: Crit. Pol. Ec./Pref. is the one given on p. 539, n. 75.
2. M: Grundrisse, 484.
3. E: Anti-Dühr./Prep. Writ., in Anti-Dühr. (59), 486.
4. On this use of *state*, see the fn, Ch. 11, p. 245.
5. E: Anti-Dühr. (59), 205.
6. Ibid., 224.
7. For ex., see M: Notebk. on Maine, 294 and passim in the following pages.
8. Ibid., 247, 248.
9. Ibid., 248-249.
10. Tökei: *Sur M. P. A.*, esp. 61-63.
11. M: War Qu., N. Y. Tribune, 5 Aug. 1853, in ME: On Colon., 79. M: Cap. 3:619. M: Theor. S. V. 3:412 [MEW 26.3:420]. E: Anti-Dühr. (59), 243-244.

12. M: Cap. 3 in MEW 25:338 [tr. 3:321].
13. M: Cap. 3:325, rev. after MEW 25:343.
14. M: Cap. 3 in MEW 25:798; this passage is quoted below, p. 569.
15. M: Grundrisse, 18; there are unimportant references to tribute on 9, 26.
16. M: Future Res. Brit. Rule, in ME:SW 1:494.
17. See esp. Ch. 19, pp. 468-475; also Ch. 5, p. 118f, with mentions at Ch. 3, p. 86f; Ch. 8, p. 171; Ch. 14, p. 321f.
18. This letter was cited on p. 527.
19. M: Brit. Rule in Ind., in ME:SW 1:492-493.
20. M: Ltr to Zasulich, 8 Mar. 1881/1st Draft, in ME Archiv, 1:325; not included in tr. in ME:SW 3:158 because it occurs in a stricken passage; similar formulation repeated in 3d Draft, ibid., 1:338-339.
21. Same/1st Draft, in ME Archiv, 1:323-324 [tr. ME:SW 3:157].
22. E: On Soc. Rel. Russ., in ME:SW 2:394.
23. E: Anti-Dühr./Prep. Writ., in Anti-Dühr. (59), 483.
24. E: Anti-Dühr. (59), 250.
25. M: Revol. Spain/I, in ME: Rev. in Spain, 25.
26. Ibid., 26.
27. M: Cap. 1:514.
28. M: Revol. Spain/I, in ME: Rev. in Spain, 21-23.
29. Ltr, E to Bebel, 18 Jan. 1884, MEW 36:88 [ME: On Colon., 309].
30. Ltr, E to Kautsky, 16 Feb. 1884, MEW 36:109 [ME:SC, 368, makes a bad error].
31. See particularly §5, p. 425f.
32. M: Opium Trade/II, N. Y. Tribune, 25 Sept. 1858, in ME: On Colon., 217; cf. also 218-219.
33. M: Chinese Aff., MEW 15:514ff.
34. See Ch. 20, p. 485 fn.
35. Wittfogel: *Oriental Desp.*, 380.
36. M: Cap. 1 in MEW 23:93 [tr. 79].
37. M: Grundrisse, 25.
38. See Ch. 22, p. 549.
39. M: Cap. 1:598; cf. MEW 23:625.
40. See Ch. 21, p. 520.
41. M: Civ. War Fr./1st Draft, in ME: Wr. Par. Com., 165-166.
42. E: Frankish Age, MEW 19:477; cf. also 478.
43. M: Theor. S. V. 3:416 [MEW 26.3:408, 581].
44. Ibid., 435 [MEW 26.3:428, 587].
45. M: Theor. S. V. 3 in MEW 26.3:391 [tr. 400].
46. See p. 553 (point 3).
47. M: Theor. S. V. 3:412 [MEW 26.3:420].
48. M: Cap. 3 in MEW 25:802-803, 804 [tr. 775, 776].
49. Cited above, §3, p. 552.
50. M: Grundrisse, 75; the preceding exposition begins on 73. Cf. also 81.
51. M: Cap. 1:333-334, or MEW 23:353; the passage from Jones's *Text-Book of Lectures*, quoted by Marx from the 1852 ed., appeared in his *Literary Remains*, pp. 451-452.
52. M: Cap. 1:334 rev. after MEW 23:353.
53. M: Grundrisse, 337; cf. also 427.
54. M: Cap. 1 in MEW 23:537 fn [tr. 514 fn].
55. Wittfogel: *Oriental Desp.*, 382.

56. M: Cap. 3 in MEW 25:798 [tr. 771].
57. M: Cap. 1 in MEW 23:93 [tr. 79].
58. M: Cap. 3 in MEW 25:799 [tr. 771-772].
59. Ibid., 799-800 [tr. 772].
60. Ibid., 800 [tr. 772].

23. RUSSIAN CZARISM: STATE AND BUREAUCRACY

1. Ltr, E to Zasulich, 23 Apr. 1885, ME:SC, 385.
2. Ltr, M to E, 14 Mar. 1868, MEW 32:42; also cited above, Ch. 21, p. 541. For the Narodnik boast, see e.g. E: On Soc. Rel. Russ., in ME:SW 2:393 [MEW 18:562-563].
3. Ltr, M to E, 7 Nov. 1868, ME:SC, 217, rev. after MEW 32:197.
4. See Ch. 21, p. 555f.
5. M: Cap. 3:329.
6. M: Pol. Eur. Mission, in *Le Socialisme*, 4, 5; E: Turk. Qu., N. Y. Tribune, 19 Apr. 1853, in ME: Russ. Men., 134; M: War Qu., N. Y. Tribune, 5 Aug. 1853, in M: East. Qu., 75; M: Financial Fail., N. Y. Tribune, 12 Aug. 1853, in ME: Russ. Men., 167 (cf. also 169); ltr, M to Kugelmann, 17 Feb. 1870, MEW 32:650; M: Secr. Dip. Hist., 111, 121, 125, 126.
7. E: Afterword/On Soc. Rel. Russ., in ME:SW 2:408 [MEW 22:433].
8. M: Ltr to Zasulich, 8 Mar. 1881/2d Draft, in ME Archiv, 332 [tr. ME: Russ. Men., 222].
9. Ltr, E to Danielson, 22 Sept. 1892, in ME: Corr. (35), 498-499.
10. Ltr, E to Faerber, 22 Oct. 1885, MEW 36:375.
11. Ltr, E to M, 25 Aug. 1877, MEW 34:73-74.
12. E: Infantry, 180.
13. E: For. Pol. Russ. Cz./Time, Part III, 540.
14. Ltr, E to Danielson, 18 June 1892, ME:SC, 445.
15. E: Afterword/On Soc. Rel. Russ., in ME:SW 2:407, rev. after MEW 22:432-433.
16. Ltr, E to Danielson, 18 June 1892, retrans. from MEW 38:364 (orig. in Eng.).
17. M: Grundrisse, 406-407 [tr. 111]; cf. also 655.
18. E: For. Po. Russ. Cz./Time, Part III, 533-34.—On breeding capitalists, see also ltr, E to Bebel, 1 Oct. 1891, MEW 38:160 ("The Russian bourgeoisie . . . is what it is through the state," etc.).
19. ME: Russo-Turk. Difficulty, N. Y. Tribune, 25 July 1853, in ME: On Colon., 73.
20. M: War Qu., N. Y. Tribune, 5 Aug. 1853, in ME: On Colon., 78; M: Future Res. Brit. Rule, N. Y. Tribune, 8 Aug. 1853, in ME:SW 1:495.
21. M: Ltr to Zasulich, 8 Mar. 1881/1st Draft, in ME Archiv, 327 [tr. 159-160].
22. Ibid., 328 [tr. 160].
23. Same, 2d Draft, in ME Archiv, 334.
24. E: Afterword/On Soc. Rel. Russ., MEW 22:433 [ME:SW 2:408].
25. M: Pol. Eur. Mission, in *Le Socialisme*, 4.
26. M: Notebk. on Maine, 330.
27. M: Secr. Dip. Hist., 125.
28. E: Afterword/On Soc. Rel. Russ., MEW 22:434-435 [ME:SW 2:409].

29. E: What Is to Become of Turk., N. Y. Tribune, 21 Apr. 1853.
30. Ibid.
31. E: article (no title) in N. Y. Tribune, 23 Dec. 1858.
32. E: On Soc. Rel. Russ., in ME:SW 2:388 [MEW 18:557].
33. Ibid., 390 [MEW 18:559].
34. See Ch. 20, §6.
35. Ltr, E to Danielson, 18 June 1892, in ME:SC, 446.
36. E: On Soc. Rel. Russ., in ME:SW 2:394, rev. after MEW 18:563 f.
37. See Ch. 20, p. 499 and fn; Ch. 16, p. 415.
38. See Ch. 14, p. 328f.

Special Note A. MARX AND
THE ECONOMIC JEW STEREOTYPE

1. See Dagobert Runes, ed.: *A World Without Jews,* by Karl Marx, an alleged
    translation; the reader is not told that the title is Runes's invention; there are
    other distortions in the text.
2. For the *usurer* definition, see any good German-English dictionary (e.g.,
    Muret-Sanders, 1920, or Wildhagen-Héraucourt, 1970) as well as, say, the
    1843 edition of Flügel's, under *Jude, Judelei, judeln,* etc. Cf. *Encyclopaedia
    Judaica* (Berlin, 1932—pre-Hitler), v. 9, p. 530. English was no different: in
    the Oxford English Dictionary, under *Jew* and its forms, see the examples
    cited from writers like Byron, Coleridge, Cobbett, Washington Irving, D. G.
    Rossetti, going back to Chaucer. (In 1973 this dictionary was sued on the
    demand that it should suppress this corner of philology.) For the German
    Jews' tendency to abandon *Jude* as a dirty word by the beginning of the
    19th century, see Graupe: *Entstehung Mod. Jud.,* 235; also the comment in
    Waldman: *Goethe,* 255.
3. Bauer: *Jewish Prob.,* 10, 114, 123; Silberner: *Soz. z. Jud.,* 117; Sterling:
    Judenhass, 101.
4. Silberner: *Soz. z. Jud.,* 117; Sterling: *Judenhass,* 101.
5. Stirner: *Ego,* 20-21, 48, 135.
6. Massing: *Rehearsal,* 253, n. 15; Silberner: *Soz. z. Jud.,* 126; Diamond:
    Marx's First Thesis, 544; Mehring: *Gesch. Deut. Soz.-Dem.,* 1:121-122.
7. Cornu: *K. M. et F. E.,* 2:273, 330 fn. 1; Silberner: *M. Hess,* 191-192;
    McLellan: *Yg. Heg. & K. M.,* 153-154.
8. Hess: *Phil. Soz. Schrift.,* 345-346; Silberner: *M. Hess,* 188-189, also partly
    quoted in his *Soz. z. Jud.,* 184-185, in both without the least comment. Cf.
    also Cornu: *K. M. et F. E.,* 2:273-274, 323-330.
9. Silberner: *M. Hess,* 130; and his *Soz. z. Jud.,* 184.
10. Silberner: *M. Hess,* 26-28, 48, 85.
11. Sterling: *Jewish Reac. to Jew-Hatred,* 110-112.
12. Silberner: *Soz. z. Jud.,* Ch. 10; Footman: *F. Lassalle,* 119-120.
13. Heine: *Works* (Leland), 8:75, 78; cf. also 510-511.
14. Rose: *H. Heine,* 132; cf. also 101.
15. Sterling: *Judenhass,* 101.
16. Lowenthal: *Jews Ger.,* 239; Reissner: *Rebel. Dilemma,* 179; Meyer: *Orig.
    Mod. Jew,* 181.

17. Silberner: *Soz. z. Jud.*, 127; cf. 167. Avineri: *Heg. Th. Mod. State,* 17-19, 55.
18. Krieger: *Ger. Idea Freed.*, 181; Silberner: *Soz. z. Jud.*, 170-172.
19. Sterling: *Judenhass,* 100-101.
20. Silberner: *M. Hess,* 86.
21. Mayer: *Early Ger. Soc.*, 410. Cf. also the example of W. Menzel mentioned incidentally in Silberner: *M. Hess,* 34.
22. Glickson: *Jewish Compl.*, 29.
23. Waldman: *Goethe,* 246-268, esp. 249.
24. Silberner: *Soz. z. Jud.*, 126-127.
25. Rosdolsky: *NRZ & Juifs,* 61.
26. Szajkowski: *Jewish St.-Simonians,* 60. For Fourierism, ibid., 46-50 esp.; Silberner: *Ch. Fourier* (all); also his *Att. of Fourierist School* (all), and his *Soz. z. Jud.*, 16-43. On Voltaire, Gay: *Party of Hum.*, 97-108, esp. 102. A good account on France is contained in Hertzberg: *French Enlight. & Jews.*
27. On Proudhon, Schapiro: *Lib. & Challenge,* 358-359; Draper: *Note on Father of Anarch.*, 80. On Bakunin, Carr: *M. Bakunin,* 145, 369, 371, 459; Pyziur: *Doctr. Anarch. Bak.*, 38 n.; Silberner: *Soz. z. Jud.*, Ch. 18. For James Guillaume, Bakunin's chief lieutenant, see his book *Karl Marx Pangermaniste,* which throughout carefully identifies as Jews all the possible enemies of humanity; also cf. Silberner: *Soz. z. Jud.*, 276.
28. See e.g. Harney's *Democratic Review,* editorial, v. 1, p. 352; Ernest Jones's *Notes to the People,* article on "The Jews in Poland" (probably not by Jones himself), v. 1, 1851, no. 11; for Bronterre O'Brien, see Collins & Abramsky, 253 and fn; about an O'Brienite, see Plummer: *Bronterre,* 268; Silberner: *Soz. z. Jud.*, Ch. 15.
29. Avineri: *M. & Jewish Emanc.*, 447.
30. Symons: *T. Carlyle,* 232; Wilson: *T. Carlyle,* 3:405, 409; 4:162-163, 373, 379, 451-452.
31. Quoted in Rocker: *London Yrs.*, 117, 119.
32. Summations of this economic-historical research may be found in: Ruppin: *Jews in Mod. World,* Part III, esp. 109-115, 122-123, 130-135; Reich: *Econ. Struc.*; Hertzler: *Sociol. Anti-Sem.*, 86-91; Graupe: *Entstehung Mod. Jud.*, 239-241; Cohen: *Jewish Life,* 182-213; Léon: *Jewish Qu.*
33. Sterling: *Judenhass,* 29-30; re the last sentence, see also Elbogen: *Gesch. Jud. Deutsch.*, 196-197, 222.
34. Ibid., 79.
35. For insight into lower-class anti-Jewish feeling, see Sterling: *Anti-Jewish Riots* (on 1819). Bloom: *K. M. & Jews,* 8. Mayer: *Early Ger. Soc.*, 417.
36. For one silly example of this trend, see Miriam Beard: *Anti-Sem.*, which is anthologized under the rubric "The Mirage of the Economic Jew."
37. Namier, in Ruppin: *Jews in Mod. World,* xvi; see also the presentation of the question in Graupe: *Entsteh. Mod. Jud.*, 239-241. For "others," Cohen: *Jewish Life,* 188 ff; Engelman: *Rise of Jew,* 93 ff.
38. Léon: *Jewish Qu.*, 219.
39. Ibid., 129-135.
40. M: *Grundrisse,* 134, 165, 167.
41. Greenberg: *Myth Jewish Paras.*, 223, 229; 223-234, 224-225.
42. Ibid., 225.
43. *Encyclopaedia Judaica* (Berlin, 1929), v. 4, pp. 974-975. On Syrkin, see e.g., Syrkin: *Ess. Soc. Zion.*, 23; or *Labor Zionist Handbk.*, 6.

44. McLellan: *M. bef. Mxism*, 141-142; also his ed. of *M: Early Texts*, 112; Tucker: *Phil. & Myth.*, 111.
45. Ruppin: *Jews Mod. World*, 133. Mayer: *Early Ger. Soc.*, 420; see also his explanation on 419-420. Sterling: *Judenhass*, 33; cf. use of *Schacherjuden* by young Engels in his Cond. Wkg. Cl. Eng., in MEW 2:487 [ME: On Brit., 314]. See also Meyer: *Orig. Mod. Jew*, 69.
46. Dühring: *Ueberschätz. Lessing's*, esp. but not only Ch. 3.
47. Lessing: *Nathan der Weise*, Act II, sc. 3; III, 4; IV, 4; III, 6; II, 9.
48. Quoted in Sterling: *Kampf Emanz. Jud.*, 285.
49. Lessing: *Sämt. Schrift.*, 6:160-161.
50. Gay: *Party of Hum.*, 97ff. "Voltaire's Anti-Semitism" is the chapter title.
51. Locke: *Ltr on Toler.*, 145 (for all quotations given).
52. Preface by Prof. Raymond Klibansky, in ibid., xxx.
53. Gay: *Party of Hum.*, 99-100.
54. Ibid., 103.
55. Engels' praise of Börne is so constant that one need simply look up Börne in the name index to MEW Eb. 2; some typical examples are at p. 395, 413, 420-421, 426, 430, 434. Later Engels qualified the relationship of Börne to Young Germany; cf. E: Rev./A. Jung, MEW 1:437.
56. E.g. E: Hungary, *NRZ* 19 May 1849, MEW 6:507, 514.
57. Ltr, E to W. Graeber, 30 July 1839, MEW Eb. 2:414-415; the same, 8 Oct. and 15 Nov. 1839, in ibid., 419, 432; the same, 15 Nov. 1839, ibid., 431; cf. E: Ger. Chapbks, MEW Eb. 2:16; also see his ref. to an essay "The Jews in Bremen" following month, ibid., 437 (not extant). E: E. M. Arndt, MEW Eb. 2:122.

Special Note B. RHYME AND REASON:
THE CONTENT OF MARX'S JUVENILE VERSE

1. Mehring: *K. M.*, 38-39; Mehring, ed.: *Aus lit. Nachlass*, 1:25-28.
2. Ltr, M to his father, 10 Nov. 1837, in M: Wr. Yg. M., 41-42, 46, 48. For Laura Marx Lafargue's letter on how her parents laughed about "this youthful foolishness," see Mehring, ed.: *Aus lit. Nachlass*, 1:25-26.
3. Cf. Ollivier: *ME Poètes* (the most ambitious effort); Johnston: *K. M.'s Verse*; Demetz: *ME & Poets*, 47-56; Ryazanov: intro. to MEGA I, 1.2:xiv-xv. Not counted is the gutter school of marxology (R. Payne, Künzli).
4. Mehring, ed.: *Aus lit. Nachlass*, 1:26.
5. MEW Eb. 1:676, n. 136. In the new English ME: Collected Works, see 1:756-7 (n. 191-194).
6. MEGA I, 1.2:3-89.
7. MEGA I, 1.2:51.
8. Published in a Berlin Young Hegelian weekly, *Athenäum*, for 23 Jan. 1841.
9. The *Athenäum* version (followed here) is in MEW Eb. 1:604-605 and MEGA I, 1.1:147. The original (notebook) version is in MEGA I, 1.2:57-58.
10. The *Athenäum* version is followed here; it is in MEW Eb. 1:605 and MEGA I, 1.1:148. The original version is in MEGA I, 1.2:9-10.
11. Johnston: *K. M.'s Verse*, 267.
12. Mehring: *Aus lit. Nachlass*, 1:28.
13. MEGA I, 1.2:81.

14. Ibid., 16.
15. MEW Eb. 1:608, or MEGA I, 1.2:42.
16. Ltr, M to Lassalle, 19 Apr. 1859, in ME:SC, 117.
17. MEW Eb. 1:609, or MEGA I, 1.2:43.
18. MEW Eb. 1:610-611, or MEGA I, 1.2:43-45.
19. MEW Eb. 1:607-608, or MEGA I, 1.2:41-42.
20. Ryazanov: intro. to MEGA I, 1.2:xiv.

Special Note C. THE STATE AS POLITICAL SUPERSTRUCTURE: MARX ON MAZZINI

1. In the form of a pamphlet: Joseph Mazzini, *To Louis Napoleon,* published in London.
2. A. J. C. A. Dureau dé la Malle: *Economie Politique des Romains,* 2v., Paris, 1840.
3. Montesquieu: *Considérations sur les Causes de la Grandeur des Romains et de Leur Décadence,* Amsterdam, 1734.
4. Joachim Lelewel: *Considérations sur l'Etat Politique de l'Ancienne Pologne et sur l'Histoire de Son Peuple,* Paris, 1844.
5. M: Mazzini's New Manif., N. Y. Tribune, 13 Oct. 1858; written 21 Sept.
6. M: Mazzini's Manif., N. Y. Tribune, 17 June 1859.

Special Note D. THE "STATE PARASITE" AND THE "CAPITALIST VERMIN"

1. Sanderson: *Interp. Pol. Ideas,* 55, 64, 68; also his *ME on State,* 951-953.
2. M: 18th Brum., in ME:SW 1:477.
3. M: article (no title) in N. Y. Tribune, 22 Feb. 1858.
4. M: Civ. War Fr., 2d Draft, in ME: Wr. Par. Com., 200.
5. Draper: *Death of State,* 293ff.
6. M: Civ. War Fr., 2d Draft, in ME: Wr. Par. Com., 196-197; see also 212, and for vampire image, 201.
7. M: Civ. War Fr., in ME:SW 2:221-222.
8. Ibid., 225.
9. Cf. the expletives bowdlerized (replaced by dashes) by the Russian editors, in ME: Wr. Par. Com., 106 (following the original publication), likewise in all available editions, e.g. MEW 17:496.
10. ME: Wr. Par. Com., 126, 129, 149, 153, 154. Other phrases of interest are on 124, 140, 146, 158, 160; for near cases, also 156, 166.
11. Ibid., 148.
12. Ibid., 149, 154, 156.
13. M: Notebk. on Maine, 329.
14. ME: Wr. Par. Com., 154.
15. See Ch. 20, p. 500.
16. M: Theor. S. V., 1:170.
17. From Jefferson's letter to William Ludlow, 1824.
18. M: Theor. S. V., 1:171 rev. after MEW 26.1:145.

19. Lenin: *Coll. Wks.,* 25:407; see also 430-431.
20. M: Theor. S. V., 2:16 [MEW 26.2:8].
21. See M: Cap. 3:583, 596; also compare p. 325 vs. 585; on 580, trade and usury are called twin brothers.
22. Ch. 23, p. 580.
23. M: Cond. Fact. Lab., N. Y. Tribune, 22 Apr. 1857.
24. M: Civ. War Fr., 1st Draft, in ME: Wr. Par. Com., 149.
25. E: On Soc. Rel. Russ., in ME:SW 2:390.
26. E: Orig. Fam., in ME:SW 3:323 rev. after MEW 21:161.
27. M: Grundrisse, 539; cf. also 643 on France.

Special Note E. ORIENTAL DESPOTISM
BEFORE MARX: THE WITTFOGEL FABLE

1. For the Comintern program, see Degras: *Com. Int. Docs.,* 2:506.
2. For the history of this question under Stalin, see Chesneaux: *Mode Prod. Asiat.,* 37-39. In *Recherches Int.* #57-58, see Suret-Canale, 10-11; Pecirka, 60 ff; other articles in this collection illustrate the pattern. A fuller account is in Sofri: *Über asiat. Prod.,* 99-127.
3. For this part of the story, see Parain: *Mode Prod. Asiat.,* 3-5; Chesneaux: *Mode Prod. Asiat.,* 34-35. The account in Encausse & Schram, 92-96, is worthless. For Tökei's work, see Bibliography.
4. Nikiforov: *Discussion,* 242.
5. Kautsky: *Labour Rev.,* 89.
6. Wittfogel: *Ruling Bur.,* 353.
7. Ibid., 350.
8. Wittfogel: *Oriental Desp.,* 5-6, 372.
9. Ibid., 373.
10. Wittfogel: *Ruling Bur.,* 350.
11. Ibid., 352.
12. Mill: *Rep. Govt.,* 274; 244, 245, 247.
13. Wittfogel: *Oriental Desp.,* 4.
14. Ibid., 6.
15. Ibid., 380; see also his *Ruling Bur.,* 352.
16. Wittfogel: *Oriental Desp.,* 381; likewise, for Bernier, in his *Ruling Bur.,* 354.
17. Wittfogel: *Oriental Desp.,* 380.
18. M: Grundrisse/Intro., in M: Crit. Pol. Ec., 211. M: Theor. S. V., 3:399, also 402; cf. also M: Cap. 1:598. Derogation of J. S. Mill runs through *Capital:* see M: Cap. 3:856, also 1:15-16, 518; also M: Grundrisse, 510, 644.
19. Packe: *Life of J. S. Mill,* 388-389; cf. also whole section, 387-391.
20. On Jesuits, Kautsky: *T. More,* 72. Lach: *China & Era Enlight.,* 209-211; Reichwein: *China & Eur.,* 78; Maverick: *China,* Ch. 1.
21. Wittfogel: *Oriental Desp.,* 1.
22. Rowbotham: *Missionary,* 277, 278; Rowbotham: *China,* 201. Maverick: *China,* 60.
23. Jacoby: *Bürokr. d. Welt,* 69-70; the valuable discussion here owes much to Tocqueville (see next note).
24. Tocqueville: *Old Regime & Fr. Rev.,* 8; highlights of the analysis will be found on 68, 146, 158-167, 189 esp.

25. Ibid., 167.
26. M: Herr Vogt, MEW 14:499-500.
27. M: Cap. 1:366. Cf. Hegel: *Philo. Hist.*, 206.
28. Maverick: *China*, 12-13, 18-19, 112; Lach: *China & Era Enlight.*, 215; Rowbotham: *China*, 183.
29. Lach: *Pref. to Leibniz*, 8-9, 31, 37-38, 65, 72 fn; the quotation is from 61.
30. Ibid., 49 (from a letter by Leibniz, tr. revised); Leibniz: *Nov. Sinica*, 70.
31. Jacoby: *Bürokr. d. Welt*, 71-74. For E's ref. to *policé*, see E: Orig. Fam., in ME:SW 3:283.
32. Herder: *Ideen z. Philo.*, 39, 12, 13; see also 7, 33, 86, 89.
33. M: Deeds of H. of Hohenzollern, MEW 6:477.
34. Rowbotham: *Voltaire* (all); also his *Missionary*, 282-284; Lach: *China & Era Enlight.*, 219-220.
35. Maverick: *China*, 27-33.
36. Jącoby: *Bürokr. d. Welt*, 78.
37. Bernier: *Travels*, 145 (qu.), also 195, 226; for description of the hierarchy, see esp. 205 ff, also 10, 204, 225-236. For 1688 work, Maverick: *China*, 16-17.
38. For Montesquieu, see e.g., Carcassonne: *Chine*, passim.
39. By Reichwein: *China & Eur.*, 105.
40. Quesnay: *Despotism in China*, 141; description of bureaucracy, 239-254; 215; administration, 235-237, 228, 219; 197; 172; classes, 200ff, 175. ("Confucius of Europe": Rowbotham: *Missionary*, 285.)
41. Tocqueville: *Old Regime & Fr. Rev.*, 161-163.
42. Ibid., 162-163.
43. Ibid., 164.
44. Rowbotham: *China*, 199 fn.
45. M: Theor. S. V. 1:65.
46. ·M: Cap. 3:765; cf. also Grundrisse, 235. On Physiocrats' combination of laissez faire and despotism, see Gide & Rist.: *Hist. Econ. Doct.*, 35-37.
47. On England, Rowbotham: *China*, 201 fn; Lach: *Pref. to Leibniz*, 57 fn. Rowbotham: *Missionary*, 288.
48. Schulin: *Weltg. Erf. Orients*, 42, 41.
49. Hegel: *Sämt. Werke*, 10:420-421.
50. Hegel: SW 11:181-182, 224 [tr. *Philo. Hist.*, 130-131, 165].
51. Ibid., 159 and cf. also 163 [tr. 112, 116]; 151 f, 150 [tr. 105, 104].
52. Hegel: SW 7:284 [tr. *Philo. Right*, 133].
53. Ibid., 380, 394, 412 [tr. 180, 188, 292 f].
54. Hegel: SW 11:133, 129-129 [tr. *Philo. Hist.*, 89, 85-86].
55. Hegel: SW 7:284 [tr. *Philo. Right*, 133].
56. Hegel: SW 17:130.
57. Hegel: SW 7:453 [tr. *Philo. Right*, 220].
58. Hegel: SW 11:182, 170, 178 [tr. *Philo. Hist.*, 131, 121, 127 f]; 201, 191 [tr. 147, 138].
59. Ibid., 174 [tr. 124].
60. Hegel: SW 13ː15. SW 7:341 [tr. *Philo. Right*, 280]. SW 11:150 [tr. *Philo. Hist.*, 104], 152 [tr. 105].
61. Hegel: SW 11:219, 251, 161 [tr. *Philo. Hist.*, 161, 188, 113].
62. Ibid., 219 [tr. 161]. SW 7:362 [tr. *Philo. Right*, 173]. SW 11:160 [tr. *Philo. Hist.*, 113].
63. Hegel: SW 11:174 [tr. *Philo. Hist.*, 124].

64. Ibid., 174-178 [tr. 124-127].
65. Ibid., 174 [tr. 124].
66. Ibid., 177 [tr. 127].
67. ME: Ger. Ideol., 174, 176, 180.
68. For Hegel, see *Sämt. Werke*, 11:162-163, 191, 234 [tr. *Philo. Hist.*, 115-116, 142, 173]; ibid., 7:453 [tr. *Philo. Right*, 220].
69. *Unter dem Banner des Marxismus*, Dec. 1931, Jg 5, p. 346ff. (Wittfogel's own ref. is only to p. 354, apparently a mistake.) Wittfogel: *Oriental Desp.*, 372 fn, 370.
70. Cornu: *K. M. et F. E.*, 1:133 (Ger. ed., 1:124).
71. Hess: *Phil. Soz. Schrift.*, 325; Silberner: *M. Hess*, 226.
72. E: Cond. Eng./Engl. Const., in ME: Art. Brit., 35.
73. Cornu: *K. M. et F. E.*, 3:64-68 (Ger. ed., 2:86-92); MEW 2:664, n. 115.
74. Rubel, in edit. notes in ME: Russ. Komm., 288-289; Grandjonc: *Vorwärts 1844*, 20, 25 n; Groh: *Russland & Selb. Eur.*, 184-191.
75. Custine: *Russia*, 1:271, 2:294 (cf. 2:6), 3:65, and elsewhere.
76. Ibid., 1:183, 228, 2:258. On officialdom: 1:121, 214; 2:15.
77. Ibid., 3:91, 150; last qu. from 3:150-151.
78. Ibid., 3:224-225.
79. Campbell: *Mod. Ind.*, 75-76; administration, 77 ff.
80. *Larousse du XIXᵉ Siècle* (1869), 4:127.
81. *New American Cyclopaedia* (1859), 5:101-102, 7:39. Hegel: *Philo. Hist.*, 204.

Special Note F. ORIENTAL DESPOTISM AND ENGELS

1. See pp. 522-527 above; for E's letter of 6 June 1853, MEW 28:259-261 (part tr. in ME:SC, 82-83).
2. For M's follow-up letter of 14 June 1853, see pp. 526-527 above; E's silence is indicated in ltr, M to E, 8 July 1853, MEW 28:272.
3. E: On Soc. Rel. Russ., in ME:SW 2:394.
4. E: Revol. Upris., MEW 6:525.
5. E: Orig. Fam., in ME:SW 3:293.
6. E: Orig. Fam., in MEW 21:170 [ME:SW 3:332].
7. M: Grundrisse, 484.
8. For this term, see E: Orig. Fam., MEW 21:97, for example.
9. E: Orig. Fam., in ME:SW 3:284 [MEW 21:116].
10. See ibid., 272 [MEW 21:102] for the case of Athens, for example.
11. Ltr, E to Sorge, 10 Nov. 1894, in ME:SC, 476 [MEW 39:310].
12. E: Afterwd./On Soc. Rel. Russ., in ME:SW 2:398-399 [MEW 22:421].
13. Kautsky: *Mod. Nat.*, 396.
14. Ibid., 397.
15. Ibid., 398.
16. Ltr, E to Sorge, 6 Apr. 1887, MEW 36:635 [ME: Ltrs. Amer., 180].
17. E.g., Mayer: F. Engels, 2:470-471.

BIBLIOGRAPHY

This list provides bibliographic data for titles referred to in the Reference Notes or in the text. In the first three sections—writings by Marx and Engels, writings by Marx, writings by Engels—titles are given first in English, followed by the original language (in italics), or by a double degree sign (°°) if the original was in English. The form of citation is the same for different kinds of writings— articles, books, or whatever. The following information is provided for individual writings: date of writing (W) or dateline (D); date of first publication by the author (P); source of the original text cited in this book (S); and an English translation, if any, used in this book (Tr). The CAPITALIZED titles are for published books, mainly collections of writings. When two entries are given for the same title, the lower-case entry deals with the writing as such; the capitalized entry represents a book published with that title, but often containing other writings as well. In the fourth section of this list (books and articles by others), entries list the edition used in this book. For abbreviations, see the note introducing the Reference Notes.

WRITINGS BY MARX AND ENGELS

The Address Question. *Die Adressfrage* (M/E). (P) 8 June 1848 in NRZ. (S) MEW 5:53.

The Alleged Schisms in the International. *Les Prétendues Scissions dans l'Internationale.* (D) 5 Mar. 1872. (P) May 1872, as General Council brochure. (S) *Mouvement Socialiste*, Paris, July-Aug. 1913. (Tr.) ME:SW 2:247, with an inaccurate title.

ARTICLES IN THE NEW AMERICAN CYCLOPAEDIA. Hal Draper, ed. Berkeley, Independent Socialist Press, 1969.

ARTICLES ON BRITAIN. Moscow, Progress Pub., 1971.

British Politics—Disraeli—The Refugees—Mazzini in London—Turkey.°° (P) 7 Apr. 1853 in N. Y. Tribune. Engels wrote only the section "Turkey."

THE COLOGNE COMMUNIST TRIAL. R. Livingstone, tr. New York, International Pub.; London, L&W, 1971.

The Communist Manifesto. *Das Kommunistische Manifest* (originally *Manifest der Kommunistischen Partei*). (P) brochure, Feb. 1848. (S) MEW 4:459. (Tr) ME:SW 1:98.

THE COMMUNIST MANIFESTO. D. Ryazanoff, ed. (including other writings). London, M. Lawrence, 1930.

CORRESPONDENCE 1846-1895. A SELECTION . . . (Binding title: *Selected*

Correspondence) D. Torr, ed. & tr. (Marxist Lib., 29) New York, International Pub., 1935.

Fall of the Camphausen Ministry. *Sturz des Ministeriums Camphausen* (M/E). (P) 23 June 1848 in NRZ. (S) MEW 5:96.

First Press Prosecution of the Neue Rheinische Zeitung. *Der erste Pressprozess der "Neuen Rheinischen Zeitung."* (W) delivered as defense speeches by M. and E., 7 Feb. 1849. (P) 14 Feb. 1849 in NRZ. (S) MEW 6:223.

The Freedom of Deliberations in Berlin. *Die Freiheit der Beratungen in Berlin.* (P) 17 Sept. 1848 in NRZ. (S) MEW 5:405. (Tr) ME: Rev. 48/49, 128.

The German Ideology. *Die deutsche Ideologie* . . . (W) Sept. 1845 to ca. summer 1846. (S) MEW 3:9. (Tr) next entry.

THE GERMAN IDEOLOGY. Moscow, Progress Pub., 1964. (This edition contains the complete work.)

GESAMTAUSGABE (full title: *Historisch-kritische Gesamtausgabe* . . .). Marx-Engels Institute, Moscow, ed. Frankfurt/Berlin/Moscow, 1927-35. There are two series of volumes: Series (*Abteilung*) I comprises vols. 1-7 plus an unnumbered 8th; Series III comprises vols. 1-4 (correspondence). Series II & IV never published; others never completed. In Series I, vol. 1 comprises two volumes, here called vol. 1.1 and 1.2.

Gottfried Kinkel. (P) NRZ Revue, no. 4 (May 1850). (S) MEW 7:299.

The Great Men of the Emigration. *Die grossen Männer des Exils.* (W) May-June 1852. (S) MEW 8:233. (Tr) ME: Cologne Communist Trial, 135, titled "Heroes of the Exile."

The Holy Family . . . *Die heilige Familie oder Kritik der kritischen Kritik* . . . (W) Sept.-Nov. 1844. (P) as book, Feb. 1845. (S) MEW 2:3. (Tr) next entry.

THE HOLY FAMILY, OR CRITIQUE OF CRITICAL CRITIQUE. R. Dixon, tr. Moscow, FLPH, 1956.

Hüser. *Hüser* (M/E). (P) 1 June 1848 in NRZ. (S) MEW 5:18.

IRELAND AND THE IRISH QUESTION. Moscow, Progress Pub., 1971.

Letter to the Brunswick Committee (Executive Committee) of the Social-Democratic Workers Party. *Brief an den Ausschuss der Sozialdemokratischen Arbeiterpartei.* (W) 22-30 Aug. 1870. (P) 5 Sept. 1870, leaflet. (S) MEW 17:268. (Tr) ME:SC, 245.

LETTERS TO AMERICANS 1848-1895. L. E. Mins, tr. New York, International Pub., 1953.

Life-and-Death Questions. *Lebens- und Sterbensfragen* (M/E). (P) 4 June 1848. (S) MEW 5:29.

The New Charter of the State of Siege. *Die neue Standrechts-Charte* (M/E). (P) 16-17 May 1849 in NRZ. (S) MEW 6:493.

ON BRITAIN. 2d. ed. Moscow, FLPH, 1962.

ON COLONIALISM. 4th enl. ed. Moscow, Progress Pub., 1968.

ON RELIGION. Moscow, FLPH, 1957.

Program of the Radical-Democratic Party and the Left Wing in Frankfurt. *Programme der radikal-demokratischen Partei und der Linken zu Frankfurt.* (M/E). (P) 7 June 1848 in NRZ. (S) MEW 5:39. (Tr) ME: Rev. 48/49, 30.

Review [January-February 1850]. *Revue* [in German]. (P) Mar. 1850 in NRZ Revue, no. 2. (S) MEW 7:213. (Tr) ME: On Colon., 17, in part.

[Review of] "Les Conspirateurs," par A. Chenu . . . [In German] (P) Mar. 1850 in NRZ Revue, no. 4. (S) MEW 7:266.

Review. May to October. *Revue / Mai bis Oktober.* (P) Nov. 1850 in NRZ Revue, no. 5/6. (S) MEW 7:421.

REVOLUTION IN SPAIN. (Marxist Lib., 12) New York, International Pub., 1939.

THE REVOLUTION OF 1848-1849. ARTICLES FROM THE NEUE RHEIN-

ISCHE ZEITUNG. S. Ryazanskaya, tr.; B. Isaacs, ed. New York, International Pub., 1972.
THE RUSSIAN MENACE TO EUROPE. A COLLECTION . . . P. W. Blackstock & B. F. Hoselitz, eds. Glencoe, Ill., Free Press, 1952.
DIE RUSSISCHE KOMMUNE. KRITIK EINES MYTHOS. M. Rubel, ed. Munich, Hanser, 1972.
The Russo-Turkish Difficulty—Ducking and Dodging of the British Cabinet— Nesselrode's Last Note—East India Question.°° (P) 25 July 1853 in N. Y. Tribune. (S) ME: On Colon., 70, last section only; all in M: East. Qu., 58.
SCRITTI ITALIANI. G. Bosio, ed. Milan/Rome, Ed. Avanti, 1955.
SELECTED CORRESPONDENCE. I. Lasker, tr.; S. Ryazanskaya, ed. 2d. ed. Moscow, Progress Pub., 1965.
SELECTED CORRESPONDENCE. Moscow, FLPH, n.d. [1955].
SELECTED WORKS IN THREE VOLUMES. Moscow, Progress Pub., 1969-70.
SELECTED WORKS IN TWO VOLUMES. Moscow, FLPH, 1955.
The Speech from the Throne. *Die Thronrede* (M/E). (P) 1-2 Mar. 1849 in NRZ. (S) MEW 6:314.
The Stupp Amendment. *Das Amendement Stupp* (M/E). (P) 21 June 1848 in NRZ. (S) MEW 5:90.
Valdenaire's Arrest—Sebaldt. *Valdenaires Haft—Sebaldt* (M/E). (P) 19 June 1848 in NRZ. (S) MEW 5:83.
WERKE. Institut für Marxismus-Leninismus beim ZK der SED, ed. Berlin, Dietz, 1956-68. Thirty-nine volumes plus supplements; Vol. 26 (*Theories of Surplus Value*) in three parts, 26.1, 26.2, 26.3; supplementary volume (*Ergänzungsband*) in two parts, Eb.1, Eb.2.
WRITINGS ON THE PARIS COMMUNE. Hal Draper, ed. New York, Monthly Review Press, 1971.

WRITINGS BY MARX

Affairs in Holland—Denmark—Conversion of the British Debt—India, Turkey and Russia.°° (P) 9 June 1853 in N. Y. Tribune.
Affairs in Prussia.°° This is the title of several articles in the N. Y. Tribune during 1858-1860.
Afterword to the Second German Edition of *Capital* (vol. 1). *Nachwort zur zweiten Auflage* . . . (D) 24 Jan. 1873. (S) MEW 23:18. (Tr) as pref. to 1887 English ed. by Engels, in M: Cap. 1:12 or ME:SW 2:91.
The Association for Administrative Reform. *Die Administrativreform-Assoziation.* (P) 8 June 1855 in Neue Oder-Zeitung. (S) MEW 11:266. (Tr) ME: Art. Brit., 233.
The Attack on Francis Joseph—The Milan Riot—British Politics—Disraeli's Speech —Napoleon's Will.°° (P) 8 Mar. 1853 in N. Y. Tribune.
The Banning of the Leipziger Allgemeine Zeitung. *Das Verbot der "Leipziger Allgemeinen Zeitung."* (P) 1-16 Jan. 1843 in RZ, as seven articles each with own title; over-all title by MEW. (S) MEW 1:152.
The Bill on the Abolition of Feudal Burdens. *Der Gesetzentwurf über die Aufhebung der Feudallasten.* (P) 30 July 1848 in NRZ. (S) MEW 5:278. (Tr) ME: Rev. 48/49, 71.
Bolivar y Ponte.°° (W) Jan. 1858. (P) 1858 in *New American Cyclopaedia.* (S) ME: Rev. in Spain, 170, or ME: Art. N.A.C., 125.
Bonaparte's Present Position.°° (P) 1 Apr. 1858 in N. Y. Tribune.

A Bourgeois Document. *Ein Bourgeoisaktenstück.* (P) 5 Jan. 1849 in NRZ. (S) MEW 6:151. (Tr) ME: Rev. 48/49, 206.

The British Army.°° (P) 14 Apr. 1855 in N. Y. Tribune.

British Commerce and Finance.°° (P) 4 Oct. 1858 in N. Y. Tribune.

The British Constitution. *Die britische Konstitution.* (P) 6 Mar. 1855 in Neue Oder-Zeitung. (S) MEW 11:95. (Tr) ME: Art. Brit., 221.

British Incomes in India.°° (P) 21 Sept. 1857 in N. Y. Tribune, untitled. (S) ME: On Colon., 168, titled as shown.

The British Rule in India.°° (P) 25 June 1853 in N.Y. Tribune. (S) ME:SW 1:488.

Capital. *Das Kapital. Kritik der politischen Okonomie.* (W) Aug. 1863 to Feb. 1866; for vol. 1 as published, Feb. 1866 to Aug. 1867. (P) Vol. 1: Sept. 1867; vol. 2 (Engels, ed.): 1885; vol. 3 (Engels, ed.): 1894. (S) MEW 23, 24, 25. (Tr) next entry.

CAPITAL . . . Vol. 1: S. Moore and E. Aveling, trs.; Engels, ed. Moscow, FLPH, n.d.; vols. 2-3 (Untermann tr. revised): Moscow, FLPH, 1957-59.

The Centralization Question. *Die Zentralisationsfrage* . . . (W) May 1842; unfinished. (S) MEW Eb.1:379. (Tr) M: Writings of the Young Marx, 106.

The Chartists.°° (P) 25 Aug. 1852 in N. Y. Tribune. (S) ME: On Brit., 358.

Chinese Affairs. *Chinesisches.* (P) 7 July 1862 in Die Presse, Vienna. (S) MEW 15:514.

The Civil War in France. Address of the General Council . . .°° (W) May 1871. (P) June 1871, pamphlet. (S) ME:SW 2:202.

The Civil War in France. First Draft.°° (W) Apr.-May 1871. (S) ME: Writings on Paris Commune, 103.

The Civil War in France. Second Draft.°° (W) May 1871. (S) ME: Writings on Paris Commune, 179.

The Class Struggles in France 1848 to 1850. *Die Klassenkämpfe in Frankreich 1848 bis 1850.* (W) Jan.-Nov. 1850. (P) Mar.-Nov. 1850 in NRZ Revue, nos. 1, 2, 3, 5/6, as series of articles. (S) MEW 7:9. (Tr) ME:SW 1:205.

Comments on the Latest Prussian Censorship Instructions. *Bemerkungen über die neueste preussische Zensurinstruktion.* (W) 15 Jan. to 10 Feb. 1842. (P) Feb. 1843 in Anekdota [&c.], Switzerland, bd.1, 1843. (S) MEW 1:3. (Tr) M: Writings of Young Marx, 67.

Communism and the Augsburg Allgemeine Zeitung. *Der Kommunismus und die Augsburger "Allgemeine Zeitung."* (W) 15 Oct. 1842. (P) 16 Oct. 1842 in RZ. (S) MEW 1:105. (Tr) M: Writings of Young Marx, 131.

The Communism of the Rheinische Beobachter. *Der Kommunismus des "Rheinischen Beobachters."* (P) 12 Sept. 1847 in Deutsche Brüsseler Zeitung. (S) MEW 4:191. (Tr) part in ME: On Relig., 81.

Condition of the Factory Laborers.°° (P) 22 Apr. 1857 in N. Y. Tribune.

Confessions.°° [A game] (W) early 1860s; there are three extant versions: Laura's (pub. in Reminisc. M. E., 266); Jenny's (facsim. of original in MEW 31: opp. 596); Zalt-Bommel's (pub. in Internatl. Rev. of Soc. Hist., vol. 1, 1956, pt. 1, p. 107).

The Constitution of the French Republic Adopted November 4, 1848.°° (P) Notes to the People, London, no. 7, June 1851, vol. 1, p. 125.

Contribution to the Critique of Political Economy. *See* Critique of Political Economy.

CONTRIBUTION TO THE CRITIQUE OF POLITICAL ECONOMY. S. W. Ryazanskaya, tr.; M. Dobb, ed. New York, International Pub., 1970.

Corruption at Elections.°° (P) 4 Sept. 1852 in N. Y. Tribune. (S) ME: On Brit., 370.

The Crisis in England.°° (P) 24 Mar. 1855 in N. Y. Tribune. (S) ME: On Brit., 423.

Critical Notes on "The King of Prussia and Social Reform." *Kritische Randglossen zu dem Artikel "Der König von Preussen und die Sozialreform . . ."* (P) 7-10 Aug. 1844 in Vorwärts, Paris. (S) MEW 1:392. (Tr) M: Writings of Young Marx, 338.

Critique of the Gotha Program. *Kritik des Gothaer Programms . . .* (W) Apr.-May 1875. (S) MEW 19:15. (Tr) ME:SW 3:13.

Critique of Hegel's Philosophy of Right: Introduction. *Zur Kritik der Hegelschen Rechtsphilosophie. Einleitung.* (W) end of 1843 to Jan. 1844. (P) Feb. 1844 in DFJ. (S) MEW 1:378. (Tr) M: Writings of Young Marx, 249.

Critique of Hegel's Philosophy of Right (Manuscript). *Aus der Kritik der Hegelschen Rechtsphilosophie. Kritik des Hegelschen Staatsrechts (§§261-313).* (W) Summer 1843. (S) MEW 1:201. (Tr) next entry.

CRITIQUE OF HEGEL'S 'PHILOSOPHY OF RIGHT.' A. Jolin & J. O'Malley, trs.; J. O'Malley, ed. Cambridge, University Press, 1970.

Critique of Political Economy. *Zur Kritik der politischen Ökonomie.* (W) Aug. 1858 to Jan. 1859, on basis of M: Grundrisse. (P) 1859, as book. (S) MEW 13:3. (Tr) M: Contrib. to Crit. Pol. Ec. (70); pref. only in ME:SW 1:502.

Debates on Freedom of the Press. *Debatten über Pressfreiheit . . . (Die Verhandlungen des 6. rheinischen Landtags. Erster Artikel).* (W) Apr. 1842. (P) 5-19 May 1842 in RZ. (S) MEW 1:28.

Debates on the Wood-Theft Law. *Debatten über das Holzdiebstahlsgesetz. (Verhandlungen des 6. rheinischen Landtags. Dritter Artikel).* (W) Oct. 1842. (P) 25 Oct. to 3 Nov. 1842 in RZ. (S) MEW 1:109.

The Democratic Party. *Die demokratische Partei.* (P) 2 June 1848 in NRZ. (S) MEW 5:22. (Tr) ME: Rev. 48/49, 27.

The Deeds of the House of Hohenzollern. *Die Taten des Hauses Hohenzollern.* (P) 10 May 1849 in NRZ. (S) MEW 6:477.

The Divorce Bill. *Der Ehescheidungsgesetzentwurf.* (P) 19 Dec. 1842 in RZ. (S) MEW 1:148. (Tr) M: Writings of Young Marx, 138.

Doctoral Dissertation: Difference Between the Democritean and Epicurean Philosophies of Nature. *Doktordissertation: Differenz der demokritischen und epikureischen Naturphilosophie.* (W) 1840 to Mar. 1841. (S) MEW Eb.1:257.— Dedication. *Widmung/Zueignung.* (W) Mar. 1841. (S) MEW Eb.1:259.— Foreword. *Vorrede.* (W) Mar. 1841. (S) MEW Eb.1:261.—Notes. *Anmerkungen.* (W) Mar. 1841. (S) MEW Eb.1:311.—Notebooks . . . *Hefte zur epikureischen, stoischen und skeptischen Philosophie.* (W) from early 1839. (S) MEW Eb.1:13.

The Duchess of Sutherland and Slavery.°° (P) 12 Mar. 1853 in People's Paper; 9 Feb. 1853 in N. Y. Tribune as part of another article. (S) ME: Art. Brit., 143.

EARLY TEXTS. David McLellan, tr. & ed. New York, Barnes & Noble, 1971.

THE EASTERN QUESTION. A REPRINT OF LETTERS [articles] . . . Eleanor Marx Aveling & Edw. Aveling, eds. New York, 1897, repr. 1968.

Echoes of Erfurt in 1859. *Die Erfurterei im Jahre 1859.* (P) 9 July 1859 in Das Volk, London. (S) MEW 13:414.

Economic and Philosophic Manuscripts of 1844. *Ökonomisch-philosophische Manuskripte aus dem Jahre 1844.* (W) Apr.-Aug. 1844. (S) MEW Eb.1:465. (Tr) next entry.

ECONOMIC AND PHILOSOPHIC MANUSCRIPTS OF 1844. M. Milligan, tr.; D. J. Struik, ed. New York, International Pub., 1964.

The Eighteenth Brumaire of Louis Bonaparte. *Der achtzehnte Brumaire des Louis Bonaparte.* (W) Dec. 1851 to Mar. 1852. (P) May 1852 in Die Revolution, New York. (S) MEW 8:111. (Tr) ME:SW 1:398.

The Elections—Tories and Whigs.°° (P) 21 Aug. 1852 in N. Y. Tribune. (S) ME: On Brit., 351.

Electoral Corruption in England.°° (P) 4 Nov. 1859 in N. Y. Tribune.

English Prosperity—Strikes—The Turkish Question—India.°° (P) 1 July 1853 in N. Y. Tribune. (S) part in M: East. Qu., 40; part in ME: On Colon., 42.

Excerpt-Notes on James Mill's Book 'Elements of Political Economy.' *Auszüge aus James Mills Buch "Elémens d'économie politique."* (W) first half 1844. (S) MEW Eb.1:443. (Tr) M: Writings of Young Marx, 265.

Financial Failure of Government—Cabs—Ireland—The Russian Question.°° (P) 12 Aug. 1853 in N. Y. Tribune.

Foreword to 'Socialism Utopian and Scientific,' French edition. *Avant-propos à 'Socialisme Utopique et Socialisme Scientifique,' 1880.* (W) May 1880 as foreword to pamphlet pub. in June. (S) M: Lettres et Doc., 205.

France.°° (P) 30 Apr. 1858 in N. Y. Tribune.

The Frankfurt Assembly. *Die Frankfurter Versammlung.* (P) 23 Nov. 1848 in NRZ. (S) MEW 6:43. (Tr) ME: Rev. 48/49, 169.

The French Crédit Mobilier.°° [Three articles] (P) 21 June, 24 June, 11 July 1856 in N. Y. Tribune.

The French Trials in London.°° (P) 27 Apr. 1858., in N. Y. Tribune.

The Future Results of British Rule in India.°° (P) 8 Aug. 1853. (S) ME:SW 1:494.

General Rules and Administrative Regulations of the International Working Men's Association, 1871.°° (W) Sept.-Oct. 1871. (P) Nov. 1871. (S) Gen. Council F.I. '70-71 [4], 451; the General Rules only in ME:SW 2:19.

GESAMMELTE AUFSÄTZE, VON KARL MARX. Hrsg. H. Becker. Cologne, 1851. Called 1. Heft (no more pub.).

Grundrisse [commonly so called in English]: Fundamentals of the Critique of Political Economy. *Grundrisse der Kritik der politischen Ökonomie (Rohentwurf).* (W) 1857-58. (S) next entry. (Tr) pp. 375-413, M: Pre-Capitalist Economic Formations, q.v.—The Introduction. *Einleitung.* (W) Aug.-Sept. 1857. (S) next entry, pp. 3-31; or MEW 13:615. (Tr) M: Contrib. to Crit. Pol. Ec. (70), 188.

GRUNDRISSE DER KRITIK DER POLITISCHEN OKONOMIE (ROHENTWURF) 1857-1858. ANHANG 1850-1859. Marx-Engels-Lenin Institute, Moscow. Berlin, Dietz, 1953. 2d ed. (The rare 1st ed. was published in 2 vols., 1939-41.)

Herr Vogt. *Herr Vogt.* (W) Jan.-Nov. 1860. (P) Dec. 1860, as book. (S) MEW 14:381.

A Historic Parallel.°° (P) 31 Mar. 1859 in N. Y. Tribune.

Judicial Inquest Against the Neue Rheinische Zeitung. *Gerichtliche Untersuchung gegen die "Neue Rheinische Zeitung."* (P) 11 July 1848 in NRZ. (S) MEW 5:198.

Karl Marx Before the Cologne Jury. *Karl Marx vor den Kölner Geschwornen.* (W) Marx's defense speech at trial, 8 Feb. 1849. (P) 25-27 Feb. 1849 in NRZ; pamphlet under this title pub. 1885. (S) MEW 6:240. (Tr) ME: Rev. 48/49, 227.

Kossuth and Louis Napoleon.°° (P) 24 Sept. 1859 in N. Y. Tribune.

Kossuth, Mazzini and Louis Napoleon.°° (P) 1 Dec. 1852 in N. Y. Tribune.

Kreuznach Excerpts [from notebooks], 1843. *Kreuznacher Exzerpte 1843.* (W) summer 1843 in Kreuznach. (S) MEGA I, 1.2:118.

Lasalle. *Lasalle.* (P) 4 Mar. 1849 in NRZ. (S) MEW 6:320.

The Leading Article in No. 179 of the Kölnische Zeitung. *Der leitende Artikel in Nr. 179 der "Kölnische Zeitung."* (P) 10, 12, 14 July 1842. (S) MEW 1:86. (Tr) ME: On Relig., 16.

Letter to the Daily News, London, of 19 Jan. 1871.°° (D) 16 Jan. 1871. (P) 19 Jan. 1971 titled "Freedom of the Press and of Speech in Germany." (S) ME:SC, 254.

Letter to the Labour Parliament.°° (D) 9 Mar. 1854. (P) 18 Mar. 1854 in People's Paper. (S) ME: On Brit., 416.

Letter to V. I. Zasulich of 8 March 1881: Drafts. [Original in French] (S) Marx-Engels-Archiv, Frankfurt, D. Ryazanov, ed., Bd. 1, p. 318-42, incl. four drafts and final version. (Tr) 1st draft only in ME:SW 3:152; final version in ME:SC, 339.

Letters from the Deutsch-Französische Jahrbücher. *Briefe aus den "Deutsch-Französischen Jahrbüchern."* (W) Mar.-Sept. 1843; perhaps revised for pub. (P) Feb. 1844 in DFJ. (S) MEW 1:337. (Tr) M: Writings of Young Marx, 203.—For the letters by others than Marx, MEGA I, 1.1:557.

LETTRES ET DOCUMENTS DE KARL MARX 1856-1883. (Texts in original languages.) In Istituto G. Feltrinelli, Milan, *Annali*, Anno I, p. 149.

The "Liberal Opposition" in Hanover, *Die "Liberale Opposition" in Hannover.* (P) 8 Nov. 1842 in RZ. (S) MEW Eb.1:387.

The Local Election of Deputies to the Diet. *Die hiesige Landtagsabgeordnetenwahl.* (P) 9 Mar. 1843 in RZ. (S) MEW Eb. 1:426.

Lord Canning's Proclamation and Land Tenure in India.°° (P) 7 June 1858 on N. Y. Tribune, untitled. (S) ME: On Colon., 190.

MANUSKRIPTE ÜBER DIE POLNISCHE FRAGE (1863-1864). W. Conze & D. Hertz-Eichenrode, eds. The Hague, Mouton, 1961.

Mazzini and Napoleon.°° (P) 11 May 1858 in N. Y. Tribune.

Mazzini's Manifesto.°° (P) 17 June 1859 in N. Y. Tribune.

Mazzini's New Manifesto.°° (P) 13 Oct. 1858 in N. Y. Tribune.

The Militia Bill. *Der Bürgerwehrgesetzentwurf.* (P) 21, 22, 24 July 1848 in NRZ. (S) MEW 5:243 (authorship not ascribed).

MISÈRE DE LA PHILOSOPHIE. Réponse à La Philosophie de la Misère de M. Proudhon. (Oeuvres Complètes de Karl Marx) Paris, Ed. Sociales, 1968.

The Monetary Crisis in Europe.°° (P) 15 Oct. 1856 in N. Y. Tribune.

Montesquieu LVI. [In German] (P) 21-22 Jan. 1849 in NRZ. (S) MEW 6:182.

Moralizing Criticism and Critical Morality. *Die moralisierende Kritik und die kritisierende Moral. Beitrag zur deutschen Kulturgeschichte gegen Karl Heinzen* . . . (P) 28 Oct. to 25 Nov. 1847 in Deutsche Brüsseler Ztg. (S) MEW 4:331.

Morning Post versus Prussia—Character of the Whigs and Tories. *"Morning Post" gegen Preussen—Charakter der Whigs und Tories.* (P) 18 May 1855 in Neue Oder-Ztg. (S) MEW 11:217.

The Nationalization of the Land. (W) Mar.-Apr. 1872. (S) Labour Monthly, Sept. 1952, p. 415, but erroneously identified. Revised version by Dupont published 15 June 1872 in the International Herald, titled as shown, repr. in ME:SW 2:288.

The New Treaty Between France and England.°° (P) 14 Feb. 1860 in N. Y. Tribune.

Notebook on the Paris Commune. Press Excerpts, April-May 1871. (P) original text, mostly French, in Arkhiv Marksa i Engel'sa, Moscow, vol. 15, 1963, p. 22.

NOTES ON INDIAN HISTORY (664-1858). Moscow, FLPH, n.d.—These notes were written in Marx's last years.

Notes on the Charges in the Ministerial Order. *Randglossen zu den Anklagen des Ministerialreskripts.* (W) 12 Feb. 1843. (S) MEW Eb.1:420.

On Protective Tariffs. *Über Schutzzölle.* (P) 22 Nov. 1842 in RZ as ed. note. (S) MEW Eb.1:398.

On the Divorce Bill. *Zum Ehescheidungsgesetzentwurf. Kritik der Kritik.* (P) 15 Nov. 1842 in RZ as ed. note. (S) MEW Eb.1:389. (Tr) M: Writings of Young Marx, 136.

On the Jewish Question. *Zur Judenfrage.* (W) Autumn 1843. (P) Feb. 1844 in DFJ. (S) MEW 1:347. (Tr) M: Writings of Young Marx, 216.

The Opium Trade—I and II.°° (P) 20 and 25 Sept. 1858 in N. Y. Tribune, untitled. (S) ME: On Colon., 213 and 217.

The Paper Tax—The Emperor's Letter.°° (P) 22 Aug. 1860 in N. Y. Tribune.

Parties and Cliques. *Die Parteien und Cliquen.* (P) 8 Feb. 1855 in Neue Oder-Ztg. (S) MEW 11:44.

Peace or War.°° (P) 25 Mar. 1859 in N. Y. Tribune.

Pelissier's Mission to England.°° (P) 15 Apr. 1858 in N. Y. Tribune.

Poland's European Mission. (W) Speech at London meeting, 22 Jan. 1867, in English; original text not extant. (S) French version in Le Socialisme, 15 Mar. 1908, "Un Discours Inédit de Marx . . ."

Political Movements—Scarcity of Bread in Europe.°° (P) 30 Sept. 1853 in N. Y. Tribune.

The Poverty of Philosophy. *Misère de la Philosophie. Réponse à La Philosophie de la Misère de M. Proudhon.* (W) Dec. 1846 to Apr. 1847; foreword d. 15 June 1847. (P) July 1847, as book. (S) see entry under French title. (Tr) next entry.

THE POVERTY OF PHILOSOPHY. Moscow, FLPH, n.d.

PRE-CAPITALIST ECONOMIC FORMATIONS. J. Cohen, tr.; E. Hobsbawm, ed. New York, International Pub., 1965. (Tr. of 375-413 of M: Grundrisse, q.v.)

Preface to the Second Edition of The Eighteenth Brumaire of Louis Bonaparte. *Vorwort zur . . .* [etc.] (D) 23 June 1869. (P) July 1869. (S) MEW 16:358. (Tr) ME:SW 1:394.

Preparations for War in Prussia.°° (P) 8 Nov. 1860 in N. Y. Tribune.

Provisional Rules of the Association.°° (W) 21-27 Oct. 1864. (P) 1864, as pamphlet. (S) Gen. Counc. F.I. 64-66 |1|, 288. (See also M: General Rules . . .)

The Prussian Press Bill. *Der preussische Pressgesetzentwurf.* (P) 20 July 1848 in NRZ. (S) MEW 5:240.

Result of the Elections.°° (P) 11 Sept. 1852 in N. Y. Tribune.

Revolution in China and in Europe.°° (P) 14 June 1853 in N. Y. Tribune. (S) ME: On Colon., 19.

Revolutionary Spain.°° (Series of eight articles) (P) 9 Sept. to 2 Dec. 1854 in N. Y. Tribune. (S) ME: Revolution in Spain, 19-84.

The Rule of the Pretorians.°° (P) 12 Mar. 1858 in N. Y. Tribune.

The Russian Victory—Position on England and France.°° (P) 27 Dec. 1853 in N. Y. Tribune. (S) part in M: East. Qu., 180.

Scorpion and Felix (full title: Some Chapters from Scorpion and Felix, a Humorous Novel). *Einige Kapitel aus Scorpion und Felix / Humoristischer Roman.* (W) Feb. to ca. Mar. 1837; part of Poems of 1837; see Special Note B, first footnote. (S) MEGA I, 1.2:76.

Secret Diplomatic History of the Eighteenth Century.°° (P) as a series of articles, in part June-Aug. 1856; complete Aug. 1856 to Apr. 1857 in *Free Press*, London; as pamphlet, ed. by Eleanor Marx, 1899. (S) next entry.

SECRET DIPLOMATIC HISTORY OF THE EIGHTEENTH CENTURY and THE STORY OF THE LIFE OF LORD PALMERSTON. L. Hutchinson, ed. New York, International Pub., 1969.

Speech on the Question of Free Trade. *Discours sur la Question du Libre Echange. Prononcé à l'Association Démocratique de Bruxelles* . . . (W) speech given 9 Jan. 1848. (P) Feb. 1848, as pamphlet, Brussels. (S) M: Misère de la Phil./68, 197. (Tr) M: Pov. Phil. (FLPH), 207.

The State and Political Problems. *Die bürgerliche Gesellschaft und die kommunistische Revolution.* (W) early 1845, prob. Jan. (S) MEW 3:537, titled as shown. (Tr) ME: Ger. Ideol./64, 655, "Draft Plan for a Work on the Modern State." (English title above is mine.)

A Superannuated Administration—Prospects of the Coalition Ministry, &c.°° (P) 28 Jan. 1853 in N. Y. Tribune.

The Supplement to Nos. 335 and 336 of the Augsburg Allgemeine Zeitung on the Estates Committees in Prussia. *Die Beilage zu Nr. 335 und 336 der Augsburger "Allgemeine Zeitung" über die ständischen Ausschüsse in Preussen.* (P) 11, 20, 31 Dec. 1842 in RZ. (S) MEW Eb.1:405.

Theories of Surplus Value. *Theorien über den Mehrwert.* (W) Jan. 1862 to July 1863 in notebooks. (P) as ed. & rev. by Kautsky, in 1905-10. (S) MEW 26.1, 26.2, 26.3. (Tr) next entry.

THEORIES OF SURPLUS VALUE (VOLUME IV OF CAPITAL). Three vols. by various translators, called Parts I to III. Moscow, FLH (vol. 1 only) & Progress Pub. (vol. 2-3) n.d., 1968, 1971.

Theses on Feuerbach. *Thesen über Feuerbach.* (W) Spring 1845. (P) in Engels' edited version, 1888; Marx's original, 1932. (S) MEW 3:5 for original, 533 for Engels'. (Tr) ME: Ger. Ideol. (64), 645 for original, 651 for Engels'.

Trouble in Germany.°° (P) 2 Dec. 1859 in N. Y. Tribune.

The Turkish War Question—The New-York Tribune in the House of Commons— The Government of India.°° (P) 20 July 1853 in N. Y. Tribune. (S) last sec. in ME: On Colon., 61.

Vindication of the Moselle Correspondent. *Rechtfertigung des ††-Korrespondenten von der Mosel.* (P) 15-20 Jan. 1843 in RZ. (S) MEW 1:172. (Tr) part in M: Writings of Young Marx, 143.

Wage-Labor and Capital. *Lohnarbeit und Kapital.* (W) articles based on lectures delivered in Dec. 1847, but (P) 5-11 Apr. 1849 in NRZ, series unfinished; revised ed. by Engels 1891. (S) MEW 6:397; Marx's original text in MEGA I, 6:473.

The War Prospect in Europe.°° (P) 31 Jan. 1859 in N. Y. Tribune.

The War Question—Doings of Parliament—India.°° (P) 5 Aug. 1853 in N. Y. Tribune. (S) part in M: East. Qu., 71; part in ME: On Colon., 77.

WRITINGS OF THE YOUNG MARX ON PHILOSOPHY AND SOCIETY. L. D. Easton & K. H. Guddat, eds. New York, Doubleday, 1967.

WRITINGS BY ENGELS

The Abdication of the Bourgeoisie. *Die Abdankung der Bourgeoisie.* (P) 5 Oct. 1889 in Sozialdemokrat. (S) MEW 21:383. (Tr) ME: Art. Brit., 395.

Afterword to 1894 Edition of the Pamphlet 'On Social Relations in Russia.' *Nachwort (1894) zu "Soziales aus Russland."* (W) Jan. 1894. (P) Jan. 1894 in Engels' book *Internationales aus dem "Volksstaat" (1871-1875).* (S) MEW 22:421. (Tr) ME:SW 2:398.

Anti-Dühring (full title: Herr Eugen Dühring's Revolution in Science). *Anti-Dühring (Herrn Eugen Dührings Umwälzung der Wissenschaft).* (W) Sept. 1876 to June 1878. (P) Jan. 1877 to July 1878, as series in Vorwärts; 1878 as book. (S) MEW 20:1. (Tr) next entry.

ANTI-DÜHRING. HERR EUGEN DÜHRING'S REVOLUTION IN SCIENCE. 2d ed. Moscow, FLPH, 1959.

Anti-Dühring—Preparatory Writings. *Vorarbeiten zum "Anti-Dühring."* (W) Part I in 1876; Part II in 1877. (S) MEGA I, [8]:372, complete; or MEW 20:573, excerpts. (Tr) of MEW excerpts in preceding entry, 463.

Army.°° (W) Aug. to Sept. 1857. (P) 1858 in New American Cyclopaedia, 2:123. (S) ME: Art. N.A.C., 64.

The Beginning of the End in Austria. *Der Anfang des Endes in Österreich.* (P) 27 Jan. 1848 in Deutsche Brüsseler Ztg. (S) MEW 4:504.

The Berlin Debate on the Revolution. *Die Berliner Debatte über die Revolution.* (P) 14-17 June 1848 in NRZ. (S) MEW 5:64. (Tr) part in ME: Rev. 48/49, 35.

British Disaster in the Crimea.°° (P) 22 Jan. 1855 in N. Y. Tribune. (S) M: East. Qu., 506.

Bruno Bauer and Early Christianty. *Bruno Bauer und das Urchristentum.* (P) 4-11 May 1882 in Sozialdemokrat. (S) MEW 19:297. (Tr) ME: On Relig., 193.

Cola di Rienzi. *Cola di Rienzi. Ein unbekannter dramatischer Entwurf.* (W) 1840 or 1841, únfinished. (P) under above title, Michael Knieriem, ed. Wuppertal, Peter Hammer Verlag, 1974.

Communism in Germany.°° (P) Dec. 1844 to May 1845 in the New Moral World; three articles, untitled. (S) MEGA I, 4:339, titled as shown.

The Conciliation-Session of July 4 (Second Article). *Vereinbarungssitzung vom 4. Juli (Zweiter Artikel).* (P) 11 July 1848 in NRZ. (S) MEW 5:190.

Conciliationist Debates. *Vereinbarungsdebatten.* (P) 8 June 1848 in NRZ. (S) MEW 5:48.

The Condition of England: 1. The Eighteenth Century. *Die Lage Englands: 1. Das achtzehnte Jahrhundert.* (W) Feb. 1844. (P) 31 Aug. to 11 Sept. 1844 in Vorwärts, Paris. (S) MEW 1:550. (Tr) ME: Art. Brit., 9.

The Condition of England: 2. The English Constitution. *Die Lage Englands: 2. Die englische Konstitution.* (W) Mar. 1844. (P) 18 Sept. to 19 Oct. 1844 in Vorwärts, Paris. (S) MEW 1:569. (Tr) ME: Art. Brit., 32.

The Condition of England, 'Past and Present' by Thomas Carlyle . . . *Die Lage Englands: "Past and Present" by Thomas Carlyle, London 1843.* (W) Jan. 1844. (P) Feb. 1844 in DFJ. (S) MEW 1:525.

The Condition of the Working Class in England. *Die Lage der arbeitenden Klasse in England.* (W) Nov. 1844 to Mar. 1845. (P) as book, Leipzig, 1845. (S) MEW 2:225. (Tr) ME: On Brit., 1.

Continental Movements.°° (P) 3 Feb. 1844 in the New Moral World. (S) MEGA I, 2:455.

CORRESPONDENCE / FREDERICK ENGELS / PAUL AND LAURA LA-FARGUE. Three vols. Moscow, FLPH, 1959-196-?

The "Crisis" in Prussia. *Die "Krisis" in Preussen.* (P) 15 Jan. 1873 in Volksstaat. (S) MEW 18:290.

The Debate on the Jacoby Motion. *Die Debatte über den Jacobyschen Antrag.* (P) 18-25 July 1848 in NRZ. (S) MEW 5:222. (Tr) part in ME: Rev. 48/49, 63.

The Debate on Poland in Frankfurt. *Die Polendebatte in Frankfurt.* (P) 9 Aug. to 7 Sept. 1848. (S) MEW 5:319. (Tr) part in ME: Rev. 48/49, 82.

The Debate on the Poster Law. *Die Debatte über das Plakatgesetz.* (P) 22, 27 Apr. 1849 in NRZ. (S) MEW 6:434.

Decay of Feudalism and Rise of National States. *Über den Verfall des Feudalismus und das Aufkommen der Bourgeoisie.* (W) probably end of 1884; unfinished ms. (S) MEW 21:392, titled as shown. (Tr) E: Peas. War Ger. (56), 210, titled as shown.

The Dissolution of the Democratic Associations in Baden. *Die Auflösung der demokratischen Vereine in Baden.* (P) 28 July 1848 in NRZ. (S) MEW 5:276.

English View of the Internal Crises. *Englische Ansicht über die innern Krisen.* (P) 8 Dec. 1842 in RZ. (S) MEW 1:454.

Ernst Moritz Arndt. [In German.] (P) Jan. 1841 in Telegraph für Deutschland. (S) MEW Eb.2:118.

For 'Peasant War.' *Zum "Bauernkrieg."* (W) end of 1884, as notes for revision of E: Peas. War Ger. (S) MEW 21:402, as shown. (Tr) E: Peas. War Ger. (56), 222, titled as shown.

The Foreign Policy of Russian Czarism. *Die auswärtige Politik des russischen Zarentums.* (W) Dec. 1889 to Feb. 1890. (P) May 1890 in Neue Zeit. (S) MEW 22:11. (Tr) ME: Russ. Men., 25.—A translation made with Engels' collaboration (Ch. 2-3 probably by Engels) in Time, London, Apr. and May 1890, p. 353 and 525. (*Abbreviated* E: For. Pol. Russ. Cz./Time.)

The Frankfurt Assembly. *Die Frankfurter Versammlung.* (P) 1 June 1848 in NRZ. (S) MEW 5:14. (Tr) ME: Rev. 48/49, 22.

Frankish Age. *Fränkische Zeit.* (W) 1881-82, ms. (S) MEW 19:474.

Friedrich Wilhelm IV, King of Prussia. *Friedrich Wilhelm IV., König von Preussen.* (W) ca. Oct. 1842. (P) July 1843 in Herwegh, ed.: *Einundzwanzig Bogen* (q.v.). (S) MEW 1:446.

The German Campaign for the Reich Constitution. *Die deutsche Reichsverfassungskampagne.* (W) Aug. 1849 to Feb. 1850. (P) Mar.-Apr. 1850 in NRZ Revue, nos. 1-3. (S) MEW 7:109.

German Chapbooks. *Die deutschen Volksbücher.* (P) Nov. 1839 in Telegraph für Deutschland. (S) MEW Eb.2:13.

The German Social Democrats.°° (P) 3 Mar. 1890 in Newcastle Daily Chronicle.

German Socialism in Verse and Prose. *Deutscher Sozialismus in Versen und Prosa.* (W) end of 1846 to beginning of 1847. (P) 12 Sept. to 9 Dec. 1847 in Deutsche Brüsseler Ztg. (S) MEW 4:207.

The Housing Question. *Zur Wohnungsfrage.* (W) May 1872 to Jan. 1873. (P) June 1872 to Feb. 1872, as series in Volksstaat; 1872-73, as pamphlet. (S) MEW 18:209. (Tr) ME:SW 2:305.

The Hungarian Struggle. *Die Magyarische Kampf.* (P) 13 Jan. 1849 in NRZ. (S) MEW 6:165. (Tr) ME: Russ. Men., 56.

Hungary. *Ungarn.* (P) 19 May 1849 in NRZ, untitled. (S) MEW 6:507.

Immermann's 'Memorabilien.' *Immermanns "Memorabilien."* (P) Apr. 1841 in Telegraph für Deutschland. (S) MEW Eb. 2:141.

The Imperial Cortege. *Der Kaiserzug.* (P) Feb. 1841 in Telegraph für Deutschland; poem. (S) MEW Eb.2:139.

Infantry.°° (W) Sept.-Oct. 1859. (P) 1860 in New American Cyclopaedia, 9:519. (S) ME: Art. N.A.C., 177.

The Internal Crises. *Die innern Krisen.* (P) 9-10 Dec. 1842 in RZ. (S) MEW 1:456.

Introduction to Marx's 'The Civil War in France.' *Einleitung zu Karl Marx'*

"Bürgerkrieg in Frankreich." (D) 18 Mar. 1891. (P) 1891 in Neue Zeit. (S) MEW 22:188. (Tr) ME:SW 2:178.

Introduction to Marx's 'The Class Struggles in France 1848 to 1850.' *Einleitung zu Marx' "Klassenkämpfe in Frankreich 1848 bis 1850."* (W) Feb.-Mar. 1895. (D) 6 Mar. 1895. (P) in bowdlerized form, Mar.-Apr. 1895, in Neue Zeit, then in book. Engels' original text first published 1930. (S) MEW 22:509. (Tr) ME:SW 1:186.

Introduction to 'Socialism Utopian and Scientific,' English Edition of 1892.°° (W) Feb.-Apr. 1892. (D) 20 Apr. 1892. (P) 1892 in book. (S) ME:SW 3:95.

Irish Internationalists for Political Prisoners and Right of Assembly. London Letters [no. 3]. *Gli Internazionalisti Irlandesi in Favore dei Condannati Politici e per il Diritto di Riunione. Lettere da Londra [no. 3].* (P) 17 Nov. 1872 in La Plebe. (S) ME: Scritti Ital., 110. (Tr) ME: Art. Brit., 363.

The Kölnische Zeitung on English Conditions. *Die "Kölnische Zeitung" über englische Verhältnisse.* (P) 1 Aug. 1848 in NRZ. (S) MEW 5:284.

The Late Butchery at Leipzig . . . [&c].°° (P) 13 Sept. 1845 in the Northern Star. (S) MEGA I, 4:475.

Letters from London. *Briefe aus London.* (P) May-June 1843 in Schweizerischer Republikaner; four articles. (S) MEW 1:468. (Tr) part in ME: Ire. & Ir. Qu., 33.

Letters from the Wuppertal. *Briefe aus dem Wuppertal.* (P) Mar.-Apr. 1839 in Telegraph für Deutschland; two articles. (S) MEW 1:413.

Ludwig Feuerbach and the End of Classical German Philosophy. *Ludwig Feuerbach und der Ausgang der klassischen deutschen Philosophie.* (W) beginning of 1886. (P) 1886 in Neue Zeit; 1888 as booklet; Engels' Foreword dated 21 Feb. 1888. (S) MEW 21:259. (Tr) ME:SW 3:335.

The Manifesto of M. de Lamartine.°° (P) 13 Nov. 1847 in the Northern Star. (S) MEGA I, 6:339.

The Mark. *Die Mark.* (W) Sept.-Dec. 1882. (P) 1882, as appendix to German ed. of E: Socialism Utop. Sci. (S) MEW 19:315. (Tr) E: Peas. War Ger. (56), 161.—Included is the 1883 addition by Engels for a separate printing entitled *Der deutsche Bauer. Was war er? Was ist er? Was könnte er sein? (Abbreviated* E: Mark/1883).

Marx and the Neue Rheinische Zeitung. *Marx und die "Neue Rheinische Zeitung" 1848-1849.* (W) Feb.-Mar. 1884. (P) 13 Mar. 1884 in Sozialdemokrat. (S) MEW 21:16. (Tr) ME:SW 3:164.

The Movements of 1847. *Die Bewegungen von 1847.* (P) 23 Jan. 1848 in Deutsche Brüsseler Ztg. (S) MEW 4:494. (Tr) ME: Com. Manif./Ryazanoff, 272.

Notes on Germany: 1. Introduction, 1500-1789. *Varia über Deutschland: 1. Einleitung 1500-1789.* (W) end of 1873 to beginning of 1874; ms. notes. (S) MEW 18:589, titled as shown. (Tr) E: Peas. War Ger. (56), 223, titled as shown.

Notes on the War.°° (W) July 1870 to Mar. 1871. (P) 29 July 1870 to 2 Feb. 1871, as series in Pall Mall Gazette, London. (S) as book: *Notes on the War. Sixty Articles Reprinted from the "Pall Mall Gazette" 1870-1871.* Friedrich Adler, ed. Vienna, Wiener Volksbuchh., 1923.

The Oath of English Soldiers. *Der Eid der englischen Soldaten.* (P) 9 Mar. 1849 in NRZ. (S) MEW 6:332.

On Certain Peculiarities in England's Economic and Political Development. *Über einige Besonderheiten der ökonomischen und politischen Entwicklung*

Englands. (W) 12 Sept. 1892; ms. note probably for his Cond. Wkg. Cl. Eng. (S) MEW 22:331. (Tr) ME: Art. Brit., 409.

On the History of the Communist League. *Zur Geschichte des Bundes der Kommunisten.* (D) 8 Oct. 1885. (P) Nov. 1885 in Sozialdemokrat; as introduction to 3d German ed. of Marx's *Revelations on the Communist Trial in Cologne,* 1885. (S) MEW 21:206. (Tr) ME:SW 3:173.

On the Italian Panama. *Vom italienischen Panama.* (P) 1-3 Feb. in Vorwärts. (S) MEW 22:358.

On Social Relations in Russia. *Soziales aus Russland.* (P) 16-21 Apr. 1875 in Volksstaat, titled *Flüchtlingsliteratur, V.;* as pamphlet, titled as shown, Leipzig, 1875; in book *Internationales aus dem "Volksstaat" (1871-1875),* 1894. (S) MEW 18:556. (Tr) ME:SW 2:387, titled as shown. – For the Afterword, see E: Afterword/On Social Rel. Russ.

The Origin of the Family, Private Property and the State. *Der Ursprung der Familie, des Privateigentums und des Staats. Im Anschluss an Lewis H. Morgan's Forschungen.* (W) end of Mar. to 26 May 1884. (P) Oct. 1884, as book. (S) MEW 21:25. (Tr) ME:SW 3:191.

Outlines of a Critique of Political Economy. *Umrisse zu einer Kritik der Nationalökonomie.* (W) end of 1843 to Jan. 1844. (P) Feb. 1844 in DFJ. (S) MEW 1:499. (Tr) M: Econ. Ph. Mss. (64), 197.

The Peasant Question in France and Germany. *Die Bauernfrage in Frankreich und Deutschland.* (W) 15-22 Nov. 1894. (P) Nov. 1894 in Neue Zeit. (S) MEW 22:483. (Tr) ME:SW 3:457.

The Peasant War in Germany. *Der deutsche Bauernkrieg.* (W) summer 1850. (P) Nov. 1850 in NRZ Revue, no. 5/6, dated May-Oct. 1850; as book, Leipzig, Volksstaat, 1870. (S) M 7:327. (Tr) next entry.

THE PEASANT WAR IN GERMANY. Moscow, FLPH, 1956.

Persia–China.°° (P) 5 June 1857 in N. Y. Tribune. (S) ME: On Colon., 120.

Position of the Political Party. *Stellung der politischen Partei.* (P) 24 Dec. 1842 in RZ. (S) MEW 1:461.

Preface to the Communist Manifesto, English Edition of 1888.°° (D) 30 Jan. 1888. (P) in the first English ed., 1888. (S) ME: Selected Works (55), 1:25. (Not in ME:SW.)

Preface to the Communist Manifesto, German Edition of 1890. *Vorwort zur . . .* (D) 1 May 1890. (P) in the edition, London, 1890. (S) MEW 22:52. (Tr) ME:SW 1:102.

Preface to 'Karl Marx Before the Cologne Jury.' *Vorwort zu "Karl Marx vor den Kölner Geschwornen.* (D) 1 July 1885. (P) in the pamphlet, 1885, q.v. (S) MEW 21:198.

Preface to 'On Social Relations in Russia.' *Vorbemerkung zu der Broschüre "Soziales aus Russland."* (W) May 1875. (P) in the pamphlet, 1875, q.v. (S) MEW 18:584. (Tr) ME: Russ. Men., 274, 203-05.

Prefatory Note to 'The Peasant War in Germany.' *Vorbemerkung zu "Der deutsche Bauernkrieg."* (W) ca. 11 Feb. 1870, for the first pamphlet ed.; supplement, for the 1875 ed. dated 1 July 1874. (P) 2 and 6 Apr. 1870 in Volksstaat; pamphlet published Oct. 1870. Supplement published in the 1875 ed. (S) MEW 16:393 for 1870 note; MEW 18:512 for 1875 supplement; both in MEW 7:531 and 537. (Tr) ME:SW 2:158, 165.

Principles of Communism. *Grundsätze des Kommunismus.* (W) end of Oct. to Nov. 1847; untitled draft. (S) MEW 4:361. (Tr) ME:SW 1:181.

Progress of Social Reform on the Continent.°° (P) 4 and 18 Nov. 1843 in the New Moral World. (S) MEGA I, 2:435.

The Prosecution of Montalembert.°° (P) 24 Nov. 1858 in N. Y. Tribune.

The Prussian Constitution.°° (P) 6 Mar. 1847 in the Northern Star. (S) MEGA I, 6:253.

The Prussian Military Question and the German Workers Party. *Die preussische Militärfrage und die deutsche Arbeiterpartei.* (W) Jan.-Feb. 1865. (P) Feb. 1865, as pamphlet. (S) MEW 16:37.

Prussian Schnaps in the German Reichstag. *Preussischer Schnaps im deutschen Reichstag.* (P) 25 Feb. to 1 Mar. 1876 in Volksstaat. (S) MEW 19:37.

Rapid Progress of Communism in Germany.°° (P) 13 Dec. 1844 to 10 May 1845 in the New Moral World; three articles. (S) MEGA I, 4:339.

Real Causes Why the French Proletarians Remained Comparatively Inactive in December Last.°° (P) Feb.-Apr. 1852 in Notes to the People, London; three installments.

[Review of] *Alexander Jung, Vorlesungen über die moderne Literatur der Deutschen* . . . (P) July 1842 in Deutsche Jahrbücher. (S) MEW 1:44.

Revolution and Counter-Revolution in Germany.°° (W) Aug. 1851 to Sept. 1852. (P) 25 Oct. 1851 to 23 Oct. 1852 in N. Y. Tribune; series of articles. As book, Eleanor M. Aveling, ed., 1896. (S) ME:SW 1:300.

The Revolutionary Uprising in the Palatinate and Baden. *Die revolutionäre Erhebung in der Pfalz und in Baden.* (P) 3 June 1849, untitled. (S) MEW 6:524.

The Role of Force in History. *Die Rolle der Gewalt in der Geschichte.* (W) end of Dec. 1887 to Mar. 1888; unfinished ms. (P) 1896 in Neue Zeit, titled *Gewalt und Ökonomie bei der Herstellung des neuen deutschen Reichs;* as book, 1946, *Über die Gewaltstheorie. Gewalt und Ökonomie* . . . (S) MEW 21:405. (Tr) ME:SW 3:377.

Savoy, Nice and the Rhine. *Savoyen, Nizza und der Rhein.* (W) Feb. 1860. (P) Apr. 1860, as brochure. (S) MEW 13:571.

Siegfried's Home. *Siegfried's Heimat.* (P) Dec. 1840 in Telegraph für Deutschland. (S) MEW Eb.2:105.

The Socialism of Herr Bismarck. *Le Socialisme de M. Bismarck.* (W) end of Feb. 1880. (P) L'Egalité, Paris, 3 and 24 Mar. 1880.

Socialism, Utopian and Scientific. *Socialisme utopique et socialisme scientifique.* (W) Jan. to Mar. 1880, as revised version of chapters from *Anti-Dühring* for France. (P) 20 Mar. to 5 May 1880 in La Revue Socialiste; in 1880 as pamphlet. (Tr) ME:SW 3:115, reproducing Aveling translation pub. 1892.

Speech at the Graveside of Karl Marx. *Das Begräbnis von Karl Marx.* (W) Speech, 17 Mar. 1883, in English. (P) in German article by Engels, titled as shown, in the Sozialdemokrat, 22 Mar. 1883. (S) MEW 19:335. (Tr) ME:SW 3:162, "verified with the ms. in English"; English ms. not published.

The State of Germany.°° (P) 25 Oct. to 4 Apr. 1846 in the Northern Star; three articles ("letters"). (S) MEGA I, 4:481.

The Status Quo in Germany. *Der Status Quo in Deutschland.* (W) Mar.-Apr. 1847; unfinished ms. for pamphlet. (S) MEW 4:40.

The Suppression of the Clubs in Stuttgart and Heidelberg. *Die Unterdrückung der Klubs in Stuttgart und Heidelberg.* (P) 20 July 1848 in NRZ. (S) MEW 5:238.

The Third Member of the Alliance. *Der dritte im Bunde.* (P) 4 May 1849 in NRZ, untitled. (S) MEW 6:469.

The "Times" on German Communism.°° (P) 20 Jan. 1844 in the New Moral World. (S) MEGA I, 2:450.

To the Spanish Workers for May 1, 1893. (Original in Spanish, untitled.) (W) Apr. 1893, in French. (P) 1 May 1893 in El Socialista, Madrid. (S) cited here from the German in MEW 22:405.

The Triumph of Faith . . . *Der Triumph des Glaubens* . . . (full title: *Die frech, bedräute, jedoch wunderbar befreite Bibel. Oder: Der Triumph des Glaubens* . . . etc.). (W) June-July 1842, in collaboration with Edgar Bauer. (P) as pamphlet, Dec. 1842. (S) MEW Eb. 2:283.
The True-Socialists. *Die wahren Sozialisten.* (W) Jan.-Apr. 1847; unfinished ms. (S) MEW 4:248. (Tr) ME: Ger. Ideol. (64), 597.
The Turkish Question.°° (P) 19 Apr. 1853 in N. Y. Tribune. (S) ME: Russ. Men., 133.
Two Speeches in Elberfeld. *Zwei Reden in Elberfeld.* (W) speeches given 8 and 15 Feb. 1845, worked up for publication. (P) Aug. 1845 in Rhein. Jahrb. f. gesellsch. Reform. (S) MEW 2:536.
The War in the East.°° (P) 30 Nov. 1854 in N. Y. Tribune.
What Is to Become of Turkey in Europe?°° (P) 21 Apr. 1853 in N. Y. Tribune.
The Workingmen of Europe in 1877.°° (P) 3-31 Mar. 1878 in the Labor Standard, New York.

BOOKS AND ARTICLES BY OTHERS

Acton, H. B. *What Marx Really Said.* London, Macdonald, 1967.
Albrow, Martin. *Bureaucracy.* London, Pall Mall Press, 1970.
Annenkov, P. V. *The Extraordinary Decade. Literary Memoirs.* A. P. Mendel, ed.; I. R. Titunik, tr. Univ. of Michigan Press, 1968.
Aristotle. *The Politics of Aristotle.* E. Barker, tr. New York, Oxford, 1958.
Avineri, Shlomo. *Hegel's Theory of the Modern State.* Cambridge, University Press, 1972.
———. "Marx and Jewish Emancipation," *Journal of the History of Ideas* (July-Sept. 1964), p. 445.
———. *The Social and Political Thought of Karl Marx.* Cambridge, University Press, 1968.
Baritz, Loren. *The Servants of Power.* New York, Wiley, 1965.
Bauer, Bruno. "Die Fähigkeit der heutigen Juden and Christen, frei zu werden," in Georg Herwegh, ed., *Einundzwanzig Bogen aus der Schweiz.* Zurich, 1843.
———. *The Jewish Problem.* H. Lederer, tr. (Readings in Modern Jewish History) Cincinnati, Hebrew Union College-Jewish Institute of Religion, 1958.
Beard, Miriam. "Anti-Semitism—Product of Economic Myths," in I. Graeber & S. H. Britt, *Jews in a Gentile World.* New York, Macmillan, 1942.
Bendix, Reinhard, and Lipset, S. M. "Karl Marx' Theory of Social Classes," in Bendix and Lipset, eds., *Class, Status and Power.* Glencoe, Ill., Free Press, 1953.
Berle, A. A., Jr. *The 20th Century Capitalist Revolution.* New York, Harcourt, Brace.
Bernier, François. *Travels in the Mogul Empire, A.D. 1656–1668,* 2nd ed. A. Constable, tr. London, Milford/Oxford, 1914.
Bestor, Arthur E., Jr. "The Evolution of the Socialist Vocabulary," *Journal of the History of Ideas* (June 1948), p. 259.
Bloom, Solomon F. "Karl Marx and the Jews," *Jewish Social Studies* 4 (1942), 3.
Brazill, William J. *The Young Hegelians.* Yale Univ. Press, 1970.
Briefs, Goetz A. *The Proletariat; a Challenge to Western Civilization.* New York, McGraw-Hill, 1937.

Brisbane, Albert. *A Mental Biography.* Boston, Arena Pub. Co., 1893.

Bukharin, Nikolai. *Historical Materialism. A System of Sociology.* New York, International Pub., 1925.

Campbell, George. *Modern India: A Sketch of the System of Civil Government.* London, J. Murray, 1852. [Marx used this ed., not the rev. ed. of 1853.]

Carcassonne, E. "La Chine dans 'L'Esprit des Lois,' " *Revue d'Histoire Littéraire de la France,* 31e année, no. 2 (April–June 1924), p. 193.

Carr, E. H. *Michael Bakunin.* New York, Vintage, 1961.

Chang, Sherman H. M. *The Marxian Theory of the State.* Philadelphia, The author, 1931.

Chaunu, Pierre. *Eugène Sue et la Seconde République.* (Coll. du Centenaire de la Révolution de 1848) Paris, P.U.F., 1948.

Chesneaux, Jean. "Le Mode de Production Asiatique: Quelques Perspectives de Recherche," *La Pensée* (Paris), Apr. 1964, p. 33.

Christophersen, Jens A. *The Meaning of "Democracy" as used in European ideologies from the French to the Russian Revolution. An Historical Study in Political Language.* (Univ. i Oslo. Institutt for Statsvitenskap. Skrifter, Nr. 5) Oslo, 1966, 2d printing 1968.

Cobban, Alfred. *A History of Modern France,* vol. 2: *From the First Empire to the Fourth Republic, 1799-1945.* Penguin, 1962.

Cohen, Israel. *Jewish Life in Modern Times.* New York, Dodd, Mead, 1914.

Collins, Henry, and C. Abramsky. *Karl Marx and the British Labour Movement. Years of the First International.* London, Macmillan, 1965.

Conze, Werner. "Vom 'Pöbel' zum 'Proletariat.' Sozialgeschichtliche Voraussetzungen für den Sozialismus in Deutschland," in *Vierteljahrschrift für Sozial- und Wirtschaftsgeschichte,* Wiesbaden, 41. Bd., 1954, Heft 4, p. 333.

Cornu, Auguste. *Karl Marx et Friedrich Engels; leur vie et leur oeuvre* (4 vols. published so far). Paris, P.U.F., 1955-1970. [The French version is not identical with the German edition cited next.]

——. *Karl Marx und Friedrich Engels: Leben und Werk.* (3 vols. published so far). Berlin (DDR), Aufbau-Verlag, 1954-1968.

Custine, Astolphe de. *Russia. Translated from the French,* 3 vols., 2nd ed. London, Longman, Brown, Green & Longmans, 1844. [1st ed. 1843; tr. of *La Russie en 1839.*]

Cuvillier, Armand. *Hommes et Idéologies de 1840.* Paris, Rivière, 1956.

——. *Proudhon.* Paris, Ed. Sociales, 1937.

Degras, Jane, ed. *The Communist International 1919-1943, Documents.* 2 vols. Oxford, 1956-1960.

Delfgaauw, Bernard. *The Young Marx.* F. Schütz and M. Redfern, trs. Westminster, Md., Newman Press, 1967.

Demetz, Peter. *Marx, Engels, and the Poets.* J. L. Sammons, tr. Univ. of Chicago Press, 1967.

Diamond, S. "Marx's 'First Thesis' on Feuerbach," *Science & Society,* Summer 1937.

Dommanget, Maurice. *Les Idées Politiques et Sociales d'Auguste Blanqui.* Paris, Rivière, 1957.

Dorn, Walter L. "The Prussian Bureaucracy in the Eighteenth Century," *Political Science Qu.* (Sept. 1931), p. 403.

Draper, Hal. "The Concept of the 'Lumpenproletariat' in Marx and Engels," *Economies et Sociétés* (Cahiers de l'I.S.E.A., Série S), no. 15, Dec. 1972, p. 2285.

——. "The Death of the State in Marx and Engels," in *The Socialist Register 1970,* R. Miliband and J. Saville, eds. London: Merlin, 1970, p. 281.

———. "Karl Marx and Simon Bolivar: A Note on Authoritarian Leadership in a National-Liberation Movement," *New Politics* (Winter 1968), p. 64.

———. "Marx and the Dictatorship of the Proletariat," *Etudes de Marxologie* (Cahiers de l'I.S.E.A., Série S), no. 6, Sept. 1962, p. 5.

———. "A Note on the Father of Anarchism," *New Politics* (Winter 1969), p. 79.

———. *The Two Souls of Socialism.* Berkeley, Independent Socialist Committee, 1966.

Dubnov, Simon. *History of the Jews.* vol. 4. New York, Yoseloff, 1971.

Dühring, Eugen. *Die Ueberschätzung Lessing's und dessen Anwaltschaft für die Juden.* Karlsruhe, H. Reuther, 1881.

Dulaure, Jacques Antoine. *Histoire de Paris et de ses monuments.* Nouvelle édition. L. Batissier, ed. Paris, Furne, 1846.

Dupré, Louis. *The Philosophical Foundations of Marxism.* New York, Harcourt, Brace, World, 1966.

Easton, David. "Political Science," in *International Encyclopedia of the Social Sciences,* vol. 12.

Eccarius, J. George. *Eines Arbeiters Widerlegung der national-ökonomischen Lehren John Stuart Mill's.* Berlin, Verlag A. Eichhoff, 1869. [Expanded revision of author's article-series in *The Commonwealth* (London), 1866–1867, under somewhat different title.]

———. "A Workingman's Refutation of the Political Economy of J. Stuart Mill," in *Labor Standard* (N.Y.), 30 Dec. 1876 to 26 May 1877 (18 installments). [Translation of most of the preceding item; left incomplete.]

Elbogen, Ismar, and Eleonore Sterling. *Die Geschichte der Juden in Deutschland. Eine Einführung.* (Bibliotheca Judaica) Frankfurt, Europ. Verlagsanstalt, 1966.

Emge, Carl A. "Bürokratisierung," *Kölner Zeitschrift für Soziologie,* 3. Jg., 1950/51, Heft 2, p. 179.

Encausse, H. C. d', and S. R. Schram. *Marxism and Asia. An Introduction with Readings.* London, A. Lane/Penguin, 1969.

Engelman, Uriah Z. *The Rise of the Jew in the Western World.* New York, Behrman's, 1944.

Ex libris Karl Marx und Friedrich Engels. Schicksal und Verzeichnis einer Bibliothek. Bruno Kaiser, ed. Berlin, Dietz, 1967.

Footman, David. *Ferdinand Lassalle, Romantic Revolutionary.* Yale Univ. Press, 1947. [Brit. ed. titled *The Primrose Path: A Life of . . .*, 1946.]

Fourier, Charles. *Design for Utopia. Selected Writings . . .* J. Franklin, tr. New York, Schocken, 1971.

Fried, M. H. "State. I. The Institution," in *International Encyclopedia of the Social Sciences,* vol. 15.

Gans, Eduard. *Rückblicke auf Personen und Zustände.* Berlin, Veit, 1836.

Gay, Peter. *The Party of Humanity. Essays in the French Enlightenment.* New York, Knopf, 1964.

The General Council of the First International . . . (Series: *Documents of the First International*) Five unnumbered volumes published, each beginning as above, followed by the years covered. Moscow, FLPH (for vol. 1) or Prog. Pub., n.d.—Vol. [1] *G.C.F.I. 1864–1866. The London Conference. Minutes.* [2] *G.C.F.I. 1866–1868. Minutes.* [3] *G.C.F.I. 1868–1870. Minutes.* [4] *G.C.F.I. 1870–1871. Minutes.* [5] *G.C.F.I. 1871–1872. Minutes.*

Ghent, W. J. *Our Benevolent Feudalism.* New York, Macmillan, 1902.

Gide, Charles, and Ch. Rist. *A History of Economic Doctrines . . .* R. Richards, tr. Boston, Heath, n.d.

Glickson, Moshe. *The Jewish Complex of Karl Marx.* J. S. Abba, tr. (Herzl Inst. Pamph., 20) N.Y., Herzl Press, 1961.

Grandjonc, Jacques. *"Vorwärts!" 1844. Marx und die deutschen Kommunisten in Paris.* Berlin, Dietz Nachf., 1974.

Graupe, Heinz M. *Die Entstehung des modernen Judentums. Geistesgeschichte der deutschen Juden 1650-1942.* Hamburg, Leibniz-Verlag, 1969.

Greenberg, Hayim. "The Myth of Jewish Parasitism," in *Jewish Frontier Anthology 1934-1944.* New York J. F. Assoc., 1945. |Orig. pub. in *Jewish Frontier* Mar. 1942.|

Groh, Dieter. *Russland und das Selbstverständnis Europas.* Neuwied, Luchterhand, 1961.

Guillaume, James. *Karl Marx Pangermaniste et l'Association Internationale des Travailleurs de 1864 à 1870.* Paris, Colin, 1915.

Guizot, François. *De la Démocratie en France.* Paris, Masson, 1849.

Gurvitch, Georges. *Les Fondateurs Français de la Sociologie Contemporaine. I. Saint-Simon: Sociologue.* (Les Cours de Sorbonne) Paris, Centre de Doc. Univ., n.d. |1961, Foreword d. Feb. 1955|.

――. *Proudhon, sa vie, son oeuvre.* Paris, P.U.F., 1965.

H. "Karl Marx. Interview with the Corner-Stone of Modern Socialism . . ." *Chicago Tribune,* 5 Jan. 1879, p. 7. (Datelined London, Dec. 18, "Special Correspondence of the Tribune.") Cited here from pamphlet reprint, *An Interview with Karl Marx in 1879* [sic: read 1878], T. W. Porter, ed. (American Inst. for Marxist Studies, Occas. Papers, 10) New York, 1972.

Hegel, G. W. F. *The Philosophy of History.* J. Sibree, tr. New York, Dover, 1956.

――. *Hegel's Philosophy of Right.* T. M. Knox, tr. London, Oxford, 1967, repr. 1971 (first pub. 1952).

――. *Sämtliche Werke. Jubiläumsausgabe in 20 Bänden.* H. Glockner, ed. Stuttgart, Fromann, 1927-1930.

Heine, Heinrich. *Works* . . . 12 vols. C. G. Leland, tr. London, Heinemann, 1891-1905.

Heller, Hermann. "Political Science," in *Encyclopedia of the Social Sciences,* vol. 12.

Herder, J. G. *Ideen zur Philosophie der Geschichte der Menschheit. Dritter Theil.* 1787. In his *Sämmtliche Werke,* B. Suphan, ed., Bd. 14. Berlin, Weidmannsche, 1909.

Hertzberg, Arthur. *The French Enlightenment and the Jews. The origins of modern anti-Semitism.* New York, Shocken, 1970.

Hertzler, J. O. "The Sociology of Anti-Semitism Through History," in I. Graeber and S. H. Britt, eds., *Jews in a Gentile World.* New York, Macmillan, 1942.

Herwegh, Georg, ed. *Einundzwanzig Bogen aus der Schweiz.* Zurich, 1843.

Hess, Moses. *Philosophische und Sozialistische Schriften 1837-1850. Eine Auswahl.* A. Cornu and W. Mönke, eds. Berlin, Akademie-Verlag, 1961.

Hirsch, Helmut. *Denker und Kämpfer. Gesammelte Beiträge zur Geschichte der Arbeiterbewegung.* Frankfurt, Europ. Verlagsanstalt, 1955.

――. "Karl Friedrich Köppen, der intimste Berliner Freund Marxens," *International Review for Social History* (Amsterdam), vol. 1.

――. "Karl Marx und die Bittschriften für die Gleichberechtigung der Juden," *Archiv für Sozialgeschichte* 8 (1968), 229.

――. "Marxiana Judaica," *Etudes de Marxologie,* no. 7 (Aug. 1963), 5.

Hodges, D. C. "Engels' Contribution to Marxism," in *The Socialist Register 1965,* London, 1965, p. 297.

Hofstadter, Richard. *The Progressive Historians. Turner, Beard, Parrington.* New York, Vintage, 1970.

Hook, Sidney. *From Hegel to Marx* . . . New York, Humanities Press, 1950 [reprint].

——. *Towards the Understanding of Karl Marx. A Revolutionary Interpretation.* New York, John Day, 1933.

Hume, David. *A Treatise of Human Nature.* L. A. Selby-Bigge, ed. Oxford, Clarendon, 1888, repr. 1955.

Iggers, Georg G., ed. and tr. *The Doctrine of Saint-Simon: An Exposition; First Year, 1828–1829.* Boston, Beacon, 1958.

Jacoby, Henry. *Die Bürokratisierung der Welt. Ein Beitrag zur Problemgeschichte.* Neuwied/Berlin, 1969.

Johnston, William M. "Karl Marx's Verse of 1836–1837 as a Foreshadowing of His Early Philosophy," *Journal of the History of Ideas* (Apr.-June 1967), p. 259.

Kant, Immanuel. *Religion Within the Limits of Reason Alone.* T. M. Greene and H. H. Hudson, trs., 2d ed. La Salle, Ill., Open Court, 1960.

Kautsky, Karl. *The Labour Revolution.* H. J. Stenning, tr. London, Allen & Unwin, 1925.

——. "Die moderne Nationalität," *Neue Zeit,* Jg. 5, 1887, p. 392.

——. *Thomas More and His Utopia.* H. J. Stenning, tr. London, Black, 1927. [Orig. pub. in German 1890.]

Köppen, Karl Friedrich. *Friedrich der Grosse und seine Widersacher. Eine Jubelschrift.* Leipzig, 1840.

Krieger, Leonard. *The German Idea of Freedom. History of a Political Tradition.* Boston, Beacon, 1957.

Labor Zionist Handbook. The Aims, Activities and History of the Labor Zionist Movement in America. New York, Poale Zion Zeire Zion of America, 1939.

Lach, Donald F. "China and the Era of the Enlightenment," *Journal of Modern History* (June 1942), p. 209.

——. *The Preface to Leibniz'* Novissima Sinica; *commentary, translation, text.* Univ. of Hawaii Press, 1957.

Ladendorf, Otto. *Historisches Schlagwörterbuch. Ein Versuch.* Strassburg, Trübner, 1906.

Landor, R. "The Curtain Raised. Interview with Karl Marx, the Head of L'Internationale. [etc.]" in *The New York World,* 18 July 1871. (Datelined: London, July 8.) Cited from: *New Politics* (Fall 1962), p. 128.

Lassalle, Ferdinand. *Nachgelassene Briefe und Schriften,* vol. 3: *Der Briefwechsel zwischen Lassalle und Marx.* Gustav Mayer, ed. Stuttgart, 1922.

Laveleye, Emile de. *The Socialism of Today.* G. H. Orpen, tr. London, Leadenhall Press, n.d. [1884]. [Tr. of *Le Socialisme Contemporain,* 1881.]

Lehning, A. M. "The International Association (1855–1859) . . ." *International Review for Social History* (Amsterdam) vol. 3 (1938).

Leibniz, G. W. *Preface to* Novissima Sinica. (orig. pub. 1697, rev. version 1699; Leibniz wrote only the preface, the book being a compilation). Included in Lach: *Preface to Leibniz* (q.v.), p. 68.

Lenin, V. I. *Collected Works.* 45 vols. Moscow, FLPH/Prog. Pub., 1960–1970.

Léon, A. *The Jewish Question. A Marxist Interpretation.* Mexico, Pioneras, 1950. Currently available in New York, Pathfinder Press, 1971.

Leroy, Maxime. *Histoire des Idées Sociales en France.* 3 vols. Paris, Gallimard, 1946–1962.

Lessing, G. E. *Sämtliche Schriften.* K. Lachmann, ed. 3d ed. vol. 6. Stuttgart, Göschen, 1890.

708   *Bibliography*

Lindsay, A. D. *Karl Marx's Capital. An Introductory Essay*. London, Oxford, 1937, pub. 1925.

Locke, John. *A Letter on Toleration. Epistola de Tolerantia.* Latin text and English. tr. by J. W. Gough. Oxford, Clarendon, 1968.

Lowenthal, Marvin. *The Jews of Germany.* 1936; repr. ed. New York, Russell, 1970.

Lowy, Michael. *La Théorie de la Révolution chez le Jeune Marx.* Paris, Maspero, 1970.

McGovern, A. F. "The Young Marx on the State," *Science & Society* (Winter 1970), p. 430.

McLellan, David. *Marx Before Marxism.* New York, Harper & Row, 1970.

———. *The Young Hegelians and Karl Marx.* London, Macmillan, 1969.

Marcuse, Herbert. *Reason and Revolution. Hegel and the Rise of Social Theory,* 2d ed. London, Routledge & Kegan Paul, 1941, repr. 1955.

Massing, Paul W. *Rehearsal for Destruction. A Study of Political Anti-Semitism in Imperial Germany.* New York, Harper, 1949.

Maverick, Lewis A. *China a Model for Europe,* 2 vols. in 1. San Antonio, Anderson, 1946. [For vol. 2, see Quesnay.]

Mayer, Gustav. "Early German Socialism and Jewish Emancipation," *Jewish Social Studies* 1 (1939), 409.

———. *Friedrich Engels: eine Biographie.* 2. Aufl. The Hague, Nijhoff, 1934. 2 vols.

Mehring, Franz, ed. *Aus dem literarischen Nachlass von Karl Marx. Friedrich Engels und Ferdinand Lassalle.* 4 vols. Stuttgart, Dietz Nachf., 1902. [Vol. 1-3 = *Gesammelte Schriften von K. M. und F. E.*]

———. *Geschichte der deutschen Sozialdemokratie.* 2 vols. (His *Gesammelte Schriften,* 1-2) Berlin, Dietz, 1960.

———. *Karl Marx; the Story of His Life.* E. Fitzgerald, tr. R. and H. Norden, eds. New York, Covici Friede, 1935. [Orig. pub. 1918.]

———. *The Lessing Legend.* Abridged tr. by A. S. Grogan. Intro. by J. Kresh. (Critics Group Pamph., 11) New York, 1938.

Mészáros, István. *Marx's Theory of Alienation.* London, Merlin, 1970.

Meyer, Michael A. *The Origins of the Modern Jew.* Detroit, Wayne State Univ. Press, 1967.

Mill, James. *The History of British India.* 4th ed. by H. H. Wilson. 8 vols. London, Madden, 1840.

Mill, John Stuart. *Prefaces to Liberty. Selected Writings.* B. Wishy, ed. Boston, Beacon Hill, 1959.

———. "Representative Government," in his *Utilitarianism, Liberty, and Representative Government* (Everyman's Lib., 482) London, Dent, 1910, repr. 1929, p. 171.

———. "[Review of] *Armand Carrel, his Life and Character.* From the French of D. Nisard . . ." *London & Westminster Review,* vol. 6 (28), 1838, no. 11 (54), Oct. 1837.

Mohl, Robert von. "Ueber Bureaukratie," in his *Staatsrecht, Völkerrecht und Politik.* Bd. 2 (*Politik,* 1. Bd.) Tübingen, 1862, p. 99. [Originally pub. 1846 in periodical.]

Money, J. W. B. *Java; or, How to manage a colony . . .* London, Hurst & Blackett, 1861. 2 vols.

Morton, A. L. *The Life and Ideas of Robert Owen.* New York, Monthly Review Press, 1963.

Nicolaievsky, Boris, and O. Maenchen-Helfen. *Karl Marx, Man and Fighter*. David and E. Mosbacher, trs. Philadelphia, Lippincott, 1936.

Nikiforov, V. "Une Discussion à l'Institut des Peuples d'Asie," in *Recherches Internationales* . . . (q.v.), p. 240.

Nock, Albert Jay. *Our Enemy, the State*. New York, Morrow, 1935.

Ollivier, Marcel. *Marx et Engels Poètes*. Paris, Bergis, 1933.

Packe, Michael St. John. *The Life of John Stuart Mill*. London, Secker & Warburg, 1954.

Pankhurst, Richard K. "Fourierism in Britain," *International Review of Social History*, vol. 1, 1956, pt. 3, p. 398.

Parain, Charles. "Le Mode de Production Asiatique: Une Etape Nouvelle dans une Discussion Fondamentale," *La Pensée* (Paris) no. 114 (Apr. 1964), p. 3.

Paul, William. *The State: Its Origin and Function*. Glasgow, Socialist Labour Press, n.d.

Plummer, Alfred. *Bronterre. A Political Biography of Bronterre O'Brien 1804–1864*. London, Allen & Unwin, 1971.

Proudhon, P.-J. *Carnets de P.-J. Proudhon*. P. Haubtmann, ed. 4 vols. published so far. Paris, Rivière, 1960-1968.

Pyziur, Eugene. *The Doctrine of Anarchism of Michael A. Bakunin*. Milwaukee, Marquette University Press, 1955.

Quesnay, François. *Despotism in China*, vol. 2 of Maverick: *China* . . . (q.v.) [Tr. of *Le Despotisme de la Chine*, pub. 1767.]

Raffles, Thomas Stamford. *The History of Java*. (Oxford in Asia. Historical Reprints) 2 vols. Oxford, 1965 (repr. of first ed., 1817).

Recherches Internationales à la Lumière du Marxisme, Paris. Double no. 57-58, Jan.-Apr. 1967, *Premières Sociétés de Classe et Mode de Production Asiatique*.

Reich, Nathan. "The Economic Structure of Modern Jewry," in Louis Finkelstein, *The Jews. Their History, Culture and Religion*, vol. 2. New York, Harper, 1949.

Reichwein, Adolf. *China and Europe. Intellectual and artistic contacts in the eighteenth century*. New York, Knopf, 1925.

Reissner, Hanns. "Rebellious Dilemma: The Case Histories of Eduard Gans and some of his Partisans," in Leo Baeck Institute (London), *Year Book* 2 (1957), 179.

Reminiscences of Marx and Engels. Moscow, FLPH, n.d.

Rocker, Rudolf. *The London Years*. Jos. Leftwich, tr. London: Anscombe, 1956.

Rosdolsky, Roman. "La Neue Rheinische Zeitung et les Juifs," *Etudes de Marxologie*, no. 7 (Aug. 1963), 53.

Rose, William. *Heinrich Heine; Two Studies of His Thought and Feeling*. Oxford, Clarendon, 1956.

Rotenstreich, Nathan. "For and Against Emancipation; The Bruno Bauer Controversy," *Leo Baeck Institute* (London Book) *Year Book* 4 (1959), 3.

Rowbotham, A. H. *China and the Age of Enlightenment in Europe*. Reprinted from *The Chinese Social and Political Science Review* 19, no. 2 (July 1935).

———. *Missionary and Mandarin. The Jesuits at the Court of China*. Univ. of Calif. Press, 1942.

———. "Voltaire, Sinophile," in Modern Language Association *Publications*, Dec. 1932, p. 1050.

Rubel, Maximilien. *Bibliographie des oeuvres de Karl Marx. Avec en appendice un*

Répertoire des oeuvres de Friedrich Engels. Paris, Rivière, 1956. [A *Supplément* was published 1960.]

——. *Karl Marx devant le Bonapartisme.* Paris, Mouton, 1960.

Ruppin, Arthur. *The Jews in the Modern World.* London, Macmillan, 1934.

Sanderson, John. *An Interpretation of the Political Ideas of Marx and Engels.* London, Longmans, 1969.

——. "Marx and Engels on the State," *Western Political Quarterly* (Dec. 1963), p. 946.

Schapiro, J. Salwyn. *Liberalism and the Challenge of Fascism. Social Forces in England and France (1815–1870).* New York, McGraw-Hill, 1949.

Schiller, F. P. "Friedrich Engels und die Schiller-Anstalt in Manchester," *Marx-Engels-Archiv,* Frankfurt, Bd. 2, p. 483.

Schoyen, A. R. *The Chartist Challenge; a Portrait of George Julian Harney.* New York, Macmillan, 1958.

Schulin, Ernst. *Die Weltgeschichtliche Erfassung des Orients bei Hegel und Ranke.* (Veröff. d. Max-Planck-Instituts f. Geschichte, 2) Göttingen, 1958.

Schulz, Hans. *Deutsches Fremdwörterbuch.* Bd. 1, Strassburg, Trübner, 1910–1913.

Silberner, Edmund. "The Attitude of the Fourierist School Towards the Jews," *Jewish Social Studies* 9 (1947), 339.

——. "Charles Fourier on the Jewish Question," *Jewish Social Studies* 8 (1946), 245.

——. *Moses Hess; Geschichte seines Lebens.* Leiden, E. J. Brill, 1966.

——. *Sozialisten zur Judenfrage. Ein Beitrag zur Geschichte des Sozialismus vom Anfang des 19. Jahrhunderts bis 1914.* Berlin, Colloquium Verlag, 1962.

Sismondi, J. C. L. Simonde de. *Etudes sur l'Economie Politique.* 2 vols. Paris, 1837.

Sofri, Gianni. *Über asiatische Produktionsweise. Zur Geschichte einer strittigen Kategorie der Kritik der politischen Ökonomie.* Frankfurt, Europ. Verlagsanstalt, 1972.

Sombart, Werner. *The Jews and Modern Capitalism.* M. Epstein, tr. London. T. Fisher Unwin, 1913.

Southall, Aidan. "Stateless Society," in *International Encyclopedia of the Social Sciences,* vol. 15.

Spargo, John. *Karl Marx: His Life and Work.* Manchester, National Labour Press; New York, B. W. Huebsch, 1910.

Spitzer, Alan B. *The Revolutionary Theories of Louis Auguste Blanqui.* (Columbia Studies in the Social Sciences, 594) New York, 1957.

Stein, Hans. "Karl Marx und der rheinische Pauperismus des Vormärz," *Jahrbuch des kölnischen Geschichtsvereins* 14 (1932) 130.

Stein, Lorenz von. *Geschichte der sozialen Bewegung in Frankreich von 1789 bis auf unsere Tage.* 3 vols. Munich: 1921. This is a reprint of Stein's work published in 1850, which is revised and enlarged from his 1842 book *Der Sozialismus und Kommunismus des heutigen Frankreichs,* Leipzig, Wiegand, 1842. (This first ed. was not available to me.) A 1-vol. English abridgment of the 1850 work was published as *The History of the Social Movement in France, 1789–1850,* K. Mengelberg, ed. and tr. Totowa, N. J., Bedminster Press, 1964.

Sterling, Eleonore. "Anti-Jewish Riots in Germany in 1819: A Displacement of Social Protest," *Historica Judaica* (Oct. 1950), p. 105.

——. "Jewish Reaction to Jew-Hatred in the First Half of the 19th Century," in *Leo Baeck Institute* (London) *Year Book* 3 (1958): 103.

———. *Judenhass. Die Anfänge des politischen Antisemitismus in Deutschland (1815-1850).* Frankfurt, Europ. Verlagsanstalt, 1969.

———. "Der Kampf um die Emanzipation der Juden in Rheinland," in *Monumenta Judaica; 2000 Jahre Geschichte und Kultur der Juden am Rhein. Handbuch im Auftrage der Stadt Köln.* K. Schilling, ed. 2d ed. vol. 2. Cologne, J. Melzer Verlag, 1964.

Stirner, Max [Schmidt, Johann Kaspar]. *The Ego and His Own.* S. T. Byington, tr. New York, Modern Lib., n.d. [Tr. pub. 1907.] [Tr. of next entry.]

———. *Der Einzige und sein Eigentum.* Leipzig, Verlag E. Stolpe, 1929. [Orig. pub. 1845; written 1843-Apr. 1844.]

Sue, Eugène. *The Mysteries of Paris.* New York: A. I. Burt, n.d. "Complete ed." [Tr. of his *Les Mystères de Paris,* orig. pub. 1842-1843.]

Symons, Julian. *Thomas Carlyle. The Life and Ideas of a Prophet.* New York, Oxford, 1952.

Syrkin, Nachman. *Essays on Socialist Zionism.* New York, Young Poale Zion Alliance of America, n.d. [1935].

Szajkowski, Zosa. "The Jewish Saint-Simonians and Socialist Anti-Semites in France," *Jewish Social Studies* 9 (1947), 33.

Thalheimer, August. *Introduction to Dialectical Materialism. The Marxist World-View.* Sixteen lectures delivered at the Sun Yat-sen Univ., Moscow. G. Simpson and G. Weltner, trs. New York, Covici Friede, 1936.

Thompson, J. M. *Louis Napoleon and the Second Empire.* New York, Norton, 1967.

Thorner, Daniel. "Marx on India and the Asiatic Mode of Production," *Contributions to Indian Sociology* (Paris and The Hague) 9 (Dec. 1966), 33.

Tocqueville, Alexis de. *The Old Régime and the French Revolution.* S. Gilbert, tr. New York, Doubleday Anchor, 1955. [Originally pub. 1856.]

Tökei, Ferenc. "Sur le Mode de Production Asiatique," *Studia Historica* (Academiae Scientiarum Hungaricae) no. 58, Budapest, Akadémiai Kiadó (1966), p. 6.

Tucker, Robert C. *Philosophy and Myth in Karl Marx.* Cambridge Univ. Press, 1961.

Ullrich, Horst. *Der junge Engels . . . Erster Teil.* Berlin, VEB Deut. Verlag der Wissenschaften, 1961.

Walbank, F. W. *The Decline of the Roman Empire in the West.* New York, Henry Schuman, 1953.

Waldman, Mark. *Goethe and the Jews.* New York, Putnam's, 1934.

Williams, Raymond. *Culture and Society 1780-1950.* New York, Doubleday Anchor, 1960.

Wilshire, Gaylord. *Socialism Inevitable. (Wilshire Editorials)* New York, Wilshire Book Co., 1907.

Wilson, David Alex. [Six biographical vols. on Carlyle, unnumbered]. London, Kegan Paul, T. & T., 1923-1934.—[Vol. 3] *Carlyle on Cromwell and Others, 1837-1848.* 1925. [4] *Carlyle at His Zenith, 1848-1853.* 1927.

Wittfogel, Karl A. *Oriental Despotism. A comparative study of total power.* Yale Univ. Press, 1957.

———. "The Ruling Bureaucracy of Oriental Despotism: A Phenomenon That Paralyzed Marx," *Review of Politics* (July 1953), p. 350.

Woodcock, George. *Pierre-Joseph Proudhon.* New York, Macmillan, 1956.

Zaniewski, Romuald. *L'Origine du Prolétariat Romain et Contemporain; Faits et Théories.* (Université de Louvain, Collège de l'Ecole des Sciences Politiques et Sociales, 153), Louvain and Paris, 1957.

INDEX

This Index does not cover the Reference Notes, the Bibliography, or the note on "The Scope of Forthcoming Volumes" at the end of the Foreword. There is no listing for *Marx* or *Engels*, or for four geographical areas, *Germany, Prussia, England, France*, since these names occur so abundantly that a large mass of page numbers would be less than useful; topics should be sought under headings of narrower scope. The same applies to some subject headings, for example, *bourgeoisie*. In other cases, such as *proletariat* and *state*, only selected aspects are indexed, as shown in the entry. Titles of writings by Marx and Engels are indexed only for substantive references, not if merely quoted or mentioned as a source. The same applies to names of periodicals in which they wrote, such as *Rheinische Zeitung* and *New York Tribune*. References include appended footnotes and reference notes, but may be to the footnote only, as in 199n.

n = note (footnote).

f = following page.

... means *passim;* for example, 178...199 means that the subject is implicit on pages 178-199 but may not be specifically mentioned on each page.

Olympus, 213
Opium War, 518
Oppenheim, Dagobert, 111
Oriental despotism, 247, 276, 284n,
469, 473, 485n, 515...571, 572,
574, 629...664
Oriental society. *See* Asia, Oriental
despotism
Orleanists, 392...394, 456, 458
Orsini, Felice, 452f, 458, 619
Owen, Robert, 59, 105, 148, 213, 233
Owenism, 97, 132, 148, 152, 155, 157,
159, 185, 213, 218. See also *New
Moral World*

Pacific Ocean, 519
Packe, Michael St. John, 638n
Panama scandal, 269
Panamino scandal, 269
pantheism, 121
Paraguay, 640
parasites, 228, 300, 323, 325, 396,
401, 453, 455, 513f, 601, 622...628
Paris, 146, 152, 228, 391, 403, 432,
443, 452, 466n, 592; Marx in, 96,
104, 135, 136-38, 172, 184, 220;
movements and clubs in, 98, 99,
104, 132, 136-38, 146, 153, 188,
284, 308, 387; Haussmann's reconstruction, 261, 457; Treaty of, 576;
Mysteries of Paris: see Sue, Eugène
Paris Commune of 1871, 82n, 212,
215, 259, 283, 302, 305, 317, 408,
432, 435, 493, 624-26
Paris-Journal, 259
Parkinson, C. N., 312
parliamentarism, 47, 296, 315-17, 337,
392, 397f, 408; parliamentary
cretinism, 399. *See also* constitu-
tionalism, representative government
party, 153, 188n, 279; the term, 153n;
one class, one party, 332n, 389n;
party coalitions, 337. *See also* Whigs
and Tories *and other party names*
passion, 12, 196-98, 212, 514
Paul, William, 240n
Peasant War, 141, 213n, 274, 475
peasants, 42, 165f, 259, 271, 273, 414,
480, 562, 601; in Prussia, 63, 79,
154, 413, 599; in Rhineland, 35, 37,
40n, 600; in France, 387, 391, 397,

401f, 406, 408, 432, 435, 452-54,
458, 462, 499, 620, 625; in Russia,
573-75, 578-82, 584, 602; in
Austria, 479; in Scotland, 520; in
classical society, 467, 542; in Asiatic
society, 518, 548, 558, 562, 569.
See also Moselle peasants, Peasant
War, serfdom
Pecqueur, Charles, 450
Peking, 642, 654
Peking man, 537, 539
Pennsylvania, 117
Pereire brothers, 440, 443, 445, 450
permanent revolution, 59, 283, 286
Persia, 57, 239, 523, 525, 550, 650,
658
Peru. *See* Incas
Peter the Great (Czar), 582
Peterswaldau (Petrvald), 175
petty-bourgeoisie, 16, 267n, 387, 391,
393, 395, 406, 501-3, 509. *See also*
shopkeepers
philanthropism, 158, 213, 228, 231,
261, 511, 520
Philippson, Gustav, 126
Philips, Lion, 195n
philosophy, 99, 126, 159, 202, 256f,
594, 595, 638, 641; Marx's relation
to, 11, 12, 256f; in young Marx, 31,
37, 58, 61, 64, 66, 67, 74-75, 77-79,
82, 95, 101, 105, 106, 136, 139-42,
147f, 162n, 166, 171, 189, 197,
209, 219-21, 225f, 232, 234, 618;
his dissertation, 203-5; Engels and,
156, 159, 189, 216f. *See also* ends
and means, Feuerbach, Hegel,
materialism, Young Hegelians
Phoenicians, 601n
Physiocrats, 643-46
Piedmont, 621
Pietism, 150f, 198
Pinsker, Leon, 602
Platen, August von, 612
Plato, 275, 640, 649
Poitiers, rue de (club), 337
Poland and Polish movements, 175,
188, 277, 433, 435, 578, 621
police, police controls, 43, 51, 53, 70,
75, 185, 188, 192-93, 209, 229n,
255-56, 258, 289-90, 294-95, 299,
305, 391, 397-98, 404, 419, 432,

STD & Reg:

& M - 180 - 9000

ST   Re -

consency   no conseny.
5yy3   TB

SPB - 1000

30 v my7 42·9

200 v - 620 → 100Vac + 2Vj

1 5 5 → ⊘ < S3

5. No1 org name | SPB uro

SENECA
FINCH
COLLEGE LIBRARY